How to Use This Book

If you want to learn the essentials of 3D Studio MAX 2.5 and then put that knowledge to immediate use in designing state-of-the-art animation and 3D graphics, then you've come to the right place. Beginning with the essentials of the MAX interface and then quickly—but completely—working through fundamental concepts of design, lighting, cameras, and finally output, *Sams Teach Yourself 3D Studio MAX 2.5 in 14 Days* is the ideal learning companion as you start your journey into the exciting world of computerized 3D graphics and animation. By highlighting all the essential topics with insightful, step-by-step exercises, as well as providing illustrative examples on the accompanying CD-ROM, *Sams Teach Yourself 3D Studio MAX 2.5 in 14 Days* will soon have you creating the ultimate in computerized graphics and animation.

Who Should Read This Book?

Anyone who has a desire to learn about one of the most powerful tools available for creating 3D graphics and animation. Although covering so much material in only 14 days may seem daunting, the combination of "the learn at your own pace" writing style, exercises highlighting important concepts, and the accompanying, example-packed CD-ROM help you to quickly understand this complex—but exciting—topic. In addition to learning the essentials of MAX, several sections of the book discuss other helpful tools and related concepts, which serve to both illustrate the discussion at hand and to show you how to get more out of your creative 3D experiences.

Paul Kakert

David J. Kalwick

SAMS
Teach Yourself
3D Studio Max 2
in 14 Days

SAMS

A Division of Macmillan Computer Publishing
201 West 103rd St., Indianapolis, Indiana, 46290 USA

Sams Teach Yourself 3D Studio MAX 2 in 14 DAYS

Copyright © 1998 by Sams Publishing

International Standard Book Number: 0-672-31268-9

Library of Congress Catalog Card Number: 98-84317

Printed in the United States of America

First Printing: June 1998

Interpretation of the printing code: the rightmost double-digit number is the year of the book's printing; the rightmost single digit, the number of the book's printing. For example, a printing code of 94-1 shows that the first printing of the book occurred in 1994.

Printed in the United States of America

Trademarks

PUBLISHER
Jordan Gold

EXECUTIVE EDITOR
Alicia Buckley

DEVELOPMENT EDITOR
John Gosney

MANAGING EDITOR
Brice Gosnell

SOFTWARE DEVELOPMENT SPECIALIST
Adam Swetnam

PROJECT EDITOR
Kevin Laseau

COPY EDITOR
San Dee Phillips

TECHNICAL EDITOR
Mark Gerhard

COVER DESIGNER
Aren Howell

BOOK DESIGNER
Gary Adair

INDEXER
Joy Dean Lee

PRODUCTION
Marcia Deboy
Michael Dietsch
Jennifer Earhart
Cynthia Fields
Maureen West

Overview

Contents

Dedication

To Peg, my wonderfully understanding and patient wife, and my two daughters who can't wait each day until Dad is done with work.—Paul Kakert

Für meine Omi, with love. —David Kalwick

Acknowledgments

David Kalwick—I would like to thank my wife and children for their patience while I was locked away working on this project and Alicia Buckley, Laura Frey, and Michelle Newcomb for releasing me when it was completed. Seriously, it takes the efforts of many people, both directly and indirectly to produce a successful project. This project would not be possible without the understanding of my family, the persistence of the publisher and patience of the editors including, John Gosney and Mark Gerhard. Many thanks to Kinetix for their support and a great product.

Paul Kakert—Thank you to Kinetix for writing such a powerful and fun program for 3D animation, and to Macmillan Computer Publishing for allowing me the opportunity to be involved in the writing of this book. Kudos to the talented and helpful Macmillan staff who helped in every part of this book, including my co-author Dave Kalwick. This was a tremendous team effort that has resulted in a book in which we can all take great pride.

About the Authors

Paul Kakert is president and founder of Fresh Look Design, Inc., a multimedia company in Davenport, IA. His company also does business as Forensic Media, offering technical presentations for use in the courtroom. Paul has written numerous articles on 3D graphics and animation for *3D Artist* magazine since 1996 and has been a contributing author for two *Inside 3D Studio MAX* books from New Riders Publishing. His experience and opinions on the forensic animation industry have been featured in major trade journals and Internet e-zines such as the insurance industry's *Best's Review*, and the National Science Foundation's *Why Files*. Paul has been an Autodesk/Kinetix software user since the 3D Studio DOS release 1. He has created animations for use in broadcast, CD-ROM, and Internet Web sites. His recent animation of a pipeline explosion, created in MAX, was featured on an episode of the *Without Warning* series aired on the Discoverty Channel. Paul delivers seminars on forensic animation and 3D graphics, and may be reached at pk@forensicmedia.com.

David Kalwick is director of 3D animation at Pacific Multimedia Productions in San Diego. Though David can see the beach from his office, he prefers viewing his office from the beach. David and his company have produced animation used in medical education, broadcast television, and courtroom litigation. David is a contributing author in the *Inside 3D Studio MAX* series from New Riders Publishing, and was sole author of *3D Graphics Tips, Tricks, and Techniques* published by AP Professional. David can be reached via email at dkalwick@worldnet.att.net.

Introduction

Kinetix 3D Studio MAX release 2.5 is, without a doubt, one of the most powerful PC desktop animation packages on the market. It has gained industry recognition for its use in feature films, games, interactive presentations, and technical productions. Even in such niche markets as forensic (courtroom) presentations, MAX has become a core program for production of animations and still graphics. Reputation and industry acceptance might have been a couple of your main justifications for buying MAX in the first place. Regardless of what reasoning led you to decide on MAX for your 3D software, the most important thing to realize is your fun has just begun. Although complex in its offerings, MAX is relatively easy to use if you put some time into learning the basics.

Whether you are a seasoned animator or a graphic designer who has never worked in 3D, you'll find value in this book. Even those new to MAX, but not new to animation, will find it a fast way to get up to speed with a new and complex piece of software. For beginners, this book will help answer the question of where to begin. With a program as in depth as MAX, users who are very familiar with the software are constantly finding features they haven't tried yet or never knew existed. This book is for everyone.

Sams Teach Yourself 3D Studio MAX 2.5 in 14 Days is designed to teach you the basics of MAX. After covering the fundamentals outlined in the 14 chapters, you'll have laid the ground work for endless hours of experimentation and learning on your own. And don't forget the hours of fun you'll have creating animations and graphics from Day 1.

We suggest you work your way through this book in a day-by-day setting, starting with Day 1 and working through Day 14. Although each day focuses on a separate topic or function of MAX, the skills you learn in one day will carry over to the days that follow. We applied a hand's on method of learning MAX, so you'll need to be at your computer while you read. Every day includes specific step-by-step instructions covering the many features you'll use every day in MAX. The accompanying CD-ROM includes example .max files and rendered digital movies that you'll use in each day's lessons.

Where applicable, we have inserted notes, tips, or warnings regarding the topic being covered. These expert insights are meant to help you through some of the common struggles new users to animation and MAX often experience. They also provide a reference to other areas you might want to explore if you need additional information. Take special note of these sidebars; they might be one of the most valuable parts of the book.

Target Audience

This book is intended as an instructional stepping stone to the creation of computer generated imagery and animation using one of the industry's most successful 3D packages—
3D Studio MAX 2.5. Although this book is extensive in the material covered, it is geared
to be used as a daily tutor. By reading and following the exercises found in a single day,
you can quickly learn the concept of the day. This incremental procedure of learning is
extremely effective when studying difficult topics such as 3D graphics or animation. The
lessons show the participant how to avoid some common pitfalls, as well as create a
mode of thinking for working in three dimensions with a two-dimensional medium.

Two Weeks at a Glance

By reading through the book and working the exercises along the way, you can quickly
become comfortable creating and working in 3D. Because of the intensity of the subject
matter, it is essential that you also work through the exercises for each topic. Learning to
create realistic 3D graphics cannot be done through osmosis, so follow along each day's
lessons and don't be afraid to get your mouse dirty.

Though some lessons are shorter than others, it is suggested that only one chapter be
studied per day. If you feel particularly energetic, go back to assure that you understand
all the concepts thoroughly. The intention of this book is to build on concepts learned in
previous chapters and therefore, as the book progresses, some concepts are quickly
glossed over under the assumption that you understood them before moving on.

Your itinerary for the next two weeks is described briefly here.

- *Day 1*   The first day opens with an in-depth discussion on the world of 3D graphics. General topics such as the general components of a geometric object and coordinate systems are discussed. An overview of the 3DS MAX 2.5 environment is
  also given during the first day.

- *Day 2*   After becoming familiar with the 3DS MAX 2.5 environment, you can
  begin modeling objects in Day 2. Creating primitives and shape objects are discussed, as well as how to access the components of objects. You will also use
  object transforms on all axes and coordinate systems.

- *Day 3*   By the third day, you will be comfortable enough to begin model modification. Such concepts as Boolean logic, extruding, and lathing are taught. Although
  considered advanced modeling techniques, the lessons are structured to ease you
  through the process through active participation. The Modifier Stack is also used
  extensively in these lessons.

Introduction

... are the discussion of the day. These ... ating Loft objects. The exercises in ... plex Loft objects and working with ... ers.

... modeling topic, the NURBS model. ... a standard PC platform. As such, ... in outside this book. These lessons ... nd guide you through building ... ool set found in 3DS MAX 2.5. ... ch modeling is also explained in these ... nd how they compare to NURBS

modeling.

- *Day 6* Creating materials is an important aspect of creating a finished 3D model. Today's lessons introduce you to the 3DS MAX 2.5 Material Editor, one of its most powerful tools. Topics of discussion include the various material types and how they are used, as well as how to design, build, and manage materials.

- *Day 7* Advanced Materials and their tools are the topic of discussion for Day 7. Advanced topics such as UVW coordinates and mapping parameters are also discussed. In this chapter, you learn the skills necessary to create sophisticated materials.

- *Day 8* Lighting and Atmosphere are an essential part of any animation or 3D rendering. Adding the right amount of light and shadow to your scene gives it depth and adds life to the scene. Effects giving atmospheric conditions to the scene add another level of reality. This day, you learn the basics of adding light and how to render special effects using atmosphere.

- *Day 9* Cameras are your audience's eyes to your scene. You are the director of your own virtual movie set. You learn the best ways to set up cameras, have them animate through your scene, and how to have them include the right amount of the scene you create.

- *Day 10 and 11* There are so many animation fundamentals; we cover them over two days. You learn animation techniques carried over from traditional cell animation and many basic techniques found in MAX.

- *Day 12* What would animation be without special effects? MAX provides two effects systems called Space Warps and Particles. Today you learn how to use both to create virtually any effect you can dream up.

- *Day 13*   Rendering your animation is the last thing you do with your scene, but it requires some forethought before your project ever begins. The right amount of planning makes for a smooth production process. This chapter shows you the basics and helps prepare you for the decisions you encounter in almost every project.
- *Day 14*   Compositing images and animations is another exciting part of animation production. MAX provides you with a full-blown video editing package with its built-in Video Post feature. You explore how to use Video Post to create a complete digital movie, all within MAX.

Summary

Animation is simple. Move an object from point A to point B over a period of time. When you play it back via videotape or some digital format, you have animation—at least in the simplest of definitions. However, most animations don't simply consist of object moving; they consist of complex model creation and deformations, interactions and reactions between the models in the scene, and special effects you haven't even dreamed up yet. Enter 3D Studio MAX 2.5. It's the collection of tools enabling you to leap from the simple to the fantastic; MAX is a truly professional level tool that's fun to use. Be warned before proceeding—USING MAX IS ADDICTIVE. Inform your family and friends you will be increasingly hard to reach unless power failure or unforeseen computer meltdown forces you to leave MAX's side. With that said, I believe you're ready to turn the page. Enjoy!

WEEK 1

DAY 1

Getting Started with 3D Studio Max 2.5

Welcome to the World of 3D

Welcome! You just entered an exciting new world. By reading this, you decided that you want to push the envelope. Although you might not realize it, you are joining the ranks of the Chuck Yeagers of the computer graphics industry. Computer-generated imagery, also referred to as CGI, is just about the most processor-intensive thing you can do with a computer. It is also the most exciting.

Whether you intend to create 3D text for the next quilt patchwork newsletter or for *Jurassic Park 6*, you need to know what makes 3D graphics appear three-dimensional and how to build these wonderful objects.

Because this is your first day, let me just assure you that you can relax. Today, you will get acclimated to the 3D Studio MAX 2.5 environment and to loading and importing models and scenes. You are embarking on a wonderful journey—enjoy the ride!

From Points and Polygons to Primitives and Beyond

Let's assume that we've all seen a wireframe model. As the name implies, it appears as a distinguishable shape that is constructed entirely of lines. Figure 1.1 depicts various forms of wireframe models.

FIGURE 1.1.

Some typical wire-frame models.

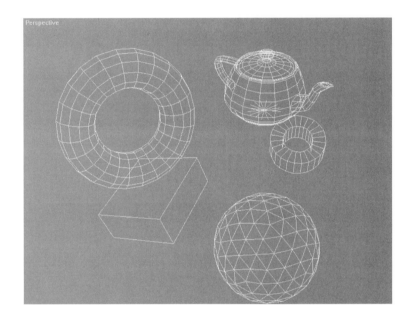

The first question you might have is "How are the wireframe models created?" Although the question is simple, the answer is not so obvious. The vague answer is that the models were created using a variety of tools as a means to manipulate points. Is that vague enough? The truth is, any model can be created in a variety of ways, but each is basically a collection of points.

Tip

Dissect your models. Prior to creating any model, a 3D artist must decide how to build an object based on the objects' characteristics. Object shape, animatable properties, and final output are just a few of the influencing factors that must be considered when building a model.

So how do the points become models? To understand how points become models, you must first subscribe to the idea that points are merely a representation of a location in space. Points cannot be seen but are merely used as endpoints or starting points for line segments. (This does not apply to particle systems, which are explained on a later day.) When used in polygons, points are called *vertices*, or *vertex* when referred to singularly.

Multiple line segments are joined together to build polygons. Polygons are what is seen when the object is rendered. A *polygon* is, in most basic terms, a closed two-dimensional shape. By connecting three or more line segments, polygons can be created. It is these polygons that collectively create an object's surface. Figure 1.2 shows a variety of objects and their polygons.

FIGURE 1.2.

Objects are created by lots of two-dimensional shapes called polygons, seen here as triangles.

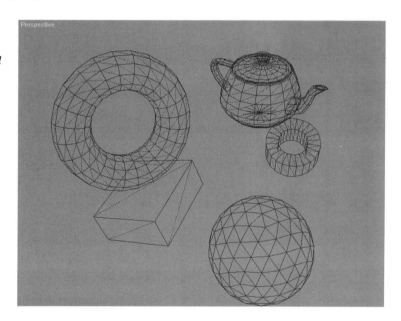

As you might notice, each progressive step gets closer to something recognizable. Because a polygon is a closed shape, such as a triangle (in a polygon with three vertices), the polygon can be given color. In fact, polygons can be given an array of various attributes using surface materials. Materials are explained in Day 6 and 7, but realize that the polygon (also called faces) is what causes the object to be rendered with some type of surface attribute, such as glass, wood, or concrete.

By now, you might be asking yourself how the polygons can be given a surface that looks like wood or any other material. Although it's not magic, it is pretty close. Through intense mathematical calculations, the color is calculated based on the angle of the polygon in relation to light projected on the model. This angle is calculated based on a surface normal that extends as a perpendicular vector from the center of every polygon (see Figure 1.3).

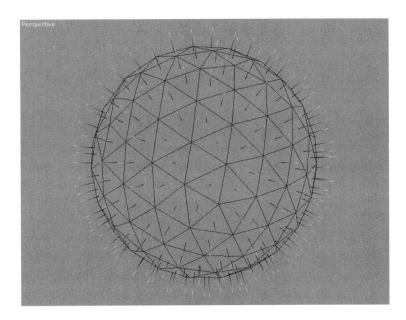

Though surface normals are important for rendering, they are equally important to the 3D artist. By adjusting the angle of the surface normals, the artist can achieve different effects on a surface material. A quick example of how surface normals are adjusted by the artist (although indirectly) is through the use of bump maps. For example, though the basic shape of an orange is spherical, the surface of an orange has lots of pits and bumps that make the surface irregular. Modeling these pits would be nearly impossible and definitely inefficient. By tweaking the surface normals, the surface can appear to have many bumps and pits, when it is actually a smooth sphere (Figure 1.4).

When a bump map is applied, additional surface normals are simulated to give the effect of ridges, bumps, and grooves. The surface normals are tweaked during rendering time based on the luminance value of a grayscale image used as a bump map. Luminance values approaching white are rendered higher whereas values approaching black are rendered lower. Figure 1.5 shows how luminance affects the bump. The bump map used is shown as an inset.

FIGURE 1.4.

A bump map adjusts the surface normals so that the surface of the orange looks pitted.

FIGURE 1.5.

The surface normals on the left have no maps applied and reflect unadjusted normals. On the right, a map has been applied reflecting in normals that are not so regular.

Though normals are used extensively, it is not always a primary concern for beginning 3D artists. For the purpose of this discussion, it is adequate to know that surface normals exist and that you can adjust them to create shading effects.

Getting Coordinated with 3DS MAX 2.5 Coordinate Systems

One of the problems explaining 3D to newcomers is the perception of depth in a 2D environment such as the computer monitor. Every 3D software package must create its own environment to build and position objects. This environment is called its *universe*. In order to know where every object is, there is an artificially set position from which all other objects are measured. This point is called the *origin* and exists in the center of the software's artificial universe. Because the computer calculates objects' positions in space relative to the origin of the 3DS MAX 2.5 universe, an artificial system of measure must be implemented. This is where coordinate systems come into play.

A *coordinate system* is one in which distance can be measured in every direction relative to a starting point. The starting point in the 3D universe is called the origin. This represents a point from which all distances are measured. Using three planes, any point in space can be accurately represented. The three planes (called axes) used are the X,Y,Z axes.

The 3DS MAX 2.5 world coordinate system (seen in Figure 1.6) is stationary and is used to position every object within the scene using the following criteria:

- *X Axis*   Horizontal plane with increasingly positive values moving toward the right.
- *Y Axis*   Depth plane, increasingly positive moving away from front view.
- *Z Axis*   Vertical plane with increasingly positive numbers moving up.
- *Axis Icon*   Used to show the orientation of every object, the axis icon looks like a tripod attached to an object (see Figure 1.7). At the end of each 'leg' on the tripod is the axis indicator. This enables users to visually reference which axis is being transformed at any given time.

In 3DS MAX 2.5, there are seven coordinate systems to choose from. When using the View or Screen coordinate systems, the Y and Z axes are switched, with the Y axis moving vertical and Z used for depth. These coordinate systems are relative to the screen and never change, regardless of the rotation of the view. (The local coordinate system is relative to the Selection Set and rotates as the selection itself is rotated).

FIGURE 1.6.

The three-axis coordinate system used in 3DS MAX 2.5.

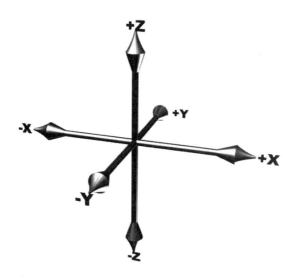

FIGURE 1.7.

MAX Axis tripods.

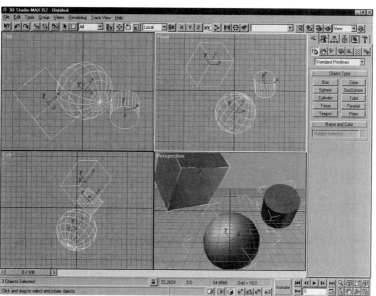

Whether or not you have any geometry training, the coordinate system is simple to understand once you grasp the concept. In Figure 1.8, the location of the sphere is easy to calculate by adding the grid lines along both the X and Y axes. The position of the object is determined by its pivot point, represented by the Axis icon. In this case, the sphere is located at position 2 along the X (horizontal) axis and position 1 along the Z (vertical) axis. To represent this location in a three-dimensional environment, you use the representation of (X,Y,Z) or (2,?,1). Given this representation, you cannot visually tell what the value is for the Y axis. In order to see the value of the Y axis, you need to view the model from an angle that permits you to see the Y axis. Viewing from either the top or bottom, or from one of the side views, you can see that the value of the Y axis is 3.

FIGURE 1.8.

The dot in this example is located at (2,3,1), indicating that it is a distance of 2 horizontal units and 1 vertical unit from the origin. From a Side or Top view, you can see that the object is 3 units along the Y axis.

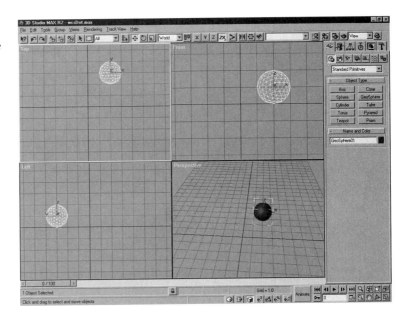

The different views are covered later in this chapter, but for now, know that you must use at least two views to see all axes. As you might have noticed, when MAX is loaded, the default configuration presents the artist with four small windows. These windows enable you to see a model from four different perspectives at the same time.

Note

When creating a three-dimensional model, you must view the model from at least two different angles in order to see all three coordinate axes. Using a four-window setup (such as the default in MAX) is a great place to start when creating geometry.

Introduction to Lights and Cameras

Using a 3-axis coordinate system enables you to place objects exactly where desired, including cameras and lights. In real life, you see things because of the light they reflect. This is also true in MAX. By adding different types of lights to a scene, you can create any mood using harsh, dark shadows, soft warm shadows, and every shadow type in between.

1

When you first open a scene, MAX provides default lighting so that objects are visible without having to add lights. This is great for modeling and scene composition, but for more accurate lighting effects, it is best to set up your own lighting. Day 8 covers lighting in more detail, so for now, enjoy the default lighting provided by MAX without worrying that the lighting might not be exactly what you were looking for.

The default lighting provided by MAX is intended for modeling only and very rarely is it acceptable for final render output. The default lighting utilizes two Omni lights, placed at opposite corners of the scene. When viewed from a Front view, the lights are placed at the upper-left and lower-right corners of the scene. These lights are not visible and are removed as soon as a single light is added by the user, which might make the scene appear darker if only one light is added. To correct this, add two or more lights to your scene, placed at opposite corners. You might also want to use backlighting and other techniques employed in filmmaking.

Unlike the default lighting provided, default cameras are not provided in 3DS MAX 2.5. Instead, a perspective view is used. The perspective view simulates the lens of the human eye to view models with some perspective. Day 9 covers cameras in detail, so until then, use the Perspective view to give the effect of viewing your scene through a camera lens.

Creating Output—Rendering Basics

As you become more in tune with the concepts of 3D, you will hear more and more talk about rendering. Rendering is where the true colors of the computer shine. *Rendering* is the process in which all colors and materials applied to models come to life. During the rendering process, lights, shadows, reflections, transparencies, and all other photorealistic characteristics are calculated. These calculations are then translated into RGB (Red, Green, Blue) color values. To create an image on a computer screen, each dot on the screen (called a *pixel*——a derivative of an original phrase describing the "picture element") must be calculated for the correct color to correspond to the image created by the computer. The number of pixels is also used to define the resolution of the image. An image rendered at video resolution of 720×486 contains 349,920 pixels. Because the color value for each of those pixels must be calculated, the rendering times can be long, especially when producing animation for video at 29.97 frames per second. At that rate, the computer must calculate 629,226,144 pixels for each minute of video. Figure 1.9 shows a rendered image compared to the wireframe models seen in the viewports.

FIGURE 1.9.

A rendered image compared to the wireframe models seen in the 3DS MAX 2 environment.

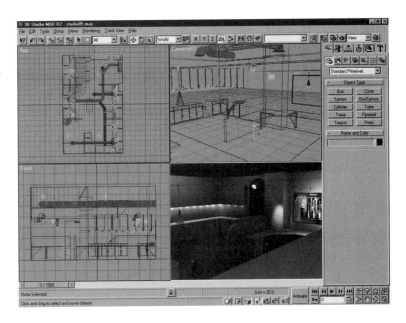

Although the rendering process is the culmination of all your hard work on modeling, lighting, and animating, you will soon learn that the rendering process reminds you that your machine is always due for a processor or memory upgrade.

The hardest thing for new 3D artists to get used to is rendering time. Although MAX is quick and efficient, and today's machines are faster than ever (the image that took days years ago might only take a few minutes today), the first time a new 3D artist renders a complex scene, it seems painfully slow.

For animation the wait gets even worse. *Animation* is the process of displaying many images very quickly. Each image is slightly different than the previous one, giving the illusion of fluid motion. For computer animation, each of the frames must be rendered. For a ten-second animation sequence playing at 30 frames per second, you end up with 300 frames. At one minute per frame, that's 300 minutes or five hours of computer time.

Tip

> Work while you are at play! When not using your computer, let it work for you. Use the time when you are busy doing other things to render your images. At the end of the day, I like to set up a group of images to render overnight, so upon returning to work in the morning, my images are ready for proofing.

Views, Your Window to the World of 3D

Working in three dimensions on a two-dimensional screen requires that you can see an object from at least two different angles to view all axes and to build objects properly. It is for this reason that MAX starts with a default four viewport interface. The standard setup of Top, Front, Left, and Perspective views enables the modeler to see an object from many different sides at one time. This setup is demonstrated in Figure 1.10.

FIGURE 1.10.

When MAX is launched, the standard four window environment appears. With this configuration, you can view models from all axes, as well as with perspective.

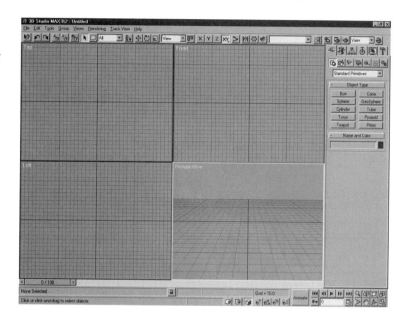

The concept of a viewport (or view) is relatively simple. Instead of having to move an object around to see all sides, have a viewport along each of the axes instead. In drafting and architecture, a similar process is used. Drawings are made of a building from the front, top, side, and finally a perspective drawing (or rendering) so that the three-dimensional aspects of the building can be seen and built properly. Using the computer, you can artificially view the object from all axes just by setting a view.

Orthographic Versus Perspective Views

If you look at a cube object placed in the center of all views, you notice that the object looks exactly the same in all views except the Perspective view (see Figure 1.11). This is because the Top, Front, and Left views are Orthographic views.

FIGURE 1.11.

Notice how the cube looks exactly the same in all views except the Perspective view. This is because the other views are orthographic and therefore do not show depth.

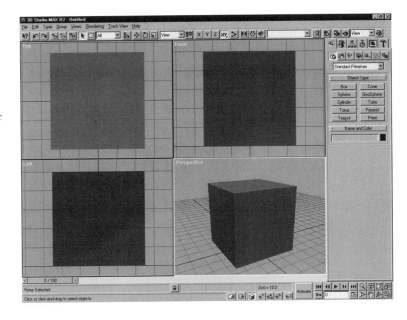

An *Orthographic* view is one in which depth has been removed. If you look at the two spheres in Figure 1.12, you notice that although they look exactly the same size in the Front view, the Left view reveals that there is a distance of about 25 units between them. This is the result of an Orthographic view. As you can see in Figure 1.13, an Orthographic view does not provide you the vanishing point that a perspective does. Comparing the two spheres in an Orthographic view provides no details as to their relative distance along the View's Z axis (Depth), whereas the same view with perspective added provides more clues as to the actual distance between the spheres.

Note

It is nearly impossible to model correctly or accurately without an Orthographic view. Use the Orthographic views such as Front, Left, and Top to model in and the Perspective views to see your models in a more realistic manner.

Orthographic views are necessary during the modeling process so that vertices and lines can be drawn precisely. When building objects, not only is precise placement required, but you also need to judge size and distance accurately, both of which are impossible using a Perspective view. One way to quickly appreciate Orthographic views is to try building even a simple model within a Perspective view and without any reference to an Orthographic view.

FIGURE 1.12.

Because these are Orthographic views, there is no depth to the objects viewed. From the Front view, they appear to be two spheres, the same size, side by side. The Top view reveals that they are indeed the same size, but there is great distance between them.

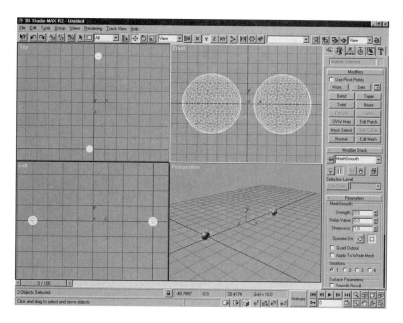

FIGURE 1.13.

Viewing both spheres from a Front view set at orthographic and a Front view with perspective reveals the distance between the two spheres.

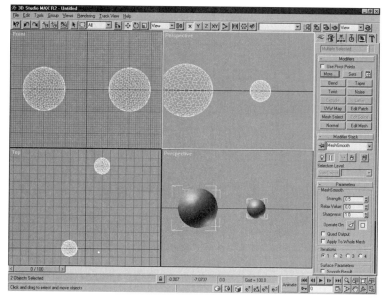

Selecting a View

Working in an Orthographic view has many advantages. There are times though, when you would like a Perspective view to get a realistic look at your model or scene. In 3DS MAX 2.5, you can quickly change to any other view, including that of an existing camera or light. In fact, though there are default views, you can rotate any view to accommodate any angle. Although the view angle is changed from a default angle by the user, the view label will change to "User."

User views are simply views in which the user changes the angle of view. The View mode is still Orthographic when in User mode, meaning that the view does not accommodate for distance. To change to a view with proper perspective, simply press the P key or right-click on the view label and select Perspective from the Views menu. Any view can also be made to fill the screen by pressing the W key or using the Min/Max toggle button on the lower tool bar. The Min/Max toggle button is described in more detail later in this chapter.

Note   The current view (called active view) is the viewport with the white border on the inside. When the Animate button is invoked, the white border of the current view is replaced with a red border.

Changing views is facilitated by right-clicking the mouse on the viewport label. This presents a pop-up menu with various view options, such as displaying grids, shading mode, and type of view. Selecting the Views options invokes an additional menu revealing the eight default views, Track views, and Grid options and can be seen in Figure 1.14. When releasing the mouse on any of the view types, the current view is replaced with the selected view.

Changing views can also be accomplished using keystrokes. For example, pressing the F key changes the current view to the Front view. The following are default keystrokes for changing views. These can be changed in the Preferences section.

- *F*   Front view
- *K*   Back view
- *T*   Top view
- *B*   Bottom view
- *L*   Left view
- *R*   Right view
- *P*   Perspective view
- *U*   User view

FIGURE 1.14.

To change views, right-click on the view name label and select a view from the Views menu.

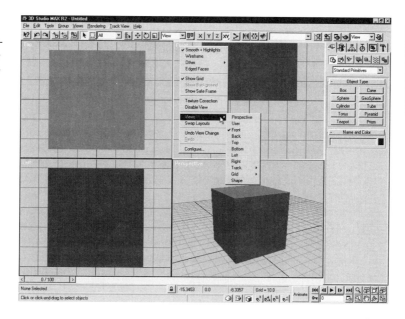

1

Note

When pressing the P for Perspective view, the current view angle is not changed; it is merely given perspective. This is helpful when you look at an object from a Left view (for example) and want to see the object from the Left side with perspective.

As mentioned earlier, you can also change the view from its current state to that of an existing camera or light in the scene. Because adding lights and cameras are discussed in Days 8 and 9, let's assume they exist and only discuss how to change the view.

To Do: Changing the view

▼ To Do

1. Right click the mouse on the view name label in the upper-left corner of the current view. A drop down menu appears

2. From the drop down menu, drag down over Views to reveal a list of all available views. Releasing the mouse over one of the listed views will change the view in the current viewport to the view selected from the list. Figure 1.15 shows an example of lights and cameras available for the current scene. The available camera and light views change with each scene, but the list is formatted with available cameras in the top section, lights, then standard views.

▲

Adjusting Views

Views can also be adjusted through zooming, panning, and rotating. This is done through the View Navigation buttons located in the lower-right corner of the MAX interface. Through the use of these tools, you can change the orbit, rotation, or distance of the view in relation to the scene, as well as zoom the current view, or all views simultaneously.

- *Zoom*   Used to magnify (or zoom) the view of the scene, this button enlarges the view of the scene while keeping the size of the view window the same. Dragging the mouse up zooms in, whereas dragging the mouse down zooms out, or makes the objects seem farther away.

- *ZoomAll*   This tool performs the same zooming action as the Zoom button but applies it to all views.

- *Zoom Extents Selected*   To zoom in on a selected object, click on this button. The view centers the selected object in the current view, based on the extents (physical boundaries) of the object. This button contains a flyout that can switch between zooming on the selected objects or all visible objects in the scene.

- *ZoomExtentsAll*   This button performs the same functions as the Zoom Extents button but works on all views, not just the current view. This button also consists of a flyout to choose between zooming on selected or all objects.

- *RegionZoom*   When working in an Orthographic view, the Region Zoom button

enables the user to drag a region to zoom in. MAX zooms in the current window to the extents of the drawn region.

- *FieldOfView*   When a view is labeled Perspective, the Region Zoom becomes a Field of View button. Because perfect regions are not definable in a Perspective view, one must change the field of view. The Field of View button works like the Zoom button in that you simply drag in a viewport up or down to change the field of view. This is like changing the lens size of a real-world camera.

- *Pan*   In order to scroll a view along the horizontal and vertical direction, use the Pan tool. Using this tool, you can "grab" the scene and move it in any direction. This tool comes in handy when zoomed into a group of objects and you need to see other parts of the scene at the same zoom level. Using this tool, you can avoid the zoom–out-and-zoom-in dance when viewing different parts of the scene.

- *ArcRotate*   Using the Arc Rotate tool, you can alter the angle of the view to any degree along any axis. This tool superimposes a Trackball icon on the current view. On the trackball are handles that you can use to rotate the view along any axis. After changing the rotation of any view, the view label reflects this change by naming the view User, indicating that the rotation is not one of the standard views.

- *Min/MaxToggle*   When working with 3D models, there always seems to be a shortage of screen space. Invariably, you will want to see your scene up close and with as much detail as possible. Clicking on the Min/Max toggle button causes the current view to fill the screen, while the other views disappear. Click the Min/Max toggle button again, and all views reappear as they were.

Zooming

Zooming is a term used to describe the view moving toward or away from the object or scene. In terms of the coordinate system, zooming moves along the local Z axis of the current view. By zooming a view, objects can appear to be closer (thereby larger in the view) or further away (causing objects to look smaller). By zooming in, a smaller portion of the model or scene can be seen in greater detail. This is an indispensable tool during model building and scene composition.

To zoom a view, select the Zoom tool from the view navigation tools in the lower-right corner of the MAX interface, and drag in a view. Dragging up with the mouse button pressed zooms in; dragging down zooms out.

Panning

Though zooming is restricted to the view's local Z axis, panning uses both the X and Y axis. In other words, using the Pan tool, you can move the view in relation to the scene along both the horizontal and the vertical planes.

Panning is great when you zoom in to see detail and need to view other portions of the scene at the same detail level. Using the Pan tool, you can grab and move the view's relative position within the scene.

Note When the Pan tool is used, only the view's position is changed. Objects within the scene are not moved.

Rotating

Both the Zoom and Pan tools are used to move a view's relative perspective on a scene. To rotate a view, you must use the Arc Rotate tool. The Arc Rotate tool is used to rotate along any of the three axes. By rotating the view, you can view the contents of a scene from any angle without changing the position of the objects in the scene. The Arc Rotate tool rotates the scene based on either the entire scene or the selected objects, depending on which flyout option you choose.

When the Arc Rotate tool is selected, a circle (called a *trackball*) is superimposed in the current view. The circle also contains four small squares along the perimeter of the circle called *handles* (see Figure 1.16). These handles are used to rotate the view along a constrained axis. The Arc Rotate tool uses the view's local coordinate system for rotation. As a result, regardless of how the view is positioned, each time the Arc Rotate tool is used, a new local coordinate system is established, with the X axis being horizontal, Y being vertical, and the Z being depth perpendicular to the view.

- *Top and Bottom handles* Used to rotate the view constrained along the View's X axis. Drag the mouse on a Top or Bottom handle to change the view rotation. Drag the mouse up for a positive X rotation and down for a negative rotation. Objects in the scene appear to tip toward or away from the camera.

FIGURE 1.16.

The Arc Rotate
Trackball.

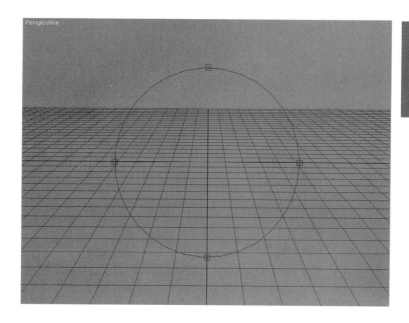

1

- *Left and Right handles*   Rotates the view constrained along the view's Y axis. Dragging left causes negative rotation, whereas dragging to the right causes positive rotation.

- *Outside Trackball*   Dragging the mouse outside the trackball rotates the view along the view's Z axis. Clicking on the left side of the trackball and dragging up rotates the view in the negative direction, whereas the opposite is true on the right side.

- *Inside Trackball*   When dragging the mouse inside the trackball, the view rotation is in the free mode. Dragging the mouse inside freely rotates the view along all axes. Hold the Shift key down to constrain the free rotation along the first axis rotated about.

Note

The View navigation tools work using the view's local coordinate system. This means that any adjustments are made along relative planes and not on the world coordinate system's absolute axis. When using the Arc Rotate tool, the center of rotation is the center of the current view. This can cause objects to rotate out of view if they are positioned near the edge of the current view and Arc Rotate All is used. To avoid "loosing" objects, select the Arc Rotate Selected option. Rotation will be based on the local axis provided by the selection set.

Min/Max Toggle

Regardless of the size of your monitor, you can always use more viewing real estate. For this reason, you can expand any view to fill the MAX view environment. By expanding a view, you replace four views with one larger view. To expand a view, use either of the following methods:

- *W*   Pressing the W key toggles the current view between full-screen and current layout size.
- *Min/Max Toggle*   Clicking on the Min/Max Toggle expands the current view to full size.

When using the Min/Max Toggle, regardless of which of the methods you use, all other views are closed. As you can see in Figures 1.17 and 1.18, instead of four views, toggling the Min/Max Toggle to full size overwrites all other views.

FIGURE 1.17.

All views in the Minimum state.

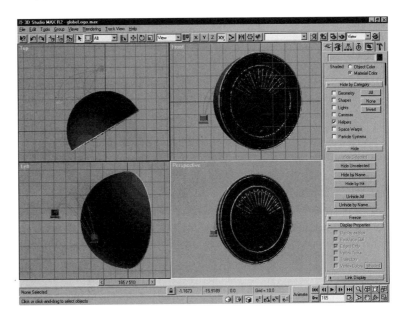

When in full-screen mode, you can still retain full viewport and interface functionality. When in full-screen mode, it is often necessary to use shortcut keys to toggle between various views, such as Front, Top, Side, and Perspective views, while retaining full-screen status.

FIGURE 1.18.

The Perspective view with the Min/Max Toggle set to Max.

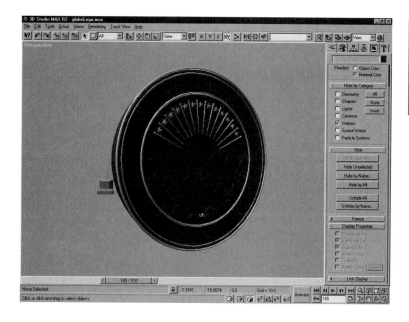

1

> **Note**
>
> To further increase the size of the modeling environment, you can switch to Expert mode by selecting Expert Mode under the Views menu. When working in Expert mode, all menus and toolbars are removed, providing maximum room for modeling and animating. Without being familiar with the shortcut keys, functionality is extremely limited in this mode. To exit Expert Mode, simply click on the Cancel Expert Mode in the lower-right corner of the screen.

Managing Resources with the Asset Manager

Creating all these models, images and scenes can really clutter your workspace. Time to organize. It is essential in any endeavor to be organized, and 3D creation is no different. There are models, textures, materials, scenes, maps, images, and animation, just to name some of the components of a single 3D project.

One way to keep components organized is to have a directory for each project. Within each project directory, create directories for each of the component types, such as rendered frames, models, and scene files. A typical directory structure might look like this:

ProjectName

Backups

Frames

Images

Maps

Models

Scenes

Finding and Opening Scenes and Models

By creating the directory structure just described, finding and opening specific components becomes much easier. When MAX is started, the default is a new scene file. To
open an existing file, select Open from the File Menu.

The standard Windows File Open dialog box is presented, starting at the MAX default
Scene path. Double-click on the desired file to load the scene. Only valid MAX Scene
files are shown.

Because MAX saves all MAX 2.5 formatted models and scenes in the same format,
native MAX models will be saved with the .max extension. In other words, whether you
save a single model or an entire scene with hundreds of objects, the file extension is the
same and you can load each just as easily.

 Note

> When opening a scene saved with a previous version of MAX, you might
> get an obsolete data error. The file is fine, but due to extensive changes in
> 3DS MAX 2.5, the scene file should be saved to update the internal scene
> structure.

Merging Models and Scenes

It's a good practice to build models separately and then add them as needed. In a real 3D
studio or animation house, more often than not, many people will work on the same animation separately. It is for this reason that models should be built to scale and saved separately. (When models are built to scale, it alleviates the problem of scaling complex
models that are incorrect in size.)

Once models are created, they need to be merged to create a 3D scene. In some cases, entire scenes will be combined and merged with existing scenes to build up a more complex scene. Merging models and scenes together is a common and efficient modeling practice. This allows the 3D artist to share models and work together while working independently.

To Do: Merging models and scenes

1. With MAX open, select Open from the File menu. Navigate to the CD-ROM accompanying this book and open scene Day1_1.max, found in the /Scenes/Day1 directory.

2. To merge an existing model or scene, select Merge from the File menu. Again, you are presented with a standard Windows file dialog box.

3. Navigate to the CD-ROM accompanying this book and double-click on Day1_2.max, found in the /Scenes/Day1 directory.

Upon double-clicking on the scene to merge, MAX displays a dialog box containing all the items in the scene file being merged (see Figure 1.19). You can select all or some of the components to merge with the scene, by clicking on a named item from the list, or using the selection buttons located on the bottom of the dialog box.

FIGURE 1.19.

The Merge file object box. You can select all or some of the objects in a merged scene to load.

Duplicate Objects and Materials

Occasionally, you might merge two files together where objects or materials contain common names. 3DS MAX 2.5 can recognize this problem and presents the user with dialog boxes to prevent replacing duplicates. When a duplicate object is merged, a dialog box appears (see Figure 1.20) offering a number of options.

FIGURE **1.20.**

The Duplicate Name
dialog box.

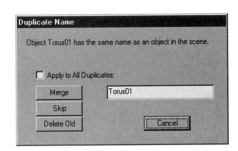

- Change the name of the imported object. By changing the name of the merged object in question, you avoid any confusion of duplicate names. 3DS MAX 2.5 allows two objects to have the same name, but when a scene contains a large number of objects, it might become difficult to distinguish between objects of the same name.

- Choose the Merge option to merge the object with the current scene. The object is then using the name specified in the Name text box.

- When the Skip option is selected, the object in question is not merged with the scene.

- Using the Delete Old option, the object is merged with the scene and replaces the object of the same name. It is important to know that the object you replace is deleted from the scene.

- When the Apply to All Duplicates check box is checked, the option (as previously specified) is applied to all duplicate objects in the scene. For instance, skipping the current object from merging causes all duplicate objects of any name to be skipped.

When duplicate materials are encountered, the dialog box in Figure 1.21 appears. The problem occurs when merged objects share a common name with a material already loaded with different attributes.

FIGURE **1.21.**

The Merge Materials
options dialog box.

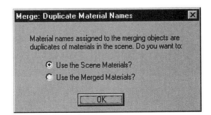

- Choose Use the Scene Materials if you want to use the materials already loaded in the current scene. This reassigns materials to any merged objects with duplicate material names.

- Choosing Use the Merged Materials causes any materials in the original scene to be replaced by the merged materials of the same name. This is a great way to update materials that have been changed and applied to the merged objects.

Merging models and scenes together is an important aspect of 3D scene composition and layout. It aids in building and animating the components of a scene independently, while seamlessly integrating with existing scenes and models.

Note

> When merging scenes, be aware of duplicate model names. Although MAX alerts you when merging components (models, lights, materials) with duplicate names, duplicate names are permitted. This can cause confusion later on when referencing an object by name. To alleviate this problem, when prompted to change a duplicate name, change the name slightly or add a numeric suffix for distinction.

Importing Models

Merging models and scenes works great if they are all 3DS MAX 2.5 files. When you need to merge files from other programs, such as 3D Studio DOS, AutoCAD, or Adobe Illustrator, you need to use the import feature.

Located under the File menu, Import loads and converts from one format to the MAX file format as the object loads into the scene. MAX can import the following formats:

- *3D Studio Mesh (.3DS, .prj)*   The .3ds format is used by 3D Studio Release 4 for saving 3D objects. The .prj format contains entire project information for 3D Studio Release 4 project files.

- *Adobe Illustrator (.ai)*   3DS MAX 2.5 can import 2D spline shapes created in Adobe Illustrator. Importing shapes in this format creates a 2D spline that can be manipulated using any of the tools available for spline manipulation. Commonly used by CorelDraw users to go from scanner to MAX.

- *AutoCAD (.dxf, dwg)*   Developed by Autodesk, this is the most common format used when transporting models between various 3D programs. Virtually every 3D program written can import files of this type. This file type does not store material attributes. DWG is the AutoCAD native format.

- *3D Studio Shape (.shp)*   This format imports 2D shape files created in 3D Studio Release 4.

- *StereoLitho (.stl)*   This format is used in rapid prototyping machines. These machines can read the data file created by 3D programs and create prototype models out of metal or plastic from the geometric information provided by the .stl file. Also a common 3D format from Architecture packages such as FormZ.

The ability to import models and shapes from other programs can be quite a time-saver. Using the Adobe Illustrator format for example, you can quickly turn flat logos into 3D objects by extruding and applying a material to the surface. Many times, models can be purchased from outside sources such as modeling houses or even independent modelers. For some projects, it might even be more efficient to purchase a model as opposed to building it.

Exporting Models

Though it is great to get models from others, it is often better to give than receive. For that reason, you might want to export your models. As easily as you have been importing models, you can export them just as easily. By selecting the Export option under the File menu, you can export either the entire scene or selected objects, depending on the export option you choose.

Actually, models are exported because they need to be used in another program. By exporting a model or scene, you are changing the file format and making it available to other programs. Although you cannot export to an Adobe Illustrator or 3D Studio Release 4 shape file (.ai and .shp respectively), all of the import file formats are also available for export. In addition to those previously mentioned, files can be exported in VRML and ASCII format.

- *VRML (.wrl)* VRML (Virtual Reality Markup Language) is used with browsers that support VRML files. When a scene is exported in this format, the browser uses the scene's cameras to move through a scene in a real-time shaded view.

- *ASCII (.ASE)* Using this format, you can export the data from any 3D scene into a readable format. This is useful if you have a program that requires you to parse the scene or model file. These files can be very large text files containing thousands of pages of data describing the scene file.

Note

Certain export modes export the entire scene, not just the selected objects. If you want to export a single object only in DXF format, for example, you must delete objects you don't want to export. Be aware of hidden objects as they too export in modes that don't support exporting selected objects only.

Saving Models and Scenes

Exporting files is great when you need to move files between a variety of programs, but more often than not, you will want to save your models and scene files to use again within the MAX environment. For this purpose, you can save entire scenes or individual objects from a scene into their own .max file.

When a scene with objects is loaded, simply choose Save under the File menu to save every aspect of the scene. Every attribute of every object is saved with the scene. For saving individual objects or saving backup files, you use the Save Selected or the Save As options respectively.

Making Yourself at Home Using Configure Paths

As you might have noticed, every time you imported, exported, or saved, MAX started in a MAX directory. These default locations are preset. You can configure these paths to any location on any local or networked drive.

To configure paths to your system, select Configure Paths from the File menu. A dialog box appears that contains all of the paths used for resources by MAX (see Figure 1.22). Select any of the components and press the Configure button to configure the path for that resource. A standard Windows File dialog box is presented. Using standard Windows navigating techniques, find the directory containing the resources you want MAX to use as the default. Any paths set in this manner will be preserved between MAX sessions.

FIGURE 1.22.

The MAX Configure Paths dialog box.

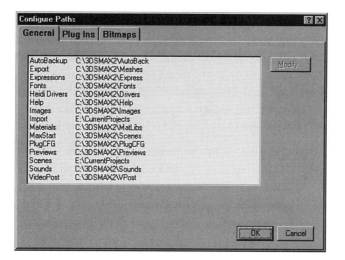

3DS MAX 2.5 Preferences

Configuring paths is a nice way to customize where MAX looks for resources. In addition to that, you can also customize the MAX environment. By setting the Preferences located under the File menu, you can build a customized environment to suit your needs (see Figure 1.23).

FIGURE 1.23.

The 3DS MAX 2.5 Preference Settings dialog box.

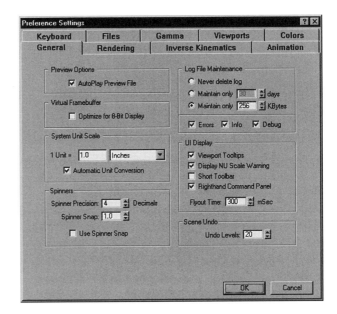

To make changes to the MAX environment, choose Preferences under the File menu. From the Preferences dialog box (pictured in Figure 1.23), you can choose from a variety of Preference settings. Preference settings made here become the default for this and subsequent MAX sessions. Changes can be made at anytime and as often as required. Though there are nine categories of Preferences, we are going to discuss the four listed.

- *General* This contains preferences for such functions as preview options, system units (inches, millimeters), decimal precision, Undo levels, and other miscellaneous interface preferences.

- *Keyboard* Used more often than others by most users, this is where you can assign shortcut keys to over 200 specific menu functions.

- *Files* From the Files tab, you can set preferences such as automatic backups and incremental saves, number of recently opened files in File menu, and archive preferences.

- *Color* Sets the default colors MAX uses to distinguish object types, such as geometry, sub-objects, Space Warps, Gizmos, and Grids.

The 3DS MAX 2.5 Toolbar System

The power of 3DS MAX 2.5 does not come without extensive tool sets. To keep tools organized, Kinetix has devised a number of strategically placed toolbars to group various types of tools. The following list explains briefly where you will find certain types of tools in the MAX interface. The tools themselves are explained in greater detail in this chapter and in other lessons throughout the book.

- *Menu Bar*   Found at the top of the screen, the menu bar contains commands to perform very specific MAX commands, as well as standard Windows commands, such as saving and opening files.

- *Toolbar*   The main toolbar is located at the top of the MAX environment, just below the menu bar. The toolbar is used for quick access to commands. Some of these commands are found in the menu bar, whereas others exist only here. Typical commands found on the toolbar include Transformation tools, invoking the Material Editor, and rendering commands.

- *Viewport Navigation*   Found in the lower-right corner of the interface, the Viewport Navigation buttons are used to change what or how objects are seen in any or all of the views. Tools for zooming and rotating the view are found here.

- *Time Controls*   Adjacent to the View Navigation buttons, on the left, are the time controls. Time controls are used to change the animation length, advancing frames, or to find key frames in an animation sequence.

- *Command Panels*   The right side of the interface is dedicated entirely to the Command Panels. The Command Panel contains numerous tabs, with each tab containing a multitude of tools and parameters. This is the heart of the 3DS MAX 2.5 interface and where most of the modeling and animation time is spent. The design of the MAX interface is such that each user can create or purchase additional tools as plug-ins that appear in the Command Panels.

- *Status Bar*   Located at the base of the interface window, the status bar is used to describe the current selection. The text in the status bar is dynamic and changes with each selection. A typical note in the status bar might be "1 object selected."

- *Prompt Line*   Found just below the status bar, the Prompt Line is used to describe the action of the current tool, such as "Click and drag to select and rotate objects."

Selecting Objects

Invariably, you will need to select an object. No need to panic—it is a very simple process. In fact, there are many methods of selecting an object. The different methods listed here aid in selecting objects while in certain modeling and animating scenarios. Although the end result is the same, there are times when one method is easier to implement than the other.

When using a selection tool, the cursor changes to a thick cross cursor when it is over a valid object. Objects are considered valid depending on the active selection filter, selection region, and the state of the selection crossing mode.

- *Select Object Tool*   Use this tool to select objects without the fear of them inadvertently being moved. When this tool is used, objects can be selected by any of the region selection methods listed here.

- *Select and Transform Tools*   When one of the transform selection tools are used, objects can be selected and transformed (Moved, Rotated, or Scaled) at the time they are selected. The Transform and Select tools also abide by the region selection methods described here.

- *Select By Name*   Instead of using the cursor to select objects, the Select by Name tool presents the dialog box pictured in Figure 1.24. From the dialog box, objects can be selected based on various filters such as type of object and alphabetical listing.

FIGURE 1.24.

The Select Objects dialog box.

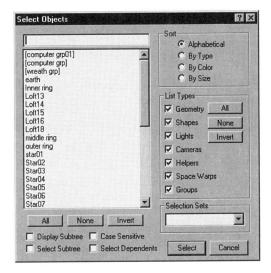

Selection Filters

Selecting an object might seem to be a trivial exercise, but the truth is, in a crowded scene, one type of selection tool is not enough. To aid in selection of only certain types of objects, MAX has a selection filter system. On the toolbar, between the Selection Region button and the Select by Name button is the Selection Filter list (see Figure 1.25). Selecting a category from the list limits the selection to that category only.

- *All*   All objects in the scene can be selected.
- *Geometry*   Geometric objects (lofts, mesh objects, NURBS, and so on).
- *Shapes*   Spline objects (Standard and NURBS).
- *Lights*   All light objects.
- *Cameras*   All camera types.
- *Helpers*   Dummy, Tape, Point, Grid, Compass, Protractor.
- *Warps*   Space Warps of any category (Geometric, Particle, Modifier based).
- *Combos*   Customized combinations of objects can be given identifiers and added to the Filter Selection List. Combos are created by selecting Combo from the list and then selecting object types from the dialog box provided.

FIGURE 1.25.

The Selection Filter list.

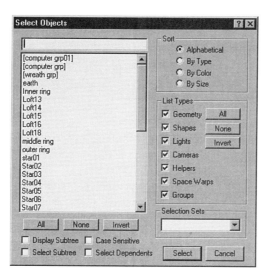

Selection Marquis

The Selection Marquis is the dotted line box created when you drag the mouse in a viewport. The Selection Marquis can be set to square, circular, or fence.

- *Rectangular Selection Region*   A selection box is drawn between the point where the mouse is first clicked in a viewport and where the mouse is released.

- *Circular Selection Region*   A circular selection region is drawn outward from the point the mouse button is clicked in a viewport to the point where the mouse button is released.

- Fence Selection Region   The Fence selection method requires the user to click the mouse in a viewport and drag out an initial marquis line. Subsequent mouse movement cause a rubber-banding effect on connecting marquis lines. Each time the mouse button is pressed in a viewport, a new line segment is drawn. This option is quite useful for creating irregular selection regions.

Selection Mode

In addition to changing the type of marquis used to create selection regions, how the region selects geometry can also be configured. There are two modes to selection: Window and Crossing (see Figure 1.26). Region selection mode can be toggled from the Selection Mode button located on the Prompt Line at the base of the MAX interface or by selecting either Window or Crossing from the Region submenu located under the Edit menu.

Window and Crossing Region Selection button

FIGURE 1.26.

The Window and Crossing Region Selection mode toggle button.

- *Window Selection*   Requires that selected objects are completely enclosed by the selection region. When drawing a selection region, objects which are not completely enclosed will not get selected. The drawing region appears as a dotted line marquis that extends from where the mouse is originally clicked to the current position of the mouse. This mode is useful when selecting objects in a crowd or for objects that are enclosed in larger objects.

- *Crossing Selection*   The selection region need only intersect any portion of the object. The most commonly used, this method requires that you merely intersect any portion of the object's geometry for it to become selected. Although easiest to use, this method makes it difficult to select objects in tight scenes or when the object is enclosed by a larger object.

- *Lock Selection*   After you make your selection, you can lock the selection by pressing the Spacebar or selecting the Lock Selection Set button located at the center of the lower toolbar. Once a selection has been locked, other items cannot be inadvertently selected or transformed.

Note

> When a selection set is locked, choosing another selection set using the Select by Name dialog box causes the new selection to replace the old and to be locked.

Transform Tools

When an object is moved, rotated, or scaled, it is referred to as a *transform*. Transforming objects in 3DS MAX 2.5 is achieved through the use of the Transform tools. Transforms are discussed in greater detail on Day 2. For greater control, each button can only perform a single type of control. This avoids accidentally rotating an object when you only intend to move it.

- *Select and Move*   When this button is active, objects can be selected and moved. Using the Axis Constraints, the Move tool can be made to move along only one axis only for a more precise move transform.

- *Select and Rotate*   To rotate objects, use the Rotate tool. Rotation can occur along any axis so that objects can be oriented to any rotational position. Like all Transform buttons, the Rotate button can also be made to rotate on a single axis only.

- *Select and Scale*   The Scale button contains a flyout that contains three different types of scaling functions. Objects can be scaled uniformly, nonuniformly, or using a squash algorithm, in which the amount of reduction in scale on one axis is applied to an enlargement on the other chosen axis.

Precision Tools

In order to have any type of precision, special tools have been developed. The tools are not typically button-type tools. More specifically precision tools consist of Units of Measure, Grids, and Snapping options.

Each of these tools adds to the modeling process and can be used to differing degrees. These tools can also be changed or turned on and off as desired.

Units of Measure

In order to build geometric models, there must be some unit of measure, such as inches or millimeters. The units of measure are used to specify distances between objects. Depending on which is more comfortable to the individual, MAX can display units of measure in either Generic, English, or Metric measurements.

To change the units of measure, select the Units Setup option found under the Views menu. From here, you can select either Metric, English, or Generic units (see Figure 1.27).

Note Using the System Unit Scale section in the General Preferences tab, found in the Preferences Settings in the File menu, is not advised for novice users. Changing the Scale property causes objects to be of a different scale than with merged objects saved at the standard scale. Use the Units Setup dialog box found under the Views menu to change the Unit of Measure.

FIGURE 1.27.

The Units Setup dialog box.

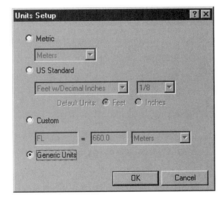

Grids

Unlike units of measure, Grids are not required to build models. They are, however, very helpful in gaining perspective, in judging distance, and for using precision modeling and transforms.

Grids can be set to any spacing desired by selecting Grid and Snap Settings from the Views menu or right-clicking on any of the Snap Toggle buttons located on the lower toolbar.

- *2D/2.5D/3D SnapToggle*   In order for objects to snap to the current grid, snapping must be turned on. Click and hold the Snap Toggle button to choose from the fly-out menu, or simply click to activate the current Snap mode.

- *AngleSnape*   When using the Select and Rotate tool, turn on the Angle Snape button to force the rotation amount to follow the snap settings. This allows for more control when rotation is performed on multiple sub-objects separately and you need to restrict the amount of rotation of each object.

- *PercentSnap*   Used with the Select and Scale buttons, the Percent Snap button constrains the amount of scaling to the specified increments.

By setting the Grid spacing, you effectively create a tighter or looser grid. The lines on the grid can then be used to snap vertices to during the modeling process or to snap objects to during a transform. The grid is also used for snapping objects to and aids in precise alignment.

Snapping to Grids

To use the grid effectively when building geometric models, you must be able to snap to a grid. Snapping to a grid ensures that models' components are properly aligned at specific points in space. Because the display environment is visually interpreted and models are mathematically calculated, what you see is not always what you get. The reason for this is that because the exact position of every vertex must be calculated, aligning by eye can never be mathematically accurate.

As you can see in Figure 1.28, MAX has very robust snap point options, allowing users to snap to the grid lines, grid points, other objects, and sub-objects.

FIGURE 1.28.

The Grid and Snap Settings dialog box.

In conjunction with the snapping options, you can choose how many dimensions the snap has active. Click and hold the mouse down briefly to reveal the Snap Toggle button flyout. Move the mouse over the desired Snap type and release. The selected Snap Toggle button is selected and snaps becomes active. Each affects the snapping options differently, as described here.

- *2D Snap*   Snapping occurs on the active construction plane only or any geometry on the same plane. The Z axis is ignored.

- *2.5D Snap*   Snapping occurs on the construction grid only. Snapping can occur with objects not on the construction plane, but the snapping point will be placed on the construction grid. It is as if all referenced snapping points were projected on a single plane.

- *3D Snap*   Snapping occurs in all dimensions regardless of planes with respect to the snapping options set. This is the default snap setting.

To use snapping during object construction, activate snapping prior to choosing one of the construction tools from the Create panel.

To apply snapping to an object after it has been constructed, you must first set some specific snap options.

To Do: Applying snapping to an object

1. Right-click the mouse on the Snap Toggle button flyout. The Grid and Snap Settings dialog box appears.

2. In Snaps tab, use the Standard snap set. Activate the Grid Point and Vertex options by clicking in the appropriate check boxes. You can click on the Clear All button to clear unwanted items, prior to setting the Grid Point and Vertex options.

3. Close the Grid and Snap Settings dialog box. Then click to turn on the Snap. Setting the Grid and Snap settings does not turn on the Snap automatically.

4. Using the Select and Move tool, select the object to be aligned with the grid. Be sure to select the object near the vertex that is to be aligned. Because vertex snapping was turned on, you can grab the object by a specific vertex and align that vertex with a position on the grid.

▲

Summary

It's been an exciting first day in the world of 3D. You covered a lot of the interface basics and some of the basic tools needed to create geometric objects. Tomorrow you will use what you learned in today's lessons to build some basic 3D objects. Though you will not do anything as controversial as cloning humans or sheep, you will be cloning 3D objects using Array and Mirror tools.

The following points recap some of the topics discussed today.

- *Points*   With the exception of NURBS objects, all objects are comprised of points, called *vertices*. Each vertex is used to connect one or more vertices to form polygons. These polygons in turn are used to create mesh faces that give an object a surface.

1

- *Coordinate systems*   In the artificial 3D environment, coordinate systems are used to keep track of where things are. 3DS MAX 2.5 uses a number of coordinate systems, each geared for a different scenario. Based on what operation you want to perform, you can change the coordinate system you use to aid in modeling and animation. Regardless of which system you use, MAX utilizes the world coordinate system to track object movement. Changing the coordinate system is for the user's convenience only.

- *Rendering*   To see what you created in geometry, you must render out the scene. Rendering uses the geometric objects in your scene plus any materials added to the objects to create a photo-realistic image. For an object to render correctly, lighting and cameras must be added to the scene for proper perspective and lighting. Models must also be supplied materials to give the geometric structure characteristics that do not exist inside a computer.

- *Views*   The only way you can see what you are doing in MAX is through views. Views can be from any angle or from any perspective. Views can also be set to view your scene from any camera or existing light source in the scene. You can also set up any configuration of views.

- *Orthographic versus Perspective*   Each view can be either orthographic or perspective. In a Perspective view, objects appear as they would in the real world (though you can change the field of view for different perspectives). Use Orthographic views for modeling because they show objects in their size relative to geometry and not relative to distance.

- *Tools*   MAX has a number of tool sets located on various toolbars around the interface. Many tools also have flyouts that supply the user with additional tools or variations on the current tool. The Command Panel is the heart of MAX and contains tools for modeling, animation, and organization.

Q&A

Q Why does the Y axis change when I switch views?

A When using the View or Screen coordinate systems, the axes are based on the view, not the object, resulting in an Axis icon that always stays the same. When object coordinate systems such as Local, or the World Coordinate System, the Axis icon reflects how the object is positioned, which causes the Y axis (and others) to look different in different views.

Q Why do my objects look strange, now that I switched to a User view?

A If you use the Arc Rotate tool on an Orthographic view, such as the Front or Top view, you change the position of the view, but the computer still wants to view objects without perspective. This can cause objects to appear deformed because their shape is based on geometry and not distance. After changing to a User view, type P to add perspective and the view will look a little more normal.

Q I've merged two scenes with duplicate objects. How do I distinguish between the two objects?

A Because 3DS MAX 2.5 allows objects to have duplicate names, it is best to change the name of the object as the scene is merged. If you answer no to the prompt alerting of duplicate names, you can still rename the object manually.

Q Why is it that when I zoom into really small objects, my grid disappears?

A In order to see the construction grid at all times, you must turn off the Inhibit Grid Subdivision Below Grid Spacing option. This is found in the Grid and Snap Settings under the Home Grid tab. Turning this option off allows MAX to dynamically change the grid spacing to accommodate for zooming in beyond the specified grid spacing.

WEEK 1

DAY 2

Modeling Basics

Now that you are familiar with the 3DS MAX 2.5 interface and some basic 3D principles, it's time to move on to the fun stuff—creating 3D models. The first thing to remember about creating geometric 3D models is that it is an exercise in dissection. Objects must first be analyzed and then dissected, either mentally or physically. The truth is, unless you use primitives as they are, all models are made up of multiple parts woven together to create the illusion of a single object. Examine the light in Figure 2.1. Although it is only a simple light fixture, there are 25 components. With the exception of the reflective cone, everything was constructed of primitives.

FIGURE 2.1.

Analyzing objects prior to modeling them saves lots of time and reduces the amount of time spent modeling parts incorrectly. At first glance, you might think that this simple model has only a few parts, when in reality there are 25 pieces to this simple light fixture.

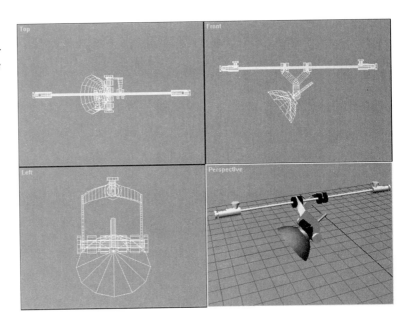

Because models are composed of many other objects, the components used to create all the parts are discussed first. In many cases, even the parts are made up of smaller parts. In today's lessons, you examine the tools needed to create some of the parts. You learn how to create primitives and two-dimensional shapes because both are used to create more complex shapes. You also learn how to Transform objects, which is the process of moving, rotating, and scaling objects. As you proceed through this chapter, keep in mind that each model you create is a process in both dissection and evolution.

Turning Concepts to Reality with the Create Panel

From the Create Panel, you begin all object creation (see Figure 2.2). From here, you can create a simple box or the most complex living creature from the dark crevices of a distant planet.

The Create Panel is where all 3DS MAX 2.5 creation begins. The Create Panel contains tools to create objects from 2D shapes to 3D Primitives to organic NURBS shapes. The Create Panel is divided into seven sections, each containing different classifications of objects.

FIGURE 2.2.

The Create Panel.

2

- *Geometric*   Contains all the 3D Primitives, NURBS surfaces, and Compound Objects.

- *Shapes*   Holds 2D creation tools for creating shapes such as circles, arc, rectangles, and other splines. Also contains NURBS curve creation tools.

- *Lights*   All lights are created through this panel, including Omni, Direct, and Spotlights.

- *Cameras*   From this tab, you can add cameras to your scene. 3DS MAX 2.5 uses two types of cameras: Free Cameras and Target Cameras. Each of these cameras can use a variety of aspect ratios applied through the rendering options dialog box.

- *Helpers*   Grids, Tapes, and Dummys are just some of the helpers you can find here. These are used as aids in modeling and animation.

- *Space Warps*   Used to create deformations in World Space. From this tab, you can choose from a variety of Space Warps to affect all types of objects.

- *Systems*   Intended as a place for plug-ins, systems can range from animation helpers to complex geometry builders to dynamic lighting capabilities. The systems that ship with 3DS MAX 2.5 have limited capability and are intended as samples only.

Modify Panel

The Modify Panel is where all objects are modified (see Figure 2.3). Modification can be as simple as changing the radius of a sphere or as complex as adding multiple Modifiers and manipulating the stack. During the modeling process, more time is spent in the Modify Panel than any other panel in 3DS MAX 2.5.

Unlike any of the other Panels in 3DS MAX 2.5, the Modify Panel is dynamic in that the displayed parameters are based on the type of object currently selected. In general, there are three sections: the Modifiers, Modifier Stack, and Parameters sections.

FIGURE 2.3.

The Modify Panel is where you find object base parameters and Modifiers.

- *Modifiers* This section contains all loaded Modifiers, which are used to change the geometry as an aid in modeling and animation. The set of Modifier buttons can be customized for each user using the Configure Button Sets button. Because the list of Modifiers is extensive (over 45 modifiers ship with 3DS MAX 2.5), you use a More button to access additional Modifiers not represented in the Modifiers section with a button.

- *Modifier Stack* As Modifiers are applied to geometric objects; a history list is maintained called the Modifier Stack. From the Modifier Stack, Sub-Object selections (vertices, faces, segments) can also be attained. Because the Modifier Stack is intended to be a nondestructive form of modeling, you can edit or remove Modifiers from the Modifier Stack with controls found in this section.

- *Parameters* Based on individual objects, the Parameters section is intended to change the various parameters with each object and each Modifier. Parameters vary with each type of object and Modifier. The radius of a sphere or the height of a cylinder are examples of typical parameters. After you select an object, you can open the Modify Panel to access the selected object's creation parameters or Modifier parameters.

Primitives: The Most Basic of Models

2

The most basic of models is the primitives. They are so basic that they are nearly drag and drop. In actual practice, they are drag and create. By dragging and creating, you can select a primitive type and then use the mouse to drag and create the parameter values. For example, creating a sphere requires that you select the sphere button and then click the mouse in a view for the center point and drag to create the radius. The sphere is created as you drag the mouse and is completed when you release the mouse button. Figure 2.4 depicts the standard primitives that ship with 3DS MAX 2.5.

FIGURE 2.4.

The 3DS MAX 2.5 standard primitives.

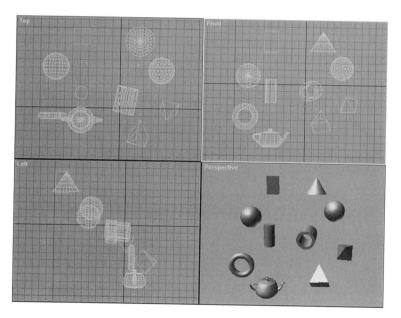

Though their name is a slight misnomer, primitives are the most simplistic of 3D models. The equations that describe their shape have been analyzed and optimized internally by 3DS MAX 2.5. Because of their simplistic nature and clean shape, primitives are essential building blocks for other 3D objects. By using the essential shapes as building blocks, you can create other shapes through shape manipulation and modification using Modifiers.

Though primitives are simple in structure, they are used extensively as the foundation for building more complex models. Start by getting familiar with the primitives.

To Do: Creating a Box

1. To select a primitives, select the Standard Primitive class of Geometric tool from the Create Panel.

2. Using the default four-view setup, select the Box tool and click and drag in a Top view. Release the mouse button and drag the mouse up or down to add height. Click when the desired height is reached.

   Notice how you create the box by clicking in a view and dragging to get the desired dimension. Releasing the mouse invokes the next dimension on the object. This is standard with all multidimensional primitives. For spheres and cubes, only a single click and drag is needed because all sides are equal. When creating a cube, for instance, you merely need to click and drag to achieve the desired radius.

When creating primitives, do not worry that the dimensions are not exactly what you want. Most objects are created roughly and then refined until the exact dimensions and shape is achieved. The refinements are done primarily through the Modify Panel.

All Standard Primitives and most Extended Primitives have a Keyboard section for creating objects from keyboard input. From the Keyboard section, you can enter exact dimensions and World Space Coordinates. Click the Create button to create the object after inputing the specified dimensions.

Modifying Creation Parameters

For every object created in 3DS MAX 2.5, there are the base parameters that define the initial shape. Called the creation parameters, these are set when the object is created. Afterwards, you must open the Modify Panel to change the creation parameters. The primitives contain the most basic creation parameters, so you need to learn about those first.

To Do: Modifying a Box

1. Create a Box by starting in the Top view. You might use either the Keyboard or click-and-drag method. Create the Box with any Length, Width, or Height values you want. Leave all other values as they are.

2. With the Box still selected, click on the Modify Panel. The bottom half of the Modify Panel shows the object's creation parameters. From here, you can adjust

▼   the Box object to more precise dimensions. Enter 20 for the Length and Width
    parameters and 100 for the height.

    Though units are not specified in this exercise, using the default of inches is fine.
    You can change units of measure using the General tab on the Preferences dialog
    box found under the File menu. Units can be either Inches, Feet, Miles,
    Millimeters, Centimeter, Meters, and Kilometers.

  As you enter the parameters, the object's shape will be redrawn to reflect the new para-
▲ meters instantly.

Segments: Another Basic Parameter of Models

The previous scenario is very common and is used for nearly every object created. In
addition to length, width, and height parameters when creating curved objects, such as
cylinders and spheres, the number of segments and sides must also be considered.
Segments are adjusted by using the Segments Spinner found in the Parameters section of
primitives. By adjusting the spinner or by typing in a value, you change the number of
segments as well as the number of faces used to generate the shape. In Figure 2.5, the
top row of objects uses minimum segments, whereas the bottom row of objects utilizes a
more realistic segment and side count.

FIGURE 2.5.

*In each of the views,
the top row of objects
use minimum seg-
ments, whereas the
bottom row uses a
denser mesh through
increased sides and
segments.*

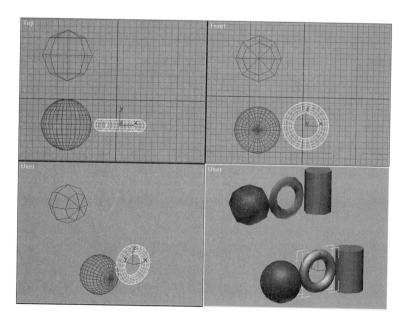

With curved objects, increasing the number of segments produces a smoother object through the curve. As you can see in the close-up shot in Figure 2.6, the denser the mesh, the smoother the curve. Unfortunately, the denser the mesh, the higher number of polygons, and therefore the longer the rendering time.

FIGURE 2.6.

A denser mesh through increased segments or sides makes for a smoother curve. Notice how the curve on the bottom is smoother due to the increased segments used to generate the mesh. By increasing the number of segments, you are effectively subdividing the curve, making it smoother.

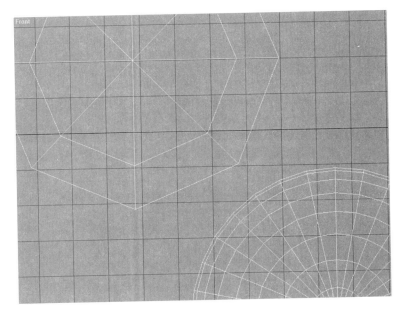

To Do: Increasing segments

1. Click Reset under the File menu to set all defaults in 3DS MAX 2.5. In a Front or Top view, create a sphere object that fills the view.

2. The default number of segments for a sphere object is 16. Click and drag the mouse up and down on the Segment slider to change the number of segments. Notice how the sphere becomes more blocky with a lower segment count and visibly smoother with more segments.

Experiment with different objects to see how the curve is affected by the number of segments and sides. For the most efficient models, use the minimum number of segments and sides to create the desired smooth effect. Although the difference between 100 polygons might not seem very much, if you saved 100 polygons on each, there would be a savings of 10,000 polygons.

Tip

> Get into the habit of using only the necessary detail for every object you create. Polygons are time, and time is money. Use the lowest segment and side count possible to create the desired curve.

Tip

> When scenes become complex and face and polygon counts get very high, there might be a decrease in performance due to the calculations needed to redraw the geometric faces. Using the Optimize Modifier, you can set up two modes of segment counts for parametric objects. This Modifier enables you to reduce the number of segments in wireframe mode but increase the segments at render time automatically for a better image.

2

Understanding and Working with Shapes

As you might have noticed, the Standard Primitives are all three-dimensional objects by nature. They have vertices that exist on all three axis when created. Shapes and splines use only two axis when created. You might recognize some of the 2D shapes in Figure 2.7, as many are cousins of the 3D primitives. In fact, three-dimensional objects are often created out of two-dimensional shapes.

FIGURE 2.7.

*Typical 2D shapes cre-
ated in 3DS MAX 2.5.*

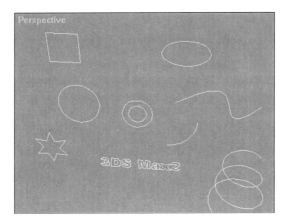

The primary use for 2D shapes and splines (interpolated curved lines) is for either creating 3D objects, lofting ribs (cross-sectional shapes), and paths (the curve that defines the shape along the local axis). Lofting ribs and paths are explained in other lessons, so this lesson concentrates on creating the 2D shapes and 3D objects from 2D shapes.

Note

Although shapes are two dimensional at initial creation, you will refer to them often as shapes and splines. This is because they are only two dimensional when first created. Through the Modify Panel, the vertices of a spline can be manipulated on any axis so that they do in fact become three dimensional.

Creating Shapes

As with the Standard Primitives, you choose a Shape tool and click and drag the mouse in a view to create a shape or spline. Some objects such as the Donut, Star, and Helix require at least two mouse actions to complete the shape. Others such as the Line tool continue to draw points as long as the user clicks and drags out line segments. Using the right mouse button or the ESC key terminates the spline creation, leaving the previous segments completed.

Although the tools for creating two-dimensional shapes and splines is adequate, you can also import 2D art from illustration and CAD packages such as Adobe Illustrator and AutoCAD. Because these illustration and drafting programs are extremely proficient at what they do, exploit the power of other tools and make your life easier.

Modifying Shapes

Typically, you need to modify a shape after it has been created. It is much easier to create a rough outline and refine it than to spend the time trying to perfectly create it the first time.

Tip

Let 3DS MAX 2.5 help with the tedious work. Do not get frustrated if the shape you create initially is not perfect. Use the tools in 3DS MAX 2.5 (such as Snapping) to massage the shape into exactly what you want.

There are three basic levels of shape modification: initial object parameters, sub-object modification, and Modifier based. Each of these levels are unique and are used to modify different aspects of a spline.

- *Initial parameters*   These parameters describe the initial creation of the shape or spline. Such attributes as the radius of a circle, or the length and width of a rectangle, are initial parameters.

- *Sub-object modification*   Vertex, segment, and spline editing are components found at the sub-object level of modification.

- *Modifier based*   When additional forces are added to the shape, they are called Modifiers. Typical Modifiers are the Bend, Twist, and Extrude Modifiers.

Modifying Initial Parameters

To modify the initial parameters, create any shape or spline, scroll down to the General Parameters, and make your changes before you create your shape. If an NGon is created, you can change the radius, whether the NGon is inscribed or circumscribed, the number of sides, and the corner radius from the Parameters section.

The General section is typical for most shapes and splines, hence the name General. These parameters are used for interpolating the number of steps used to create the shape and whether or not the spline is renderable.

- *Steps*   The number of segments used to describe the shape. Just like adding segments and sides to 3D shapes, increasing the number of steps increases the smoothness of a curve. Increasing steps can also increase polygon count and rendering time.
- *Optimize*   Check this to let 3DS MAX 2.5 use the least number of steps possible to achieve the shape.
- *Adaptive*   When Adaptive is checked, the number of steps change depending on the curve. Zero steps are used through straight segments of the shape.
- *Renderable*   When Renderable is checked, the spline renders as though it has thickness. This is an artificial attribute because by definition splines are infinitely thin. The Thickness setting is used to change the width of the spline when rendered. Regardless of this setting, the spline appears as normal in all views. This is a rendering effect and will not show up in the modeling views.

Though each shape and spline has varying parameters, the concept is the same. These parameters make up the initial shape as defined by 3DS MAX 2.5. For many shapes, this is the lowest level of change that can be made.

Sub-Object Modification

Though they are relatively simple objects, lines are made up of vertices that come in three different varieties. These three vertex types have different characteristics and effect the way the line is drawn as it passes through the vertex. The vertex types are listed under Creation Method parameters on the Line tool Create Panel button. The way each curve affects the curve is displayed in Figure 2.8.

- *Corner*   The interpolation of the line as it passes through the vertex is linear. This produces a sharp point along the spline.

- *Smooth*   As the line passes through each vertex, it is analyzed based on the previous and next vertex and is interpolated to create a smooth curve through the vertex. The distance between each vertex directly affects how smooth the curve is interpolated. This type of curve is not adjustable because the smoothing is interpolated automatically by 3DS MAX 2.5.

- *Bézier*   Like the smooth vertex type previously mentioned, the Bézier spline produces smooth curves. The difference is that the Bézier curve has adjustment handles that enable you to control the way the curve is interpolated by adjusting the handles. Bézier curves can also be changed to Bézier corners that produce independently adjustable handles on either side of the vertex. This enables a curve to be sharp as it enters the vertex and smooth as it exits, for example.

FIGURE 2.8.

The Creation Method used to create a line directly affects the way the line is produced. The Corner Creation Method was used on the top line and Smooth was used on the lower line.

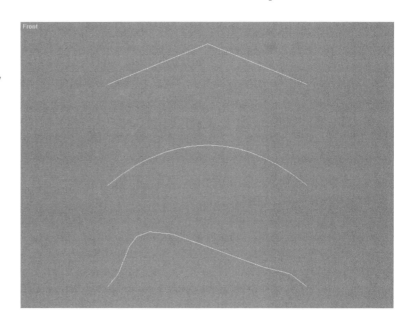

The Creation Method is also broken down into two sections. Labeled the Initial Type and the Drag Type are how the line is created based on the way the user creates the line. By selecting the vertex type for each of the creation methods, you can specify how each line is to be drawn initially, thereby eliminating the need to have to change the vertex type immediately after creation.

To Do: Creating linear lines (sharp corners)

1. Activate the Line tool from the Shapes section of the Create Panel. Located near the bottom of the Create Panel Parameters for the Line tool is the Creation Method section. Be sure that Corner is checked for Initial Type.

2. In a Front view, create the first vertex of a line by clicking toward the middle-left side of the view window. After clicking in the view with the Line tool active, the first vertex is created and a line is drawn between the current mouse position and the newly created vertex. As the mouse moves, the line also is adjusted to follow the mouse (also referred to as *rubber banding*).

3. For the second vertex, click the mouse near the middle of the view window (closer to the top of the screen than the first vertex). A new vertex is created at the top of the view connecting the first vertex to the second. The line extending from the second vertex is now rubber banding between the second vertex and the mouse pointer.

4. Click the mouse in the lower-right corner of the view window. The third vertex is created. Right-click the mouse to discontinue the Line creation process. You should have a line that looks similar to the one in Figure 2.9.

FIGURE 2.9.

A three-vertex line created using the Corner Creation Method. The Corner vertex type creates lines that are linear in their interpolation, providing sharp corners at every vertex.

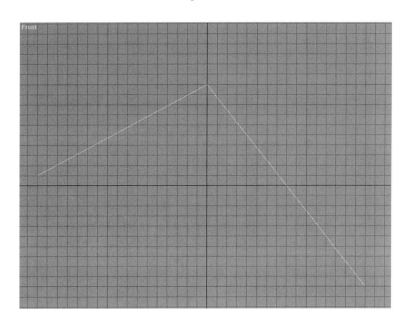

▼

As you can see, the line created is very linear, and the connecting segments enter and exit the vertices precisely. In the next two examples, you generate interpolated splines using Smooth and Bézier vertices. The following two exercises use the exact same steps as used previously so that you can fully realize the difference in how the Creation Method affects the outcome of the spline. When following the exercise, try to create the points at the same locations as the previous line.

To Do: Creating a Smooth line

1. To create a Smooth line, activate the Line tool and set the Initial Type to Smooth in the Creation Method parameters.

2. Follow steps 1 through 4 in the previous exercise. When creating vertices, try to create them as close to the previous line as possible to get a better idea of how each Creation Method affects the Line.

3. When the line is created, you have a line similar to the one in Figure 2.10.

FIGURE 2.10.

The same three-vertex line created using the Smooth Creation Method. By using the Smooth Creation Method, the smoothness of the line is based on the position and distance of each vertex. Each vertex is influenced by the vertex before and after itself along the length of the spline.

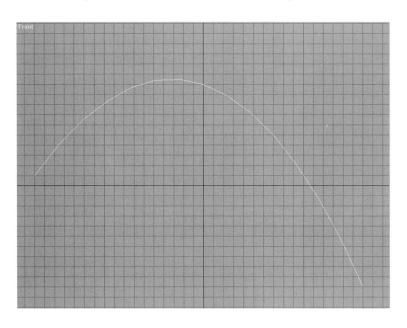

As you might have noticed, the line behaves differently during the creation process with Smooth set as the Creation Method. This is because the line is interpolated, meaning that each vertex has influence over the surrounding vertices to ensure a smooth curve.

Exercise 2.6: Creating a Bézier line

1. To create a Bézier line, activate the Line tool and set the Initial Type to Smooth and the Drag Type to Bézier in the Creation Method parameters.

2. Follow steps 1 through 3 in the exercise for creating a line. Do not create the third vertex at this point. Remember to try to create vertices as close to the previous line as possible, to get the full effect of how each Creation Method affects the Line.

3. For the third vertex, try to click the mouse in the same position you created the third vertex for the other two lines (in the previous exercises). Before you release the mouse button, drag the mouse about halfway up the view window and release the mouse. Right-click to complete the Line creation operation.

▲

Your line should look something similar to the line in Figure 2.11. As you can see, the first two vertices are the same as in the Smooth line created in the previous exercise. That is because Smooth type was used for the Initial Type vertices. The third vertex is completely different than the other three. Although it is smooth, the shape of the line into the vertex was affected by how you dragged the mouse after clicking to create that vertex. That is what is meant by the Drag Type vertex.

FIGURE 2.11.

By changing the Drag Type to Bézier and using a drag method to create the third vertex in the spline, your line has taken new dimensions. Because the third vertex is a Bézier type, the handles can be adjusted using Transform tools to radically change the shape of the spline.

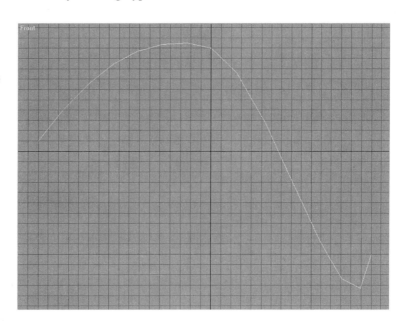

In addition to the third vertex in the previous exercise being created using the drag mode, the vertex is also of the Bézier variety. The Bézier type contains handles that enable you to alter the effect of the interpolation along the spline. In the following exercise, you adjust the Bézier curve to see how it affects the overall shape of the spline.

When you do need to change the vertices of a line after it has been created, you need to access the Sub-Objects (vertex, segment, spline). Sub-Object selection is achieved through the Modify Panel in the Modifier Stack section. Initially the Line shape and the NURBS curves are the only Shapes to have sub-object modification parameters included in the default. Other Shape objects can be given sub-object modification parameters by adding an Edit Modifier, which is discussed in another section.

Sub-object modification is the modification of the vertices, splines, and segments of a shape object. A line shape is a collection of vertices connected with line segments to form a multisided shape (unless there are just two vertices used to form a straight line).

To Do: Modifying Sub-Object parameters

1. Using the line created in the previous exercise, select the line and open the Modify Panel.

2. Midway down the Modify Panel, under the Modifier Stack section, is the Selection Level and a Sub-Object button. Click on the Sub-Object button.

3. To the right of the Sub-Object button is the Selection Level list. The default is Vertex, although Segment and Spline levels are also accessed here. Figure 2.12 shows the Modify Panel and the Sub-Object selection parameters.

FIGURE 2.12.

The Modify Panel containing the Sub-Object selection level and the Sub-Object list.

4. Using the Vertex level, you can now Transform individual or groups of vertices. The vertices are identified by the tick (small cross) marks located along the spline. Using the Select and Move tool, select and examine each vertex by dragging a region or clicking directly on it.

You might notice that vertex 1 and 2 look the same (represented by a red tick mark) when selected. More importantly, you should notice that the third vertex has handles (represented by lines with small green boxes at the end of each line). If the handles are

▼

▼   not visible, zoom out the view window so that the entire line can be seen or click on the
    Zoom Extents All button.

   5. With the Select and Move tool, click and drag the mouse on one of the Bézier han-
      dles (the green box at the end of the handle line). Drag the mouse in all directions
▲   to see how the curve of the line is affected.

By using a Bézier-type vertex, you can directly control how the line is affected, just by
making adjustments to the handles. Bézier curves are extremely useful when smooth
lines with controls are needed. By using two Bézier curves in a row along a spline, you
can move the handles into opposing directions and create very smooth 'S' type curves.

2

Note

In most cases, when in Sub-Object selection mode, you cannot select other
objects in the scene. To exit the Sub-Object mode, simply click on the Sub-
Object selection button to return to standard selection mode.

Tip

Initially, when splines are created, you might notice that the curve is somewhat choppy. Because interpolated splines can generate many faces at render time (or when used as a path for other objects), 3DS MAX 2.5 uses a
default setting to reduce the number of steps generated. By turning off the
Sub-Object selection level, you can access the interpolation steps in the
Interpolation section of the Edit Object parameters. Setting the steps to
Adaptive lets 3DS MAX 2.5 generate the number of steps needed to create a
smooth curve. If you prefer, you can increase the steps manually by setting
the steps to a higher number than the default of 6. Increasing the number
of steps can increase the rendering time by generating more faces than the
Adaptive method.

Using the Edit Spline Modifier to Edit Shapes

Unlike the initial or sub-object modification methods, Modifier-based modification
requires that you add a Modifier to the object. Though Modifiers and the Modifier Stack
are explained in detail in Day 3, you use the Edit Spline Modifier here for some basic
Shape modification.

To Do: Modifying a shape using the Edit Spline Modifier

1. Start with a fresh scene by selecting Reset from the File menu. Create a Circle shape in the Front view.

2. With the Circle shape selected, open the Modify Panel. Under the Modifiers section, click on the Edit Spline Modifier. If it does not appear in the Modifier section, click on the More button and choose it from the list.

3. When the Edit Spline Modifier is added to the Circle shape, sub-object selection is automatically invoked at the vertex level.

4. Any vertex can now be selected and Transformed using the Select and Move tool, just as you did in the Line object.

Experiment by moving vertices and segments around. Remember to click the Sub-Object Selection button to select other objects in the scene. Alternatively, you can also select the Create Panel (or any other Panel) to close the Sub-Object Selection mode.

Building Complex Shapes

When creating a shape object, the default state is that each time a Shape tool is used, a new shape object is created. If the Start New Shape button is turned off during shape creation, each subsequent shape becomes a spline within the same Editable Spline object.

To Do: Adding multiple splines

1. Create a circle shape object from the Shape section of the Create Panel.

2. After creating a single circle, remove the check from the Start New Shape check box directly below the Object Type section heading.

3. Create another circle object so that it overlaps like the two circles in Figure 2.13.

4. Right-click the mouse to exit the Create Mode for the Circle tool.

FIGURE 2.13.

The two circle objects are created as part of the same shape object. The object is now an Editable Spline object.

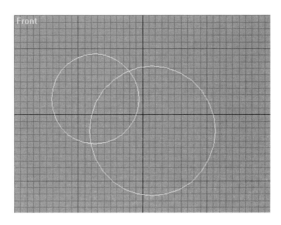

▼ As you can see, if you deselect and select either of the circles, both become selected.

▲ This is because, instead of each being a circle shape, they now form one editable spline.

 Note Even though the Circle shape does not have a sub-object selection mode, when two shape objects are combined, they automatically are converted to an Editable Spline, with vertex, segment, and spline sub-object selections.

2D Boolean Operations—Spline Tingling Cutting Tools

In the previous section, you learned how to use the vertex and segment sub-object selection to refine a shape. For more sophisticated shape refinement, you can use entire shapes to affect another shape. If you need a rectangular shape with a round hole in the middle, how can you create one? There is no "rectangle with round hole in the middle" primitive. The answer to this intriguing question is Boolean operations.

Boolean operations come in two categories: 2D and 3D. The 3D Boolean tools are found under the compound objects class in the Create Panel of the Geometry button. The 2D Booleans are found in the Spline Sub-Object selection level. The 2D Booleans work very similar to the 3D type, except that they are suited for two-dimensional objects only.

 • *Boolean Subtraction*   When selected, the shape of the second operand is subtracted from the shape of the first operand where the two shapes overlap.

 • *Boolean Union*   Two shapes can be combined using the Boolean Union. The vertices where the two shapes overlap are removed to create a single shape combination of the two operands.

 • *Boolean Intersection*   The geometry from both shapes is removed except where they overlap. The resulting shape is a single spline that outlines where the two shapes intersected.

Each Boolean operation generates an entirely new shape based on the operands. By understanding how each operation works, you can easily predict the outcome. The shapes in Figure 2.14 all use the same circle and rectangle, yet each had a different Boolean operation applied.

FIGURE 2.14.

From left to right are the original circle and rectangle, followed by results of the Boolean Union, Subtraction, and Intersection operations performed on the circle and the rectangle.

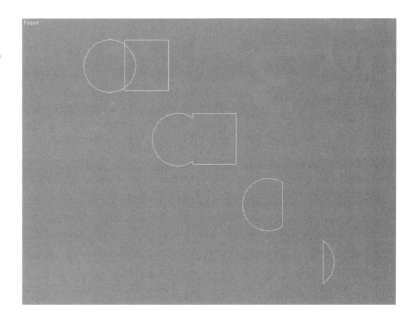

To Do: Modifying an editable spline

1. Using the objects created in the previous exercise, select the Circle object Editable Spline and open the Modify Panel. In the Modifier Stack, you can see that the object is an Editable Spline as opposed to a Circle object.

2. Turn on Sub-Object Selection and choose Spline from the Sub-Object List. You should now have some Edit Spline options such as Outline, Boolean, Mirror, and Detach.

3. For this exercise, you use the Boolean operations to create a different shape.

Boolean operations are used to change geometry through the addition, subtraction, or intersection of two objects. There are Boolean tools for both 2D and 3D objects.

4. In the Boolean section, select the middle button, one dark and one light overlapping circle. This is the Boolean subtraction button.

5. Move the mouse over the two circles and select the larger of the two circles. Because you are in sub-object selection mode, the selected spline becomes red, indicating that it is a sub-object selection.

6. Click on the Boolean button and notice that it stays pressed down and changes color. You are now in Boolean Subtraction mode.

▼

▼ 7. Use the mouse to select the other circle. As the mouse moves over the other spline, it changes to a thick cross cursor in addition to the Boolean Operation icon. This indicates that the newly selected spline will be subtracted from the first selected spline. Click on the unselected circle. The shape of the second selected spline is removed from the first (see Figure 2.15).

FIGURE 2.15.

Performing a Boolean Subtraction on the two circles creates the crescent moon-shaped spline pictured here.

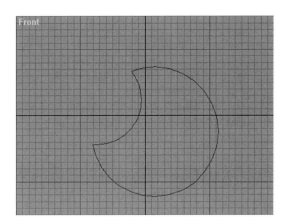

▲

As you selected the remaining spline, 3DS MAX 2.5 used that shape to subtract it from the first selected spline object. This cookie-cutter operation is a typical Boolean operation and can be done with any two splines. Right-clicking the mouse terminates further Boolean operations.

The rectangle and the circle in Figure 2.16 were created as a single Editable Spline. After a Boolean Union was performed, the results of removing the overlapping segments can be seen in Figure 2.17.

FIGURE 2.16.

This rectangle and circle are part of a single Editable Spline object. Use the Boolean Union operation to remove overlapping geometry.

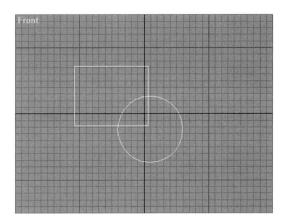

FIGURE 2.17.

The results of performing a Boolean Union on an overlapping rectangle and circle that were created as a single Editable Spline object.

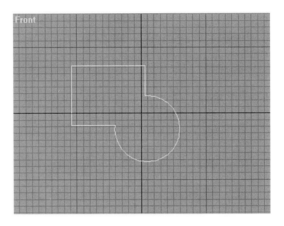

The Boolean Intersection is used to remove all geometry except that which is intersected by two objects. It is essentially the opposite of the Union operation. The geometry that was removed from the Boolean Union operation is in essence what would be left if the Intersection operation were performed instead. Figure 2.18 depicts the same rectangle and circle after a Boolean Intersection was performed.

FIGURE 2.18.

After performing a Boolean Intersection on the same overlapping rectangle and circle as in the previous exercise. The original shape is in darker gray but the results are shown in the lighter shade.

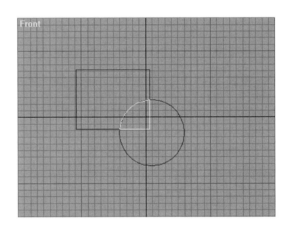

You spent all this time creating 2D shapes, editing vertices, and applying Booleans but still ending up with a two-dimensional object. Though it might not seem relevant, learning these basic 2D concepts are necessary for creating three-dimensional objects in 3DS MAX 2.5 (or any 3D program). The types of shapes that you create here are used with other tools (called Modifiers) to create more elaborate and complex shapes. For example, by using a Lathe Modifier, you can create a beautiful vase from a 2D shape representing the profile of the vase. You can also use the Loft Modifier to create very complex shapes based on 2D shapes used to describe various cross sections of the object. Fear not! You will convert these two-dimensional basic shapes into lifelike 3D objects. You must first learn some additional fundamental concepts.

Using Transforms

Transform is a term used to describe the change in position, rotation, and scale of an object. Transforms are used to position an object in a scene, animation, and in modeling. In 3DS MAX 2.5, each type of Transform has its own tool. Each of the Transform Tools are located in the toolbar located at the top of the 3DS MAX 2.5 interface.

2

- *Select & Move*   Used to select and change object position by holding the mouse button down while moving the mouse. Movement can be constrained to any one or two axes and can utilize any of the available coordinate systems.

- *Select and Rotate*   Select and rotate objects along the specified axis. Rotation is applied as the mouse button is pressed and the mouse is moved. Rotation can be constrained to any one or two axes and can utilize any of the available coordinate systems.

- *Select and Scale*   Objects can be selected and scaled using this tool. Unlike the other Transform tools (Move and Rotate), the Select and Scale tool has a flyout with three choices: Uniform Scale, NonUniform Scale, and Squash. Uniform Scale scales the object evenly on all axes. NonUniform Scale uses axis constraint to scale only selected axes. Using Squash scaling causes one axis to increase in scale while another is decreased a proportionate amount.

You can use the Transform Tools to select or to select and transform. For example, if you have the Rotation tool active and the current selection set is a cube, you can still use the Rotation tool to select another object, such as a sphere, and change its radius through the Modify Panel without causing the sphere to rotate.

However, you can select an object and apply a transform with the Current tool, all in a single motion.

Moving Objects

For a position transform, use the Select and Move tool. By selecting an object with the Select and Move tool, you can change an object's position according to the active Axis Constraints and the active Coordinate System. Transforms can be performed either manually by dragging the object or by using the Transform Type-In dialog box for precise placement.

Creating Precise Transforms

There are many instances when precise object movement is required. In fact, for good scene composition, object placement should be a precise, well-thought procedure and not a haphazard afterthought. For example, suppose you are building a model of an entire house as a mock-up design of a real house for a client. In building the scene, it is imperative that objects are built to scale so that as many features of the final image or animation will portray the house as it is to be built. In the following example, you examine how to position a handle on a cabinet door. Though it is a simple exercise, it is important if the cabinet is built from existing blueprints or needs to be representative of a real object.

To Do: Creating precise transforms

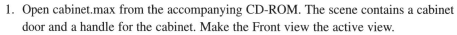

1. Open cabinet.max from the accompanying CD-ROM. The scene contains a cabinet door and a handle for the cabinet. Make the Front view the active view.

2. Using the Select and Move tool, move the handle object around on the screen. Prior to releasing the left mouse button, click the right mouse button. The object snaps back to its original position. This is a current Undo feature that comes in handy when you realize that the current operation is not what you intended. Of course, there is always the Undo button for after the fact.

3. With the cabinet handle still selected, click on the Select and Move tool to make it the active Transform tool.

4. With the cabinet handle object still selected, right-click the mouse on the Select and Move tool icon. A Type-In Transform dialog box appears. This dialog is used to type in exact world coordinate values for the placement of the current object.

In this example, you want to move the handle so that it is two inches from the base of the cabinet door and one inch from the left side. To make the change, you must edit the values found in the Transform Type-In dialog box.

5. In the Transform Type-In dialog box, type in 69.311 in the Z axis input box because you want the handle to be positioned two inches above the base of the cabinet door. Because the handle is currently placed at the base of the door, you add 2 to the Z value shown in the Transform Type-In dialog box (67.3111).

6. With the transform Type-In box still open, add one inch to the current location on the X axis to move the handle one inch from the left edge of the cabinet door. The original position is at -0.6323, and adding 1 will give you a new X position of 0.3677 (-0.6323 + 1.0).

▼ Although it seems easy enough to figure out the value of where the new coordinate should be, there is an easier way. After all, why not let the computer handle the grunt work.

7. Click on the Undo button to undo the Transform performed in step 5. You can try this again an easier way. You do not need to close the Transform Type-In window to click the Undo button.

8. Because you want the handle of the cabinet door to be positioned one inch from the left side of the edge of the cabinet door, you can perform an offset transform. This is accomplished by typing the desired Transform amount in the appropriate axis parameter. In the Offset;World X parameter, type 1.0 or simply the numeral one. Press the Return or Enter key to input the data. As you can see, the handle was moved to the same location (.3677) as when you had to do the math yourself. The offset feature saves a lot of time and possible human error by letting 3DS MAX 2.5 calculate the new coordinate based on the offset parameter.

You have just successfully completed placing an object based on exact dimensions. What wasn't covered here was that prior to changing the position of the cabinet handle, the Alignment tool was used to position the handle at the exact edge of the cabinet door. The Type-In Transform is used to type in exact transform amounts on any axis. The parameters on the left side are used for exact World Space Coordinate values, and the right side

▲ is used for inputting an offset amount from current values.

The Select and Move tool and the Transform Type-In can be used on both objects and Sub-Object selection sets. This is a precise method for transforming objects and works equally well in the Rotate and Scale Transforms.

Note During a parameter change that requires holding the mouse and dragging, clicking the right mouse button before releasing the left mouse button causes the change to be undone. This action works on spinners and any action involving a click-and-drag operation.

Pivot Points

As we move into rotating objects, it is important to realize that every object has a point designated as its pivot point. Typically, the pivot point can be located at the base or at the center of an object, but it can be moved (deliberately) to anywhere on the object or in the scene. In other words, you can have a sphere with the pivot point resting at the center of the sphere. You can also manually move the pivot point to be 100 miles away from the center of a one-inch sphere. The reason for this is that when objects are rotated, they need to pivot at some point, thus the pivot point was established.

The pivot point is an imaginary position on the object used to establish the object's position and rotation point. When viewing an object's positional data, it is based on where the pivot point is located, not necessarily where the object is located. As an example, if box A is visibly one inch from the center of the world grid, it might seem safe to assume the location of the box is somewhere around one inch, give or take a half inch. In reality, the location of the box is based on the pivot point, which can be located anywhere in the scene's universe.

Rotating Objects

As well as objects being moved, they are also frequently rotated. Rotate Transforms use the Rotate tool. Objects can be rotated around any of the three axes using any of the coordinate systems provided in 3DS MAX 2.5.

When rotating an object, you must be aware of the object's pivot point, the point from which rotation occurs. Figure 2.19 shows a few objects, each with its pivot point positioned differently.

FIGURE 2.19.

Each of the objects pictured has its pivot point located somewhere differently. The sphere has its pivot centered, while the box is at its base, and the cylinder's pivot is positioned at its top.

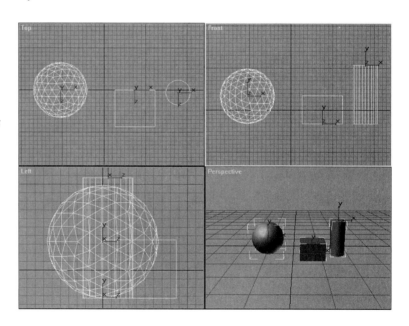

Objects are rotated around their pivot point. For this reason, as you rotate objects, you need to be aware of where their pivot points are.

To Do: Pivot Points and the Rotate Transform

1. Open rotpivot.max from the accompanying CD-ROM. The scene contains the geosphere, the box, and the cylinder object seen in Figure 2.19.

2. Using the Rotate tool, rotate each object around the various axes. Use the View coordinate system. Notice how each object rotates differently based on the pivot point.

Based on the location of the pivot point, objects can behave differently, even when given the same amount of rotation. You can adjust or move the pivot point by using the Pivot options located on the Hierarchy Panel. The Hierarchy menu and adjusting the pivot point is discussed in a later day.

Scaling Transforms

Unlike Moving and Rotating, Scaling transforms change attributes about an object's geometry. It is for this reason that many times scaling is not the desired way to change the size of an object. When possible, it is always best to change the object's initial parameters or by adjusting the sub-objects instead of scaling an object.

The problem with scaling an object is that the base parameters become misleading. If you scale a sphere with a radius of 5, the sphere still shows 5 in the radius parameter, though the true radius is somewhat different. To find out what the true radius is, you can look at the Transform Type-In by right-clicking the mouse on the Scale tool. On the left side of the dialog box, in the Absolute;Local section, is the percentage of scale for each axis. Using simple math, you can calculate the actual radius by multiplying the value in the Transform Type-In by the radius value in the parameter list.

Though advanced at this level of discussion, scaling can be accomplished in a nondestructive way. Through the use of Modifiers (discussed in tomorrow's lessons), you can apply scaling to the object using the Xform Modifier. Used in this fashion, the integrity of the original object remains intact, while accurate scaling can still be achieved.

Alternative Coordinate Systems

During the course of an animation or during the modeling process, objects are moved, rotated, and repositioned in ways that can make it difficult to make adjustments to the transforms. For this reason, 3DS MAX 2.5 has a variety of coordinate systems. Although the world coordinate system is based on the actual object transform parameters, it is often necessary to transform an object based on its local transforms, screen coordinates, or the orientation of another object in the scene. Say you want to roll a cart up or down an incline. Using the incline's local coordinate system, you can easily animate the cart to follow the angle of incline. Though this is a simple example, using the local coordinate system ensures that the cart remains on the surface of the incline as it moves.

Although it might seem confusing that there are multiple coordinate systems, you will appreciate them immensely after you become familiar with using the different coordinate systems. 3Ds MAX 2.5 uses the View coordinate system as the default because objects are transformed based on the viewport, not the object's orientation, making object transformations easier.

- *View* The default coordinate system used in 3DS MAX 2.5. This coordinate system is based on the current view. For instance, using a View coordinate system when moving along the X axis, the object always moves either left or right in the view. Depending on which view you choose, the object might actually move along the X or Y World axis. This Coordinate system was designed to speed up working in 3D, allowing you to jump from viewport to viewport and freely move your objects without worrying about changing the constraints or object orientation.

- *Screen* Similar to the View Coordinate system, this uses a coordinate system relative to the active viewport. In this case, even if the view is changed from the default views (becoming a User view), moving along the X axis causes the object to move relative to the view.

- *Local* This coordinate system uses the coordinate system for the object. As objects are transformed, their local coordinate system goes with them. In other words, as an object is rotated, its local Z axis might not point up anymore. For example, when using the local coordinate system, moving along the Z axis causes the object to move along its Z axis regardless of where it is pointed. This is extremely useful for scaling objects that have been rotated.

- *Pick* Using the Pick coordinate system, you can choose the local coordinate system of any object in a 3DS MAX 2.5 scene. This is advantageous when moving objects along the surface of another object that might be at some incline. To use the Pick Coordinate system, select Pick from the Coordinate System list and select the desired object in the scene. The object name appears in the Current Coordinate system label. Because all Constraints and Coordinate systems are based on the currently selected Transform mode, you must first select the transform that you want to use before you select Pick mode. After the Pick coordinate system has been chosen, you must then pick the object on which the coordinate system will be based. After selecting the object from the scene or from the Select By Name dialog box, the selected object's name appears in the coordinate drop-down list.

Axis Constraint

Now that you are using all these different coordinate systems, you might want to start constraining transform axes. By constraining transforms, objects in a scene can be made to move or rotate on a single axis only. This prevents inadvertent and more precise transforms. Constraining a transform axis is often used during animation and modeling, such as ball bearings rolling across a chessboard.

Axis Constraint can be implemented by either clicking on the Axis Constraint buttons (see Figure 2.20) or by using the function keys.

FIGURE 2.20.

The Axis Constraint buttons. Clicking on any of these buttons will toggle between permitting and constraining transforms along that axis.

Using the Axis Constraint function keys, you can toggle the On/Off state of any axis. The axis Constraint keys work with the active coordinate system.

- *F5* Toggles the X axis constraint.
- *F6* Toggles the Y axis constraint.
- *F7* Toggles the Z axis constraint.
- *F8* Turns on current two axis constraint. Repeated presses turn on remaining combinations (XY, YZ, ZX) of two-axis transform constraint.

In addition to the function keys, the Axis Constraints can also be changed using the accent key (`) and the tilde (~). The accent key cycles through the X, Y, and Z constraints and the tilde (~) key cycles through the two axis choices.

Transform Type-In

For the most precise transform, use the Transform Type-In box. By clicking the right mouse button on any of the Transform tools (Move, Rotate, Scale), you invoke the Transform Type-In dialog box (see Figure 2.21). From here, you can add the exact amount of movement, rotation, or scale. The Transform Type-In dialog box is Transform tool dependent. Thus, if the Select and Move tool is active, the Transform Type-In will be applied to a Move Transform only. To use a Transform Type-In for the Rotation or the Scale Transform, you must first select the appropriate Transform tool. You can also access Transform Type-in from the Tools menu.

FIGURE 2.21.

The Transform Type-In dialog box is used to transform objects with precise values.

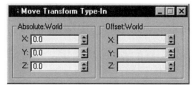

> **Note**
>
> When using the Transform Type-In dialog box, transforms are not constrained by the active axis constraints.

Transforming Pivot Points

All objects are created with a default pivot point, but that pivot point might not be in the appropriate location for the work you want to do. For example, if you want to rotate an object around its end point, but its pivot point is in its middle, you can transform the pivot point as one method to accomplish this. Although pivot points can be moved, a pivot point's position cannot be animated.

For one example, you can create a pendulum on a clock. If the pivot point were at the center of the pendulum arm, the swing would be incorrect (as can be seen in Figure 2.22) when the arm is rotated. Moving the pivot point to the top of the arm makes for an animation with more realistic motion. Figure 2.23 shows the ghost images of the swing of a correct pendulum.

FIGURE 2.22.

A pendulum with the pivot point centered. This motion is incorrect for the pendulum's swing.

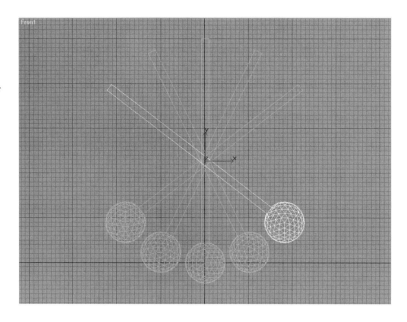

FIGURE 2.23.

With the pivot point set at the top of the pendulum arm, a more realistic swing can be achieved.

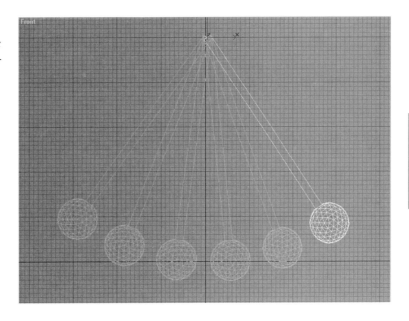

2

To Do: To transform a Pivot Point

1. Create an object and select it. In the Hierarchy Panel, click on the Pivot tab.

2. Select Affect Pivot Only. Using the standard Transform tools, you can Move, Rotate, or Scale the pivot point. You can also use the Align and Snap tools to reposition the pivot point, just as you would with any other object in 3DS MAX 2.5.

> **Note**
>
> When scaling the pivot point, even though Affect Pivot Only is selected, the entire object will be scaled, not just the Pivot Point. There is really no reason to ever scale the pivot point of an object because the pivot point has no size. The pivot point is merely a location from which transforms are applied to the attached object.

▲

Scale

Scaling is used to change the proportionate size of an object. Changing the scale of an object does not change its creation parameters. This can cause unexpected results when building other objects based on a scaled object. Both of the cubes in Figure 2.24 are 10×10×10. The box on the left has been scaled by 50 percent, yet still retains creation parameters that state that both objects are 10×10×10.

FIGURE 2.24.

Both of these cubes are identical in their size parameters. The difference is that the cube on the left has been scaled by 50 percent.

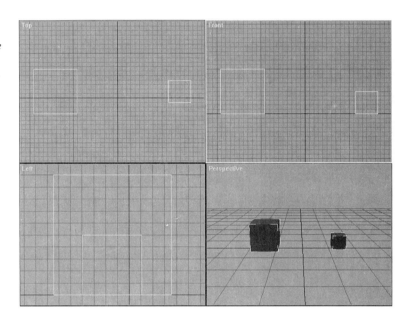

The Scale tools are available in the 3DS MAX 2.5 toolbar located at the top of the screen in the form of a flyout. This means that if you press and hold the mouse button on the Scale tool, a flyout menu appears showing the Non-Uniform and the Squash tools. To use the Scale tools, simply select the desired tool and click and drag the mouse on an object to scale. The object need not be selected prior to using the Scale tools.

There are three scale tools on the 3DS MAX 2.5 toolbar. Their usage is the same, although the results are somewhat different. Using the Non-Uniform Scale and the Squash tool at the object level causes 3DS MAX 2.5 to post a warning dialog box confirming the Scale choice. This occurs because using the Non-Uniform and Squash Scale can cause unexpected results when subsequent operations are performed on those objects.

 • *Uniform Scale*   This tool scales the object in all directions equally, regardless of the Axis Constraint options set. Clicking and dragging up with the mouse with an object selected scales the object larger (scaling smaller when the mouse is dragged down).

 • *Non-Uniform Scale*   This tool uses the Axis Constraint options to constrain the scale of any axis. When an axis is constrained, it will not be affected by the Non-Uniform Scale tool.

 • *Squash Scale*   This tool performs opposite scales on opposing axes. As one axis increases, the opposite axis decreases by the same amount.

The scale tools are best when used with sub-object selection sets and not at the object selection level. This is due to the logical manner in which 3DS MAX 2.5 applies the Scale transforms.

Note

If a situation occurs where weird things happen after you perform a Squash or Non-Uniform Scale on an object, you can reset the scale to it original state by selecting Scale in the Reset section of the Hierarchy Panel. This does not affect any object manipulation, but it does reset the scale so that subsequent transforms react properly.

2

Scale tools are best when used with sub-object selection sets, such as vertices. If you need to pinch the middle of a cylinder as in Figure 2.25, using the Uniform Scale tool on the sub-object selection of vertices makes it a snap. You can also use an Xform Modifier and then scale the gizmo. This allows you to change the scale anytime later in the life of the object.

FIGURE 2.25.

Scaling the vertices of a cylinder using the Uniform Scale tool. By selecting a middle row of vertices and scaling down, the vertices move closer together, causing the cylinder to become pinched.

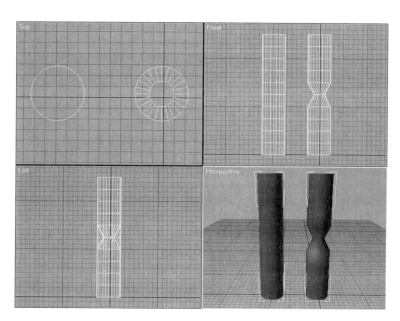

Aligning Objects

With all this transforming going on, it is inevitable that you will want to align two objects. The Alignment tool in 3DS MAX 2.5 makes this a breeze. You can align objects according to bounding boxes, pivot points, or centers. By using the Alignment tool, you can perfectly align selected objects to other objects along any of the three axes.

• *Align*   Used to align objects and Sub-Objects to other objects within a scene. This is the most commonly used Alignment tool and also the easiest to use.

 • *Normal Align*   When you need to align the normals of two objects, this is the tool to use. This works well when two objects are created independently and the results of each need to be aligned specifically along irregular edges. Using the Normal Align tool, you can align the two objects based on the Normal projected by each of the respective faces.

 • *Place Highlight*   To aid in lighting a scene, the Place Highlight tool was added. This tool aligns the selected light to a specified normal on a selected object. This tool is extremely useful when applying lights to a scene and creating the perfect light setup.

 • *Align Camera*   This tool works much the same way as the Place Highlight tool except that it works with cameras instead of lights. Again, this tool greatly aids in getting the camera aligned to exactly the correct position quickly.

 • *Align to View*   In addition to aligning to other objects, you can use the Align to View tool to align a selected object's local axis to the current view. Objects can be aligned along any of the three axes of the selected view. Views can consist of any view, including a view through a camera, light, or user view.

The Alignment button contains a variety of alignment tools, but for now you will concentrate on object alignment. The Object Alignment tool is used to align the selected object with a target object. To use the Alignment tool, select an object, choose the Alignment tool from the toolbar, and select a target object. Any two transformable objects can be aligned. You can also use the Alignment tool to align sub-object selections, pivot points, and even gizmos.

After a selection and target has been made with the Align tool, the Align Selection dialog box appears (shown in Figure 2.26). This is where all the alignment options are selected and applied.

To align two objects, select from which points the objects are to be aligned. The alignment points are explained next. Figures 2.27 and 2.28 show two simple boxes aligned using the Minimum and Maximum settings.

• *Align Position*   This is the axis that is to be affected. You can affect one or more axes at a time.

• *Minimum*   The closest edge of the object's bounding box to the target object.

• *Center*   The center of the object's bounding box.

FIGURE 2.26.

The Align Selection dialog box is used to choose the axis of alignment and to that aspect the objects are to be aligned.

- *Pivot Point* The object's Transform Pivot Point.
- *Maximum* The farthest edge of the object's bounding box.
- *Apply* Use the Apply button to apply the currently selected alignment options. This is useful if different axes need to be aligned differently. Apply does not close the dialog box, allowing for further alignment.
- *OK* Performs and closes the Alignment operation.

FIGURE 2.27.

Two boxes aligned using Minimum to Minimum along the Y axis.

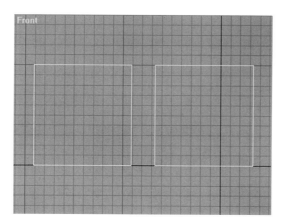

FIGURE 2.28.

*Two boxes aligned
using Minimum to
Maximum along the
Y axis.*

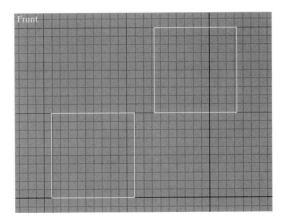

Cloning Objects

Though not very difficult, it is important that you become familiar with alignment before working on cloning. *Cloning* is used to create multiple copies of objects without building each one separately. There are a number of scenarios where cloning is used, such as creating half a head and cloning the other side to form a complete head or cloning the tires on a bicycle. After an object has been cloned, it can also be adjusted to differentiate it slightly from other clones, for added realism.

Copying can be done either by holding the Shift key while dragging a selected object or by selecting Clone from the Edit menu. When either option is employed, the Clone Options dialog box in Figure 2.29 appears.

FIGURE 2.29.

*The Clone Options
dialog box.*

Note

When using the Shift/Drag method of cloning, the Clone Options dialog box contains an extra parameter for the number of clones. When using the Clone menu item, only one clone is created.

There are only a few parameters in the Clone Options dialog box. Each is explained here.

- *Copy*   A clone of an object is created with exactly the same parameters as the original.

- *Instance*   A linked clone of the original object is created. When a change (excluding Transforms) is made to any instanced geometry, the changes are reflected in all instances. This includes changing Materials, Space Warps, base parameter changes, and Modifiers.

- *Reference*   This is like a one-way street for instanced geometry. Any referenced object will have the same parameters as the original and will reflect any subsequent changes made to the original. Again, this does not include transforms. Changes made to the referenced objects will not be reflected in the original or any of the other referenced objects.

- *Controller*   Selecting either Copy or Instance clones the object's transform controllers.

Mirror

In addition to using the Shift/Drag method or the Menu, you can create clones using the Mirror tool. The difference with the Mirror tool is that when objects are created, they mirror the original shape. Figure 2.30 compares the same object cloned and mirrored.

FIGURE 2.30.

The two objects toward the left-top side are copies of each other, whereas the two in the lower-right side are mirrored.

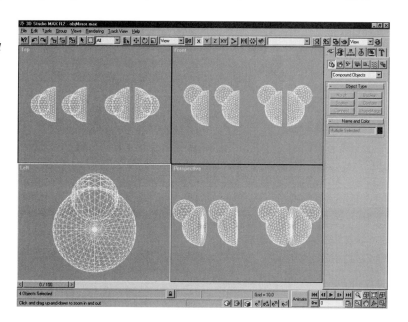

There are two sections in the Mirror Options dialog box, labeled Mirror Axis and Clone Selection. The following options describe how you can clone an object:

- *Mirror Axis*   This option is used to clone the object according to the specified axis.
- *Offset*   The distance between the original and mirrored object.
- *No Clone*   Under clone selection, if you choose No Clone, the original object will be mirrored but not duplicated.
- *Copy, Instance, Reference*   These clone options are the same as in all cloning options and the same rules apply as mentioned earlier in the cloning section.
- *Mirror IK Limits*   When using Inverse Kinematics, this option mirrors the IK limits as well.

To Do: Mirroring objects

1. To use the Mirror tool, select any object. For demonstration purposes, use a teapot object so that you can distinguish the different sides of the object.
2. With an object selected, click on the Mirror tool. Immediately, the Mirror: Screen Coordinates dialog box appears, which contains all mirror options.

3. Select the desired options, set the offset, and click OK to create a mirrored object.

Array

The previous cloning options work well when creating a few copies of an object, but for power-house cloning, use the Array tool. The Array tool is used to create mass quantities of clones that have a relational transform applied. This means you can create a row of objects, such as a chair, as easily as creating one chair. Taking the array further, you can also create an entire auditorium of chairs easily using the correct array settings. As you can see in Figure 2.31, a simpler example of cloning would be the spokes on a wagon wheel. In the wagon wheel example, each spoke was rotated 36 degrees.

An *array* is a group of identical objects that are created in a methodical pattern. Arrays are used primarily when multiples of an object need to be copied in an organized manner. The chairs of a stadium, bowling pins, or venetian blinds are all examples of when an array would work better than duplicating objects manually.

At first look, the Array dialog box might seem intimidating (see Figure 2.32). But once you understand the principles behind the elements, it is very basic.

FIGURE 2.31.

An array of wagon wheel spokes.

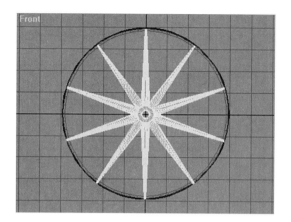

FIGURE 2.32.

The Array dialog box.

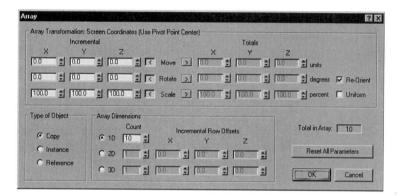

There are three major sections in the Array tool: Array Transformation, Type of Object (Cloned), and Array Dimensions. When creating an array of clones, these parameters are applied to each of the individual clones. How these parameters are set dictates how the array will look.

- *Array Transformation* Describes the transforms to be applied to each of the individual clones. This includes all three transformations (Move, Rotate, and Scale).

- *Type of Object* Standard clone option of Copy, Instance, or Reference.

- *Array Dimensions* Describes on which axes the array is to be built. This is positioning objects only, so scale and rotation are not included in this section. For scaling and rotational transforms, use the Array Transformation section.

- *Reset All Parameters* Use this button to clear out any previous parameters that were set. This is useful because 3DS MAX 2.5 saves the array settings between uses of the Array tool (although not across 3DS MAX 2.5 sessions).

Note When using the Array tool to create clones, keep in mind that the Array Count is the total number of objects in the array, including the original. This is not the number of objects that will be cloned from the original.

Array Transformation

Using the Array Transformation section, you can create a collection of repetitive objects such as steps, fences, or spokes on a wagon wheel. You can easily create arrays with applied transformations. Using a simpler version of the wagon wheel example, create a simple array.

To Do: Using an array to create a wagon wheel

1. Open spokeRA.max. This scene contains objects to create a wagon wheel. For this exercise, you need only apply the Array tool parameters.

2. With the spoke object selected, click on the Array tool. Press the Reset All Parameters to ensure that all values are reset. Click on the right arrow (looks like a greater than symbol) between the Rotate parameters. This instructs 3DS MAX 2.5 to use total values and to calculate individual clone transforms.

3. Use a value of 360 degrees along the Z axis rotation parameter. In the Array Dimensions section, set the Count parameter to 10 (the array options should look the same as the dialog box in Figure 2.33) and then click the OK button.

FIGURE 2.33.

The Array Transformation parameters for the wagon wheel example.

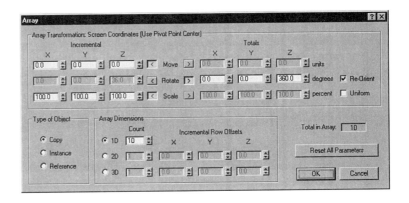

▼   Setting the Array Count parameter tells 3DS MAX 2.5 to create an array with a total of
ten elements. In this case, nine more spokes will be added to the original to create a total
of 10 spokes. As you can see, individual spokes were rotated 36 degrees from the previous spoke created. Using the Array tool Totals parameter, you ensure that all spokes are
evenly distributed through the 360 degrees of the circle.

- *Incremental*   This method is used to increment each clone with the value specified
  in the axis parameter. Values reflected here will be updated in the Totals side based
  on the number of clones requested.

- *Totals*   Using the Totals parameter is nice when you know that you need a certain
  distance or revolution covered. In the wagon wheel example, you wanted the
  spokes to encircle 360 degrees. This saves having to calculate how many degrees
▲   each spoke has to be rotated to be evenly spaced around the hub of the wheel.

> When using the Totals to cover a certain distance, the calculations might
> appear to be off. The reason for this is that when creating an array, the
> total number in the array is used to calculate the distance, when in fact the
> actual number created is one less than the total clones in the array, thereby
> shortening the distance by the distance covered by one element.

Array Dimensions

The Array Dimensions section is used to specify the number of clones in the entire array
(including the original), the dimensions of the array, and the offset of each row if building a multidimensional array. Here are the following options:

- *Count*   The entire number of elements in the array, including the original object.

- *1D, 2D, 3D*   The dimensions of the array. A one-dimensional array consists of a
  single row of the number specified in count. A two-dimensional array consists of
  the number of rows specified in the 2D count parameter plus the number specified
  in the count.

- *Incremental Row Offset*   When using two- and three-dimensional arrays, the X, Y,
  Z values specify the distance between each of the rows.

Summary

In today's lessons you learned some of the most basic principles behind creating very
simple models. It is imperative that the concepts in today's lessons are understood for
continued success through the entire book.

- *Primitives*   Primitives are the most basic geometric 3D objects. Typical primitives are the box, sphere, cylinder, cone, and torus. These objects are considered primitives because they are shapes that are the simplest to define and they are symmetrical.

- *Shapes*   In 3DS MAX 2.5, two-dimensional splines are called shapes. Some standard shapes are line, arc, circle, rectangle, and NGon. Similar to the 3D primitives, these too have predefined, optimized shape definitions. Though the line might have many vertices, the basic principle is still the same in defining the segments.

- *Transforms*   Transform is a term used when an object changes position, rotation, or scale. Transform data is kept in the Transform matrix of each object and is based on a relative offset from the world coordinate system.

- *Alignment*   Objects can be aligned to other objects based on the bounding box, pivot point, or center of either object. Alignment can also be used on sub-object selections, such as points, segments, and splines.

- *Cloning*   In the world of 3D, cloning is not only ethical, it is rampant. Cloning objects is essential when creating mass quantities of identical objects. When cloning objects, the clones can be either Copies, Instances, or References.

- *Copy*   A copy of an object is an unlinked duplicate of an object and all modifiers applied to the stack at the time of cloning. After the copy is made, there is no connection between the two objects.

- *Instance*   When an object is Instanced, it is cloned with the intention that this clone is linked to the original object. Any modifiers added to any of the Instanced clones are applied to every other Instance of this object.

- *Reference*   A Referenced object is a one-way Instanced clone. Any modifications made to the shape of the original is reflected in all the Instanced and Referenced objects. Unlike the Instanced clones, the Reference clones can be modified without affecting the original object.

Q&A

Q What is the difference between primitives and other 3D objects?

A Primitives are the most fundamental three-dimensional geometric objects and therefore have been optimized in 3DS MAX 2.5 from which many other objects can be derived. Primitives have parameters that can be changed to alter the object.

Q **How do I know how much an object has been scaled if the dimension parameters remain the same?**

A The Transform Type-In is a viewport into the Transformation matrix used for each object. Viewing the Scale percentages through the Scale Transform Type-In discloses the percentage of scale along each axis for the selected object.

Q **Can I constrain an axis when transforming vertices or sub-object selections?**

A Axial constraint can occur with any sub-object selection, including vertices, and it's quite common during the modeling process.

Q **Why is the Z axis up in the world coordinate system and the Y axis up in the local coordinate system?**

A To confuse the user. No, actually Z is up in the world coordinate system because that's the convention 3D Studio MAX has adopted. The local coordinate system is based on how an individual object was created. If you create one box in the front viewport and a second in the Left viewport, they will have different Y-axis directions in the local coordinate system.

Q **Can I use the Alignment tool to align the pivot point of an object?**

A The Alignment tool can be used to align two or more objects, any sub-object selection, or the pivot point. Using the Hierarchy Panel, select Affect Pivot Point Only, and then apply the Align Tool.

Q **I've tried to create an array through rotational transforms, but the objects ended up on top of each other. How do I get them to rotate correctly around a central object?**

A Use the Align tool to align the pivot point of the original array object to the point around which you would like to rotate. After the pivot point has been aligned, the object will rotate correctly, building the correct array.

2

DAY 3

Advanced Transforms and Modifiers

Today you learn how to apply some of the most common advanced modeling techniques in 3DS MAX 2.5. Advanced modeling requires that you understand the basic principles behind an object and the world coordinate system. You learn the following concepts

- Boolean operations
- Connect Objects
- Object Modifiers
- The Modifier Stack

Building Compound Objects

Compound objects are just what their name implies; they are created from multiple objects. Today you focus on 3D Boolean operations and the Connect Object. Both types use multiple objects to influence how a single object appears. By applying the geometry of one or more objects together, you can create far more complex geometry.

As more and more effects are applied to geometry, you can coax a more complex shape from a simple sphere, box, or cylinder. It is important to realize that 3D modeling is an evolutionary process. Objects are not merely punched out of a sheet of metal; they must be persuaded out of nothing and massaged into a form that becomes more refined as each tool is applied.

3D Boolean Operations

Start with the most basic of compound objects, Boolean operations. These 3D Boolean operations are the same as the Booleans found in the Spline Sub-Object Selection Level for Editable Splines. The only difference is that instead of working on two dimensions, they work on all three.

When performing a Boolean operation, the geometry of one object is applied to another. You can use Booleans for any two mesh objects. Actually, Booleans can be applied to NURBS objects, but they are converted to mesh objects in the process.

In 3DS MAX 2.5, the three types of Boolean operations are Union, Subtraction, and Intersection. Figure 3.1 shows the effects of each of the Boolean operations as applied to two geospheres.

FIGURE 3.1.

A geosphere and a cube demonstrate the Boolean operations. The results shown from left to right are the Union, Subtraction, and Intersection operations.

By using the geometry of one object to affect another, you can create shapes that would be very tedious to shape by pushing points around. The three Boolean operations listed here and found in MAX are used to either join geometry (Union), remove geometry (Subtraction), or save only the intersecting geometry of the two objects (Intersection).

- *Union* The geometry of both objects is combined to create a single object. Redundant geometry (intersecting geometry) is removed.

- *Subtraction* The geometry of one object is carved out of 88 or removed from another. Like a three-dimensional cookie cutter, you can remove the exact shape of one object from another.

- *Intersection* This operation removes all geometry except where the two objects intersect.

In the following exercise, you use the Boolean Subtraction to remove the geometry of one object from another. In this scenario, you remove the bent cylinders from the block to create a drip channel for the cutting board.

To Do: Using Boolean subtraction

1. Open file boolSub.max from the accompanying CD-ROM. The scene contains two objects labeled cutboard and channel.

2. Select cutboard and click on the Create Panel. From the Create Panel's object class list, select Compound Objects.

3. From the Object type section, click on the Boolean button. The button turns green to indicate it is the active function.

4. Near the bottom of the Boolean parameter panel is the Operation section. Subtraction (A-B) should be checked as the default; if not, select it. This indicates that the second object selected will be subtracted from the first object selected. Choosing Subtraction (B-A) would have the opposite effect.

5. In the Pick Operand B section, choose Move. Using Move causes the Operand B geometry to be removed from the scene after it is applied to the Operand A object. Choosing Copy or Instance leaves a copy of the original Operand B intact.

6. Click on the Pick Operand B button. It too turns green to indicate that it is active. Select the channel object by clicking on it or by choosing it from the Select by Name button on the main toolbar.

7. After you choose Operand B, the Boolean operation is applied. Right-click on the mouse to terminate the operation. Notice now how the geometry of the channel object was used to carve out a channel around the cutting board.

8. With the cutting board still selected, choose the UVW Map Modifier from the Modify Panel. If it is not listed, click on the More button and choose it from the list. This adds a planar material mapping parameters by default to the new cutting board object. Leave the parameters as they are.

Render out the Camera view by clicking in the Camera view to make it active. Then click on the Render Last button from the main toolbar.

> **Tip**
>
> When two objects have complex mapping coordinates, these coordinates are not transferred through the Boolean operation. Use the Unwrap UVW Modifier to create complex mapping after a Boolean operation if you need to.

Though this is a basic object, the channel would have been difficult to model without the use of the Boolean Subtraction function. Without the channel, the cutting board would have a lower degree of realism. It is the subtleties of 3D modeling that make the big difference in attaining realism.

Modifying Boolean Objects

Once a Boolean object has been created, how is it modified? Good question, and one not often answered in other programs. The power of MAX is that even though the operands are hidden, they are still adjustable. Say that you used a cylinder to bore a hole through a block and later found out that the cylinder was too large or too small. Using Sub-Object selection methods and the Modifier Stack, you can change the parameters of the operands.

To Do: Modifying an operand after the fact

1. Open boolMod.max from the accompanying CD-ROM. This file contains a cylinder and a geosphere.

2. Apply a Boolean Subtraction to the geosphere using the cylinder. The object seen in Figure 3.2 appears. If you need a refresher, refer to the previous exercise on Boolean operations.

3. With the geosphere still selected, open the Modify Panel. Click on the Sub-Object selection button to activate Sub-Object Selection mode.

4. In the Parameters section, click on Operand B in the parameter list, denoted by the entry B;B_Cylinder01 (as seen in Figure 3.3). The item appears highlighted when selected.

5. In the Display section of the Parameters rollout, click on Show Hidden Ops. The cylinder appears in wireframe.

FIGURE 3.2.

The geosphere after the cylinder was subtracted using a Boolean operation.

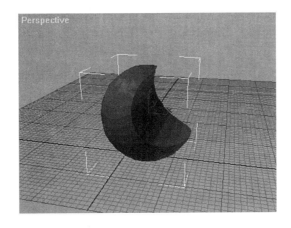

FIGURE 3.3

The Operands Parameters section is located below the Modifier Stack section in the Modify Panel.

6. In the Modifier Stack section, click on the Modifier List and select the Cylinder01 object directly under the Boolean entry (see Figure 3.4).

FIGURE 3.4.

The Modifier Stack showing the cylinder in the list.

7. After selecting the Cylinder01 operand, the Modify Panel becomes populated with the parameters of the cylinder object. From here you can adjust any of the parameters of the cylinder. Set the Radius to 100 and the Height to 175. Notice how the geosphere's shape changes to reflect the change in parameters (see Figure 3.5).

▲

FIGURE 3.5.

The Modify Panel becomes populated with the cylinder's parameters after it is chosen from the Modifier Stack. The Modifier Stack is covered in more detail later in this chapter.

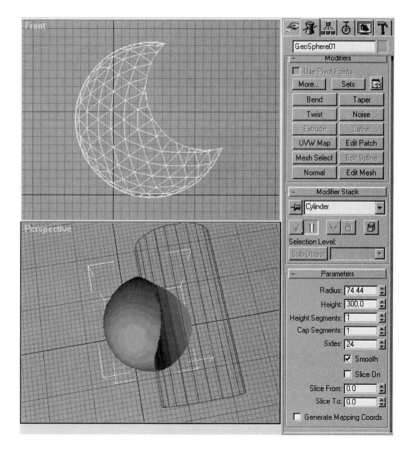

Tip

As with all concepts covered in this book, to fully understand the Boolean operations, it is best to experiment. Use different operands and adjust the parameters in various ways. Become familiar with the Modifier Stack, as it is an integral part of successful modeling in MAX. If you find that you are experiencing unexpected results, it might be advisable to collapse the object's stack to create an Editable Mesh. Depending on the topology of the object, collapsing the stack might mean the difference between successful Booleans and frustration.

Bridging the Gap with the Connect Tool

Although the Boolean tool can add or subtract geometry, the Connect tool is used only to create a bridge between two objects. The Connect tool is sort of a hybrid Boolean Union in that two objects will be joined together by a geometric bridge that spans the distance between the two objects. The Connect tool is not intended to be used on geometry that overlaps, as in the Boolean Union.

3

To clarify, the Connect tool adds geometry to bridge the distance between two objects, as can be seen in the eyelet shown in Figure 3.6. The technique is to remove some faces from each of the operands, and the Connect tool creates a bridge between the holes in each.

FIGURE 3.6.

A torus and a cylinder connected by the Connect tool. The objects on the top are the originals, prior to applying the Connect tool.

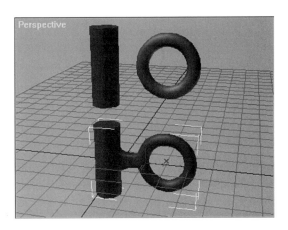

In the real world, most edges are smooth, and where two pieces of a material meet, the connection normally contains a smooth fillet. The Connect tool is very useful for creating fillets between joined objects.

To Do: Creating an eyelet using the Connect tool

1. Open connect.max from the accompanying CD-ROM. The scene contains a cylinder and a torus.

2. Select the cylinder and collapse to a Mesh object. This is performed by opening the Modify Panel and clicking on the Edit Stack button. From the pop-up menu, choose Editable Mesh. Once the cylinder is converted, you can edit its vertices, face, and edges.

3. Set the Perspective viewport to Wireframe; then click on the Sub-Object selection button and choose Face as the selection level (see Figure 3.7). Select a few of the faces that are closest to the torus. The selected faces become red, indicating the active Sub-Object selection.

FIGURE 3.7.

Choose Faces from the Sub-Object Selection Level.

4. If too many faces are selected, hold the Alt key down and deselect unwanted faces by touching them with the mouse pointer. Only a few faces remain selected.

5. When you are satisfied with the number of faces selected, delete them. This can be done by either pressing the Delete key (while in Sub-Object selection mode) or by pressing the Delete button in the Miscellaneous section of the Sub-Object parameters. Delete any isolated vertices if requested by an alert from MAX.

6. Turn off Subobject Mode. Then repeat the entire procedure for the torus. Remember to convert the torus to an editable mesh first. You should now see two objects similar to the one pictured in Figure 3.8.

   You delete the faces because this is where the Connect tool bridges the gap between the two objects. The Connect tool will not work if faces aren't deleted.

7. Now that the proper faces have been deleted, select the cylinder object again. You have to exit the Sub-Object selection mode if you haven't already done so.

8. With the cylinder selected, open the Create Panel and choose Compound Objects from the Object Class list. Click on the Connect tool.

9. The Connect button turns green to indicate it is the active tool. Click on the Pick Operand button and you can now select the torus.

FIGURE 3.8.

*The cylinder and the
torus after removing
the appropriate faces.*

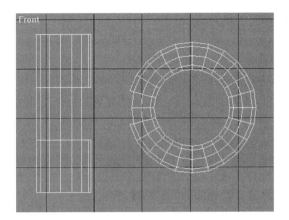

3

10. Set the Interpolation Segments to 3 and then adjust the tension. Increasing the seg-
    ments and adjusting the tension affects the smoothness of the bridge. The tension
    parameter will draw the geometry toward its center, adding more or less curve in
    the bridge depending on the setting.

You see that a bridge is generated between the cylinder and the torus where the faces
were deleted. You can adjust the parameters to create a smoother shape. Other Connect
parameters are explained next.

- *Delete Operand*   Because you can connect more than one object, an Operands list
  is created showing the objects that have been connected to the original object. Any
  operand can be deleted by selecting it from the list and clicking on the Delete
  Operand button. As operands are deleted, MAX tries to bridge to a remaining
  operand, if any.

- *Segments*   This changes the segments used to create the bridge between the object
  and the operands. Increasing the segments creates a denser mesh but also a
  smoother bridge. This can be adjusted as necessary.

- *Tension*   Used to interpolate the curve between the bridge geometry and its attach-
  ment to the operands. A tension of zero creates the straightest possible path for the
  geometry used. Adjust the tension until the desired curvature is reached. This
  varies with geometry type and the relative position of the faces deleted on the original operands. Negative values will bulge the bridge, whereas positive values taper
  it inward.

- *Smooth Bridge*   This adjusts the smoothing used when the object is rendered. By
  checking Smooth Bridge, MAX applies smoothing groups to the new geometry so
  it is not rendered with sharp edges.

- *Smooth Ends*   Checking this box causes MAX to apply smoothing groups to the
  new geometry to match the smoothing of the original objects so
  there will be no sharp edges rendered where the bridge is created.

Nondestructive Modeling with Object Modifiers

When using the Boolean and Connect tools, you might have noticed that the original geometry is lost. Though that is not entirely true (its parameters are available through Sub-Object Selection), the geometry itself is no longer readily available. With Object Modifiers, the geometry of the original object is always available.

The best way to describe Modifiers is that they are applied to an object as layers. Layers can be added, deleted, or moved around to different layer positions. This layering effect is called the Modifier Stack.

The Modifier Stack is used to keep a history of all the Modifiers added to an object. Figure 3.9 shows a Modifier Stack that contains a few Modifiers. Notice the original object (the rectangle) on the bottom of the stack, and all the Modifiers layered on top of it.

FIGURE 3.9.

The Modifier Stack. The original object (the rectangle) is listed at the bottom of the stack, with Modifiers listed above in order of application.

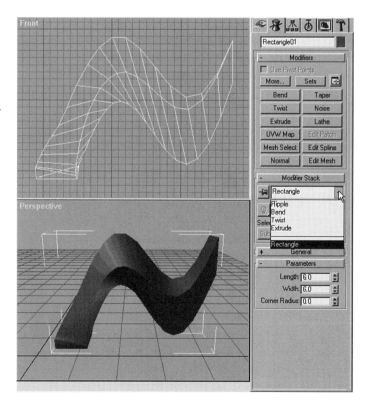

Why use Modifiers? The best reason is that they are nondestructive. Any Modifier added to an object can be removed by selecting the Modifier from the Stack and clicking on the Trash Can icon. Modifying the Stack is covered later, but for now we will discuss some of the most common Modifiers.

From 2D to 3D with the Extrude Modifier

Arguably the most common and easiest to use, the Extrude Modifier is used to extend a 2D shape a specified distance, creating 3D geometry out of the 2D shape. It is very similar to pushing dough through a cookie cutter. The cookie cutter defines the profile of the object, and the thickness of the dough is how far it is extruded.

In Figure 3.10, several shapes have been extruded along side of their original 2D shapes. The Extrude Modifier is applied through the Modify panel to any 2D shape.

FIGURE 3.10.

The Extrude Modifier applied to various 2D shapes.

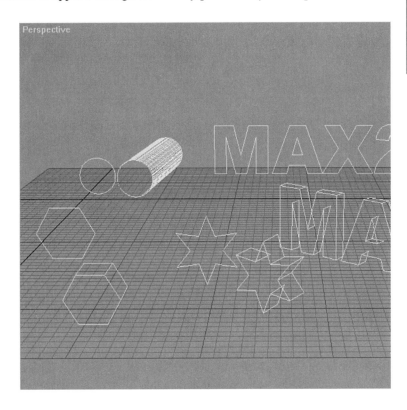

3

To Do: Extruding a logo

1. Open extlogo.max from the accompanying CD-ROM. This scene contains a single shape object that is made up of some text and logo splines.

2. Select the shape and open the Modify Panel. With the shape selected, choose Extrude from the Modifiers section. If it does not appear in the set of buttons, click on the More button and select it from the list of Object Modifiers.

3. The first time Extrude is used in any MAX session, the Amount Parameter is 0.0. Change this to .5. Leave all other parameters as they are.

Congratulations! You just applied your first Modifier. You can still go back and edit either the logo shape or the Extrude Modifier parameters by choosing the appropriate object from the Modifier Stack.

As you might have noticed, you did not use all the Extrude parameters. In many cases, you would not adjust all the parameters of the Modifier. Here are the Extrude parameters.

- *Amount*   The distance the Extrude is applied. This is the depth of the extrude and can be any negative or positive number. Use the spinner or type in any value. This value is expressed in current MAX Units.

- *Segments*   The number of segments along the axis of the extrusion. Unless you intend to bend or sculpt the object, you rarely use more than one segment. Each segment adds a row of vertices dividing the extruded shape along the extrusion axis.

- *Capping*   A term used to describe whether the original shape is placed at the start or the end of the extrusion. Not checking either of these removes the shape from that face. In the previous exercise, remove the check mark from the Cap End check box and watch how the face of the extruded shape disappears.

- *Output*   Common to many Modifiers, this specifies to MAX the class of shape that is created. The default is Mesh, though Patch and NURBS output might also be used. Depending on the requirements of the specific model, you can change this parameter. For most models, Mesh is the most appropriate choice.

Creating Curved Objects Using the Bend Modifier

Like the Extrude Modifier, the Bend is also straightforward. The Bend Modifier requires a little more preparation of an object prior to applying. In general, when using the Bend parameter, you need to increase the Segments of your original model.

Note   Study the exercises in this section. Though the Bend Modifier is considered basic, many fundamental principles that you can use carry over to other Modifiers.

To Do: Bending a cylinder

1. Reset Max by choosing File/Reset. In a Top view, create a cylinder. In the Parameters rollout, adjust the Radius to 10 and the Height to 50. Click on the Zoom Extents All tool in the lower-right corner of the lower toolbar.

2. Open the Modify Panel and apply a Bend Modifier. If the Bend Modifier is not visible in the Modifier section, click on the More button and select Bend from the list of Object Modifiers.

Note

As you might notice, MAX places an orange box around the cylinder. This is used to visualize what the Modifier is doing. Whenever a Modifier is applied to an object, a box is placed around the object to simulate the settings of the Modifier.

When MAX applies the Bend Modifier, the default value for the Angle and Direction parameters is 0.0. You adjust these parameters to make the Bend work.

3. In the Angle parameter of the Bend Modifier, type in a value of 90. Leave all other parameters as they are. Notice that the cylinder doesn't bend, but the Modifier shows a smooth bend along the length of the Modifier box (see Figure 3.11).

FIGURE 3.11.

Though the Bend Modifier shows a smooth bend, you don't have enough segments in the cylinder to create the Bend effect.

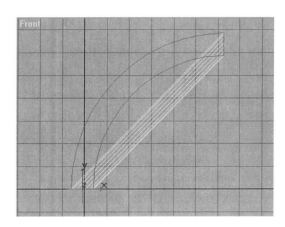

4. Because models can only bend where there are segments, you need to add more segments to the cylinder. With the cylinder selected, click on the Modifier Stack list to reveal the list (see Figure 3.12). Select Cylinder from the list.

FIGURE 3.12.

*The Modifier Stack list.
The cylinder is the
original object and is
listed at the bottom of
the Stack.*

5. When the cylinder is selected from the Modifier Stack, you can change any of the original creation parameters. In this case, you need to increase the segments to 3. Type 3 in the Height Segments parameter box.

   Notice when you increase the segments count to 3, the cylinder begins to curve. Although this is progress, you need to increase the number of segments so that the curve is smooth.

6. Increase the number of segments to 20. The cylinder now has a very smooth curve to it and renders smoothly.

> **Tip**
>
> When increasing the segment count, be careful to not just increase to a high number. Adding more segments increases the number of faces and rendering time.

Advanced Bend Parameters

Although the Bend Modifier worked great for the cylinder, you can apply other Bend parameters. The function of each parameter is listed here, followed by an explanation of how it affects the object. Read through the parameters and then follow the exercise to apply the new parameter changes.

- *Bend Direction*   This specifies the angle of rotation around the specified axis the Bend is applied. This value can be 0 to 360 degrees.
- *Bend Axis*   This is the axis in which the Bend is applied. Changing the Bend axis can have dramatic effects.
- *Limits*   By enabling Limit Effect, you can localize where the Bend Modifier is applied on an object. The Upper and Lower Limits are used to specify in units where the effect is to be applied.

By changing the Direction parameter, the Bend rotates around the specified axis by the amount specified in the Direction parameter. To get an idea of how this works, enter a value of 90 in the Direction parameter for the previous exercise. The Bend is rotated 90 degrees around the Z axis.

To Do: Using Limit Effect

1. Use the previous exercise to demonstrate the effects of Limits. With the cylinder selected, open the Modify Panel and click on the Limit Effect check box of the Bend Modifier.

2. If the Upper and Lower Limit values are still at their default of 0.0, you see no change in effect. In the Upper Limit parameter, type in 30.

As you can see, the Bend is now limited to the lower-half of the cylinder. The effect has been limited to the first 30 units of measure along the length of the cylinder.

Applying a value to the lower limit seems to make the cylinder rotate. When the Bend starts at the base of an object, this is the effect. You need to move the Bend along the length of the cylinder. This is where Gizmos help.

Gizmos are used as the mechanics that cause the object to be modified. By changing the position of the Gizmo on the object, the effect can be manipulated even further.

To Do: Working with Gizmos

1. Using the same cylinder example as in the previous exercise, select the cylinder, open the Modify Panel, and change the Limit values to 15.0 in the Upper Limit and -15.0 in the Lower Limit. You should end up with a cylinder pointing up about 45 degrees as in Figure 3.13.

FIGURE 3.13.

The cylinder with Limits turned on and set at 15.0 for the Upper Limit and -15.0 for the Lower Limit.

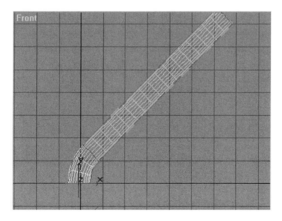

2. Click on the Sub-Object Selection. Gizmo and Center are the Sub-Object choices. Choose Gizmo. You see a yellow box surrounding the cylinder; this is the Gizmo object that surrounds the object.

3. Using the local coordinate system, constrain the Move axis to the local Z axis.
    Select the yellow cross located at the base of the Gizmo and move it along the
    local Z axis. As you move the Gizmo along the Z axis, notice how the Bend moves
    along the axis as well (Figure 3.14).

FIGURE 3.14.

By moving the Gizmo along the Bend axis, the Bend can be placed anywhere along the object.

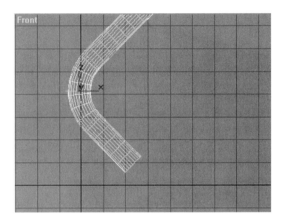

Because you used limits on the Bend Modifier, you were able to move the entire
90 degree Bend anywhere along the length of the object.

4. Because you used the Limit Effects option, the Bend was constrained to 30 units
    (-15 to 15). Turn off the Limit Effects option.

Because the Limits were turned off, the Bend Modifier is now applied to the entire
length of the object. When the Gizmo is moved, the object seems to rotate, but this is the
same effect as if the center of the Bend were moved.

The Twist Modifier

Though it might sound redundant, the Twist Modifier is used to twist objects. If you ever
had the hankering for modeling licorice twists, this is the perfect way to achieve that
effect.

The Twist Modifier is very similar to the Bend Modifier. In fact, the only difference in
the parameter structure is that the Twist Modifier uses a Bias parameter where the Bend
Modifier uses a Direction parameter.

*   *Angle*   This determines to what degree the object is twisted. A value of 360
    degrees means that one end of the object is turned 360 degrees in relation to the
    other end of the object along the specified axis.

- *Bias*   Used to cause the twist to be stronger or weaker toward the Gizmo center instead of uniformly interpolated across the surface of the affected object. Values range from -100 to 100 with negative values moving the bias away from the center of the Gizmo and positive moving toward the center.

Using the Lathe Modifier to Create 3D objects from Silhouettes

Unlike the Bend and Twist Modifiers, which work with 3D objects, the Lathe Modifier works with 2D shapes. The Lathe Modifier is very much like the real-world lathes used to create things such as legs for tables and chairs. The concept of the Lathe Modifier is that by drawing an outline of an object, you turn or revolve it around an axis, creating multiple segments from which faces are created (Figure 3.15).

FIGURE 3.15.

The outline on the left was used to create the glass on the right using the Lathe Modifier.

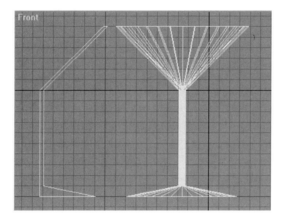

Though the Lathe parameters are not as simplistic as the Bend or Twist Modifiers, they are still relatively simple.

- *Degrees*   Used to specify the amount of the lathe operation. Partial lathes (less than 360 degrees) produce objects that seem to have a pie slice taken out of them.
- *Weld Core*   When checked, eliminates redundant vertices that lie on the axis of rotation. Due to the nature of lathing, any vertices that lie on the lathe axis will be reproduced for each segment. This causes excess vertices that occupy the same position in space. Check Weld Core unless the Lathe object is used in Morphing.
- *Flip Normals*   When the surface normals of the segment's faces point inward, checking the Flip Normals box causes them to face outward.

Normals can be pointed in, depending on the axis rotation and the vertices that make up the object profile.

- *Segments*   As with any object, increasing the segment count creates a smoother surface across curves. Increasing segments also increases rendering time and face count.

- *Capping*   When the Degree parameter is less than 360 degrees, the first and last segment of the Lathe will be exposed. If either of the Capping options are not checked, the object will have a hole where that face should be. If the Degree parameter is set at 360, Capping has no effect.

- *Morph/Grid*   Determines the shape of the faces used in the Capping. Using Grid creates faces that are evenly space and more appropriate for subsequent Modifiers.

- *Direction*   The axis of rotation for the lathe operation.

- *Align*   Used to align the lathe rotation axis to either the Minimum or Maximum extents of the object, or at the center point of the object.

Note

> Depending on the vertices and the rotation of the 2D shape, you might need to flip normals. You can tell if the normals need to be flipped by looking at the model in a shaded view. If the shading looks peculiar or it seems as though the model is inside out, you might need to flip the normals.

To Do: Creating a glass using a Lathe Modifier

1. Create an outline for your glass or open glass.max. Notice that the line is not a closed spline (all the vertices do not connect with segments on both sides). Vertices that lie on the axis of rotation do not need to be closed because they will become redundant vertices anyway.

2. From the Modify Panel, add a Lathe Modifier. If not found on the Modify Panel, click on the More button and choose Lathe from the Object Modifier list.

3. You should end up with an object that looks similar to the one pictured in Figure 3.16.

4. With the lathe object selected, choose Min from the Align section to align the axis of rotation. Changing this parameter moves the axis of rotation to align with either the Minimum, Maximum, or Center of the object extents. Notice how the shape looks more like what you want (see Figure 3.17).

5. As an alternative method to step 4, click on the Sub-Object selection and choose Axis. A yellow line appears indicating the lathe axis. Using the Select and Move tool, the axis can be moved back and forth until the desired shape is achieved.

FIGURE 3.16.

The glass goblet shape after applying the Lathe Modifier. It looks incorrect because the axial alignment needs to be adjusted.

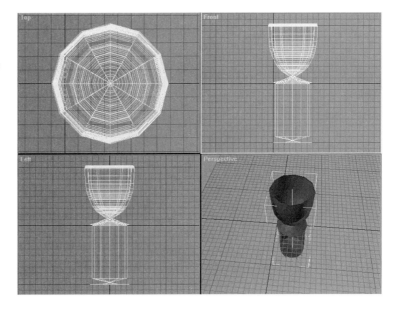

3

Note

One caveat when moving the axis manually: Because manually moving the axis on a Lathe Modifier relies on visual placement, holes or self-intersecting geometry is always possible if the axis isn't placed properly. Though holes are sometimes desired through the center of a Lathe object, self-intersecting geometry is not a desirable effect and will not render properly.

▲   6. Increase the segment count to 32 for a smooth goblet.

While working in the goblet example, experiment with the other parameters. By decreasing the segments, you can create a completely different look.

In the following example, you see how the number of segments affects the object. This exercise will also adjust the axis for a completely new dimension on the Lathe Modifier.

To Do: Modifying the axis and segments of the Lathe modifier

1. Open frame.max from the accompanying CD-ROM. This file contains a single 2D shape, which is the profile for your frame.

2. With the frame profile object selected, apply a Lathe Modifier by selecting Lathe from the Modify Panel. Click on the Zoom Extents All tool so that you can see the frame in all views.

FIGURE 3.17.

The axis has been aligned to the Minimum extents. The correct position of the axis alignment is dependent on the placement of the vertices and the lathe degrees as well as the desired effect.

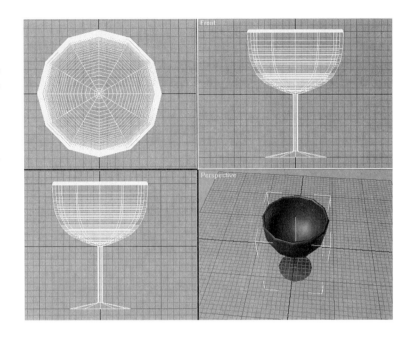

3. Change the number of segments to 4. The frame looks more like a frame but is still not quite right. The axis of revolution is too close to the shape.

4. Set the alignment to Max. Though the frame looks better, it is still not enough. You need to adjust the Axis.

   Adjusting the Axis is necessary when the object being Lathed forms a gap through its center. A frame is that type of object because it is really made up of four carved pieces of wood (or any other material).

5. With the frame still selected, click on the Sub-Object selection from the Modify Panel. Because Axis is your only choice, you don't need to choose anything from the Sub-Object list.

   Now that Sub-Object selection has been turned on, you see a yellow line going through the center of the frame. This is the Axis of revolution that the Lathe operation is based upon.

6. In a Front view, use the Select and Move tool to drag the yellow axis line to the right. Notice how the frame opens up and looks more like a picture frame (Figure 3.18).

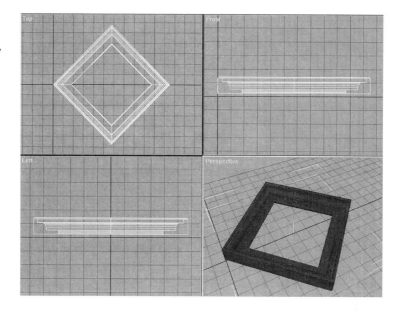

FIGURE 3.18.

The lathe object looks more like a frame, now that you moved the axis outward.

By changing the relative position of the axis of revolution, you widen the lathe operative and can create different objects with the same profile shape. As you might have noticed, even though the axis constraints were not on, the axis of revolution constrains itself to the perpendicular of the Direction chosen for the Lathe Modifier.

Note

Use the segment count to your advantage. If you want to create an intricate picture frame, create a 2D profile of the frame; then use the Lathe Modifier with only four segments. Presto! A perfect picture frame.

Modifiers and the Modifier Stack

Now that you have experience with Modifiers, you need to look more closely at the Modifier Stack. The Modifier Stack is used by MAX to keep track of the modifications made to an object's geometry.

Most simply, the Stack is a hierarchical system that tracks external object modifications. Whenever Modifiers or Space Warps are applied to an object, the binding shows up in the Modifier Stack. This section describes the different options and how they affect the overall object.

The Stack Controls

There are a number of control options related to the Modifier Stack. These controls are used to manipulate the Stack and its contents and can be a very powerful aid when using the Stack to model objects. The Stack controls appear as buttons just below the Modifier Stack list and can be seen in Figure 3.19.

FIGURE 3.19.

The Modifier Stack controls. From left to right, they are Active/Inactive toggle, Show End Result, Make Unique, Remove Modifier, and Edit Stack.

- *Active/Inactive Modifier*   When this toggle button is engaged, the current Modifier becomes inactive and is not applied to the object geometry, though it remains in the Modifier Stack. This toggle button is also a flyout. Pressing and holding this button reveals a two-button menu from which you can choose either Active/Inactive Modifier or Active/Inactive in Viewport. The default of Active/Inactive Modifier affects the Modifier in the Stack. Active/Inactive in Viewport only affects the object when seen in the modeling viewports. When rendered, the effect is applied.

- *Show End Result*   Frequently when working with the Modifier Stack, you go back to make changes to either the original geometry or previous Modifiers. When you traverse through the Modifier Stack, the effects of Modifiers that appear higher in the Stack are not seen by default. This is similar to a history list. You can only see the results up to that point in history. By toggling the Show End Result button, you can make changes at the current level and view how the change affects the other Modifiers higher in the Modifier Stack.

- *Make Unique*   When a Modifier has been applied to a number of objects at the same time, it becomes an Instanced Modifier. Changes to any object that contain that particular instance of the Modifier affect all objects that contain that Modifier in their Modifier Stack. By clicking on the Make Unique button, you can make the Modifier unique; any changes to its parameters by the current object will not affect any other instanced Modifiers.

- *Remove Modifier*   This removes the Modifier from the Stack permanently. Unlike the Active/Inactive toggle, when the current Modifier is deleted, it has to be reapplied.

- *Edit Stack*   The Edit Stack button contains a number of options that you can use primarily for moving Modifiers around in the stack or collapsing the entire stack to a single mesh object..

As you can see, the Modifier Stack offers a number of options. In fact, the Modifier Stack is the heart of 3DS MAX 2.5's modeling strength. By applying Modifiers to a stack, nondestructive modeling can easily be achieved.

Editing the Modifier Stack

You examined some of the Modifier Stack's basic options, but now look at some of the power behind the Modifier Stack, or Stack, as it is also referred to.

So why edit the Stack? You edit the Stack for a number of reasons, including removing Modifiers, changing the hierarchy, or converting to Mesh or NURBS objects. In fact, every time you add a Modifier, you manipulate the Modifier Stack. The next exercise shows a basic example of why editing the Stack is not only desirable, but necessary.

To Do: Removing a Modifier from the Stack

1. Open file ModStack.max from the accompanying CD-ROM. You notice a single box twisted out of control by a Taper, Bend, and Twist Modifier.

2. To demonstrate how the Show End Result button works, select the box and open the Modify Panel. Click on the Modifier Stack list and select Bend from the list (Figure 3.20). Though Bend is the current Modifier, you can still see what the object looks like with all active Modifiers applied.

FIGURE 3.20.

Selecting the Bend Modifier from the Modifier Stack.

3. Turn off the Show End Result by clicking on its toggle button. The result is that only Modifiers up to the current Modifier are shown. The Twist Modifier's effects are not seen. Toggle the Show End Result button on and the Twist Modifier's effects are seen again. Leave the toggle on.

   You can not only turn Modifiers off, but they can be easily removed from any point in the Stack as well.

   With ModStack.max still open, you can remove a Modifier from the Stack. But first, hold a copy of the scene in memory in case you decide to abort some of the changes.

4. From the Edit menu, choose Hold from the menu items. This preserves the current status of the scene in RAM memory. This way, you can later retrieve the scene by choosing the Fetch item, and any changes you make will be aborted.

5. At the top of the Stack is the Twist Modifier. Select it from the list and click on the Trash Can icon just below the Modifier Stack. Clicking this button removes the current Modifier from the Stack permanently. Notice how the Bend Modifier becomes the top item in the Stack and the shape of the box changes to the Modifier Stack.

   Modifiers can be removed from any point in the Stack. The only stipulation is that the current Modifier is removed when clicking on the Remove Modifier button.

6. Bring back your scene by clicking on the Edit menu and choosing Fetch. When asked if OK, choose yes. This warning tells you know that you made changes that will be lost when you Fetch the previous file.

7. Now that you have the original file, Edit the Stack. Select the box and click on the Edit Stack button to bring up the Edit Modifier Stack dialog box (see Figure 3.21).

Note

Because Holding and Fetching a scene requires knowing when you begin making edits that you might want to change, the Undo feature might be a better alternative. Right-clicking the mouse on either the Undo or Redo buttons displays the history list commands performed, including removing and adding Modifiers. Simply select the items to undo from the list and press the Undo button to remove them. Undo items might only be removed sequentially from the list.

Figure 3.21.

Use the Edit Modifier Stack dialog box to move Modifiers and collapse the Stack.

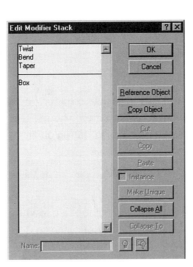

From this dialog box, you can easily remove, reposition, or collapse any Modifiers associated with this object.

8. Select the Taper Modifier and click on the Cut button. Notice how the object changes prior to clicking OK. This is a preview mode that enables you to see the results prior to making the commitment. If only real life were this way.

9. Move the dialog box around so that you can view the changes to the box. With the Edit Stack dialog box still open, select the Twist Modifier and click on the Cut button.

10. Although the Twist Modifier has been removed from the Stack, it is not lost. Select the solid line below the Bend Modifier in the Edit Stack dialog box (see Figure 3.21). Click on the Paste button. The Twist has been moved to appear prior to the Bend Modifier. Leave the Edit Stack dialog box open for now.

This is how Modifiers are repositioned in a Modifier Stack. Through this method, you can easily change the way an object is affected without having to delete and reapply Modifiers.

During complex modeling, the Modifier Stack can become very long. Each Modifier in the list also requires a certain amount of memory. When the list gets long, you can convert the list to single Mesh object. This applies all the Modifiers to the object and removes them from the Stack. This saves memory; the Modifier history and the ability to change their parameters are lost when you collapse the stack into a single Mesh.

11. In the Edit Stack dialog box, select from the Twist Modifier to the box object by dragging on them in the list.

12. Notice how the Collapse All and Collapse To buttons become active in the lower portion of the Edit Stack dialog box (Figure 3.22).

13. When one or more Modifiers are selected, you can collapse the stack from the bottom of the list to the highest selected Modifier. Click on the Collapse To button.

14. A warning box appears letting you know that this converts this Modifier to an Editable Mesh object, and any animated parameters will be lost. Click yes for this exercise.

The Stack now contains just the Mesh and the Bend Modifier. The solid line is used to denote where the object geometry begins and where the Modifiers begin.

15. Collapse the remaining Stack items by clicking on the Collapse All button. You now have a single Editable Mesh that has internalized all the Modifiers you applied. If you were to click on the Cancel button, all these changes would abort and you would have your original object and Modifiers.

FIGURE **3.22.**

The Collapse All and Collapse To buttons are used to either collapse the entire stack or just up to the selected Modifiers.

Though you only manipulated simple Modifiers, you can easily see the power of the Stack. By moving Modifiers around, they affect the object in different ways. Modifier order plays a big role in the resultant object.

Note

> The Modifier Stack can become quite long and, in some cases, unwieldy. If the length of the Stack becomes a problem, due to memory or logistical issues, collapse either a portion or the entire Stack. The Modifier Stack uses memory for each Modifier in the Stack. By collapsing a portion of the Stack that you know you will not need to change, you can make the tack more efficient.

Modifier Order as a Matter of Preference

When adding multiple Modifiers, it is important to remember that the order in which the Modifiers are applied can greatly affect the resulting object. In the previous exercise and Figure 3.23, when the Twist Modifier was placed prior to the Bend Modifier, a more desirable result was achieved.

Note

> If you find that the result of your Modifier is not what you expected, you might need to adjust the axis of application or reposition the Modifier in the Stack.

FIGURE 3.23.

FIGURE 3.23.

Identical objects with the order of the Bend and Twist Modifiers reversed. On the right, the Twist Modifier was applied prior to the Bend.

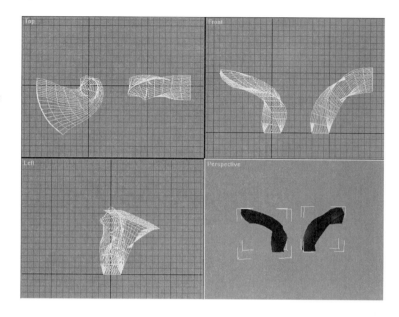

Applying Modifiers to Sub-Object Selections

Although Modifiers work great on objects, they can be applied equally well on Sub-Object selections. By applying a Modifier to a Sub-Object selection, you can localize the effect to a specified selection of vertices, faces, or segments.

To Do: Applying Modifiers to Sub-Object selections

1. Open file subMod.max from the accompanying CD-ROM. This scene contains a single box object, which was created with 10 segments along each dimension.

   In order to apply a Modifier to a Sub-Object selection, you first need to make a Sub-Object selection. Because the box in this exercise is not an Editable Mesh object, you can either apply an Edit Mesh or Mesh Select Modifier or right-click on the Edit Stack button and choose Convert to Editable Mesh (see Figure 3.24).

FIGURE 3.24.

Convert the box to an Editable Mesh object by right-clicking on the Edit Stack button and choosing Editable Mesh from the pop-up menu.

2. Though applying the Edit Mesh Modifier gives you the advantage of removing it later, for this exercise, use the Edit Stack option from the Modify Panel to convert the box to an Editable Mesh.

3. Now that the box has been converted, click on the Sub-Object selection button and make Vertex the selection choice.

4. Select the top five rows of vertices (as in Figure 3.25) and add a Twist Modifier by clicking on the Twist Modifier button. If the Twist is not available in the Modifier list, select the More button and select Twist from the Object Modifier list.

FIGURE 3.25.

The top five rows are selected to apply a Modifier to a Sub-Object selection.

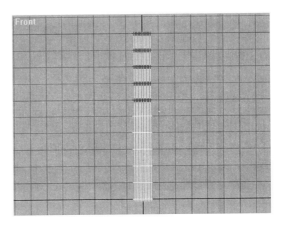

In the Modifier Stack, you notice that the Twist Modifier has an asterisk next to it. This indicates that this Modifier has been applied to a Sub-Object selection set.

5. In the Twist Modifier parameters, set the Twist angle to 180. As you can see, the 180 degree twist is only applied to the selected vertices.

6. Go into the Modifier Stack and select Editable Mesh from the list. You notice that the vertices are still selected. Select a set of vertices located in the center of the box. Click on the Show End Result button to view the results of the parameter change. Notice that the Twist Modifier is now applied to the newly selected set.

7. Select the Twist Modifier from the Stack list without deactivating the Sub-Object selection. The operation was a success. The Modifier was applied to a Sub-Object selection.

▲

Note

When applying Modifiers to a Sub-Object selection, you must leave the Sub-Object selection button active. If you turn the Sub-Object selection off, the Modifier will be applied to the entire object instead of the specified Sub-Object selection set.

Summary

In this chapter, you learned some important concepts leading to the creation of more advanced modeling. Through the use of the Modifier Stack, you can continually refine the model until the complex model emerges.

- *Sub-Objects*   The vertices, segments, and faces of a 3D object; they can also be transformed just as entire objects can.

- *Boolean Objects*   Can be fused together using the Boolean tools. Through the use of the Boolean functions, the geometry of one object can also be subtracted from another.

- *Modifying Booleans*   Through Sub-Object selection, the operands used in a Boolean object can be modified even if the operands are no longer visible.

- *Connect Objects*   Using the Connect object, you can connect two or more objects by geometric bridges. These bridges are generated where the faces of the operands have been removed.

- *Modifiers*   You can apply Modifiers to objects as a nondestructive method of modeling. Modifiers can be turned on and off, removed from the Stack, or collapsed to become a permanent part of the object's geometry.

Q&A

Q I've used the Boolean function, but I can't see the operands in the Modifier Stack. Where are they?

A Because the Boolean is a class of object and not a Object Modifier, it does not appear in the Modifier Stack. The operands are accessible through the Boolean parameters section. When selected from the list, the object's base parameters can be adjusted. In order to visually see the operands, click on the Show Hidden Ops. Check box under the Display section of the Boolean object.

Q I've used the Boolean on two objects and I want to reposition one of the operands, but can't. How can an operand be repositioned after the Boolean has been applied?

A To reposition an operand that was used during a Boolean operation, two criteria must be met. First, you must be sure the Boolean Display parameter is set to Operands, not Result. Secondly, you can move only the operand through its Sub-Object selection. If the operand does not have a Sub-Object selection available, you need to apply an Edit Mesh Modifier, select all the faces, and reposition them as needed.

Q Why does it seem that the Boolean doesn't work well on a group of objects?

A When using the Boolean on a group of objects, MAX does not recognize the group structure and selects the single item only. If you need to use a group of objects in a Boolean operation, ungroup them and apply the Boolean Union to each of the objects in the group to create a new object. Then use the Boolean on the new object. You can also use the Collapse Utility if you have many object that you want to turn into one object for a Boolean Union.

Q I've created a mesh object and two holes for the Connect object to bridge from. Why does only one hole get bridged?

A In order for the Connect tool to bridge two objects, the holes must be facing each other. The Connect tool works on the basis of the imaginary normals from the deleted faces. In order for the Connect tool to work, the normals of the missing faces from each object must be facing each other.

Q When I apply more than one Bend Modifier, the result is not what I expect. Why does the output seem strange or unpredictable?

A Because the Modifiers work on the entire object, adding multiple Modifiers requires a little forethought. Typically, the problem might be due to the Limit Effects Parameters or the position of the Gizmo. When using the Bend Modifier, start at the top of the object and work back toward the object's pivot point.

Q When using Lathe, why does the object seem to be inside out?

A Due to the position of the vertices and the axis direction of the Lathe operation, many times the normals are generated inside the object. To correct this, check the Flip Normals option in the Lathe parameters.

Q When I used a Modifier on a Sub-Object, the effect did not stick. Why does this occur?

A When working with Modifiers on a Sub-Object selection, you need to keep the selection active. If you close the Sub-Object selection (by clicking on the Sub-Object selection), you loose the Sub-Object selection set.

Q Can I add a Modifier to both a Sub-Object selection and the entire object?

A In order to add a Modifier to both a Sub-Object selection and the entire object, you need to add an Edit Mesh Modifier after the Sub-Object Modifier has been applied. Because the order of the Modifiers can change the shape dramatically, you need to experiment with you shape and Modifiers to get the effect you want.

DAY 4

Spline-Based Modeling and Lofting

Splines can be used in a number of modeling solutions. In terms of modeling, splines are used as cross-sectional shapes as well as paths. Splines can also be nested within a single shape, such as the donut shape, where one circular spline is nested inside a larger one.

Lofting is a term derived from the old ship-making days. Cross-sectional ribs were created outlining the shape of the boat. The ribs were then covered to create the body of the boat. Lofting in the 3D world is very much the same, except that 2D splines are used. These splines are linked together so that MAX can generate a "skin" over them, thereby creating the three-dimensional objects seen in Figure 4.1.

FIGURE **4.1.**

Typical Loft objects.

Though spline objects and 2D objects are used interchangeably many times, the truth is they are not really interchangeable. Although splines can look like 2D objects, in actual practice, many times a spline's vertices lay on three planes. Because of the many uses of splines (such as animation and modeling paths), spline objects can just as easily be two or three dimensional.

There are two classes of splines that ship with MAX: Standard splines and NURBS curves. The Standard splines are such splines as the Line, Rectangle, and the Circle. NURBS curves are classified as either Point curves or CV curves. The NURBS curves are explained in Day 5, so today we will concentrate on creating Loft shapes with the Standard splines.

Standard Splines

The Standard splines in MAX are what most consider to be two-dimensional shapes. These include, among others, the circle, rectangle, ellipse, and line objects. The Standard splines are used primarily as components of more complex shapes. Through the use of Lathing, Lofting, and Extruding, three-dimensional shapes can be created. Splines (as seen in Figure 4.2) are also often used as motion paths during animation.

Note

> Splines are curves that are interpolated. This means that the curve is created by control points that have influence over the shape of the curve. Unlike standard lines, which are straight as they enter and exit a point, splines use the control points to influence the shape of the curve. NURBS and Bézier curves are examples of interpolated spline curves.

FIGURE 4.2.

Splines come in all shapes and sizes, each with a variety of uses.

Creating and Editing Standard Splines

4

As with any object created in MAX, creating a spline is done through the Create Panel. Simply select the Object Type button and begin by clicking the mouse where selected vertices are to appear.

Note

By turning off the Start New Shape button, each subsequent shape you create becomes part of a single shape. Through this method, you can create complex shapes or even generate holes in geometry by nesting shapes.

As with any MAX object, splines can also be edited. The spline's components (vertices, segments, or splines) can be edited using any of the Transform tools. For more information regarding the Transform tools, refer to Day 2 lessons regarding modifying shapes and splines.

With the exception of the Line tool and the NURBS curves, to edit splines, you must first either add an Edit Spline modifier or convert the spline to an editable spline using the Edit Stack button. Regardless of which method you choose, you can edit either the vertices, segments, or an entire spline (when working with spline objects that have multiple splines).

To Do: Creating and editing a spline

1. Start with a new MAX scene by selecting Reset from the File menu. Open the Create Panel and select the Shapes button. You notice a number of buttons under the Object Type section. The buttons coincide with the Spline-type objects available to MAX during this session (see Figure 4.3).

FIGURE 4.3.

The Standard spline types that ship with MAX.

2. Create an NGon by selecting the NGon button and dragging the mouse in the Front view with the mouse button pressed.

3. With the NGon selected, open the Modify Panel and set the Sides parameter to 3. This creates a two-dimensional triangle shape.

4. Apply an Edit Spline Modifier by selecting the Edit Spline Modifier from the Modifier Panel or by clicking on the More button in the Modifiers section of the Modify Panel. The spline can now be edited as needed through any of the Sub-Object Selection levels available.

   Notice that after an Edit Spline Modifier is applied to the object, the Sub-Object Selection level is opened to the Vertex level of Sub-Object Selection. After the Modifier has been applied, Sub-Object Vertices, Segments, or Splines can be edited for this object. Because a Modifier has been used, these changes are nondestructive and the Modifier can be removed if it is later decided that the changes are not needed.

5. Instead of adding an Edit Spline Modifier, the shape can be converted to an Editable Spline by right-clicking on the Edit Stack button. Unlike the Modifier version, the Editable Spline is destructive in that the original shape object is lost when converted.

Note

Adding an Edit Spline Modifier is not the same as converting the shape to an Editable Spline. Though both access the same Sub-Object Selection levels, the Edit Spline Modifier can be removed to discard changes, leaving the original shape intact. Conversely, the converting the shape to an Editable Spline offers an adaptive setting that creates a smoother curve through adaptive segmenting of the shape (see Figure 4.4).

FIGURE 4.4.

Both these shapes are clones of the same three-sided NGon. The shape on the left had an Edit Spline modifier attached, whereas the shape on the right was converted to an Editable Spline. Notice how much smoother the shape on the right is along the lower curved edge.

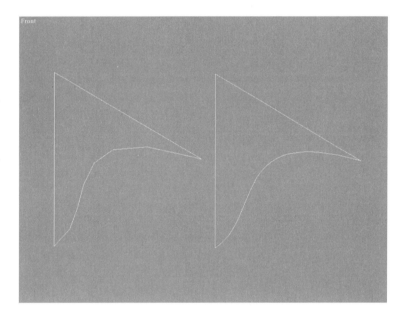

4

Loft Objects

Understanding the basics of shapes and splines is vital for understanding how lofting works. Lofting is the process of combining one or more shapes (of spline class) with a path (also a spline) to create a three-dimensional object. Figure 4.5 depicts objects created using the Loft method of modeling.

The path is used as the basis for the frame of the object, and the shapes are used as cross sections along the length of the path. There might be any number of cross-sectional shapes along the length of the path.

Figure 4.5.

Typical Loft objects.

> **Note**
>
> As with most aspects of MAX, the Loft object's parameters can be animated. This includes the position and shape of any of the associated splines, including the cross-sectional shapes and the path itself.

Valid Loft Shapes and Paths

To create a Loft object, you must first create splines to represent the cross-sectional shapes and the path. There are valid and invalid loft shapes. Although almost any spline can be used as either the path or the cross-sectional shapes, you have a few restrictions as noted here.

- *Paths must be single splines*   Compound shapes such as text and the Donut shape do not qualify as valid path shapes.

- *Cross-section splines count*   Each cross-sectional shape must have the same number of splines. Shapes with nested splines work if each shape has the same number of nested splines.

- *Spline nesting order*   Each cross-sectional shape must have the same nesting order of its splines. Nesting order refers to the placement of sub-object splines within a single shape object. For example, if one spline is completely enclosed in another in a particular shape, only shapes that also have one spline completely enclosed within another will have the same nesting order. In Figure 4.6, all the shapes, except the circle intersecting the circle (lower left), have the same nesting order and can be used in the same loft.

FIGURE 4.6.

This image depicts two different nesting order scenarios. When referring to nesting order, shape isn't considered, position is. The two upper shapes and the shape on the lower-right all have the same nesting order and can easily be used in the same Loft object. The shape on the lower left cannot be used in the same Loft object as any of the other shapes in this image.

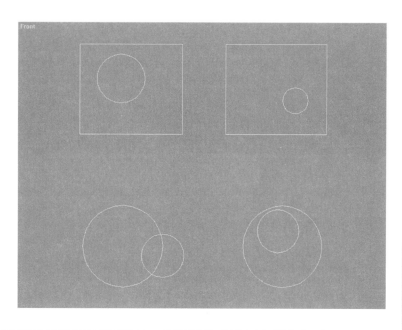

Note

When choosing shapes and paths for Loft objects, MAX will not allow you to select an invalid shape. If you try to select a shape and it does not become selected, chances are the shape is not valid for the Loft object. Typically, the problem is due to the nesting order on compound shapes.

After you create valid shapes, you can select them and place them along the path. The following exercise is intended to point out the distinction between valid and invalid loft shapes.

To Do: Choosing loft shapes

1. Open file loftsimp.max from the accompanying CD-ROM. This file contains a line, two circles, and a star.

2. With the star shape selected, open the Create Panel; then open the Geometry tab and select Loft Object from the Object class list. Select the Line shape and click on the Loft button.

▼   3. From the Creation Method section, choose Instance and click on the Get Shape
             button. The button turns green to indicate it is active.

           4. Move the mouse over the large circle and notice how the cursor gets a halo with a
             line through it. This indicates that the circle is a valid Loft shape. Click on the
             large circle object. The circle becomes attached to the path and a cylinder is creat-
             ed at the position of the line (path object).

           5. Notice that the Get Shape button is still active. Click on star shape. The circle
             cross section is replaced by the star shape and the Loft object is now a lofted star
▲   (see Figure 4.7).

     If you click the mouse on the small circle, the star is replaced by the circle. Because we
     haven't changed the path parameter, each time a new shape is selected, it replaces the
     previous. We will cover changing the position later in the day.

FIGURE 4.7.

*The star is lofted along
the spline path.*

     As easily as you can choose shapes, you can also choose your paths. There are many
     times when you might want to loft the same shape along different paths. Suppose you
     were modeling an octopus with eight legs, each in varying positions. Though the cross-
     sectional shape of the legs would be the same, the legs would each have their own
     unique pose and, therefore, their own unique Loft path. For such a case, select the shape
     first and get the path shape for the loft.

To Do: Creating lofts using Get Path

To Do

1. If loftsimp.max is still open, select and remove any Loft objects created in the previous exercise. Otherwise, load the file from the accompanying CD-ROM.

2. Select the large circle shape and click on the Loft button from the Create Panel, under the Loft Object class list.

3. Click the Get Path button from the Creation Method section. Leave the Creation Method at Instance. Select the Line object as the path for the loft. The Loft object is created at the position of the circle object.

4. With the Loft object still selected, click on the Get Path button again. This time, click on the star shape. The star shape becomes the path and the Loft object takes on the look of a rounded star object.

▲

5. With the Loft object still selected, click on the Get Shape button and select the smaller circle object. The Loft object changes again and can be seen in Figure 4.8.

As you can see, the Loft object can be changed very quickly just by changing the shape or the path objects. This is the power of the Loft. Choose Unhide All from the Hide section on the Display tab to reveal some more paths and shapes. Experiment with the other shapes and paths by alternating uses for each shape as both a path and a shape for more unique Loft objects.

4

FIGURE 4.8.

The new star object after changing the Loft path and shape.

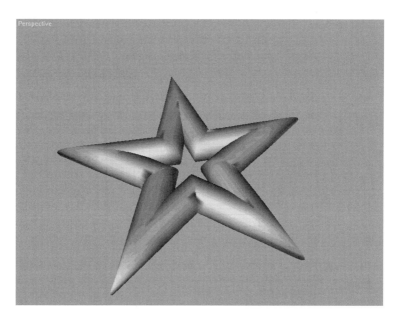

Note

> When creating Loft objects, the resulting object is created at the position of the object that was selected prior to the Loft operation. Attached objects are moved to the location of the primary object, regardless of whether the primary object was a path or a shape object.

Skin Parameters

Because the shapes and paths used to create a Loft object can vary greatly, the skin that is generated can also have different characteristics. For example, paths with irregular curves require more segments at varying positions along the path. By adjusting the Skin parameters, MAX can accommodate and create the most optimized shape. Changing the skin parameters can also change the density of the mesh and alter the way the mesh appears when rendered.

- *Shape Steps*   When a shape is created, the number of steps between the vertices can be set in order to limit the number of faces generated. Increasing the Shape Step parameter increases the number of steps between each vertex of the shapes associated with the current Loft object.

- *Path Steps*   Like the Shape Steps, the Path Steps are used to increase the smoothness of any curves along the path by increasing the number of steps between each path division. A path division occurs at every vertex along the path.

- *Optimize Shapes*   By optimizing the shape, the number of faces can greatly be reduced, saving rendering time and unneeded polygons. Shapes are optimized only along corresponding segments that are straight for all shapes along the path.

- *Adaptive Path Steps*   When checked, MAX recalculates the Loft object and adds divisions when needed to create the smoothest mesh object. Main divisions on the Loft path occur at the location of every shape on the path, and every vertex.

- *Contour and Banking*   These controls are used to keep the cross-sectional shapes oriented properly along the length of the Loft path. When Contour is checked, the shape turns with the path so that the shape is perpendicular through the entire length of the path, regardless of how the path might bend. Banking is used when the path is three dimensional in its curves. When Banking is turned off, the shape remains at the same angle along its Z axis along the entire length of the path as it was at step 0 of the path (see Figure 4.9). When Banking is turned on, MAX automatically rotates the shape along its local Z axis to coincide with the curvature of the path.

- *Constant Cross-Section*   As shapes are lofted along the length of a path, curves might be encountered. As the shape enters the curve, the shape begins to intersect itself if the curve is too sharp in relation to the size of the shape. Checking this option adjusts the size of the shape through the curves to avoid pinching the Loft geometry.

- *Linear Interpolation*   Though the change is subtle, Linear Interpolation causes the segments generated between steps to become straight. When Linear Interpolation is turned off, the segments between the path steps are smoothed, creating a smoother curve between shapes.

FIGURE 4.9.

The top Loft object has Contour and Banking turned on, whereas the same Loft without Banking is seen below.

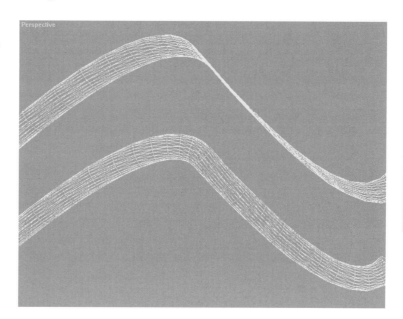

Surface Parameters

Whereas the Skin parameters are used to change the criteria for creating the object's geometry, the Surface parameters are used to affect the way the geometry is rendered. As with most objects in MAX, you can control how the mesh is rendered. Through Smoothing and Mapping controls, you control how MAX renders the Materials and the shading applied to a Loft object.

- *Smoothing*   When checked, the specified faces utilize a smoothing algorithm so that the faces appear smoother through curved surfaces. This can be applied along a Loft object's length or width. When not checked, faceted edges are created instead. This is achieved through the surface normals and does not affect the geometric structure at all.

- *Apply Mapping*   When checked, Loft mapping coordinates are generated for the Loft object. Checking this option activates the ability to control the tiling method and count for both the length and width of the Loft object.

- *Normalize*   Mapping coordinates are generated according to the vertices of a Loft object. Because the vertices can occur in higher concentrations along different points in the path, mapping can become skewed when Normalize is turned off. For most applications, leave Normalize checked. When you want to apply a material according to vertices, turn Normalize off.

Editing Loft Sub-Objects

When using multiple shapes, they are placed at different levels along the length of the Loft path to change the shape of the loft. To do this, you change the Path value in the Path Parameters section prior to selecting the shape. A yellow X placed along the path corresponds to the Path value.

In the following exercise, you edit both the Loft Sub-Object shape and path. To fully understand Loft objects, it is important to understand how to edit their components.

To Do: Editing loft sub-Objects

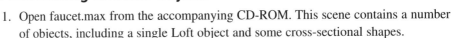

1. Open faucet.max from the accompanying CD-ROM. This scene contains a number of objects, including a single Loft object and some cross-sectional shapes.

2. Select the faucet Loft object and open the Modify Panel. In the Skin Parameters section, turn off Skin in the Display section. This removes the wire frame from any view that is set to Wire Frame mode and facilitates working with Loft Sub-Objects.

3. From the Modifier Stack section, click on the Sub-Object button, select Path from the Sub-Object list, and select Line from the Modifier Stack. The line in the Loft object appears red in the wire frame views.

4. With the Line still selected, again click on the Sub-Object Selection button to access the vertices of the Line shape. Click and drag a selection region over the entire Line shape. This selects all vertices of the Line object.

5. With all the vertices selected, right-click the mouse on any of the selected vertices. The vertex properties menu (seen in Figure 4.10) appears, from which you can change the vertex type. Select Bezier Corner.

6. With the vertices all converted to Bezier Corners, select and rotate the corner vertices to round off the ends of the faucet (see Figure 4.11).

By selecting and changing the vertex type, you can create a smoother curve for the Loft object. If you view the Loft in the Perspective shaded view, you notice the faucet has a smoother curve now.

7. To create the handles for the faucet, select the Handle Path from the Select by Name dialog box. Create a Loft object by opening the Create Panel, clicking on the Geometry button, opening the Loft Object panel, and clicking on the Loft button.

8. Leave the Creation Method at Instance and click on Get Shape. The Get Shape button turns green to indicate it is active. Click on the Handle Base shape (the large Circle).

   As you can see in the shaded Perspective view, the Handle loft looks very much like a short cylinder. To create a more realistic handle, you need to add additional shapes to the Loft object.

9. The Loft object should still be selected. If not, select it and open the Modify Panel. If it is still selected, you can make changes from where you are. In the Path parameters section, change the Path percentage from 0.0 to 100.0. A small yellow X appears at the end of the Loft object path. This indicates where 100 percent is along the path. Any value typed in the Path percentage value will be represented along the path with a yellow X.

10. If the Get Shape button is not active, activate it by clicking on the Get Shape button. Click on the Handle Top shape (the rounded star) to place it on the Path at the 100 percent mark.

    As you can see, the handle now looks more realistic with the circle smoothly blending into the star shape.

▲

FIGURE 4.10.

The Vertex properties pop-up menu. From here you can change the vertex type for all selected vertices.

FIGURE 4.11.

*Select the Bézier han-
dles and rotate to
round off the corners.
The corner on the right
has already been
rounded.*

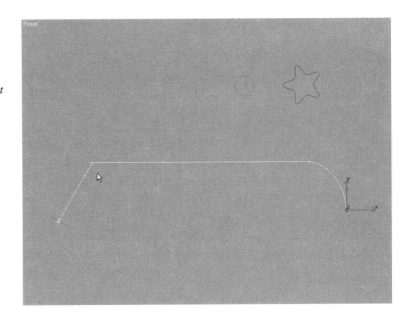

Using Multiple Shapes

Although the Loft object is similar to the Extrude, there are some major differences. The
most obvious is that the Loft can use a curved path, whereas the Extrude path is perpendicular to the face being extruded. The second difference is that Loft objects can use
multiple shapes along the length of the path.

When using different shapes along the path, MAX creates a smooth mesh between the
cross-sectional shapes. Shapes can be of any size or type and do not need to have the
same vertex count. The only stipulation when using multiple shapes on a Loft object is
that each shape must have the same number of splines.

Objects such as text and compound shapes have multiple splines. In text, each letter is
considered its own spline. Within each letter, there might also be more than one spline
(as seen in Figure 4.12) used to create the shape.

Although the rule holds true that all shapes must have the same number of splines, there
are ways of dealing with objects with varying numbers of splines. The secret: reconfigure each shape in the loft so that the number of splines is equal.

Though not a difficult task, discretion must be used when deciding where the splines
should be split, as this affects how the shape is lofted. When creating Loft objects with
multiple shapes, it is essential to use the Compare tool within the Loft object Shape
Commands to ensure proper lofting. See the section "Aligning Shapes" for more information regarding the Compare command.

FIGURE 4.12.

All the shapes on the left are made up of single splines, whereas the shapes on the right all contain multiple splines. When using multiple shapes on a Loft object, shapes must have the same number of splines.

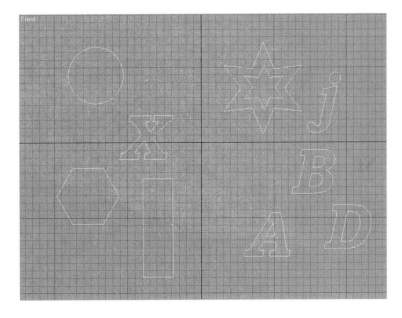

Aligning Shapes

When using multiple shapes in a Loft object, vertex count isn't as important as alignment. When the starting vertex of the cross-sectional shapes do not align, the result is geometry that can become contorted as in Figure 4.13. Normally, this is not the desired result. To correct this problem or to change the alignment for a twisting effect, you can compare and align shapes.

Loft objects become twisted when the start vertices of all the Loft shapes are not aligned. By default, MAX attempts to align the start vertices of all shapes applied to the Loft object. To manually align the cross-sectional shapes of a Loft object, use the Shape Commands.

The Shape Commands are located in the Loft object's Modify Panel, at the Shape Sub-Object Selection level. Here are the Commands and their functions:

- *Compare* Pressing the Compare button displays an interactive dialog box that is used to display selected shapes from the Loft object. As shapes are selected, they appear in the Compare dialog box.

- *Reset* When aligning shapes, you might use either the Select and Move tool or the Rotate tool. Pressing reset will undo any transforms performed on the Loft object cross-sectional shapes.

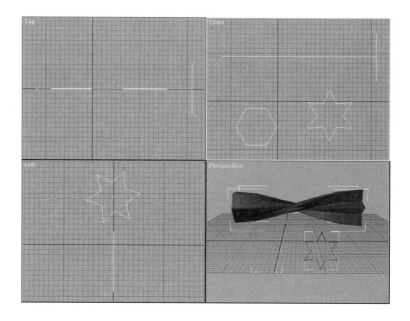

FIGURE 4.13.

The Shapes used to create this Loft object have vertices that are not aligned, as is evidenced by the twisted Loft object.

- *Delete*   Removes the selected Loft cross-sectional shape from the Loft object. If Move was used as the Creation method, the shape will no longer exist in the scene. If you need to preserve the shape but want to remove it from the Loft, use the Put tool.

- *Align tools*   Each of the various alignment tools are used to align the selected shape to the path. By default, the shapes are aligned via their pivot points. Using these alignment tools aligns the shape via its bounding box. The alignment shapes are also progressive in that if you align a shape to the left and then to the top, the shape will be aligned to the Left and to the Top of the path. The Default button aligns the shape as it was when attached to the Loft object (via the shape object's pivot point), whereas Center aligns via the bounding box.

- *Put*   Using the Put button will generate either a copy or an instance of the selected shape and place it in the scene, separate from the Loft object.

Using the Compare tool, you can visually see how selected Loft shapes compare in alignment. In Figure 4.14, you can see that the shapes used for the previous figure do not have aligned starting vertices (shown as small boxes along each shape's spline).

FIGURE 4.14.

The small squares located on the spline indicate the starting vertex of each shape. Notice they are not aligned with each other.

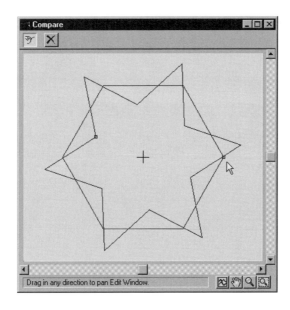

To Do: Comparing loft cross sections

1. Open loftComp.max from the accompanying CD-ROM. Select the Loft object and open the Modify Panel.

2. Click on the Sub-Object Selection Level button and choose Shape as the selection level. At this level, the Shape Commands are available.

3. In the Shape Commands section, click on the Compare button to invoke the Compare tool. An empty dialog box appears as seen in Figure 4.15.

FIGURE 4.15.

The Compare tool dialog box with no cross-sectional shapes selected.

4

▼ 4. Click on the Pick shape icon to add a shape to the Compare dialog box (Figure 4.16). At this point, the cursor becomes a thick cross cursor with an augmented Plus or Minus sign as the cursor rolls over the Loft shapes. Click on the Star shape along the Loft path to add it to the Compare dialog box (see Figure 4.17).

FIGURE **4.16.**

The Pick Shape button used in the Compare dialog box.

FIGURE **4.17.**

Click on the Star shape attached to the Loft path, not the Star shape that exists in the scene.

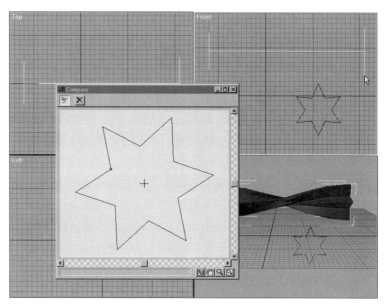

5. Using the method described in step 4, add the NGon shape located at the opposite end of the Loft object to the Compare window.

Now that the two cross-sectional shapes have been loaded into the Compare window, you can correct the twisting geometry. As you will notice, the two shapes are not

▼ aligned according to their starting vertices (the small boxes located on the spline).

▼ 6. Select the Select and Rotate tool and click on the Star shape to select it. Select it from the modeling window, not the Compare window. Leave the Compare window open.

7. From the Front view, click and drag the selected shape. Notice how the shape rotates in the Compare window. By adjusting the rotation of the cross-sectional shape, you can align the starting vertices of both shapes. Rotate the Star shape until its starting vertex is as close to the NGon's starting vertex as possible. Your shape's

▲ alignment should look similar to the alignment shown in Figure 4.18.

FIGURE 4.18.

The Loft shape after aligning the Loft object shape's starting vertices.

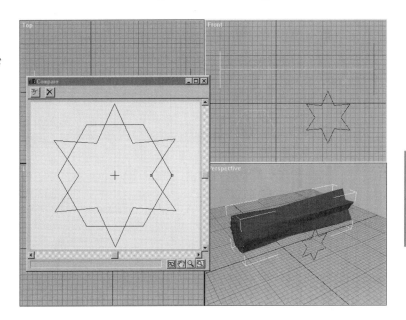

4

Notice how the Loft object has become smoother through the transition of the two shapes associated with this Loft object. In some cases, you might not want to align the starting vertices, as you did in this exercise. And as seen in Figure 4.19, you can create a twisting effect in the Loft without applying a Twist Modifier. Though used infrequently, this effect might be desirable in some modeling cases. In either case, one must be aware of the misalignment phenomenon so that unexpected twisting can be resolved (through manual alignment of cross sections).

Note

Many times, when adding multiple shapes to a Loft path, the shape will become twisted. When this occurs, you must align the vertices of the sub-object shapes. Aligning the starting points of each sub-object shape will remove the unwanted twist from your Loft object's surface.

FIGURE 4.19.

The same Loft object with the cross-sectional shapes not off alignment by 90 degrees. By doing this, you can generate a twist effect in the Loft object without adding a Twist Modifier.

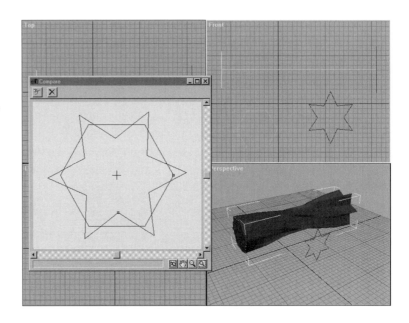

In addition to aligning the starting vertex of Loft shapes, you might want to align the cross-sectional shapes differently. Using the tools provided in the Shape Commands, you can align shapes relative to the Loft path.

> **Note**
>
> Cross-sectional shapes assigned to a Loft object are aligned to the Loft path. The default alignment is with the path passing through the shape's pivot point.

To Do: Aligning cross-sectional shapes

1. Open file cubeLoft.max from the accompanying CD-ROM. This scene contains a single loft object and a single shape.

2. Open the Modify Panel, click on the Sub-Object Selection button, and choose Shape as the Sub-Object Selection level.

3. Click the Compare button to invoke the Compare function. In the Compare window, click the Pick Shape button and click the mouse on each of the shapes attached to the Loft. You should see both the rectangle and the circle in the Compare window.

   As you might have noticed, the shapes are centered around the crosshair in the center of the window. The crosshair represents the path alignment axis. By default, the pivot point of each shape in the Loft is centered on the Loft path.

▼ 4. Leaving the Compare window open, use the Select and Move tool to select the circle shape. The shape is selected in the modeling views, not the Compare window.

5. With the circle shape selected, click on the Left button in the Align section of the Shape Commands. The left edge of the circle is aligned with the crosshairs in the Compare window.

6. Click on the Bottom button in the Align section of the Shape Commands. Notice that although the bottom of the shape is aligned to the crosshairs, the left edge is still aligned. Each alignment button works on a single axis only, therefore each axis must be aligned.

7. Using the Select and Move tool, select the rectangle shape. Click on the Right and then the Top align buttons. Notice in the Compare window that the rectangle is realigned. Also notice that the lofted shape now has a curved shape, even though
▲   the Loft path is perfectly straight.

Because MAX attempts to create a smooth skin over the cross-sectional shapes of a Loft object, the shape can become quite curvy just by changing the alignment of the cross-sectional shapes. For an additional exercise, alternate another rectangle and circle shape along the path at different percentages and change the alignment. Watch how the shape changes according to the alignment.

Loft Deformations

By aligning the cross-sectional shapes of the Loft object, you can create variations of a given loft. There are also Loft Deformations that can be used for even greater control and variation of the Loft after the cross-sectional ribs have been applied.

Loft deformations are applied to the Loft object as needed to alter the shape of the Loft object at specified positions along the Loft path. Each has its own effect, and with the exception of the fit deformation, they all work on the same basic principle. Alter the shape of the loft object by applying the deformation to various portions of the Loft.

There are five Loft deformations that ship with 3DS MAX 2.5, as listed here. The use of Loft Deformation makes it possible to create shapes that have the basic characteristics of a Loft object, but also require changes in scale or rotation in the cross sections along the path.

- *Scale* Enables you to scale the Loft object at any point along the path without adding additional cross-sectional ribs.

- *Twist* Apply a twisting motion to the ribs without having to manually rotate the ribs in the Compare window.

- *Teeter* This is used to rotate a cross-sectional shape along both the X and Y local axes. This can dramatically alter the shape of the Loft and can also cause the shape to have self-intersecting geometry. Use care when using this Loft Deformation.

4

- *Bevel*   Because nearly nothing manufactured in the real world has a razor sharp edge, the Bevel Deformation is used to take the edge off of Loft objects. Although a subtle effect, using this Deformation adds to the realism of a model.

- *Fit*   The Fit deformation works like a double axis Loft object. Two curves are used to define the top and sides of the Loft object. As the shape is lofted along the path, the Fit curves are used to limit the effect for both the X and Y axes.

The Loft Deformations can be used to create very complex shapes that are not normally possible through the standard loft parameters. If you analyze the shape in Figure 4.20, you will notice that this shape would be time-consuming to create using a standard loft because of the varying cross-sectional shapes. By using a loft deformation, only two shapes were used, and the Scale Deformation was applied to create variations in the cross-sectional ribs at different positions along the Loft path.

FIGURE 4.20.

This Loft object uses two shapes and the Scale Deformation to create its irregular look.

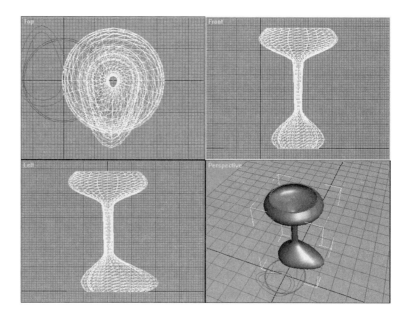

The Scale Deformation is used to scale a Loft object at various positions along the length of the loft through the use of a scale grid. The grid displays the Loft path horizontally. Edit points are placed on the path to scale the cross section at that position of the Loft path. By adding multiple edit points along the length of the path, the Loft object's shape can be changed dramatically. The following exercise demonstrates how to create and edit a Loft Scale deformation.

To Do: Using the Scale deformation

1. Open ScaleLft.max from the accompanying CD-ROM. This file contains a Loft object and the line and circle shape used to create it.

2. Select the Loft object and open the Modify Panel. Open the Deformations section located at the base of the Modify Panel and press the Scale Deformation button. The Scale Deformation grid is presented. The depressed Light Bulb icon next to the Scale button indicates the Scale Deformation is active.

The Deformation grid is used to scale a Loft object along the length of the Loft path. The grid represents the length of the Loft path in percent, starting at the left side (see Figure 4.21). The vertical representation is the percentage of scale. The deformation grid is used to change the scale of a cross section located at a specific point along the length of the spline.

FIGURE 4.21.

The horizontal values denote position along the Loft path in percent. The vertical values denote the percentage of scale for the cross section at a specified position.

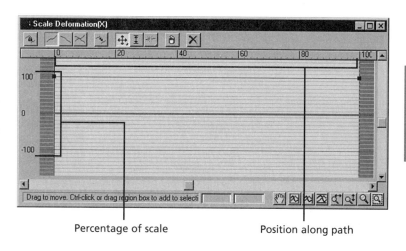

Percentage of scale   Position along path

3. In the Deformation grid, select and position the middle control point so that it is close to the zero horizontal line but not touching. Position the Scale Deformation grid window so that the Loft can be seen in the Perspective view.

4. In the Scale Deformation window, deactivate the Make Symmetrical button (see Figure 4.22) and view the Y Deformation Axis by clicking on the Display Y Axis button. Select and delete the center point along the Deformation curve by clicking the Trash Can icon. You now have a Scale Deformation along the X axis only.

Because the Y axis deformation was removed, the Loft object became flattened in the center without affecting the Y axis (see Figure 4.23). Using this type of deformation makes it easy to simulate something such as a piece of hot pipe being struck with a hammer.

FIGURE 4.22.

The Scale Deformation window is used to scale a Loft object along the X and Y axis. Each axis can be scaled independently or as a single locked deformation.

The Make Symmetrical button · The Display Y Axis button · The Move Control Point tool

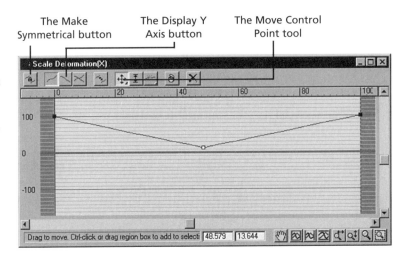

FIGURE 4.23.

Because Lofting occurs along the Z axis, scaling can be done along the X and Y axis using the Scale Deformation. When scaled along either the X or Y axis, the other axis is unaffected.

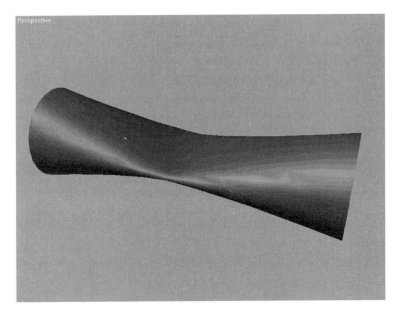

5. Change the Insert Point type by clicking and holding on the Insert Point flyout. This can be set to insert either a Corner point or a Bezier point. Choose Bezier point. Add a Bezier Point to the deformation by clicking on the horizontal path (in red). Place the point near the 20 percent point.

6. Right-click the mouse on the center edit point in the X axis Scale Deformation. The pop-up menu has three choices for point types. Choose the Bezier Smooth type.

7. Change to the Move Control Point tool and adjust the Bézier handles of the Scale Deformation edit point so that the handles are about 45 degrees off kilter with the horizontal zero grid line. Notice how the shape of the Loft object changes to reflect the Scale Deformation profile (see Figure 4.24).

FIGURE 4.24.

Adding a point to the Scale Deformation can dramatically change the shape of the original Loft object. Through this method, complex lofted objects can be created by adding points to the X or Y axis, or both simultaneously.

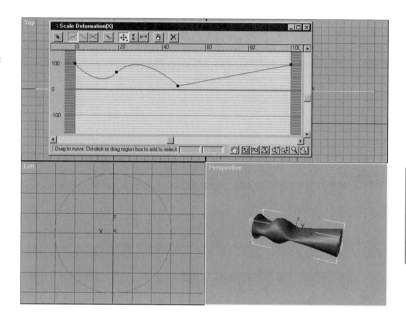

8. If working in the nonsymmetrical mode, changing to the symmetrical mode will move all points on the active deformation axis to the other axis. With the X Scale Deformation axis active, click on the Make Symmetrical button. Notice how the points are added to the Y Scale Deformation axis and the shape of the Loft object changes to reflect the newly added points (Figure 4.25).

One of the most interesting, yet somewhat complicated, Loft Deformations to use is the Fit Deformation. This deformation tool uses three shapes to define the object. One shape is used for each of the axes. The Fit Loft Deformation is really a variation on the Loft Scale Deformation. Each of the shapes are used to scale the Loft object along one of the axes. The following exercise demonstrates a basic Loft Fit Deformation.

FIGURE 4.25.

By clicking the Make Symmetrical button, the points on the X Scale Deformation axis are copied to the Y Scale Deformation axis. This process removes any existing points on the axis receiving the copied control points.

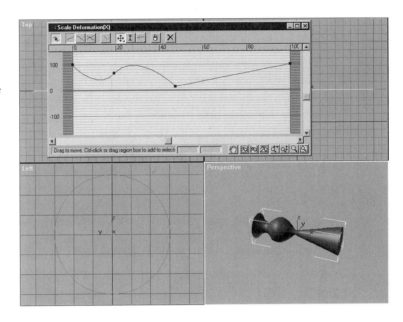

To Do 4.8: Using the Loft Fit Deformation

1. Open fitLftEx.max from the accompanying CD-ROM. This file contains four shape objects that will be used to create a Loft Fit Deformation.

2. Select the object named Line01 and create a Loft object using the Loft Create button and selecting the Star shape as the Get Shape object. This produces an extruded star-shaped object.

3. With the Lofted star object selected, click on the Modify Panel and set the Skin Display parameter to Display Skin. You use this to compare the shape of the Loft after various modifications.

4. Open the Deformations rollout and add a Fit Deformation by pressing the Fit Deformation button found at the bottom of the Deformations section rollout. The Fit Deformation grid window opens.

   Like the Scale Deformation, the Fit Deformation window has the same type of deformation grid. In this grid, Fit shapes are added that are used to scale the Lofted shape to fit the specified shape.

5. Click the Get Shape button (depicted by a hand over a wavy line) in the Fit Deformation window and click on the rounded rectangle shape. As you can see, the lofted star now has rounded edges.

▼

6. Click on the Generate Path button to match the Loft path with the size of the rounded rectangle Fit Shape. Generating a path ensures that the Loft matches the dimensions of the Fit shapes added.

7. To add a deformation to the Y axis, unlock the Make Symmetrical button and click on the Display Y Axis button. Use the Get Shape button to select the teardrop shape. The star Loft shape is now pinched at the bottom.

▲

As you can see by this example, each of the Fit shapes are used to reshape the Loft object along a specific axis. When creating shapes for the Fit Deformation, be aware that the shapes should be created to scale (in relation to the other shapes in the Fit deformation).

An Introduction to Animation—Animating Loft Paths and Shapes

One of the most powerful features of 3DS MAX 2.5 is that nearly all parameters can be animated. In many cases, this makes fundamental animating techniques trivial and complex animation much easier. The following exercise assumes that you read the chapter on animation and understand the concept of animation and how it is achieved in MAX. If not, this exercise might be difficult to follow at times.

To Do: Animating the Scale Deformation

1. Open animScal.max from the accompanying CD-ROM. This file contains four Loft objects, which have been instanced so that changes to one Loft object will propagate to the other Loft objects.

2. Select the only active Loft object and open the Modify Panel. Open the Scale Deformation window by clicking on the Scale button in the Deformations section.

3. Set MAX to Animate mode by clicking on the Animate button. Set the time slider to 50.

4. Change the Move Control Point selector to horizontal only by selecting the horizontal arrow from the Move Control Point flyout. Select the two middle points of the Scale Deformation curve and move them as one to the extreme right side of the Scale Deformation grid. Only the point on the right will be against the edge of the deformation limit. Close the Scale Deformation window and turn off the Animate button to exit the Animate mode.

5. To view a preview of the animation of the Loft object, select Preview from the Rendering menu. Check active segment and make preview. The preview will be displayed after MAX completes the preview animation.

▼ To Do

4

Summary

You learned that Loft shapes are made up of cross-sectional shapes. These cross-sectional shape are often referred to as geometric ribs over which MAX will generate a skin to create an object.

You also know that any number of ribs can be used, although the concept behind lofting is to let MAX fill in the missing ribs for a smooth flowing shape. You can, by contrast, control the density of the skin to create smoother or more segmented geometry, based on the type of object you create.

Lofting is a general all purpose tool for creating shapes that have either irregular shapes or irregular paths, unlike extruded and lathed objects that are created along a single straight path or axis.

Q&A

Q What is the difference between a Loft object and an extruded object?

A The Loft object is very similar to an extruded object, except that the extrusion path does not have to be straight in a Loft object. The Loft object also can use many shapes along the length of the path, where the extrude is performed on a single shape.

Q I have a single shape applied to my Loft object, but I want to add more. I turned on the Get Shape button, but although I clicked on a shape, why can't I select the shape I want? I can attach the shape to a new Loft but not to an existing Loft. Why not?

A If you cannot add a shape to an existing Loft object but you can create a new Loft object with it, the problem lies in the number of splines in each shape, or the nesting order of the shape. When multiple shapes are added to Loft objects, each shape must have the same number of splines and the same nesting order for the shape to be valid.

Q Why is it that when I use multiple shapes in my Loft object, the skin sometimes turns out contorted and twisted?

A Use the Compare window to check the alignment of the start vertex for each shape along the Loft path. MAX builds the skin based on the position of the start vertex for each shape in the Loft. If the start vertices are not aligned, the skin will become twisted.

Q Can Loft objects be animated?

A Not only can Loft objects be animated, but all the components can be animated, as well. You can animate any or all the shapes used in a loft object independently, as well as the path shape.

DAY 5

Modeling with NURBS and Patches

You know what splines and lofting can do, but wait until you experience the power of NURBS. Regarded as the leading technology for creating organic objects, NURBS modeling is the créme de la créme of the 3D modeling world. It seems everyone wants to work with NURBS, though many might not understand it. NURBS themselves are not difficult to understand, but the tool set can become quite extensive and the modeling approach is different than that of polygonal modeling.

NURBS, which stands for Non-Uniform Rational Basis Spline, is a special type of modeling concept. Instead of working with polygons and faces, the entire object consists of splines. The splines used are very much like the ones you used with lofting, although the nature in which they are used is somewhat different. Instead of creating a mesh object like lofting does, NURBS retains the splines during the modeling process and creates the surface during the rendering process. The result is typically a smoother surface with a more organic look to it.

Because NURBS objects are based on splines, the tessellation of their mesh can be dynamic, based on user-controlled parameters. *Tessellation* is the process in which faces are created based on an object's geometric parameters. By controlling the tessellation, one can control how dense the mesh of an object is. Although a higher-density mesh creates smoother curved surfaces, it also increases rendering time. In MAX, NURBS objects have the built-in capability for dynamic tessellation (called View Dependent). This means that tessellation can be controlled by the distance the object is from the camera. When the object is close to the camera, tessellation is higher to produce a smooth surface. As the distance between the object and the camera increases, the tessellation is reduced because the object is less significant as it moves away from the camera. This dynamic tessellation will speed up rendering time by using the lowest tessellation possible to create a smooth edge, no matter where the object is in the scene.

What Is NURBS Modeling

As with all object models, it is the surface that is rendered to give the object solidity. Without a surface, the object is merely a group of splines. Although MAX has a provision for rendering splines, this is not how splines were intended to be used. So, if NURBS are made up entirely of splines, how do you create a surface? Surfaces are created by combining together groups of NURBS curves and performing surface generating functions on them. In addition to the NURBS curves, NURBS surfaces can be created directly. NURBS surfaces are explained in detail in a later section of today's lessons.

Though generating a NURBS surface directly from the NURBS Create Panel consists of flat sheets of NURBS material, this is not the full extend of NURBS surfaces. In fact, NURBS are very complex entities, created from a variety of sources. Even the Standard MAX primitives can be directly converted to NURBS surfaces. Through the use of all these objects and manipulating Points, CVs, and surfaces, incredibly complex objects can be completed.

In short, NURBS modeling is a process by which NURBS curves are used to generate organic, renderable, and animatable models. The resulting geometry produces a cleaner surface because faces are calculated at render time and not during modeling time. Using this method, the same NURBS model can be rendered with a varying number of faces at different frames during an animation. When the object is close to the camera and the edges are seen, the tessellation can be higher than when the object is off in the distance as a background object and face count can be greatly reduced, without a substantial loss in image quality. This process is called view-dependent tessellation.

NURBS Curves, the Essence of NURBS

Before you can begin working with NURBS objects, you must first understand the NURBS curve. These curves are not much different than other splines, except that they are constantly adjusting themselves to keep the curve smooth. The NURBS curve shown in Figure 5.1 was created by creating points at arbitrary locations. Though similar curves can be created using the Standard Line tool and smooth creation method, NURBS curves use a different equation for creating smooth curves. NURBS curves can also be used to create NURBS surfaces using NURBS surface creation tools or converting directly to NURBS surfaces through the Edit Stack dialog box.

FIGURE 5.1.

This NURBS curve continues to be smooth through every point created. It is difficult to create sharp corners along a NURBS curve because NURBS curves were designed to create smooth flowing curves from point to point.

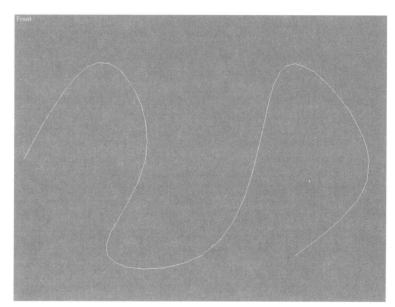

5

NURBS curves come in two flavors, Point curves and Control Vertices (CV) curves. Though both create smooth curves, there are distinct differences between them. Both can be used together in creating NURBS surfaces and each has advantages over the other.

Point Curves

If you used the Line tool with the Creation Method set to smooth, you have dealt with a curve that is close in characteristics as the NURBS Point curve. The Point curve creates a curve that passes through each point as it is created. When creating a Point curve, you might notice that the line changes as new points are added during the creation process. Though this might be somewhat confusing at first, it is an essential characteristic of

NURBS Point curves. The reason the line is adjusting is to keep the curve at a specified smoothness through every point along the line. For this reason, it is impossible to create a sharp corner using a Point curve.

To Do: Creating a NURBS Point curve

1. Reset MAX to start with a clean scene file, by selecting Reset from the File menu.

2. Open the Create Panel and open the Shapes section. From the Splines type list, select the NURBS Curves spline type. Creation buttons for the two types of MAX NURBS Curves available are in the Object Type section.

3. Prior to creating this Point curve, turn on snapping and set the Snap option to Grid Points.

4. Click on the Point Curve button to activate NURBS Point curve creation.

5. Use this exercise to see how the Point curve reacts as each point is created along the curve. Maximize the Front view and with snapping turned on and click at 0,0,0 to create the first point in the Point curve.

6. Create the second point along the vertical dark grid line at least four grid lines up from the first point. Move the mouse from side to side and watch how the Point curve reacts.

   After creating the second point and moving the mouse back and forth to the left and right of the second point, you notice that even though the segment between the first and second point is a straight line, the curve bends according to the position of the third point (which has yet to be created).

7. Create a third point on either side of the center vertical grid line and watch how the curve remains smooth.

8. Create a fourth point as close to the second point as you can. Right-click the mouse to complete the curve.

Though it might seem as though you created a sharp edge in your Point Curve with the position of the fourth point being close to the second, it is still a smooth curve. The Point curve is ideal for creating smooth curves in which the smoothing is done automatically by MAX. For curves where the smoothness between vertices can be adjusted, check out the CV curve.

CV Curves

Like the Point curve, the CV curve (CV stands for Control Vertices) is a NURBS based curve intended to create smooth curves. The primary difference between a CV curve and a Point curve is that the curve does not pass through the CVs as in the Point curve (where the curve passes through each point). Figures 5.2 and 5.3 compare the differences between the Point and CV curves.

FIGURE 5.2.

An S curve created using the CV Curve. Notice how the CVs are used to influence the curve and do not lie directly on the curve itself.

FIGURE 5.3.

The same S curve shown in Figure 5.3, created with a Point curve. Here the points lie directly on the curve. As a result, more points are required than to create the CV Curve.

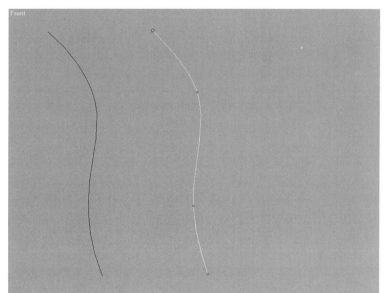

5

CV curves take some practice to create the curve you really want. Understanding how the CVs influence the curve is essential in creating the proper curve without numerous edits. When creating a CV curve, think of the CVs as tension controllers that pull the curve tighter toward them as you change the weight of the CV.

To Do: Creating a CV curve

1. Open Cvnurb.max from the accompanying CD-ROM. This scene file contains a single line shape.

2. Open the Create Panel and select the Shapes button. Select NURBS Curves from the spline Type drop-down list.

3. Select CV Curve as the Object Type. Using the line shape as a guide to create CVs, create a CV by clicking on each of the vertex points of the line shape, starting from the left.

4. Right-click the mouse to complete the curve, after creating CVs at the appropriate positions.

5. Leave this scene file for the next exercise, or save it under a new name for future reference.

As you can see, where the line curve can create a very straight line, the CV curve creates a line that flows between the CVs. For a comparison of the same line created using a NURBS Point curve, click on Unhide All from the Display Panel. The Point line looks different. In the following section, you edit the CV curve by moving CVs and changing the weight of selected CVs.

> **Note**
>
> In 3DS MAX 2.5, all Standard splines can be converted to NURBS curves, with the exception of the Helix. This greatly aids in creating perfect circles and other shapes for use in NURBS modeling. All converted splines become CV type NURBS curves.

Using CV Weighting to Control the Curve

Where the Point Curve uses points along the curve to control how the curve is created, the CV curve uses CV weighting and CV position to control how the curve appears. CV weighting is relative, with each CV trying to control the portion of the curve between the adjacent CVs. Because the control of each CV overlaps its neighboring CV's control, the effect can work together to pull the curve toward both CVs. Another difference in the CV curve is that each of the Control Vertices can exude a certain amount of influence over the CV adjacent to it. As a result, CV curves can create curves that are weighted. Figure 5.4 shows how different weighting of the CVs affects the curve.

FIGURE 5.4.

Though the two CV curves shown here are identical, the curve on the right was adjusted by weighting the two middle CVs. The second CV from the top has a weight of 9, whereas the third has a weight of 5. All other CVs were left as they were. Though not a sharp curve, weighting the CVs increases the tightness of the curve as it gets closer to the CV.

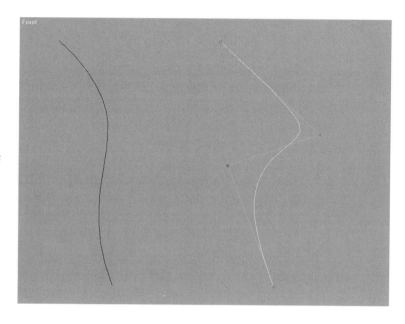

Note

The weight value of CVs is relative to the adjacent CVs. For example, if all had weight values of 1 and one CV had a weight value of 3, the CV with the value of 3 would have more influence than the others. If all CVs had a weight value of 3, the effect would be the same as if all had a weight value of 1.

5

The following exercise shows how the CV's weight can change the shape of the curve, without moving the CV. This exercise requires that you perform the exercise prior to this one so that you have the necessary splines located in your scene file.

To Do: Editing and weighting CVs

▼ To Do

1. Using the scene from the previous exercise, select the CV curve created in the previous steps. Open the Modify Panel and turn on Curve CV Sub-Object Selection.

2. Select the CV closest to the top of the view. This should be CV 02 if your curve was created following the line shape in the previous steps. You can see the name of the selected CV in the CV rollout.

3. In the CV parameters section, use the Weight spinner to increase the weight incrementally. Do this by clicking on the up arrow of the spinner.

4. Continue increasing the value of the Weight spinner using the spinner arrows and watch how the curve continues to move closer to the CV. Stop when the Weight value gets to 10.

▲

By increasing the weight parameter, the curve changes shape in the segment where the weight is changed. Though the curve continues to get tighter, it will not become a sharp point due to the nature of CV curves. It is difficult (though not impossible) to create sharp points along a NURBS curve. Though not to be taken as a challenge of drawn swords, the NURBS object is not intended for objects with sharp curves. The segment on Chamfer curves later in this chapter offers some insight on creating sharp corners on NURBS curves.

NURBS Curve Sub-Object Comparison

For editing the NURBS curve after creation, you have three levels of Sub-Object selection, as described here. Like the Standard Line shape, these Sub-Object levels are available without adding the Edit Spline modifier, as with such shapes as the circle or the arc shapes.

- *Point*   Similar to vertices on Standard splines, the Point Sub-Object is manipulated to change the curvature of the NURBS curve. Points have no independent controls because the curve is based on the relationship of adjacent points. In a Point curve, the points of the curve are located directly on the curve.

- *Curve CV*   Because the CVs, or control vertices, are not located on the curve itself, the weight of each CV is used to influence how close the curve passes to the CV. Increasing the weight value of a CV draws the curve closer to the actual location of the CV without ever actually reaching it. Because this weight value must still be interpolated along a smooth curve, the CV curve can have tighter curves than the Point Curve. CVs are only affected by the Move transform. Rotating or Scaling a CV has no effect on either the CV or the Curve.

- *Curve*   CV curves can have multiple curves as part of their Curve Sub-Object level of modification. Additional curves can be added using the Shift+drag method or by attaching existing curves.

Regardless of which NURBS curve type you are editing, either the Points or the CVs can be edited. Weighting being the only parametric difference between the CV and the Point, both have similar editing functions. In each case, the Points or CVs can be transformed, refined, or fused, to name a few examples of editing commands. For a complete list of editing commands for the NURBS curves, see the section on NURBS Curve Sub-Object Parameters.

NURBS Curve Object Parameters

At the object level, Point and CV curves have four categories of parameter editing. From these parameters, Points or CVs and curves can be added and manipulated. Rendering and curve approximation parameters can also be set.

- *General*   Contains controls used to attach or import splines.

- *Curve Approximation*   Sets the number of steps between segments or can be set to adaptive interpolation. The portion of the curve between two points is considered a segment.

- *Create Points*   Use to add Points or CVs to the curve or to add Dependent Points or CVs referenced by the curve. Dependent Points do not have to lie on the curve.

- *Create Curves*   Either Point or CV curves can be added to an existing NURBS curve. Choose the curve type and create the curve as usual. Dependent curves can also be created using the Dependent Curve tools. These tools aid in creating new curves or creating a smooth transition between existing curves.

NURBS Curve Sub-Object Parameters

At the NURBS Curve Sub-Object level, you can control the CVs of a CV curve or the Points of a Point curve. At this level, the curve can change shape based on how each CV or Point is configured. Except for the Weight and Display Lattice parameters, all the parameters described here are common to both the CV and Point curve.

- *Selection*   This selection method is used to toggle between selecting a single CV or Point on a spline or selecting All CVs or All Points. When working with NURBS curve objects with multiple curves attached, using the Select All option is useful to isolate the vertices of a single curve.

- *Name*   Each Point or CV is assigned a default name that starts with Point or CV followed by a number, based on the creation order of the Point or CV. The names can be changed to more meaningful names, by selecting the Point or CV and typing in an appropriate name. This becomes useful when using the curve for animation and a specific Point or CV is referenced individually.

- *Hide/Unhide All*   Hides the selected Point or CV or unhides all Points CVs on any curves that make up the selected NURBS curve object. This can be used to make working with complex curves easier by hiding Points or CVs that are not intended to be edited. Though the Points or CVs are hidden, their affect on the curve will remain intact.

- *Fuse/Unfuse*   Two or more Points or CVs can be fused together and controlled as a single entity. Unlike welding vertices, fused Points or CVs are still considered separate Sub-Objects, yet they are manipulated as one. Fused Points or CVs can be unfused at anytime, whereby each can be transformed independently.

- *Refine/Delete*   Using Refine, Points or CVs can be added along the curve of the same type. Points can not be added to a CV curve and vice versa. Selecting a CV and pressing the Delete button removes the Points or CV from the curve.

5

- *Extend*   Used to extend the Point or CV curve. Clicking on the curve adds an additional Point or CV to the end of the curve, (at the end closest to the mouse click) and extends the new segment to meet the mouse position.

- *Affect Region*   When checked, this option affects Points or CVs within a certain proximity, based on the Edit Curve falloff parameters. The Edit Curve parameters describe the shape of the influence exerted over the surrounding Points or CVs.

- *Weight*   The key to CV curves is in the weighting of the CV. This value can be any number, although the values are relative to the values of the surrounding CVs. For example, when the weight of all CVs is set to 1 (the default), each CV has the same influence on the curve. By increasing the weighting of another CV (say CV 1), the curve will have a stronger attraction to the CV, causing the curve to bend more toward the CV of higher weight. As the weight value is decreased (typing in zero will be replaced with .0001, using as many leading decimal places prior to the 1), the CV exerts less influence on the curve. If set to zero, the effect is a semi-straight line. Having a CV with both adjacent CVs set to 0 causes the middle CV to create a sharp point in the curve as can be seen in Figure 5.5. The Point curve has no weight control.

- *Display Lattice*   Used in the CV curve and not the Point curve, this option turns off the lattice that connects the CVs (displayed as a yellow dashed line). This option does not affect how the curve is interpolated and is for display purposes only.

FIGURE 5.5.

Compare the two CV curves. Although the right curve was cloned from the left curve, the second and fourth CVs were weighted with a value of zero.

NURBS Curve Tools

Creating NURBS surfaces from NURBS curves involves using multiple curves. Curves can be used as cross sections for Ulofts, for example. Regardless of how you use the NURBS curves, you eventually need to modify the curve or join two curves together. The NURBS Curve tools are here to help.

At the object level of both the Point and the CV curve, in the General parameters section is a NURBS Curve palette. This floating palette contains all the tools contained in the Create Points and Create Curves sections. The floating palette is a convenient method for keeping these tools within reach when creating NURBS curves.

On the floating NURBS palette, there are two categories of tools. The Points section is used to create Points on either type NURBS curve. To use these tools, select the tool from the palette and click on the curve as appropriate.

- *Create Point*   Creates a new point within the existing curve. Points can only be added to the Point NURBS curve. NURBS curves cannot contain a mixture of both Points and CVs along a single curve. The point can be added anywhere along the curve or offset from the curve.
- *Create Point Point* (Offset Point in MAX 2.5)   Creates a dependent point at the same position as an existing point or at a specified offset distance.

> **Note**
>
> In 3DS MAX 2.5, the Point Point has been renamed the Offset Point. This reflects more accurately the type of point created using this tool.

5

- *Create Curve Point*   Creates a point along a curve or at a specified offset distance from it.
- *Create Curve Curve Point*   Creates a Point at the intersection of two existing curves.

> **Note**
>
> The following features are new to MAX 2.5.
>
> - *Create Surface Point*   Creates a Point on a NURBS surface or relative to it. Surface Points can be used to change the shape of a surface or curve.
> - *Create Surface-Curve Point*   Where the Surface Point can create a Point anywhere on a NURBS object, the Surface-Curve Point is used to create a Point that lies on a Surface-Curve. This means that only curves that exists within a NURBS surface will be used to create this Surface Point. This restricts the Point to be generated along a Surface-Curve only.

The second section, "Curves," is used to generate curves for connecting existing curves or creating entirely new Dependent curves. Dependent curves are as their name implies, dependent. They are dependent on the curves that they were created from, or curves they are connected to. Curves such as the Blend, Fillet, and Chamfer are used to connect two other curves, so they are dependent upon the curves they are connected to. The Transform, Offset, and Mirror curves are dependent on the curves that created them.

- *Create CV Curve*   Creates a curve of the CV type (as opposed to a Point curve).
- *Create Point Curve*   Creates a new Point curve as part of the current curve.
- *U and V Iso Curve*   This tool creates a curve along the surface of a NURBS surface. The curve runs the length or width of the NURBS surface (based on whether U or V Iso curve was selected). The curve resides on the surface. U Iso and V Iso curves are frequently used to trim a NURBS surface.
- *Create Fit Curve*   Creates a curve between two selected curves on the current Point curve. CV curves are not included because they do not have points that can be connected.
- *Create Transform Curve*   Creates a dependent curve based on the transform applied. In essence, this is a copy of the original curve; your position, rotation, and scaling might be different.
- *Create Blend Curve*   Used to create a smooth transitional curve between two curves. The curve adjusts itself so that it retains a smooth transition between the selected curves.
- *Create Offset Curve*   Using this creates a copy of the selected curve by offsetting the vertices of the original curve. Because it is based on offsetting Points or CVs, the curve can overlap itself if offset is too high.
- *Create Mirror Curve*   Like the Mirror Object tool, the Mirror Curve tool is used to create a mirror image of the selected curve.
- *Create Chamfer Curve*   This tool creates a straight segment connecting two existing curves as opposed to creating a smooth curve between the curves.
- *Create Fillet Curve*   Creates a smooth corner type curve between two curves.

Note

The following NURBS Curve tools are new to 3DS MAX 2.5.

- *Surface-Surface Intersection Curve*   Creates a curve where two selected NURBS surfaces intersect. Both surfaces must be part of the same NURBS object and must intersect to create the dependent curve.

- *Normal Projected Curve*   This tool is used to project a NURBS curve onto a NURBS surface. By projecting a curve onto a NURBS surface, the curve takes on the topography of the surface along its local Z axis, while retaining all its X and Y axis information. This is equivalent to creating a NURBS curve, extruding it until it passes through the NURBS surface, and then performing a Surface-Surface Intersection on it. Normal Projected curves are projected onto a NURBS surface, based on the surface's normals. For this reason, the position of the curve is important. If the curve is on the wrong side of the surface's normals, the curve will not project onto the surface. Normal Projected curves are great for trimming NURBS surfaces.

- *Vector Projected Curve*   The Vector Projected curve works in the same manner as the Normal Projected curve except that instead of the normal controlling how the curve is projected onto a surface, a user controllable vector is used. Because the vector used to project the curve onto the surface is based on the current view's local Z axis, by changing the current view, the projection vector can be changed. The seed value is used to change the location of the seed value on the NURBS surface. Changing the seed value changes the way the projection is evaluated and can change a valid projection to an invalid one, and vice versa.

- *CV Curve on a Surface and Point Curve on a Surface*   Both of these tools are used to directly draw a curve on the NURBS surface. By drawing directly on the NURBS surface, the added step of projecting the curve onto the surface can be alleviated. When creating the curve, the Points or CVs are automatically projected onto the NURBS surface using the current view's local Z axis. If 2D view is checked, an Edit Curve on Surface dialog box appears. This lets you draw the curve in a 2D Edit Curve window with the surface represented in a two-dimensional view. Surface topography is not visible in the 2D Edit Curve window.

- *Surface Offset Curve*   Enables you to select a curve that is already on the surface of a NURBS object and offset it from the surface based on normals. The parent curve must exist on the surface of the object through any of the surface curve options, such as (but not exclusively) Normal and Vector projected curves and surface-surface intersection curves.

5

Note

The Trim and Flip Trim check boxes found on many of the Dependent curves are used to cut holes in the NURBS surface they are applied to. By checking the Flip Trim box, just the hole is left. This works similar to a Boolean Subtract A–B and B–A. The subtraction (called Trim in NURBS) is based on the normals of the surface the curve is applied to. If a curve is projected onto the side with normals, the checking Trim will cut a hole in the surface. If projected on the backside of the surface, just the surface inside the curve is kept. Because the trim values are based on the surface's normals, projecting a curve onto the back of a surface requires that the trim be flipped to achieve a hole.

Note

The Replace Surface and Replace Curve options found in the Dependent Curve tools are used to change the parent surface or curve. In this way, you can be working with one surface or curve independently of the current object, make changes, attach it to the current surface (if not already part of the current NURBS object), and switch surfaces or curves. This is handy if the parent surface or curve is a dependent surface independent from another NURBS surface or curve. The scenario can become complex, but if you need to replace the current surface or curve, use the Replace button found on the Dependent curve.

The following brief exercises are intended to familiarize you with the various NURBS curve tools. Because an entire NURBS project can become complex, you work with simple curves at this time.

To Do: Creating a Mirror Dependent curve

1. Open nurbTool.max from the accompanying CD-ROM. This file contains a single NURBS curve object that contains two sub-object curves.

2. Select the curve and open the Modify Panel. At the Top level of selection, open the Create Curves section and click on the Mirror button. Or using the NURBS tool palette found in the General section, click on the Create Mirror Curve tool.

Note

Using the NURBS tool palette is a handy way to quickly access all the NURBS tools. As the Selection level changes, the NURBS palette also changes to only display the appropriate tools. The NURBS tool palette also is set to float above all other windows so that it can be moved to any part of the screen and always be within reach.

3. In the Front view, use the Mirror tool to create a mirror of the larger curve. To do this, simply click and drag the Create Mirror Curve tool on the large curve. Dragging up moves the mirrored curve in the positive X direction and dragging down moves the new curve in the negative X direction. Drag the mouse up to create a new curve to the right of the original curve (see Figure 5.6).

4. When the dependent Mirror curve is selected, axis and distance parameters are available in the Mirror Curve parameters section. The curve can be mirrored on any axis, as well as any two axes combination. An offset distance from the original curve can also be set.

As you might notice, the new Dependent curve is green in color and contains no points. This is because the Dependent curve is controlled by the parent curve (or curve used to create it). Any changes made to the parent curve will be reflected in the Dependent curve. To see how this works, go to the Point Sub-Object selection and try moving some of the points on the original curve. Undo any point changes made while experimenting here.

FIGURE 5.6.

The newly created dependent curve using the Mirror Curve tool is the curve on the right. This curve is dependent on the curve that created it (shown on the left). Any changes made to the original affects the dependent curve, regardless of which tool was used to create it.

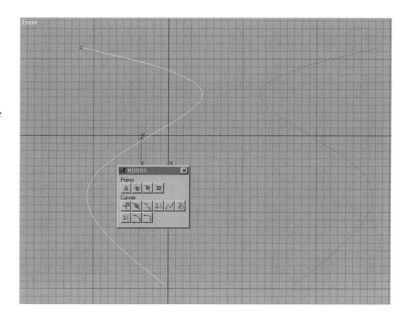

5

The Offset and Transform tools work very much like the Mirror tool in that click-ing and dragging on a curve while the tool is active creates a dependent curve of that type. Experiment on your own with these tools until you become comfortable using them. These are the simplest of the Dependent Curve tools to use because their parameters are few.

5. Continuing use of the NURBS Curve tools, delete the Dependent Mirror curve cre-ated in the previous steps. You must change to the Curve Sub-Object selection level to select and delete the dependent curve.

▲

> **Note**
>
> When the Modify Panel is open, right-click on an object to quickly change Sub-Object selection levels. The submenu that pops up in all previous ver-sions contains a selection list of all the Sub-Object selection levels for the selected object in 3DS MAX 2.5.

After deleting the Dependent Mirror curve, you use both the large and small curve for creating both a Chamfer and Fillet curve. A Chamfer curve is one in which a flat bevel is created between two curves. In this way, a sharp edge can be created along an otherwise smooth NURBS curve.

To Do: Creating a Chamfer curve

1. From the floating NURBS tool palette, select the Create Chamfer Curve tool or select Chamfer from the Dependent Curve tools in the Create Curves section at the Top level of the selected NURBS object.

2. To use the Chamfer Curve tool, you need to drag from the endpoint of one Point curve to the endpoint of another Point curve. Chamfer curves do not work with CV curves. As the mouse moves within close proximity of a NURBS curve, a blue box surrounds the closest point on the curve. Click and drag to another curve to connect the two curves with a Chamfer curve.

   After dragging between the two curves, one of three things can happen. Either the blue boxes disappears (indicating points were not established correctly), an orange line appears between the two curves (error in evaluation), or a green Chamfer curve is created. Let's hope for the latter result, but usually you need to do some tweaking first.

> **Note**
>
> When using any of the Create Curve tools, a curve that becomes colored orange is the default color indicating an error occurred in evaluating the result of the NURBS Curve tool used. Don't worry; this just means that adjustments must be made to the curve before it can be used by any other Curve tools.

3. If you received the blue boxes but then they disappeared, try dragging between the two lines again, changing the location of the initial and final position of your points. The Chamfer curve does not require that you select points directly. In fact, better results are achieved by clicking slightly away from the endpoints. Regardless of where the Chamfer is drawn, its position can be adjusted later.

4. If you got the green Chamfer line, consider yourself lucky. Step 9 explains why.

5. Because of the default values used in MAX, chances are you got the orange Chamfer line, indicating an error in the curve. Set the Sub-Object selection level to Curve and select the newly created Chamfer curve.

6. In the Modify Panel, close the Curve Common section to make the Chamfer Curve parameters more accessible. Open the Chamfer Curve parameters section, if not already open, and be sure that Trim Curve is checked for both the First and Second Curve. This enables the Chamfer to trim off the excess curve length that exists past the Chamfer.

7. The default value for the Length 1 and Length 2 parameters is 10. This is the length of the Chamfer curve and naturally is not adequate for all Chamfer curves. This value does not reflect the actual length of the curve; it is more representative of a value needed to calculate the curve needed to create an accurate Chamfer across the adjoining curves.

8. Change the values in Length 1 and Length 2 to 30. As you can see, the curve is still orange, indicating these values are not valid to create the Chamfer across these two curves.

9. Increment the Length 1 and 2 parameters by 5 alternately until either Chamfer curves become valid. There are three ways of determining if the Chamfer curve becomes valid (see Note). The valid Chamfer curve can be seen in Figure 5.7.

5

FIGURE 5.7.

The Chamfer curve is used to create a bevel or straight edge in an otherwise smooth NURBS curve. The Chamfer curve becomes a Dependent curve of the other two curves and remains that way unless made Independent.

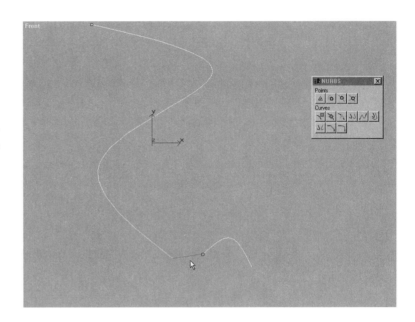

▲

Note

A Chamfer curve (as well as a Fillet or Blend curve) is valid only when it is colored green as all Dependent curves are colored. When selected, the curve will be red indicating Sub-Object selection. To tell if the Chamfer curve is valid when selected, look for the parent curves to be trimmed (if trimming is set) or that the Axis icon is centered on the Chamfer curve. When the Chamfer curve is invalid, the Axis icon will be centered over the enter NURBS object.

Note

Sometimes, incrementing the Length values by five can be tedious. Another method is to hold down the Ctrl key and drag up on the spinner values, alternately. When the Chamfer becomes valid, decrease the value by half from the last known invalid length and continue making adjustments by half to find the Chamfer value that suits your needs. By halving the value each time, you can always find the solution in the least amount of steps.

To Do: Creating a Fillet curve

To Do

Now that you spent all that hard work creating a Chamfer curve, delete it. Using the same two original curves, you will now create a Fillet curve. If you want to save your Chamfer curve for reference, save it under a different name.

1. After deleting your Chamfer curve or reopening nurbTool.max from the CD-ROM, select the NURBS curve object and open the NURBS tool palette, if not already open.

2. Select the Create Fillet Curve from the NURBS tool palette, or Fillet from the Dependent Curve section of the Create Curves palette.

3. As you did in the preceding step 6, click and drag the Fillet tool from one curve to the next, near the endpoints. This creates a Fillet curve that will either be green or orange, or if invalid positions were used, the blue boxes disappeared and no line was created. Try again if either an orange or green line were not created.

4. As with the Chamfer curve, chances are the default value of 10 did not work for this Fillet curve. That's okay. In the Fillet Curve parameters section (accessed by selected the newly created Fillet curve), you can see the Radius parameter. Increment the Radius parameter by 10 until the curve becomes valid (see the previous Note about determining if a Dependent curve is valid). You should hit a valid value at 40 with this curve.

▲

When a value of 40 is used on this Fillet curve, you see a nice smooth curve generated, which follows the contour of the adjoining curves. Fillet curves are used to generate a bend between two curves, where the Chamfer curve is used to create a straight bevel between two curves. Figure 5.8 shows the valid Fillet curve between the two original curves.

FIGURE 5.8.

The Fillet curve is used to create a rounded curve between two adjoining curves. Like other Dependent curves, changing the location or points on either of the parent curves might cause the Fillet curve to become invalid, and the Fillet Curve's Radius parameter must be adjusted.

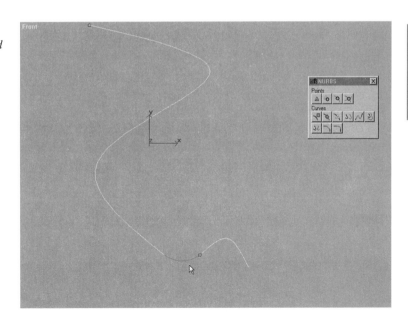

5

> **Note**
>
> Changing any attribute of a parent curve can make the Dependent curve become invalid. If the Dependent curve, such as a Fillet, Chamfer, or Blend curve, change to orange after moving a parent curve, you must go back and adjust the radius or length parameter (as appropriate) to reflect the change in the parent curve.

Like the Chamfer and Fillet curves, the Blend curve is used to create a transitional curve between two curves. Whereas the Chamfer curve creates a straight beveled curve and the Fillet creates a curve with a specified radius, the Blend curve uses the two adjoining curves and interpolates a smooth transition between them. In this regard, the Blend curve can be used to create a curve of any shape between two curves.

> **Note**
>
> Dependent curves are always dependent on the curves used to create them. In many cases, there are uses for the curve independently. To make a Dependent curve independent, select the curve and click the Make Independent button in the Curve Common parameters. Although this does make the curve independent of the other curves, there is a caveat: the resulting Independent curve will be a CV curve, regardless of the type of curve used to create it.

To Do: Creating a Surface-Surface Intersection curve

1. Create a NURBS Point Surface in any view. Create a geosphere so that it overlaps the NURBS surface by at least half.

2. Convert the geosphere to a NURBS object using the EditStack button and choosing NURBS surface as the collapse type.

3. With the Point surface selected, open the Modify Panel and choose Attach from the General parameter section. Click on the geosphere to make it part of the NURBS Point Surface.

4. Using the Surface-Surface Intersection Curve tool, click and drag from the Point surface to the geosphere. Each object turns blue when the mouse is over it, indicating it is a valid surface for this operation.

5. After releasing the mouse after dragging between the Point surface and the geosphere, a new curve is created where the Point surface and the geosphere intersect. Set the trim options to choose if either of the surfaces are to be trimmed with this operation.

For added modification, the new curve can be made independent and used for trimming other surfaces within the object using the Normal or Vector Projected Curve tool.

Choosing between Point and CV Curves

NURBS curves can be used any time a smooth curve is needed. The choice of either the Point curve or the CV curve depends on the type of control you need over the curve. Both generate smooth curves; the difference is in how the curves are controlled.

- *Point curves*   A curve is generated through each point and the curve always runs through every point. In and Out tension between points is generated by the position of the adjacent points.
- *CV curves*   The curve generated by CVs never passes through the actual Control Vertices. The CVs are used to apply tension along a segment of the curve. Each curve has a weight value that affects the curve. Weighting each CV is relative to adjacent CVs so if all CVs were given a weight value of 5, it would have the same affect as if the weight value were 1.

Now that you studied NURBS curves, you need to put them to use. The general practice of modeling in NURBS involves creating NURBS curves that describe the outline of the object, collapsing the curves into a single NURBS surface object, and applying NURBS tools to generate the surface. Typical tools used in creating a NURBS model are the Uloft, Railed Sweep, and the UV Loft tools.

NURBS Surfaces

In addition to the Point and CV curves, 3DS MAX 2.5 can also create NURBS surfaces directly. NURBS surfaces are used like organic patches of modeling material. They can be bent, sized, and modeled into any smooth configuration. By attaching additional NURBS surfaces to one another, an entire model can be created that will be very smooth and seamless. Working with NURBS surfaces is mathematically intensive and is arguably the most difficult and time-consuming modeling method used today. The results of a NURBS model, however, is a higher-quality, smoother model and is worth the extra effort.

Like the Point curves and the CV curves, NURBS surfaces also come in Point versions and CV versions. The similarities between the Point and CV surfaces and their Point and CV curve counterparts are high. The primary difference is that instead of generating a curved spline, a viewable curved surface is generated.

NURBS surfaces are accessed by selecting NURBS surfaces from the Object Class drop-down list found under the Geometry button on the Create Panel. As seen in Figure 5.9, two buttons are present from which you can choose either Point Surf or CV Surf. By selecting either of these surface creation buttons, you can drag out a rectangular section of a NURBS surface.

5

FIGURE 5.9.

NURBS Surfaces can be created as either of two types, the Point Surface and the CV Surface. The NURBS surfaces have the same characteristics as the NURBS curves, plus additional characteristics and tools to mold the surface into organic shapes.

Like their NURBS curve counterparts, the NURBS surfaces use different controls to bend their surfaces. When creating a complete NURBS surface with multiple NURBS surfaces joined together, you can use either of the surface types, as the need arises.

NURBS Point Surface

Like NURBS Point curves, the Point surface has its points located directly on the surface. As the points are moved, the surface is recalculated so that the surface runs through each of the points. In this manner, like the Point curve, the Point Surface always generates a smooth curve that passes directly through the NURBS surface.

Creating a NURBS Point surface is a relatively simple matter. The work comes when manipulating the surface to create organic objects.

To Do: Creating a NURBS Point surface

1. Reset 3DSMAX2 to start with a clean scene. Open the Create Panel and choose NURBS Surfaces from the Object Class drop-down list.

2. Click on Point Surf to activate the Point Surface Creation tool.

3. In a Top view, click and drag a rectangular NURBS Point Surface. Right-click to deactivate the Point Surface Creation tool.

   As you can see, the Point Surface looks much like a subdivided rectangle. The difference in the look is that it has points along the edges and how the points affect the surface.

4. With the Point Surface object selected, click on the Modify Panel and activate the Point Sub-Object selection level. Points appear on the surface as green dots.

5. In a Top view, select a single point located in the center of the NURBS surface. Use the Spacebar to lock the selection.

6. In a Front view, drag the point toward the top or bottom of the viewport. Adjust the Perspective view so the entire surface can be seen.

After dragging the Point either up or down, you see the surface having a smooth dimple or mound in it (see Figure 5.10). Also note how the surface geometry continues to be smooth and connected to the transformed Point.

FIGURE 5.10.

Changing the shape of a NURBS Point surface requires manipulating the Points that make up the surface. The Points of the Point surface work very much the same as the NURBS Point curve.

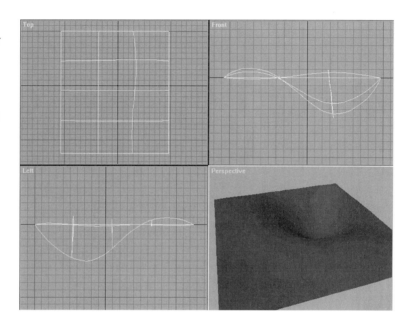

Using a Point surface is a starting point for creating complex NURBS surfaces. A typical NURBS surface requires many NURBS surfaces joined together or created as Dependent surfaces (described next). Working with NURBS can be a time-consuming and complex task, though the modeling process is much easier than using traditional methods of modeling for creating organic models.

CV Surfaces

When creating CV surfaces, you immediately notice the difference from creating Point surfaces. The CV surface contains a lattice that is used to bend and control the CV surface. In practice, the lattice works the same way that the CV points work with the CV curve. Because the CV surface is a contiguous surface, each of the CVs will be connected by two to four adjacent CVs.

By changing the position of each of the CVs, you can change the shape and bend of the CV surface. As in the CV curve, weighting can also be assigned to the CVs in the CV surface. By assigning a higher weight value to a CV, the surface will be drawn toward that CV. Figure 5.11 depicts two identical NURBS surfaces. The difference is that the CV surface on the right was given a weight value of 5, whereas all the other CVs in both surfaces were left at the default value of 1.

FIGURE 5.11.

Both of these NURBS surfaces are identical except for the weighting of one CV. On the right, the CV was given a weight value of 5, whereas all other CVs in both surfaces were left at the default value of 1.

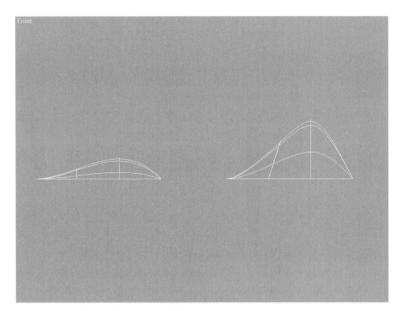

To Do: Creating a CV surface

1. Reset 3DSMAX2 to start with a clean scene. Open the Create Panel and choose NURBS Surfaces from the Object Class drop-down list.

2. Click on CV Surf to activate the CV NURBS Surface Creation tool.

3. In a Top view, click and drag a rectangular NURBS CV Surface. Right-click to deactivate the CV Surface Creation tool.

   Though the CV surface looks somewhat like that of the Point surface, notice the difference of the lattice that surrounds the object. This lattice works in the same manner as the lattice used in the CV curve.

4. With the CV Surface object selected, click on the Modify Panel and activate the Surface CV Sub-Object selection level. CVs appear on the surface as green dots connected by a yellow lattice.

5. In a Top view, select a single point located in the center of the NURBS surface. Use the Spacebar to lock the selection. Try to select the same point used when creating the Point surface, for comparison.

6. In a Front view, drag the point toward the top or bottom of the viewport. You need to drag the CV more to create the same effect you got by moving a point in a Point surface. Adjust the Perspective view so the entire surface can be seen.

One of the first differences you might have noticed is that when dragging the CV, it took a greater distance of movement to get the CV surface topology to change. This is a characteristic of the CV surface, just as in the CV curve.

A key issue to realize about the NURBS surfaces is that they work like their NURBS curve counterpart. They are, in fact created using a network of internal curves (of their respective types), which give the similar results seen in the previous exercises.

NURBS Surface Tools

There are a number of tools that are used to create and manipulate a NURBS surface. These tools can be found in the Create Surfaces parameters of both types of NURBS surfaces, as well as on the NURBS tool palette. Some of the NURBS Surface tools are similar to the NURBS Curve tools as distinguished here. NURBS surfaces can contain additional NURBS surfaces of either Point or CV in type.

- *Create Point Surf*   Creates a Dependent Point surface within the current NURBS surface.
- *Create CV Surf*   Creates a Dependent CV surface within the current NURBS surface.
- *Create Transform Surface*   Like the Transform curve, this creates a copy of the selected surface at another position, rotation, or scale.
- *Create Blend Surface*   Used to create a smooth surface between two nonconnected NURBS surfaces. This tool uses the curvature of the selected surfaces to create a smooth blend between them.
- *Create Offset Surface*   Creates a copy of the selected surface at a specified offset from the selected surface.
- *Create Mirror Surface*   Creates a copy that is a mirror to the selected NURBS surface.
- *Create Extrude Surface*   Though part of the surface tools, this is used on Dependent NURBS curves to create an extruded surface, just as with a Standard spline extrude. This has advantages to the spline extrude because the extruded surface is also part of the NURBS surface, thereby enabling the user to create additional NURBS surfaces as part of the NURBS structure.
- *Create Lathe Surface*   Also used on Dependent NURBS curves within a NURBS surface; this Lathe tool works as the Standard Lathe tool does, the results of which are also a NURBS surface.
- *Create Ruled Surface*   Using two NURBS curves (which must be part of a NURBS surface), this tool generates a surface between the selected NURBS curves. The curves can be either Point or CV.

5

- *Create U Loft Surface*   Like the Standard Loft object, the Uloft is used to generate a Loft object out of a selection of NURBS curves. The curves, however, must be part of the same NURBS surface prior to the Uloft operation.
- *Create Cap Surface*   After creating a Uloft, the Cap tool can be used to put an end cap on the NURBS surface. This closes the surface along the selected NURBS curve.

Note

The following NURBS Surface tools are new to 3DS MAX 2.5.

- *Create UV Loft Surface*   The UV Loft tool is designed to create a surface that is lofted by using cross-sectional NURBS curves for both U dimension and V dimension. To use this tool, at least four curves are needed, two each for the U and V dimensions. When laying out the curves, the U dimension curves must be perpendicular to the V dimension curves.
- *Create 1 Rail Sweep*   This tool is the NURBS equivalent of a Standard Loft object. A minimum of two curves are needed to create a 1 Rail Sweep. The first curve, called the Rail, is the path in which the sweep occurs (like the Standard Loft path). The second (and subsequent curves) are used to describe the cross sections of the Rail Sweep.
- *Create 2 Rail Sweep*   Where the 1 Rail Sweep uses a single rail as the path to sweep the cross sections, the 2 Rail Sweep uses each rail to describe an edge. In this manner, the cross sections sweep along the path of the rails, conforming the edges to the shape of the rails. Both Rail tools work best when the rails are open curves. The cross-sectional curves used in the 2 Rail Sweep tools can be open or closed curves and must intersect both rails for optimal results.
- *Create Multisided Blend Surf*   When a gap exists between NURBS surface sub-objects, the Multisided Blend Surface can be used to close the gap. Three or four sub-object surfaces can be used to create the Multisided Blend surface, but together they must completely enclose the area to be filled. To create the Multisided Blend surface, select the edges of the surfaces to be blended. Surface curves can also be used if they exist on the surface and completely enclose the fill area.
- *Create MultiCurve Trim Surf*   This tool makes it easy to trim a NURBS surface using multiple curves. When a surface needs to be trimmed based on neighboring curves, the curves can be projected onto the surface and used to trim the surface as a single entity. The curves must form a closed loop and their endpoints must be fused prior to projecting onto the NURBS surface to be trimmed.

> **Note**
>
> NURBS surfaces can also be created by collapsing the Stack on all the Standard primitives. After a primitive is converted to a NURBS surface, all the NURBS tools are available for use in editing it.

One of the most essential aspects of creating a NURBS surface is to start with NURBS curves. The NURBS curve is the essential component in creating NURBS surfaces. In the following exercises, you create NURBS surfaces by manipulating the curves contained within a NURBS surface.

To Do: Creating a NURBS surface from simple curves

1. Open appleCV.max from the accompanying CD-ROM. This scene file contains a single CV curve.

2. The first step in creating a NURBS surface from a NURBS curve is to convert the curve to a NURBS surface. To convert the curve, select it and click on the Edit Stack button and select NURBS Surface in the Convert To pop-up menu. The NURBS curve is now part of a NURBS surface that consists solely of the newly converted curve.

3. Even though the curve is now considered a NURBS surface, you still need to generate a NURBS surface. From the NURBS palette found in the General parameters section at the top level of the Modify parameters, select the Create Lathe Surface tool.

4. Using the Create Lathe Surface tool, move the mouse over the NURBS curve. You notice it turns blue, indicating the curve is a valid operand for this tool. Click on the curve. The curve is lathed and an apple is created. Right-click to deactivate the Create Lathe Surface tool.

The new NURBS surface is drawn in green to indicate it is a Dependent surface. This means that any changes made to the curve used to create this surface will be reflected in the surface interpolation. This is an important point to remember, especially if you don't intend to change your surface, but you do intend to change the curve. Even changing the position of the curve will be reflected in the dependent surface.

You continue to use this scene for a few of the following exercises, so if you feel like saving, save each under a different name. (Try the auto increment on the Save feature under the Files tab in the Preferences Settings dialog box.)

To Do: Gaining Independence

To Do

Now that you created the NURBS surface in the form of an apple, what do you do with it? When working with NURBS objects, many times, sub-objects are frequently used for other purposes, such as trimming, rails, projection curves, and many other uses. As such, there must be a mechanism to make the sub-object available to other NURBS objects, because NURBS objects can only work on sub-objects that are contained as part of the current NURBS object. For this reason, you have the Make Independent and Detach tools.

1. Select the NURBS Lathe surface created in the previous exercise. The Lathe surface is drawn in green indicating it is a Dependent surface. If you work with 3DS MAX 2.5, you can right-click the mouse over the object to change selection levels (when the Modify Panel is open). In MAX2, you must manually choose the selection level from the Sub-Object selection list in the Modify Panel. The Lathe surface turns red indicating this sub-object is selected.

2. With the Lathe surface selected, click on the Make Independent button in the Surface Common parameters section of the Modify Panel. This makes the surface an Independent surface sub-object within this NURBS surface. This also means that NURBS surfaces can have multiple surface sub-objects.

3. When the surface is Independent, changes to the curve will not affect the surface created by it. Making sub-objects independent is a commonly used method of using curves and surfaces in NURBS objects.

4. Now that the NURBS surface is independent, you need to make it its own NURBS object, with no association to the object that created it. To do this, click on the Detach button, also found in the Surface Common parameters section. You will be prompted for a name for the new object. Enter a name and press OK. The object now has no connections with the object that created it.

When Detaching an sub-object, the object does not first have to be made independent. This exercise was used to illustrate the difference between Detach and Make Independent. To summarize, Make Independent just breaks the ties to the object's creator, while the object remains a sub-object. Detach makes the sub-object independent from the object that created it and removed it as a sub-object so that it can be its own object.

Note

You might notice that the new, independent and detached object is no longer as smooth as it was when attached and dependent. By accessing the Surface Approximation section, you can change how the object is tessellated in both the viewports and the final rendering.

To Do: Blending surfaces

Frequently, two NURBS surfaces need to be joined together seamlessly. This requires the blending of two surfaces. Using the Blend Surface tool, not only can you Blend two surfaces together, but the surface necessary to fill the gap between the two surfaces is automatically generated by MAX.

1. Open blendsurf.max from the accompanying CD-ROM. This simple scene file contains a single NURBS surface with two surface sub-objects.

2. Select the NURBS surface and open the NURBS tool palette. Select the Create Blend Surface tool.

3. In the Perspective view, move the mouse over a surface and notice how the edges become blue, indicating valid sub-object selections for the current tool.

4. Select the top edge of the vertical surface and drag over to the closest edge of the horizontal surface. Release the mouse when the horizontal edge closest to the first selected edge turns blue.

5. Upon releasing the mouse, a blended edge is created between the two NURBS surfaces.

To Do: Using the ULoft tool

The ULoft tool is a NURBS version of the Standard Loft tool except no path is used. Cross sections are chosen in order and the NURBS surface is generated, based on the order of selection of the cross sections.

1. Open appleStem.max from the CD-ROM. This file contains the apple you built in the NURBS lathe exercise, with the addition of three more Point curves attached.

2. In the Front view, zoom in so that the three Point curves are visible in the view. With the apple object selected, open the Modify Panel and the NURBS tool palette.

3. From the NURBS tool palette, select the ULoft tool. Starting at the topmost curve, click and drag from the first curve to the second curve and then to the third. You see the dependent surface generated as you click on each curve.

4. Right-click to deactivate the ULoft tool and your stem is nearly complete.

To Do: Adding a Cap

1. The ULofted stem looks great, but after rendering, you notice there is no top to the stem. You can see right inside. To complete this ULoft, you need to add a cap to the top curve.

2. From the NURBS tool palette, select the Create Cap Surface tool. This tool creates a surface over any single curve.

3. Click the Cap tool on the topmost curve in the stem. A NURBS surface is generated on the topmost curve to complete the stem.

 4. Add materials to the stem and apple and serve 'em up hot with cinnamon sugar.

The following exercises are for use with 3DS MAX 2.5 only. These tools are not available in version 2.0. Because of the advanced features found in the 3DS MAX 2.5 upgrade, it is highly advisable to upgrade to 2.5 if you intend to do sophisticated NURBS modeling in MAX.

To Do: Using the 1 Rail Sweep

1. Open nurbRail.max from the accompanying CD-ROM. This scene file contains a single NURBS object with three curve Sub-Objects.

2. Creating a 1 Rail Sweep does not require that you are in the Surface Sub-Object selection level. The Rail Sweep tools (as well as many other NURBS tools) can distinguish valid sub-objects automatically. Select the 1 Rail Sweep tool from the NURBS tool palette or 1-Rail from the Surface Creation rollout. The NURBS tool palette can be opened from the top level of the NURBS object and then left on the desktop as a floating palette.

3. In the Top view, move the mouse over all three of the curves. Notice how the curves turn blue as the mouse rolls over each curve. This is an indication that this sub-object is valid for this operation. This is the standard applied to all NURBS tools, regardless of which sub-object selection level they affect.

4. With the 1 Rail Sweep tool still active, click on the left curve (with two bends in it) as seen in the Top view and in Figure 5.12. This is your Rail curve; the rail is always the first curve chosen.

   The Rail is the portion of the Rail Sweep that acts as the path in which the subsequently selected curves will be swept along. Typically, the Rail curve is an open curve.

5. After selecting the Rail curve, a rubber-banded dotted line extends from the Rail curve at the point of selection to the mouse pointer. This indicates the Rail curve was accepted and you can choose the first cross-section curve.

6. Select the rounded square CV curve (as seen in the Front view) as the cross-sectional shape.

 7. Right-click the mouse to complete the Rail Sweep object. Right-click again to deactivate the 1 Rail Sweep tool.

FIGURE 5.12.

The Rail curve is typi-cally an open curve and it defines the path of the Rail Sweep. The Rail curve is always the first curve chosen, when working with Rail Sweep tools.

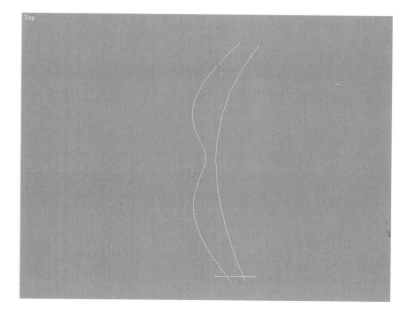

If your sweep object looks inside out, you might need to turn on Force 2-Sided in the viewport configuration dialog box. NURBS objects are surface objects, and as such con-tain normals on one side only. Because of the complex shapes that can be created using NURBS tools, many times, both sides of the NURBS object can be seen. For this reason, when rendering NURBS objects, be sure to turn 2-Sided on in the material applied to your NURBS surfaces, if both sides of the NURBS object is exposed.

The 2 Rail Sweep is not very different from the 1 Rail Sweep, although the ease in which creating the two differs tremendously. The following exercise builds on the previ-ous one to create a 2 Rail Sweep.

To Do: Creating a 2 Rail Sweep

▼ To Do

1. If the nurbRail.max scene file isn't open from the previous exercise, open it now. This scene can be found on the CD-ROM that accompanies this book.

2. From the Display Panel, click on Unhide All to display a copy of the original NURBS object worked on in the previous exercise. If you completed the previous exercise, leave the 1 Rail Sweep object you created in the scene. It will serve as a comparison with the 2 Rail Sweep. If you did not do the previous exercise, you should because the surface will not be there, otherwise.

3. Select the 2 Rail Sweep tool from the NURBS tool palette, or 2-Rail from the Surface Creation rollout.

5

4. As in the 1 Rail Sweep, in the Top view, click the vertical curve on the left as the first rail. Again, when using the Rail Sweep tools, the rails are always chosen first automatically in MAX.

5. After selecting the first rail, select the second rail (the dotted line should follow the first rail and the cursor to the second rail). The second rail will be the vertical curve to right of the first rail.

6. After selecting the second rail, select the rounded square as the cross-sectional shape again. Notice how different the shapes look.

Arguably the most important aspect to remember about NURBS is that they are relational. It is what gives them their organic look. Because of this trait, the resulting shape is not always what you might first expect. Polygonal and mesh modeling is linear between each of the cross sections, where NURBS is not. Because of the influence exerted on each cross section and the interpolation to keep the surface smooth, sometimes the surface needs a little attention after created. Here are some other modifications to get more familiar with how Rail Sweeps work:

- The Rail Sweep tools are not limited to a single cross section. After selecting the rail objects and first cross section, you can continue to select additional cross sections. A circle cross section has been included in this shape. Experiment by deleting the current surface sub-object and creating a new 1 or 2 Rail Sweep using the two cross sections included.

- After working with both Rail Sweep tools, experiment by editing the curves from within the surface. This is achieved by creating the Rail Sweep surface, selecting the surface, and clicking on the Edit Curves button in the Sweep Surface parameters section.

- Try switching the curves used in the Rail Sweep. Keep in mind that all Rail curves must be on the same axis plane and all cross sections must be on the same axis plane as other cross sections. The cross-section curves and the Rail curves must also be perpendicular to each other and must intersect for optimum results.

Using Modifiers on NURBS Objects

Because NURBS models are analytically defined by the Points and CVs that make up the object, using Modifiers on NURBS can be somewhat dicey. Unlike mesh objects, NURBS surfaces do not have a deformable mesh and therefore applying the same Modifiers with the same settings might produce entirely different results with two seemingly similar objects (see Figure 5.13). Though the surface of the NURBS object can be deformed, Modifiers such as the Ripple and Noise Modifiers might not work correctly because the CVs or Points that make up the NURBS object might be spaced further apart than the parameters needed for the Modifier to change the geometry.

FIGURE 5.13.

Both of these spheres were Standard primitives converted to NURBS surfaces. After converting one back to an Editable Mesh, the same Noise modifier was added to both. Notice the difference in the deformation of the NURBS model (seen on the left in the Front view).

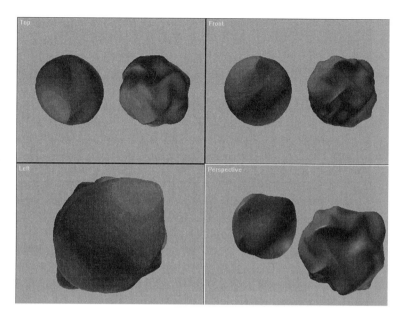

If you absolutely need to use a modifier with a NURBS object but find that it is ineffective, you might consider converting the NURBS object to a Mesh object through the Edit Stack button. Converting the NURBS object to a Mesh object is a more reliable method of applying Modifiers and might produce more predictable results. When using Modifiers with NURBS objects however, they are applied as they are with any other type of object.

Because MAX enables you to mix mesh and NURBS surfaces in the same scene, or even in the same model, you need to be clever in deciding when you use NURBS and when to use a mesh. If you can't accomplish your task using one, try the other. Use NURBS when view-dependent tessellation is essential; use meshes when the modeling tasks are easier to do with polygons.

5

Patch Modeling

Though not as advanced as NURBS modeling, Patch model affords the 3D artist with the ability to create organic mesh objects through the use of patches. As their name implies, patches are patches or sections of geometry. Each Patch is controlled by Bézier handles so that the Patch can be bent and twisted to create a smooth section of geometry. Prior to using patches, models were started with a primitive and each vertex was manipulated into position to create different shapes. Although this method can be used, it is only one step above writing the code to produce models, one vertex at a time.

Using patches enables you to create each piece of the finished object independently and then stitch them together to complete the piece. By working in smaller sections, tools can be used to affect very limited areas, instead of the entire model. Because patches can be joined directly to existing patches, it becomes a seamless harmony of many patches working together to create a more smoother shape in much less time than can be created by the old method of editing primitives.

Different Patch Surfaces

In MAX, patches can be created using either the QuadPatch or TriPatch method. Both use Bézier curves and handles to generate and manipulate their surfaces. In Figure 5.14, the difference between the QuadPatch and the TriPatch is evident through the lattice they each form. Though they are similar in their approach, their characteristics can quickly be recognized by the geometry they form when manipulated.

FIGURE 5.14.

The QuadPatch and TriPatch both are manipulated using Bézier patches. The difference is in the lattice each generates and uses during the manipulation process.

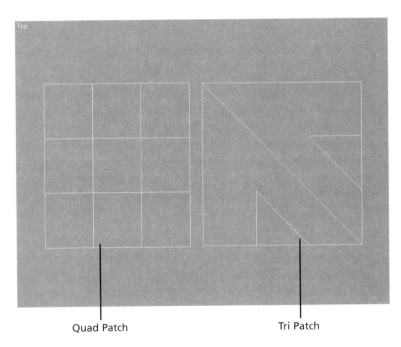

Quad Patch   Tri Patch

- *QuadPatch*   Because they are generated using quadrangles, editing one QuadPatch vertex affects both adjacent and diagonal vertices. This causes the surface to bend differently than the TriPatch.
- *TriPatch*   Generated using a triangular mechanism, the TriPatch affects vertices that share an edge. This can create curves that affect a larger portion of the patch than when using a QuadPatch. Where the QuadPatch has more of a rubbery surface, the TriPatch has a closer resemblance to paper.

Using the different patch types is dependent on the type of curved surface needed for that patch. To fully understand the nuances of the QuadPatch and TriPatch, you must work with them and experiment with different situations.

Like NURBS objects, you can also generate Patch objects by collapsing mesh geometry into patches. Simply apply an Edit Patch Modifier to a Standard primitive and then choose Collapse All. The result will be a Patch object.

Modifying Patches

Regardless of which patch type you choose to create your object, they are modified and manipulated in very much the same fashion, through the Sub-Object level. At the Sub-Object level, there are three modes of editing a Patch object. Patches can be manipulated using Bézier handles at the vertex level, by adding patches at the edge level, or by adding patches at the patch level.

Patches are not inherently editable. Prior to editing a QuadPatch or TriPatch, an Edit Patch Modifier must be added. By adding the Edit Patch Modifier, you can access the various Sub-Object levels and begin manipulating vertices, edges, and patches. The levels of patch editing are described here.

Patch Object Level Parameters

By adding an Edit Patch Modifier, you can access various levels of the Patch object. At the object level, the entire patch is affected by parameter changes. At the object level, the parameters will only affect how the object is rendered or viewed, and other than the tessellation level, these parameters will not change the shape of the object.

- *Display Lattice* Turn on or off the lattice encompassing the Patch object. This lattice is what controls the shape of the patch based on the placement of the vertices.

- *Display Surface* Checking this option permits MAX to display the surface in shaded views. This setting does not affect the patch during rendering. Use this option to turn off surfaces that are blocking the view of other surfaces that need to be accessed.

- *Topology Steps* To manually increase or decrease the number of steps used to interpolate the patch, change the Steps parameter in the Topology section. This works in the same fashion as other objects in MAX. Increasing the number of steps creates a smoother curve, at the price of more faces. Setting the Steps value to 0 causes the patch to become flat.

- *Topology Attach* Additional patches can be attached to the currently selected patch using the Attach button. Activate the Attach button by clicking on it; then select an existing patch from the scene. The patches are now part of the same patch object, regardless of whether they are of the same patch type.

- *Topology Reorient*   When attaching patches, use the Reorient button to realign the patch being added to the creation local coordinate system of the patch it will be added to. If the patch being added was created on a different angle than the one it is being attached to, the patch changes orientation to coincide with the patch it is being attached to.

- *Tessellation Viewports/Renderer*   Tessellation is the process MAX uses to generate a mesh and the faces required to render an object's surface. The Viewport/Renderer radio button toggles between changing options for the renderer and the viewports. When Viewport is selected, all the parameters set in the Tessellation rollout will be applied to the Viewport settings. Switch the setting to Renderer to affect the rendering parameters. The parameters are the same for both the Viewport and the Renderer, though their settings can be different at the same time.

- *Mesh Parameters Fixed*   When set to Fixed, the mesh remains as set by the Steps option in the Topology section.

- *Mesh Parameters Parametric*   Using the Parametric options, the tessellation of a patch is based on the U and V steps settings. In this way, the tessellation can be refine so that more tessellation occurs where needed.

- *Mesh Parameters Spatial*   This option bases the tessellation on the length of individual faces. The Edge parameter is the maximum length in current MAX units that each face can be. Setting this parameter to a lower number increases the number of faces and produces a denser mesh.

- *Mesh Parameters Curvature*   This option is optimized to increase tessellation where needed and to optimize it where it is not. This helps to smooth out curves, yet not increase the tessellation along straight edges. The Distance parameter is used to control the deviation of the tessellation from the actual shape of the patch. Decreasing the distance parameter increases the density of the mesh as well as the rendering time. Setting the Distance parameter to zero turns on this feature and lets the Angle parameter control the tessellation. The Angle parameter is used to control the maximum angle between faces of the mesh. Decreasing the Angle parameter creates smoother tessellation along curves at the price of increased rendering time. Setting the Angle parameter to zero turns off this feature and lets the Distance parameter control the tessellation. Setting both parameters to zero causes no tessellation.

- *View Dependent*   This option is available for the rendering parameters only. Setting this parameter optimizes the patch so that tessellation is dependent on the distance the patch is from the camera or perspective viewport. When rendering the patch, if the patch is in the distance, a lower tessellation rate is used, causing the object to render faster. As the patch gets closer to the camera, the tessellation is increased. This can greatly reduce the rendering time by reducing the number of unnecessary faces.

Regardless of which type of patch you use, QuadPatch or TriPatch, the object level parameters are the same. Remember, in order to edit a patch of either type, you must first add an Edit Patch Modifier.

Editing Patch Vertices

At the top of the Sub-Object level drop-down list is the Vertex level. Patches, just like spline objects, have vertices that control the surface of the patch. These vertices are Bézier in type and as such, have handles to control their orientation. Vertex-level editing can also be used to refine patches that were attached, by welding or deleting vertices.

Just as in Standard spline objects, you can right-click the mouse on a vertex to change its type. Patch objects only have two type of vertices to choose from. Their functions are described next.

- *Coplanar*   The default option for vertices on a patch object; this ensures that the Bézier handles maintain a coplanar relationship, resulting in a smooth curve through the vertex. The spline vertex equivalent is the smooth or Bézier vertex.

- *Corner*   Setting the vertex to a Corner type enables free movement of the outgoing vector. When in this mode, the vertex can be positioned so that the curve created in the patch surface is no longer completely smooth. Very much like the Bézier Corner vertex in the Standard spline object, the Corner vertex is good for changing the flow of the surface curve suddenly.

Also available to refine the patch are the Edit vertex options listed here. Some of these options are used for display purposes only, but aid in making the viewport easier to work in by clearing out unwanted data, such as vertices or vectors. Others are used to tighten any holes in the mesh by welding close vertices together. These options are found in the Topology, Display, and Filter sections of the Vertex Sub-Object level of the Edit Patch Modifier.

- *Lock Handles*   This option locks the Bézier handles so that all three move together.

- *Weld*   Used to join to vertices together to become one. When attaching patches, welding vertices ensures that the two patches will be seamless where the vertices are welded. Welding occurs only if the vertices are within the Weld Threshold. Change this threshold to accommodate for vertices that are outside the Weld Threshold or for patches with many vertices in close proximity.

5

- *Delete*   This is not your ordinary Delete button. Select a vertex or group of vertices and click the Delete button to remove the selected vertices from the lattice. This Delete button comes with a huge caveat. When deleting a vertex from a lattice, any patches that share that vertex are also removed. If two patches share a welded vertex and that vertex is deleted, both patches will also be removed.

- *Display Lattice/Surface*   This option turns the display of the Lattice and Surface of the patch. This is for the viewport only and will not affect the rendered object. This is useful when working in a crowded scene.

- *Filter Vertices/Vectors*   When either of these options are checked, they can be selected and modified. Not checking either will inhibit any inadvertent changes.

Working with Patch Edge Sub-Objects

Because the patches start out as a rectangular object, both the QuadPatch and TriPatch have four Edge Sub-Objects when created. As patches are edited, this number can change, but it will never be less than four—and normally more.

Because of the lattice structure and the fact that the vertices of patches lie on edges, working in the Edge Sub-Object mode is very common when manipulating patches. Editing patch edges enables you to subdivide the patch for smoother curves or add patches to build a framework of patches, each building on itself.

- *Subdivide*   Splits the selected edge in two at the center of the edge, creating two edges and adding a vertex connecting the two edges. Subdividing edges does not destroy the curve but adds a vertex midway through the edge while preserving the edge curvature.

- *Propagate*   When this is checked and an edge is subdivided, surrounding edges will also be subdivided. Keeping this option turned on when subdividing prevents holes from forming between the newly subdivided edge.

- *Add Tri / Add Quad*   Adds a new patch of that type to the selected edge. Patch modeling is based on building a model using multiple patches, each individually manipulated into form. The patches are then stitched together to create a seamless patched-based model. As each patch takes shape, you can add the next patch and have automatically seamlessly integration with the current patch.

- *Display Lattice/Surface*   Turns on and off the display of the lattice and the surface in the modeling views. This option does not affect the object when rendered.

Working with edges is a powerful method of adding patches to the existing patch structure. Because you can add edges directly to other edges, you can assure there are no gaps in the geometry.

Manipulating Patch Sub-Object Patches

The Patch Sub-Object level is for manipulating entire patches. At this level, you can select individual patches or groups of patches contained in a patch structure. Although all the transform functions can be used on patches, betake caution when transforming patches. If a patch is attached to an adjacent patch that is not selected, transforming the selected patch might cause gaps in the object geometry—usually an undesirable result.

Patches can also be removed or copied from the patch structure. When creating a face for instance, you might decide that you want to remove the nose or use the nose in another model. Using the Detach tool, you can create a copy of the nose as a separate patch object to be used elsewhere.

Patches can also be subdivided for further refinement. As each patch is subdivided, it's left intact, yet more edges and vertices are created, which can be edited at the appropriate Sub-Object level.

- *Detach*   Detaches and removes the selected patch or group of patches from the current patch structure. Checking the Reorient option transforms the path so that its local coordinate system is oriented to the patch from which it came. Selecting the copy option enables you to make a copy of the selected patch as a separate patch object while retaining the selected patch within the current patch structure. When detaching a patch, MAX requests a name for the new patch object or generates a default name of Patch01, Patch 02, and so on.

- *Delete*   Deletes the selected patch from the patch structure. It is possible to delete all patches from a patch object and be left holding an axis tripod. Although it renders quickly, you do not see much, and it is best to either remove the object or undo the last patch delete.

- *Subdivide*   This tool divides the selected patch into four patches. With propagation turned on, patches attached to the selected patch are also subdivided as needed. This prevents gaps in the object geometry.

- *Display*   Turns the lattice and surface display on and off in the modeling views.

- *ID*   Sets the Material ID for the selected patch or group of patches. You can change the Material ID number of any patch by selecting it and typing in a new ID number. By changing the Material ID number of patches, you can apply different materials to different patches using the Multi/Sub-Object Material type.

- *Select by ID*   When creating a patch, the entire patch is given a default Material ID of 1. By changing the Material ID as previously stated, you can easily distinguish between the patches by using the Select by ID button. When pressed, you are asked for an ID number to use as the selection criteria. By setting the Clear Selection button, any currently selected patches will be deselected and only materials with the ID number specified will be selected and highlighted.

5

Using Object Modifiers on Patch Models

Other than applying the Edit Patch Modifier, Patch objects are by their own design pliable material that is inherently smooth. By adjusting vertices and attaching multiple patches, the use of other modifiers are almost antiproductive. As with any case, you have exceptions, but the key concept to remember is that Patch objects used with an Edit Patch Modifier typically provide enough flexibility to create the desired shape or effect.

Though Modifiers are not used as often on patches themselves, Modifiers can be used with great effectiveness on an entire Patch model. After the model has been built using patches, there is no reason why Modifiers cannot be used. Using a Modifier on a completed Patch model is a viable modeling procedure. Patch models will also have a tendency to have smoother effects when working with Modifiers, such as the Bend Modifier (see Figure 5.15).

FIGURE 5.15.

A 90-degree Bend Modifier applied to identical models. The model on the left used Patches as the output method, Standard mesh for the center object and NURBS for the object on the right. As you can see, the Bend is smooth on the Patch object, whereas the Standard mesh is slightly blockier. The NURBS model is completely wrong and the shape was even changed slightly.

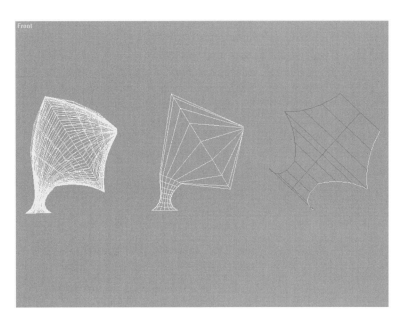

Patch Versus NURBS Modeling

Patch and NURBS modeling are similar only in the fact that both are created using sections of their associated material. Both can be manipulated like sheets of rubber, but the NURBS model uses a more accurate and controllable surface structure.

Given the fact that NURBS are more powerful than Patch models, why would anyone consider using Patches, when NURBS models are available? Because both use different methods for manipulating the surface, it is a personal preference as to which modeling type you use. NURBS are a more powerful object than Patches, yet Patch modeling has been available to the general public longer than NURBS modeling. Because of the complexity of the mathematics involved in NURBS modeling, many personal computer systems couldn't handle the work load required for NURBS modeling. For this reason, more 3D artists are more comfortable with Patch modeling than NURBS modeling.

Although MAX offers the capability to model using NURBS, this is still the first iteration of the NURBS tools. And although they work well, some tools are still required to make this a complete and robust modeling alternative. For that reason, you might find yourself modeled into a corner from which there is no way out using NURBS.

Regardless of whether you choose NURBS or Patch modeling, if the model must be converted to a mesh object to perform a specific function to achieve the results you are looking for, you lose the advantage of working with that modeling method and it might not be the appropriate modeling method for that model. There is no substitute for experience and each modeling scenario has its own set of problems to overcome. Choose the modeling method you are most comfortable with, but don't be afraid to experiment with other methods. You might just find a quicker and easier way to build the better mousetrap.

Summary

NURBS models are created using NURBS curves or NURBS surfaces. Both the surfaces and the curves can be created as Point or CV types. Point curves and surfaces are created with the points lying directly on the surface or intersected by the curve. CVs (or Control Vertices) never lie directly on the surface or the curve. CVs can also be weighted so that the curve or surface gravitates toward the weighted CV.

One of the benefits of NURBS models is that the tessellation can be dynamic. In other words, the renderer can be set to change the number of faces generated at render time based on either the curvature of the model, size of faces, or at a fixed rate. Tessellation can also be set to change with the distance from the focal point, so that the same model in the distance has less faces than when it is up close to the camera.

Patches use Bézier curves to create their surfaces. For this reason, they are easily manipulated through the manipulation of the Bézier handles. Patches can be created using either QuadPatches or TriPatches.

An additional benefit of Patch objects is that additional patches can be added directly to the edge of an existing Patch. Edges can also be subdivided for smoother curves on an individual basis, keeping the number of faces to a minimum. When subdividing faces though, keep the Propagate property turned on to avoid creating holes or gaps between the newly created patches. Subdividing patches also adds vertices and edges that expand the structure of the patch.

Though not as powerful as NURBS modeling, Patch modeling has definite advantages over modeling from primitives. Patch models offer more flexibility than Standard primitives because each patch is inherently smooth, where modifying vertices of a Standard mesh model can cause spikes to occur.

Working with Patches and NURBS objects are currently some of the most advanced modeling methods used today. In that regard, using Patches and NURBS successfully takes patience and practice. Although both NURBS and Patch modeling greatly simplify the process of creating organic models, organic models are in themselves difficult shapes to mimic. To go farther as a 3D artist, it is important to learn these modeling techniques, but perfecting them will not happen in a single day. Start slow and apply NURBS for small tasks until you become proficient at building NURBS models. When you understand the nuances of NURBS and Patch modeling, building larger and more complex models is just an exercise in methodical model building.

Q&A

Q I created a QuadPatch but cannot access the Sub-Object parameters. I've tried to do the same with a TriPatch with no luck. How do I access Patch Sub-Object levels?

A Regardless of whether you are editing a QuadPatch or a TriPatch, an Edit Patch Modifier must be added before you can edit any of the Sub-Object levels.

Q After editing at the Vertex Sub-Object level, I realized I needed to increase the segments along the length of the QuadPatch. Is there a way to increase the number of segments and avoid getting the Modifier warning?

A Because Modifiers use the original object's topology as a basis for object modification, you cannot change the original patch segments without risking object corruption. To change the segments and ensure object integrity, you must remove the EditPatch Modifier. Unfortunately any vertex, edge, or patch modifications will be lost. There is an alternative to losing your work, though. By going to the Patch Edge Sub-Object, you can subdivide an Edge, which adds a new vertex midway along the Edge's length. If you prefer not to subdivide the edge, you can always add another patch to the patch Edge.

Q How do I create a sharp corner in a single NURBS curve?

A Creating sharp curves on a NURBS curve or surface can only be achieved with a CV curve. To create a sharp point in a NURBS curve, set the weight value to zero on both CVs adjacent to the CV that is to be sharp. This causes the middle CV to come to a sharp corner.

Q Why don't the Ripple and Noise Modifiers seem to work on my NURBS surface?

A Because Modifiers work on the displacement of vertices (Point or CVs in the case of NURBS surfaces), the position of the Points or CVs is not normally dense enough to create an effective displacement. If you find that the NURBS surface must have a Modifier for the desired effect, the only option might be to convert the NURBS surface to an Editable Mesh. Unfortunately, the advantages of using a NURBS surface would be lost when converted.

5

DAY **6**

Creating Materials and Maps Part I

You put a great deal of effort into your modeling, but when you render out the scene, your outstanding models look sort of bland. The reason is materials haven't been added to your models. Materials give the model depth and personality. Materials are the equivalent of house paint; they create the color and finish of the surface of the model. Without materials, it's impossible to tell the difference between a brick, a piece of wood, or a gift box (as in Figure 6.1). Materials are used to give the model surface attributes. Without materials, the model is just a well-placed group of gray faces.

FIGURE 6.1.

All three of the objects in this image use the exact same model. By applying different materials to each object, you can achieve an entirely different look.

Tip

Creating good materials is essential for a great scene. Though many times a simple material might be used, creating good materials can drastically make up where the modeling leaves off. Materials can be used to give the object attributes that are impossible to model or too intense to render in a timely fashion.

To understand how materials work, you must understand what they are and how they are applied to objects. There are probably as many different ways to apply materials as types of materials. In today's lessons, you learn what materials are, some of the most common types used, how to create them, and how to apply them to a model.

What Is a Material

In the most basic terms, a material is an entity that allows MAX to render a model with simulated surface attributes. These attributes can be such things as reflectivity, transparency, wood grain, or any other physical attribute. The key to remember when adding materials is that the surface attributes are simulated. Through the rendering process, MAX uses the information in each material to affect how that face is rendered and ultimately how the entire scene is viewed.

What's truly unique about 3D rendered graphics is that you can create objects that do not exist in the real world. Because the attributes have a lot of flexibility, you can create such things as transparent wood or marble made from every color in the rainbow. Though the software enables you to create such materials, it is up to you to use the correct balance of the different attributes to create a material that is realistic or surreal, depending on the look you want.

After materials are created, they can be applied to objects. Because of the variety of shapes used to create models, the materials must be positioned correctly to have the correct orientation. Typically, after the material has been created and oriented correctly, the fine-tuning is done to give the object the correct look based on the lighting in the scene, where the object is in relation to the camera, or the level of detail used in the material.

Understanding the Material Editor

In 3DS MAX 2.5, materials are created, loaded, and assigned using the Material Editor. The Material Editor in 3DS MAX 2.5 is one of the most innovative ideas implemented for creating and manipulating materials. As you see in Figure 6.2, the materials are visually laid out at the top of the editor for easy viewing. The Material Editor also has tools for configuring the editor to better suit different model and material types. Such controls as number of viewable materials, sample type, and animated previews of materials are just some controls used to customize and reconfigure the Material Editor for various material needs.

6

FIGURE 6.2.

The Material Editor interface.

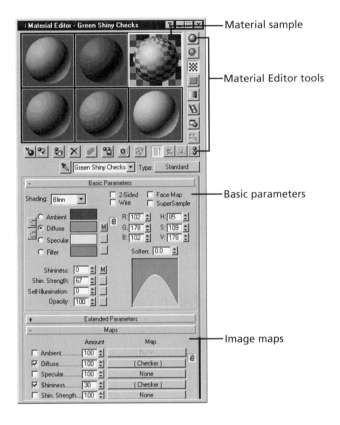

— Material sample

— Material Editor tools

— Basic parameters

— Image maps

To Do: Opening the Material Editor

1. To open the Material Editor, select Material Editor from the Tools menu.

2. Click on the Material Editor icon, located on the main toolbar at the top of the screen.

Now that the Material Editor is open, take some time to become familiarize with some of the tools and locations of the various parameter groupings. Some of the most commonly used tools are described briefly here and in more detail later in this day.

- *Get Material*   Loads a material into the Material Editor from a saved library or the scene, or used to create a new material.

- *Put Material to Scene*   Used to replace a material that was copied and then edited. When material is put to the scene, any references to the old material of the same name is replaced with the new material.

• *Assign Material to Selection*   Applies the currently selected material to an object or group of objects selected in the modeling viewport.

 • *Reset Maps/Mtl to Default Setting*   Removes any attributes changes made to a base material.

 • *Make Material Copy*   Makes a copy of the current material, so if the material is active in the scene, you can make changes to the copy without it affecting the material in the scene. By affecting the copy and not the original material, changes can be previewed and tested prior to reassigning the material. When changes have been made and approved, the material can be reassigned to all objects that use the original material by using the Put Material to Scene button (previously described).

 • *Put to Library*   Saves the currently selected material to disk and registers it in a selected Material Library.

 • *Material Effect Channel*   Using Video Post processing, materials can be given effects channels so that effects applied in Video Post can be directed to act on only those materials with the same effects channel selected.

 • *Show Map in Viewport*   When using images as part of a material, activating this option allows the image to be seen in shaded viewports.

 • *Sample Type*   Used to change the shape of the object in the Material Editor sample window. This can be set to sphere, cube, cylinder, or to any MAX mesh object.

• *Backlight*   Applies back lighting to the material sample for a more realistic sample. This does not apply any back lights to the scene; it is merely for surveying the material under back-light conditions.

 • *Background*   Applies a checkered background in the sample window. Primarily used when working with materials that have some transparency applied to judge transparency or refractive values.

 • *Select By Material*   Enables the user to select objects based on the currently selected material. Objects that use the currently selected material will be highlighted in the Select by Name dialog that appears.

 • *Material Map Navigator*   Enables you to quickly navigate through all the currently loaded materials and associated maps and sub-materials. Useful when changing parameters on a scene with many materials used or loaded.

6

Keep in mind as you read through and experiment with the Material Editor that creating materials can become a complex endeavor. Though creating materials in MAX has been greatly simplified, a large portion of the process is within the artist. Because you have so much control in MAX's Material Editor, you have a lot of information to cover. If you feel overwhelmed at any time, go back and study the section again. As you can see, this is the only topic thus far that is divided into two sections.

Loading Materials into the Material Editor

Often, especially for the beginning 3D artist, existing materials are loaded and edited to create a new material. MAX facilitates this by providing an extensive library of materials that you can edit to create new materials. Even for the experienced 3D artist, materials are often reused when needed. There is no reason to create a glass texture over again, especially if you already created one that would be perfectly adequate for a new model today.

Prior to creating new materials, you must understand the relationship between the material and the model. For this reason, it is best to start by loading an existing material and applying it to a model to examine the way the material is applied to the object. In the following exercise, you load and apply an existing material to object in a scene.

To Do: Loading and applying a material to an object

1. Open matAply.max from the accompanying CD-ROM. This scene contains the box, sphere, torus, and cylinder primitives.

2. Open the Material Editor by using the Material Editor button located on the main toolbar, or by selecting Material Editor from the Tools menu.

3. Click on the Get Material button to activate the Material/Map Browser.

   The Material/Map Browser is used to load existing materials or image maps or to create new materials by loading one of the 3DS MAX 2.5 material types. As seen in Figure 6.3, materials can be loaded from a variety of sources, including the Material Libraries and the current scene.

4. In the Browse From section, choose the Material Library radio button (if not already selected) to choose from the default MAX Material Library.

5. When you make a Browse From selection, the right-side panel becomes populated with names of available materials. Move the mouse cursor over the list of available material and the cursor changes to a hand cursor, indicating that this list is drag scrollable. In other words, clicking and dragging with the mouse on the list will scroll the list in the direction the mouse is dragged.

6. Drag-scroll the list until the Green Shiny Checks material is visible within the list.

7. Single-click the mouse on the Green Shiny Checks material. In the upper-left corner of the Material/Map Browser, a sample box shows an example of the selected material as applied to a sphere. This should be a checkerboard pattern set in green hues.

8. Because this is the material you want to load, double-click the material name to load it into the selected slot in the Material Editor. The material is now loaded and ready for use.

FIGURE 6.3.

The Material/Map Browser is used to preview and load materials from other Material Libraries, the current scene, and from other objects.

Before assigning this material to an object, take the time to use some of the other features of the Material/Map Browser. At the top of the window are two groups of tools. On the left side of the Material/Map Browser window are the selection constraints. A brief description of the buttons and their usage follows. To use the tools, simply click on the buttons. The selection criteria toggle between the radio button groups to keep the material window from becoming completely overloaded. Viewing is based on where the material currently resides in relation to the open scene file.

- *View List* Displays a list of the available materials based on the selection criteria specified in the Browse From section on the left of the interface window.

- *View List + Icons* The available list appears by name and by a small icon. The icon consists of a small sphere with the named material applied to it.

- *View Small Icons* Displays a list of available materials by icons only. The icons have the associated material applied.

- *View Large Icons* The available material list appears as large icons with the associated material applied.

6

- *Update Scene Materials from Library*   Materials used in the current scene are updated using the saved materials stored in the Material Library. Any material containing the same name as a material in the currently selected library will be replaced with the stored version, regardless of intention.

- *Delete from Library*   Removes the currently selected material (in the Browser list) from the currently opened Material Library.

- *Clear Material Library*   Removes all materials from the currently loaded Material Library.

Though there are seven types of materials in 3DS MAX 2.5, the default material type is called Standard. The material types are discussed in detail later in this chapter. The next discussion is based on the Standard material type for simplicity.

> Do not spend enormous amounts of time creating a material for an object that is not created yet. When applied to an object, the material might not look as it does in the sample window, due to the lighting and the actual shape of the object. Typically, applying materials to an object is one of the last things done in the modeling process.

Assigning Materials to Objects

When a material has been created or loaded, it must be assigned to an object to be utilized. After a material has been assigned to an object, that object's surface takes on the characteristics of the material. Materials can be assigned either directly (by assigning the material specifically to an object) or indirectly by using the material as a component in another material, such as with a Blend or Multi/Sub-Object material type. For now, examine how to assign a material directly to an object.

> When a material has been assigned to an object, each of the corners of the material's sample slot contain a small gray triangle. If the triangles in the material's sample slot are white, it means that one of the currently selected objects has that material assigned to it. Multiple materials can contain the white triangles at a single time if multiple objects are selected, each with a unique material assigned. Figure 6.4 depicts hot, cool, and hot materials assigned to currently selected objects.

FIGURE 6.4.

The sample slots show whether the material is currently used in the scene or not. Materials that are assigned to an object are considered hot and contain triangles in the corner of the sample slot.

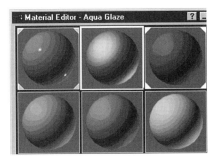

Note Materials that are assigned to an object are called hot materials. Materials that are not currently assigned to any objects in the scene are considered cool.

When assigning a material to an object, either of two methods can be employed. As part of the Material Editor tools, there is a button depicting a sphere with an arrow pointing down to a cube. This is the Assign Material to Selection button and assigns the current material to the current selection set. Regardless of the number of items selected, the material is assigned to each according to the UVW mapping properties associated with each of the individual objects.

UVW mapping coordinates are based on the object's XYZ orientation. UVW is used to distinguish between the mapping coordinate system and the World Space coordinate system, though the letters UVW refer to the XYZ coordinates, respectively. The use of the UVW coordinates allows materials to be oriented easily and correctly, regardless of the orientation of the object in world space. UVW mapping modifiers can also be added to objects and oriented by the user.

6

The second method of assigning a material to an object is through the drag-and-drop method. This involves selecting a material sample from the material editor and dragging it onto an object in the scene. This assumes that the drag-and-drop option is activated in the Material Editor. The default is for drag-and-drop to be set.

To Do: Assigning a material to an object

1. Reset the MAX environment by choosing Reset from the File menu.

2. Create a geosphere in the Top view on the left side of the view and another in a Front view positioned to the right of the first geosphere. Deliberately make each geosphere from within a different view. They should be approximately the same size.

3. With the geosphere still selected, open the Material Editor. Right-click the mouse on the first material sample. The pop-up menu shown in Figure 6.5 appears in the window. If the Drag/Copy option is not set, set it by clicking on that menu choice.

4. Click on the Get Material button and load the MAX material from the default Material Library. You might need to set the Mtl Library radio button option from the Browse From: section of the Material/Map Browser.

5. With the material loaded, click on the MAX material and drag it to each of the objects. Applying the material is not dependent on the orientation of the view.

6. Make the Perspective view active and click on the Quick Render button to perform a quick render of the two geospheres.

   Viewing the result of the render (also seen in Figure 6.6), it looks as though the material has been applied differently to each object. Actually, each object is oriented differently due to the active view during construction.

7. Select the geosphere on the left (created in the Top view) and right-click the mouse cursor on the Select and Rotate tool. Examining the parameters, you can see that the geosphere has no rotation applied to any of the three axes.

8. Select the geosphere on the right (created in the Front view) and right-click on the Select and Rotate tool. As you can see, because the geosphere was created in the Front view, the object has been rotated 90 degrees along the X axis. In the Transform Type-In window, type in a zero in the Absolute World X parameter.

9. Perform a quick render in the Perspective view. The material is positioned identically in both objects. This is because of the UVW mapping coordinates automatically generated for the geosphere object.

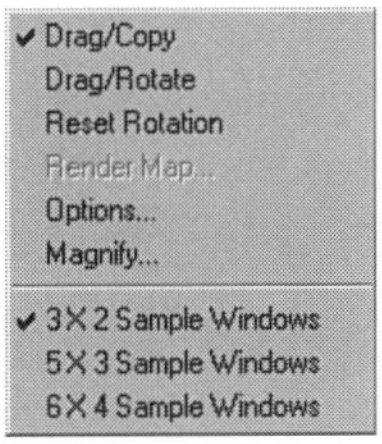

FIGURE **6.5.**

FIGURE **6.5.**

The Material Editor sample pop-up menu enables you to change the sample size, drag-and-drop options, as well as to render preference for samples.

✓ Drag/Copy
Drag/Rotate
Reset Rotation
Render Map...
Options...
Magnify...

✓ 3 X 2 Sample Windows
5 X 3 Sample Windows
6 X 4 Sample Windows

FIGURE **6.6.**

Because each of these geospheres was created in different viewports, their orientation is different. When the material is applied, it is based on the UVW mapping, which is based on the orientation of the object.

Alternately, you can apply the same material to a selection set by clicking on the Assign Material to Selection button. Using this method, materials can be assigned to entire groups of objects in a single action. To experience this, create a group of objects, position each in the scene, select all, and then apply the material using the Assign Material to Selection button. Each object has the material assigned and aligned according to the UVW mapping for each respective object.

Editing Materials

After loading and assigning a material to an object, you realize that something just isn't right. The color is not quite right or the surface seems dull, for example. Welcome: You just entered the exciting phases of fine-tuning your scene. On the one hand, you can feel good that you're entering the last stage of development for the scene and can soon sit back and watch as the rendered scene appears before you. On the other hand, this can be one of the most time-consuming areas of the entire 3D process.

6

Materials add much to the scene. In fact, between materials and lighting, no single attribute carries as much weight in determining whether a scene looks poor, good, or great. As such, this phase requires that materials and their attributes be edited or tweaked to get just the right look. Editing a material can be as simple as changing the color, or as complex as balancing refractive values with the reflectivity and opacity to create the perfect translucency for an object to appear real.

In the following exercise, you edit some basic parameters to get the feel of editing a material. Keep in mind that just about every attribute can be a material in its own right.

To Do: Editing materials

1. Start with a new scene by selecting Reset from the File menu. Create a torus in the Front view.

2. Open the Material Editor and use the Get Material button to retrieve a material from the default MAX library. Choose Material Library in the Browse From: section and double-click on the Aqua Glaze material. The Aqua Glaze material is then loaded into the scene. You can close the Material/Map Browser but not the Material Editor.

3. Select the torus and assign the Aqua Glaze material to it by dragging the Sample slot from the Material Editor to the torus. The material can also be applied by using the Assign Material to Selection button.

   Begin with some basic editing such as changing the color of the material's Diffuse property. The Diffuse property is the main color of the material when viewed in a well-lit scene.

4. To change the Diffuse property, click on the Specular color swatch. After clicking on the color swatch, the Color Selector (shown in Figure 6.7) is activated. In the large color palette on the left side of the Color Selector, click the mouse in the area of the magenta color. The change in Diffuse color is reflected in both the Diffuse color swatch and in the sample window.

▲

FIGURE 6.7.

Use the Color Selector to adjust the color for any material attribute that uses direct color values. From the Color Selector, you can adjust colors by Hue, Saturation, Value, RGB values, whiteness, or blackness.

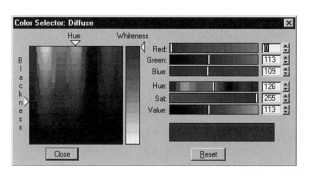

Changing the Diffuse color is a simple change to make that you can easily undo. You can use the standard Undo feature to correct erroneous changes; refining materials is an evolutionary change. It might be hours, days, or weeks later that you decide you want to change the material back to its original configuration, or somewhere in between.

To accommodate changes that might span many iterations of change, the Material Editor supports duplicate material names. This is done so that a material can be applied, the material copied, changes made to the copy, and then the new material reassigned to all objects using the original material.

To minimize the confusion, walk through a simplified process of changing an attribute of a material and reassigning it to the scene and all objects that use the original.

To Do: Refining materials with cool copies

1. Reset the current session and place a few objects in the scene. For simplicity, add some primitives such as a torus, sphere, and a box. Also, load the Aqua Glaze material from the default MAX default Material Library.

2. Select all objects and assign the Aqua Glaze material to them.

3. Click on the Aqua Glaze material sample and drag to the next material sample slot. The previous material is replaced with a copy of the Aqua Glaze material. This new copy of the Aqua Glaze material is called a cool copy of the material because it is not assigned to any objects. Keep in mind that the material still has the same name as the original material.

4. In the cool copy of the Aqua Glaze material, change the specular color to a magenta color, or some contrasting color, as you did in the previous exercise. Remember, the cool material is one not assigned to an object and therefore has no triangles in the corner of the sample slot.

5. In addition to the specular color, change the Shininess parameter to 5 and the Soften parameter to 0.8 in the cool copy of the Aqua Glaze material. There is a distinguishable difference in the two materials now.

   Judging by the sample slot, you can decide that this is the material you want to use in place of the original Aqua Glaze material. After you make these changes to the material, you can apply the changes to all the objects that use the original Aqua Glaze material. Keep in mind that you made changes to the Aqua Glaze material copy, not the original. Doing this provides you the safety of being able to change a material, yet having a backup to come back to if you decide the changes are not what you expected.

6

6. To apply the changes made to the copy to all objects that were assigned the original Aqua Glaze material, click on the Put Material to Scene button. This button takes the modified material copy and applies it to the originally assigned material of the same name. As you can see, the original copy becomes cool and the modified copy of the Aqua Glaze material becomes the hot material.

The Standard Material Basic Parameters

Regardless of which material type you choose, each material type has Basic Parameters. Though they might appear slightly different in each material type, Basic Parameters essentially encompass some of the most basic elements required of any material, such as shading algorithm and diffuse color. The Basic Parameters list here is for the Standard Material type, but similar parameters are found in almost every other material type at a sub-material level.

- *Shading*   When an object is rendered, the rendering software can be directed to use different rendering algorithms. A rendering algorithm is a method used to calculate the light as it is projected on an object surface. Different rendering algorithms are developed to satisfy certain rendering needs. In MAX, the standard rendering algorithms are Constant, Phong, Blinn, and Metal. The Constant method is used to render each face of an object with the material attributes without smoothing between faces. Objects appear faceted, but the rendering is very fast. Unlike Constant, Blinn and Phong use smoothing to create a smooth surface across faces. The algorithm, although not as fast as Constant, provides greater quality in the final render. The Blinn method offers some subtle differences from the Phong method, most notably in the area of highlights. Using the Metal shading algorithm sets parameters to produce a material that has more characteristics of metal. One of the main differences in metal materials is that the specular light closely resembles the diffuse color of the metal and not the light it is reflecting. These terms are discussed in more detail later in the chapter.

- *2-Sided*   Check this option to render both sides of the object (inside and out). This option is normally used only with objects that have transparency or refraction applied or when the object has holes in the geometry. Checking this option does increase the rendering time because the object's surface will need to be evaluated from both sides. This option should also be applied to objects that have no thickness and where both sides will be seen, such as a vase, where both sides of the lathe would be seen.

- *Wire*   When you prefer to render an object out in wire frame mode, check this option. The object will be rendered using the attributes specified in the material, though only the visible face edges will be rendered. Control which edges are rendered by designating which edges are visible and invisible at the sub-object level. If 2-Sided is checked, the edges of the faces on the back side of the object will also be rendered.

- *Face Map*   If you want to paste an image or pattern on every facet of an object, check this option. When checked, Face Map renders each facet of the object with the material applied to every face. If your material contains an image of a circle inside a square, checking Face Map renders the object so that every facet of the object has a square with a circle inside it on the rendered object.

- *Super Sample*   By comparing the surrounding pixels, Super Sampling mode creates a better antialiased edge. Turn this option on when you need better edge resolution or when rendering higher resolution images.

- *Ambient*   The swatch to the right of this button indicates the color of the object in ambient light or indirect light. Many times, the ambient light is set to something similar to the Diffuse color, though not as strong. Others even set this color to colors approaching black.

- *Diffuse*   When light strikes an object's surface, the Diffuse color is used. The Diffuse and Ambient color are closely related and as such can be locked to be sure that changes in one will be reflected in the other. Changing the diffuse color is the most influential Basic Parameter regarding the object's color.

- *Specular*   Light that is reflected off an object is called the specular light. Shininess and Shininess strength parameters control to what degree light bounces off a face. Specular light is also referred to as specular highlights. If you have a deep green material diffuse color and magenta specular color, the object appears to have magenta highlights as the lighting conditions change or the material is given a higher specular value.

- *Filter*   Because transparent objects change the color of the light that passes through it, setting the filter color to something close to the diffuse color allows light that passes through the object to pick up some of the object's color. This can be used to create more vivid transparency effects, such as in a stained glass window where the colors of the material are projected into the scene.

- *Shininess*   To simulate the effect of a shinier material, the specular highlight is changed. Increasing the shininess causes the specular highlight to become smaller, giving the appearance of a smoother, shinier surface material.

- *Shininess Strength*   This parameter increases the strength or size of the specular highlight. As the value increases, the specular highlight grows larger and more closely represents the specular color swatch.

6

- *Self-Illumination*   Self-illumination is used to control the difference between ambient values and the diffuse values. Use this parameter when you want to create objects that are unaffected by lighting. Do not confuse self-illumination with lighting. This will not cause the object to cast any light or create a glow. To create an object that casts light, hide a light inside the object and turn off the object's shadow casting capabilities. To make an object glow, you need to use a video post glow effect.

- *Opacity*   As the value of opacity decreases, the object becomes more transparent, with a value of zero equating to completely transparent. Objects can have any degree of transparency from 0 to 100 percent. When making objects completely transparent, you might need to adjust the Shininess and Shininess strength for the right effect because although the object is transparent, it can still reflect light.

- *R, G, B*   These values indicate the Red (R), Blue (B), and Green (G) values of the parameter color selected and denoted by the radio button. The RGB values are extremely useful when exact color matching is required for a material. Keep in mind that although you might set the RGB values of a material to an exact match of a real-world color (such as PANTONE colors), the colors might appear different, due to ambient color, light color, and atmospheric conditions just to name a few. Creating exact color matches to materials requires getting to know the other parameters of the Material editor as well.

- *H, S, V*   Just like the RGB values, you can also adjust the Hue, Saturation, and Value to achieve the proper color. RGB and HSV are two different methods of affecting the same colors. Again, these values are important for getting the correct color, but the overall look of a material is based on all the parameters used on the material, as well as lighting conditions in the scene.

- *Soften*   This parameter is used to soften the specular highlights of a material. The Blinn shading algorithm helps alleviate the need for this parameter, although it is still used when utilizing Phong shading. By increasing the value of the Soften parameter, the material will ease the harsh effects that can occur due to back lighting on an object's surface.

Remember, although the parameters of a material are extensive, it only means the artist has more control over the final output of a material. The only real way to understand how each material attribute works is to experiment with objects and change the parameters one at a time. Even with experience, there is a lot of trial and error in creating the material just right for the situation.

Material Types

As you were browsing through the materials, you might have noticed that some look very different than others. Some materials are reflective, some transparent, and some even seem to be a combination of multiple materials. In addition to the difference in values of some of the parameters, materials can also have different parameters altogether. By creating materials with just the needed parameters, unnecessary calculations can be avoided reducing rendering time.

Materials in MAX are divided into seven types. Each type has its own advantages whereas most share some common parameters. Choose the type of material depending on the effect or material characteristics that you are creating.

- *Standard*   Used as a general all-purpose material type, the Standard type is used more often than any other. Use this material when you want to apply a single material to an entire object. This type contains the most common attributes and can be applied to any type of object. The Standard material type is also used to create materials that are then used in other material types such as the Multi/Sub-Object type listed later. When you have an object that requires several different materials applied to portions of its surface, use Multi/SubObject Material type.

- *Double-Sided*   An object such as a vase or a cup might be made with a single set of faces (such as a lathed spline) requiring a different material on the inside from the material on the outside. For example, if you create a vase from a spline using a lathe modifier (see Figure 6.8), the inside of the vase can be plain ivory, although the outside might be ornately painted. Using a Double-Sided material type allows you to assign two materials.

6

FIGURE **6.8.**

The vase in this image was created using a spline and a Lathe Modifier. Because the vase has no real thickness, a double-sided material was used to give the back faces a different color from the front faces.

- *Multi/Sub-Object*   This truly unique material type greatly aids creating complex models. By using the Multi/Sub-Object material type, you can add different materials to Sub-Object selections of a model. This is extremely helpful in applying materials with greater accuracy. By applying a MeshSelect modifier, you can select any specific faces on a mesh (or any other Sub-Object selection), for example, and apply a transparent material to some, metallic to others, and so on. Any number of materials can be used in a Multi/Sub-Object material type. Multi/Sub-Object materials are applied based on Material ID #, which can be specified by applying a Material Modifier or in some cases directly applied within the Modify panel parameters.

- *Matte/Shadow*   The Matte Shadow material takes the Environment (the rendered background) and applies it to objects in the scene. This causes those objects to become indistinguishable from the background (called Matte objects), so geometry can appear to move behind objects in the environment bitmap. In addition, the Matte Shadow material allows these objects to receive shadows, so you can have the illusion of the geometry casting shadows into a scene that doesn't really exist (only a bitmap). You can use Matte Shadow materials to save rendering time by rendering parts of your scene and then using the rendering as a background applied to objects through Matte Shadow. This is similar to the process used with mattes in traditional filmmaking.

- *Blend*   With the Blend material type, you can use two materials on the same side of an object. Using this type of material, you can apply the characteristics of two materials to the same object as well as animate the amount of blend between the two materials. Unlike the Double-Sided material type that applies one type to each side, or the Multi/Sub/Object type that applies different materials to different faces, the Blend material type combines two materials on the same surface. How the materials are combined is controlled by the mix amount or the mixing curve. The Mix Amount parameter is the percentage of the second material mixed with the first. You cannot have 100 percent of both materials; the two values have to equal 100 percent. A Mix Amount value of 100 percent means that only the second material is seen.

- *Raytrace*   By now you might have heard the stories about how raytracing is memory-intensive. Many of the horror stories about raytracing are true. It is a memory-intensive rendering algorithm, and yet it yields very realistic results when working with reflections and refractions. Using the Raytrace material type, you can selectively choose which objects in the scene are raytraced and which are rendered using the standard MAX scanline renderer. Although the Raytrace material type can increase rendering time compared to using other material types, the quality is dramatically increased on objects requiring true reflections and refraction. The rendering time required to render an entire scene using raytracing is substantially higher than using the raytraced material method, yet the difference in quality is negligible.

- *Top/Bottom*   This material type is like a hybrid of the Blend and the Multi/Sub-Object material types. Two materials are chosen, one for the top and one for the bottom portion of the object, based on either World or Local coordinates. Each of the materials are given an adjustable amount of coverage to complete 100 percent of the object. The two materials can be gradually blended together as well so that there is a smooth transition between the materials. For example, suppose you have an old iron post with rust at the base. You can discolor the bottom portion of the iron material with the rust material and gradually blend up to iron without rust. It might or might not be obvious to see that the different material types are needed to accommodate the various types of model shapes and surface characteristics. Experience plays an important part in deciding what material type to use in what situation. There are no set rules on which type of material needs to be used when. For the most part, it is up to the artist to experiment with different values and material types to create his own customized materials.

6

Using Maps with Materials for Greater Effectiveness

In addition to adding color to a model's surface, you can also add images to the material, which in turn are applied to the surface of an object. These images are called maps. When applied as a Diffuse Map, an image is applied to the surface of the object the way wallpaper is applied to a wall.

Maps can also be used for many of the Basic Parameters described in the previous section and basically in any parameter that requires color in some fashion. Maps can also be used to control transparency, surface texture, and reflective parameters. The use of maps greatly enhances the effectiveness of a material and might also pick up the slack where modeling would be too tedious or render intensive.

Maps are applied using the UVW coordinate system. UVW was chosen because it was the three letters in the alphabet prior to XYZ. The UVW coordinates are based on the XYZ coordinate plane so that the horizontal (U) and vertical (V) positions on a two-dimensional image can be mapped to a three-dimensional object. Using an association between the coordinate system, MAX can correctly apply a map to a curved surface (as in Figure 6.9) based on the objects UVW mapping coordinates generated when the object was created. The Z axis or depth (represented by W) is used when orientation of the map is switched based on the object's Z axis.

FIGURE 6.9.

A material applied to a curved surface uses the object's UVW mapping coordinates to correctly map the material.

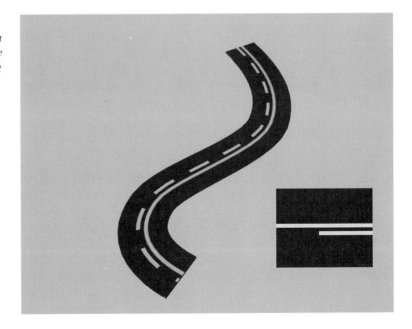

Maps are a versatile tool in material design. For example, if you want to create the effect of a broken piece of lumber as in Figure 6.10, a map can be used to create the jagged edges instead of modeling them. By using a map to create the irregular edge of the wood, you can save time in both modeling and rendering. In this example, the geometry is not broken and ragged. Instead an opacity map is used to create that effect on a box. This requires far fewer polygons and so speeds rendering and modeling time.

FIGURE 6.10.

Using a map to create the effect of transparency on an object.

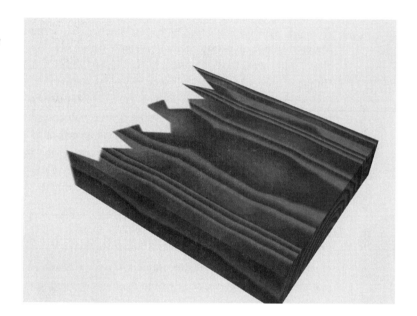

Applying a map to a material is a two-step process. In the following exercise, you start with a standard material and add a diffuse map to give the object a better looking surface.

To Do: Adding a map to a material

1. Start with a new scene in MAX. To ensure that the entire scene is new, select Reset from the File menu. When asked if you want to reset, answer Yes.

2. Open the Material Editor by choosing Material Editor from the Tools menu or clicking on the Material Editor icon on the toolbar.

3. Click in the second sample slot to make it the active material. Notice that a white band is drawn around the material sample indicating that it is the active material.

▼ To Do

6

4. Under the Basic Parameters section, notice the various parameters and an adjacent color swatch next to some of them. Some parameters also include a small square unlabeled button. Click on the button adjacent to the Diffuse color swatch. The Material/Map Browser is activated and a list of material types appears.

5. Because you want to use an image, select the Bitmap type by double-clicking on it. Though the type is Bitmap, MAX can use a number of image types including .bmp, .tif, .jpg and .tga.

6. After you select the material type, the Material/Map Browser closes and the Material Editor updates to include the new parameter. The Material Editor also changes to reveal the parameters for the newly added material type. Under the Bitmap Parameters section, click on the blank button next to the label Bitmap. A dialog box is presented allowing you to select a bitmap file located on any attached or networked drive. Unless you changed your paths, the default should point to the MAX directory that contains the maps that ship with 3DS MAX 2.5.

7. Single-click the first file in the list entitled 3DSMAXR2.TGA. Because the file was highlighted in the list and not selected, options become available in the dialog box.

8. With the first selection still highlighted, click on the View button in the Select Bitmap Image File dialog box. The bitmap appears in a separate window. Close the preview window as you would any Windows window.

9. Double-click the first file entry to load it into the Material Editor. Looking at the material sample you can see that the map was applied to the material and now covers the sample sphere.

10. Create a box object in the Perspective view and rotate the view so that you can see three sides of the box at once. Apply the material to the box by clicking in the sample sphere and dragging to the box object. The cursor changes to either an arrow with a box attached (when over a valid object) or a circle and slash cursor with a box attached (the cursor is not over a valid shape).

11. Click the Show Map in Viewport icon (the checkered cube). Now the map shows up on the box in the viewport.

12. When you applied the material to the box, UVW mapping coordinates were required so that the box could display the material that had a diffuse map. Because the box is a primitive that can have its own implicit mapping, that mapping was automatically turned on with the application of the material. If the geometry had been something other than a primitive, it would have required a UVW Mapping Modifier placed in the stack, or the material would not appear correctly.

Mapping Coordinates Parameters

Working with maps, you quickly notice a lot can be done with them. Maps can be used for virtually every attribute of a material. Because they are so versatile, understanding some of the basic mapping parameters is a necessity.

- *Texture/Environ Mapping*   Maps can be applied to an object using a variety of mapping coordinates. By selecting Texture, the map is applied using the local coordinate system of the object. The coordinates are based on UVW coordinates or on the object's planar XYZ coordinate system. If Environment is checked, the map is applied to the environment in a spherical or cylindrical manner or according to the screen (fills the frame).

- *Offset*   A value in current units, the map is offset from the UVW mapping coordinates. This parameter is used to reposition the map precisely on an object's surface.

- *Tiling*   Tiling is used to specify how many times the map is applied across the surface of an object. A value of one means the map will be stretched or shrunk to fit across the surface of an object one time. Changing the number to 2 means it will be fitted so that it will be seen two times across the surface of an object. The higher the number, the more times the map is repeated across the surface of the object.

- *Mirror/Tile*   If the tiling amount is set to more than one, the map must be duplicated across the surface of the object. The Mirror/Tile parameter is used to say whether the map is repeated end to end or mirrored with each repetition. This value is independent for the U and V parameters.

- *Angle*   Used to change the angle the map is applied to the surface of an object, based on the UVW parameters.

- *Rotate*   An interactive tool that can be used to rotate the map on a surface using a trackball mechanism, as in the view orbitor.

- *Blur/Blur Offset*   This parameter blurs the map as it is applied to a surface. Unless you have a perfect mirror, reflected objects do not normally reflect perfectly clear. By setting the Blur and the Blur Offset, you give the material a more realistic finish.

6

Using the Asset Manager to Acquire Maps

Using maps in materials greatly adds to the depth and realism of a material. Because maps can be used for so many properties, they are used extensively. In the movie *Toy Story*, over two thousand maps were used in materials. In an addition to that, over 1,300 materials that didn't use maps at all were used. As you might have guessed, sifting through that many images to add a map to a material can be a major ordeal. 3DS MAX 2.5 has a nifty Utility that will soon become indispensable to you when creating materials. The wonderful utility is the Asset Manager.

The Asset Manager is found on the Utilities Panel and is used for locating assets such as scene files, .avi files, and any image file supported by 3DS MAX 2.5. The interface of the Asset Manager (seen in Figure 6.11) closely resembles the Windows Explorer format.

FIGURE 6.11.

The Asset Manager is an indispensable tool for locating MAX scenes and image files. A thumbnail representation appears for all types of files supported, including scene files and .avi files.

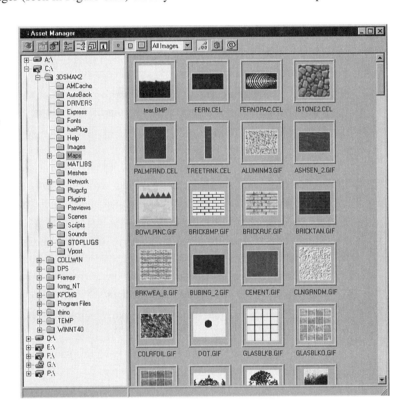

The Asset Manager works on a very simple principle. The user simply traverses through the directory structure of any mounted drives, just as in the NT Explorer window. On the left side of the window is the directory tree; on the right are the contents of the current directory. Simply click on the directories on the left to display their contents on the right. Settings at the top of the Asset Manager window enable you to filter out certain file types, making only selected file types visible to the Asset Manager.

Though that in itself is useful for discovering where your files are, there are other benefits to this tool. If the filter is set for .max scene files, you can quickly browse through a project directory and get a quick glance at what each of the scene files contain. MAX saves a thumbnail preview of the scene file.

When using the Asset Manager to find maps, productivity instantly increases. Not only can map files be located quickly, the user is also given a preview of the file in thumbnail format on the right side of the Asset Manager interface. As the user browses through the directory structure, desired maps can be viewed by right-clicking the mouse button on the thumbnail image and selecting View. Image properties can also be viewed by selecting the Properties option when right-clicking on a thumbnail sketch of the image through the Asset Manager.

Now for the big news. Although it's all well and fine that you can view images and find where they are on mounted drives, after the desired image is located, you can simply drag the map from the Asset Manager to the desired property in the Material Editor to add that map to the material. This is a tool that I highly recommend when applying maps to material properties. By centrally locating maps, even categorizing them, and using the Asset Manager, loading maps for a material property has never been easier.

Child and Parent Materials

As materials are edited, becoming more complex, a hierarchical structure evolves around the components of the material. When traversing through the hierarchical tree, the novice user can quickly become disoriented. To the unwary individual, it might appear as though the other parameters are no longer present. In reality, what has happened is that by adding a map to a material, a child material is added. As in standard 3D hierarchy, entities that are dependent on other entities are called the child. The child entity is dependent on the Parent entity. This hierarchical structure is used in everything from modeling to animation and Inverse Kinematics, as well as in the Material Editor.

Navigating Through Materials and Parameters

6

Every map applied to any attribute is a different child material to the Parent material. When a material has more than one map applied and there are multiple child materials, each of the child materials are referred to as sibling materials of each other. As sibling materials are added, a single material can become a very complex array of maps and even other materials. To access the siblings, use the material navigation buttons seen in Figure 6.12.

FIGURE 6.12.

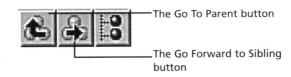

The Go To Parent button

The Go Forward to Sibling button

The material naviga-
tion buttons are used
to navigate through the
hierarchy of materials
and maps applied to a
Parent material.

Navigation can be done either by clicking the navigation arrows or by using the Material/Map Navigator. The navigation arrows provide the quickest method of returning to the previous level or accessing the next logical sibling material. The problem is that they are limited in that they traverse the tree in an orderly fashion, and it might take several clicks to get to the desired component. The navigation arrows are designed for quick access for materials with a minimum number of dependent materials and maps.

Although the Go to Parent and Go to Sibling buttons are simple and quick, the Material/Map Navigator is much more complex yet easy to use once understood. Figure 6.13 depicts a semicomplex material hierarchy. As you can see, there are a number of maps and materials under the parent material. The Material/Map Navigator is used to show the hierarchy and structure of the selected material only.

FIGURE 6.13.

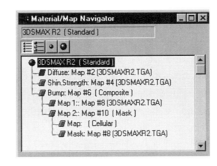

The Material/Map
Navigator facilitates
moving quickly
through the levels of
complex materials.
From this window,
any of the dependent
materials can be
accessed and adjusted
immediately.

When using the Material/Map Navigator, click on the material you want to examine, and the selected dependent's parameters appear in the Material Editor. Using this method, you can quickly access any dependent to make changes or view parameters.

Managing Materials

Good materials are just one of the prized possessions of the 3D artist. Because some materials can take several hours or days to create, the good ones are not typically tossed aside at the end of a project. In fact, many times materials are categorized into libraries that can be stored, reused, or even sold. Because old habits are hard to break, a good habit to get into is to organize your materials. Materials are saved with the scene in MAX, but materials should also be saved because you never know when that obscure transparent mahogany wood material might be required.

One of the simplest ways to categorize the materials is by scene. Though this is not the most organized, it is a method that enables you to save all the materials from a single scene into a separate library.

To Do: Creating material libraries

1. Open libex.max from the accompanying CD-ROM. This file contains a few objects and some preloaded materials.

2. Open the Material Editor and click on the Get Material button.

3. In the Browse From section of the Material/Map Browser, select scene. Choose Save As from the file section, also located in the Material/Map Browser.

4. In the Save As dialog box choose a meaningful name and add the .mat extension. Click on the Save button to save the material in the specified directory. Your materials can now be recalled at any time to reuse the materials of your choosing.

Note

When saving libraries, turn off the Root Only option in the Material/Map Browser. When checked, dependent maps will not be saved with the materials. Dependent maps are denoted by the red parallelogram in front of the material component in the Material/Map Browser. With the Root Only option turned off, the material will be self-contained and can be loaded in its entirety by anyone using MAX.

6

Summary

If only one point from this entire chapter is to be retained, it is that materials are vitally important for creating a believable image. Whether the image is part of an animation, architectural design, or an imaginary dancing baby, using the correct material can greatly enhance the image. That being said, strive to put forth a conscientious effort when creating materials. By using materials customized for each object, you gain the ability to turn an average model into an extraordinary one.

- *Maps*   Colors of materials can be changed using the color swatches, but for added realism, use maps in places where a solid color is requested. You might, for example, want to create a surface that has a reflection of a beautiful sunset. Using a sunset map in the parameter setting gives you that effect. Many times, maps are used for something completely different than the image portrays. Bump maps and reflection maps very often will use images that have nothing to do with the elements in the scene directly, but because of the image's color capabilities, it might be used to give off irregular reflections as though it is reflecting its surroundings. Animations in the form of AVI, FLC, or sequences of still images can also be used anywhere maps can be placed.

- *Materials as Properties*   In addition to being assigned to objects, materials can be built exclusively for use as an attribute in a material property. You might want an irregular procedural bump map, so you create a marble material for use in the bump property of another material. In this way, the marble material is applied indirectly to the object. Using other materials as a sub-material is a common practice, especially when you consider the blend and Multi/Sub-Object material type.

- *Material types*   Not all materials are created equal. It's a fact of life and one we can live with. By using different material types, objects can receive the most applicable material for that object. Because an object's surface is simulated, a lot of effort in creating materials is creating innovative ways to simulate new effects. By combining material types, you can gain a distinct advantage over your competition by carefully choosing your material type.

- *Editing Materials*   Materials can be edited and cloned so that the editing process becomes somewhat nondestructive. By clicking and dragging a material to another slot, the material is cloned. Changes can be made to the clone and then propagated throughout the scene by putting the material to the scene.

- *Saving Material Libraries*   After spending an inordinate amount of time on creating a material, no one wants to throw their materials away. Customized libraries of materials can be created by the 3D artist by saving the materials used in the scene to a customized Material Library. The Material Libraries can then be passed to other animators or loaded into MAX at a later date.

Q&A

Q When I apply my material to an object, it seems too large. How do I change the size of a material?

A Through the tiling property, materials can be sized to appear a specified number of times across the horizontal or vertical axis of an object.

Q I've tried to load materials into my scene, but the list of materials is empty. Why can't I load any materials?

A If the Browse From setting is not set to Material Library, you cannot load the Material Libraries. Material Libraries are kept in the MatLibs directory of the installed 3DS MAX 2.5 directory.

Q I've saved a material to a custom library, which was transported to a different computer. Why doesn't this new library work correctly on a different machine?

A When saving materials to custom libraries, it is important to turn off the Root Only option in the Material/Map Browser window. When activated, this option references any maps used by their relative path, which most likely will not exist on other machines. Turning this option off saves the materials in a self-contained format.

6

DAY 7

Creating Materials and Maps Part II

In the Day 6 lessons, you learned about the Material Editor in general. Today, you dive into material creation and the tools needed to create them. Not covered in this book, although worth mentioning, is that creating materials requires that the 3D artist can also envision how a certain material is made up. Creating the skin of a salamander, for example, would be moist and slippery, whereas the skin of a lizard would be dry. It is this attention to detail that is necessary to create believable materials.

Along with using the Material Editor found in 3DS MAX 2.5, you should also have access to a paint program such as Adobe Photoshop and a scanner to scan imagery, such as sky, tree bark, marble, and any other real-world images that would make great maps. We will discuss the uses for such maps in subsequent sections later in today's chapter.

Today's chapter requires that you already understand the fundamentals of the Material Editor. You also need to understand the basics of what materials are and their basic construction. Today we will discuss the following topics:

- *Material Editor tools*   We will focus on the tools of the Material Editor and how they are used to create, apply, and adjust materials.

- *Creating material*   Basic theory on creating and applying materials to objects.

- *Map types*   You learn about the map types used in 3DS MAX 2.5 and how they differ in both their creation and their application.

- *Material types*   MAX offers you seven different material types with endless combinations; you learn how to choose which is right for your model.

- *Dynamic Properties*   The Dynamic Properties parameters of materials are used in creating realistic animation effects based on the type of material. In this manner, objects made of steel have less resistance on objects moving over their surface than objects made of rubber.

Material Editor Tools in Detail

The Material Editor is a myriad of tools, all which have their usefulness. I find the Material Editor in 3DS MAX 2.5 to be one of the best-designed mechanisms for creating and working with materials. The drag-and-drop capabilities between material attributes and the live color wand make moving and setting attribute colors and maps a breeze.

Here are the tools available at the surface level of the Material Editor. These tools are on the bottom and right sides of the material sample slots and you use them at the highest level of material development and assignment.

- *Material Map Navigator*   Enables you to quickly navigate through all the currently loaded materials and associated maps and sub-materials. Very useful when changing parameters on a scene with many materials used or loaded.

- *Sample UV Tiling*   Sets the number of times the material is tiled in the sample slot for the selected material. The tiling set here does not affect how the material is actually tiled in the rendered object; this parameter is only for the sample slot representation. To change the tiling parameters, open the Bitmap Coordinate parameters and change the Tiling settings for the U and V Tiling parameters. You can also adjust the tiling of the UVW Mapping Coordinate. This allows one material to be tiled in different ways on different objects.

- *Video Color Check*   When creating animation for broadcast, television standards (NTSC in the United States and PAL in Europe) can cause some colors to bleed (such as red) or become fuzzy. With this button enabled, illegal colors are rendered as black in the sample slot. Use this attribute with caution. Leaving this parameter turned on will seemingly cause unexpected black patches to the rendered scene to the unwary. Many novice users complain that they have unexplained black patches in their renderings, without realizing that Video Color Check has been enabled. When rendering output for computer or print media, do not check this option.

- *Make Preview*   Use this flyout to choose between creating a preview of an animated material, playing an existing material preview, or saving the material preview to disk.

- *Show End Result*   When editing sub-materials or maps, this button toggles between displaying the final result and the result up to the current level in the sample slot of the Material Editor.

- *Go to Parent*   When working with materials that have multiple levels, such as maps, sub-materials, or multiple materials, you can use this button to move up one level in the hierarchical material tree.

- *Go to Sibling*   Used to move between materials and maps associated with a material, this button moves to the next material at the same level in the hierarchical material tree.

- *Options*   Enables you to adjust Material Editor parameters that affect how the materials are rendered in the sample slots. Options such as antialiasing, renderer used, and lighting color for the Material Editor can be set using this button.

Show Map in Viewport

One of the hardest aspects of working with bitmaps is getting them aligned correctly on irregular objects. It's easy to align a flat image on a cube, but what about materials where alignment needs to be more precise, on objects that are not so easily mapped? By setting the toggle of the Show Map in Viewport to active, you can see how the material is mapped on the object in the Modeling view. This is a major advance over just a couple of years ago. Due to the speed and power of affordable desktop computers (not to mention the geniuses at Kinetix), it is now possible to see a low-resolution version of what the material looks like in the modeling environment, without having to render the scene. Although this is not intended for final output, it greatly speeds up the process of applying and setting materials correctly.

The Show Map in Viewport button is accessed at the material level where the image map resides. By controlling the viewable mapping in selected materials, you can turn on only those materials where it is important to see the image map while in the modeling environment. Due to the increased processor workload, turning all material maps can require enormous amounts of video RAM. Even a video card with 16MB of RAM would begin to bog down after you view more than a few maps at a time in a high polygon count scene.

In the following exercise, you align a material using the Show Map in Viewport button.

7

To Do: Turning on the Show Map button

1. Open roadmap.max from the accompanying CD-ROM. This scene file contains a single lofted, curved shape representing a winding country road.

2. If not already done, maximize the Perspective window.

3. Open the Material Editor and select the road material in the first sample slot. Apply the road material to the curved shape by dragging it onto the shape or by selecting the shape and clicking the Assign to Selection button on the Material Editor. You see the road object change to the Diffuse color of the Road material.

4. Click on the small M button next to the Diffuse color swatch. This accesses the Diffuse map material directly.

5. Activate the Show Map in Viewport property by clicking on its button. The curved road shape turns black with some yellow marking near the center (see Figure 7.1).

FIGURE 7.1.

The road material when first applied to the curved road based on the default mapping coordinates produced when the Loft object was created.

As you can see, the road material is not properly assigned to the road shape. One of the advantages of MAX is that shapes can carry their own material mapping coordinates. This facilitates applying a square material to a nonsquare model, such as the road. You need to make some basic material alignment adjustments. Analyzing the map in the Perspective view, it looks as though it is off by 90 degrees along the local Z axis. To fix this, set the W parameter on the Map Angle, found in the Coordinates section of the bitmap material (Map#2 in this case) to 90.

6. Set the W Angle of the Coordinates section of the bitmap to 90. This changes the rotation of the bitmap along the curved object's Z axis. As you can see in Figure 7.2, the bitmap has been rotated but is not yet correctly applied to the road model.

7. Now that the correct angle has been applied, you need to change the number of repetitions along the length of the curve. Set the U parameter (also found in the Coordinates section of the bitmap) to 10. Be sure that Tile is checked. Figure 7.3 shows that the number of repeated material looks better, but the material is still not properly aligned to the road.

8. Move the Material Editor to the right side of the screen so that the road and Material Editor can be seen at the same time. Using the mouse, click and drag down on the U Offset spinner slowly. Watch how the road material is interactively adjusted. Center the material so that the lines run down the center of the road. This setting should be approximately –0.28 in the U offset property.

For those of you who do not realize it, having the map bend with the geometry of the road is an incredible feat. It has always been an issue to apply a rectangular map on a curved surface. In the past, 3D artists actually had to model some aspects of a material (such as the lines on the road) because applying maps cannot be properly molded to fit the geometry.

9. One final adjustment. Change the V tiling to 2.0 to make the lines on the road thinner. Readjust the U Tiling to 15. The finished road with mapping can be seen in Figure 7.4.

FIGURE 7.2.

The road material after rotating the bitmap 90 degrees along the local Z axis.

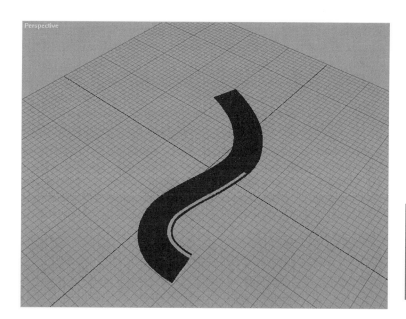

7

FIGURE 7.3.

Changing the U Tiling repeats the pattern of the lines along the entire length of the road object.

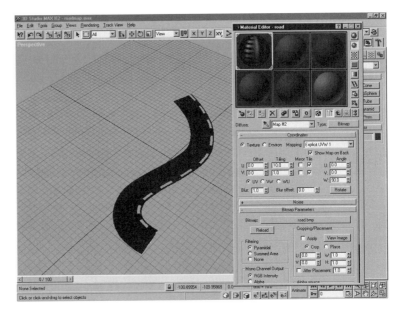

FIGURE 7.4.

After making the final adjustments, the road map is properly aligned and tiled along the length of the curved road object. Using the Show Map in Viewport gives you instant feedback, so you can make material design decisions as you model.

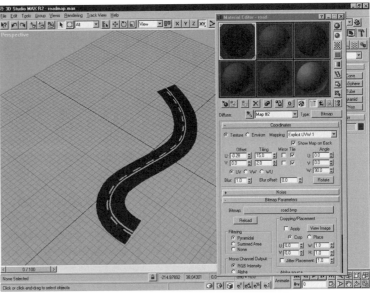

Another thing to realize while changing the material attributes, such as tiling and rotation, is that it is reflected in the sample slot of the Material Editor. Though this does not always accurately reflect the model used in the scene, it does serve as an important guide when restructuring materials. A cube can be used instead of the sphere by changing the sample type flyout. You can also instruct the Material Editor to use a specified model in the sample slot through the Material Editor options dialog box. The Custom Sample Object section contains a blank button that when pressed presents a dialog box used to load a MAX model. To load custom geometry into the sample slot, set the sample type flyout to the Question Mark icon.

Material/Map Navigator

As you create materials that become increasingly complex, you invariably find that traversing through the sub-materials can become tedious using the standard Go to Parent and Go to Sibling buttons. For this reason, the Material/Map Navigator was implemented. Through the Material/Map Navigator, you can quickly access the parameters of any map associated with a material.

Figure 7.5 shows a sample of the Material/Map Navigator with the MAX Material that ships with 3DS MAX 2.5. By highlighting any of the materials or maps in the Material/Map Navigator, you instantly have access to the materials' parameters or even sub-materials contained in a sub-material.

FIGURE 7.5.

The Material Map Editor displays all maps and sub-materials associated with a material. This dialog box provides instant access to any of the attributes of a material.

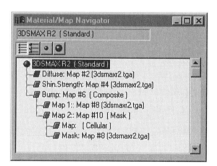

Although it has few controls, the Material/Map Navigator is a tool that expedites maneuvering through materials.

- *View Icons*   The four icons located at the top of the Material/Map Navigator are used to change the size of the icons in the Navigator list. The list can be viewed as a list only, list and small icons, small icons only, or large icons.
- *Blue Spheres*   Indicate materials or sub-materials.
- *Green Parallelograms*   Maps used on specific attributes of a material.
- *Red Parallelograms*   This indicates the map is currently assigned to an object in the scene and that the Show Map in Viewport option has been turned on.

As materials are selected from the Material/Map Navigator list, their attributes appear in the Material Editor. Maps and materials from the Navigator window can also be added to

7

other materials in the Materials Editor, using the drag-and-drop feature available to all valid MAX material buttons. As with the Material Editor, you can even drag materials from the Material/Map Navigator directly onto objects in the scene.

Using Different Map Types

To accommodate for various modeling and material needs, you can use different maps types when creating materials in MAX. Because you have different requirements for different attributes, it only makes sense that the map types used on an object's surface should match the type of surface being simulated. To that end, MAX uses five classifications of maps, as described here.

- *2D Maps*   Typically bitmaps (although they can be procedural), this mapping type is used to project an image or pattern on a surface. Because the map is only two dimensional, there might be some distortion when projecting a map of this type on curved surfaces. To experience this, apply a bitmap to a sphere and watch how the map is gathered at the poles.

- *3D Maps*   To have a map projected on three dimensions, it must be calculated procedurally. This creates a map that is projected throughout an object and not just mapped to its surface. Map types such as Wood, Smoke, and Marble are typical of procedural 3D Map types. Using this type of map, if an object were cut open with a Boolean operation, the pattern of the material would be continued throughout its geometry, where a 2D map would not.

- *Compositors*   Used to mix two maps on an object's surface. Compositing can be done using alpha channels or the maps themselves. By mixing two materials on a single surface, effects and maps can be combined for an even greater range of effects.

- *Color Mods*   Called Color Modifiers, maps of this type are used to tweak the colors of a bitmap or material that does not have color controls. Using this map type, you can affect the vertex colors, RGB values, or the Output properties.

- *Others*   Map types for reflections and refractions are found in the Others category. Raytracing, reflections, and refraction have immense calculation workloads and therefore have been optimized with their own type of mapping procedure.

The Map types previously described can be used anywhere a map might be applied, such as the diffuse color, Bump, or Reflection properties. By using different map types on the appropriate attribute, MAX can be more efficient when rendering processor intense attributes, such as raytracing.

To access the different map types, click on the Type button located just below the sample slots of the Material Editor. When the Type button is pressed, the Material/Map Browser appears, offering various material options from choosing a new type, a new material, or loading a material currently used in the scene. The following exercise describes how to go from a Standard material type to a complex material using the Blend Material type, along with the Planet and Noise Map types.

To Do: Changing a Map Type

▼ To Do

1. Reset MAX and Open the Material Editor.

2. Click on the Type button found just below the Material Editor sample slots. Adjacent to the material name is a Type button, which displays the current material type and is used to change material Types, if necessary.

3. The Material/Map opens after clicking the Type button. From here, the Browse From filter is used to filter out where materials are loaded from. Click on New to select only new material types.

4. 3DS MAX 2.5 ships with seven material types. Double-click on the Blend material type. You are immediately prompted to keep or discard the material currently occupying the sample slot. This occurs each time a material type is changed. Though it doesn't matter for this exercise, change the option to Keep the current material, just to see how it works. Choose Keep and click OK.

   The material has now been changed to the Blend material type, retaining the old material as a sub-material in the first Material position (labeled Material 1). As you can see, the Material name and type are listed on the button next to the Material 1 label. Attributes can now be adjusted or changed as needed. Even the sub-material's type can be changed to create more complex, multilevel materials.

5. Now change one of the sub-materials to a Planet material. Within the Blend material just created, click on Material 1. The Material's Basic parameters section opens.

6. Click on the Diffuse Map button found to the right of the Diffuse color swatch. The Material/Map Browser opens.

7. Select New from the Browse From filter and choose the Planet type by double-clicking on it. The Planet procedural map is placed in the Diffuse mapping parameter. The Planet material type is one that is procedural, with eight different color swatches used to create the land and water. Experiment on your own with the colors to create some interesting results. For now, make this material more complex and add a cloud layer.

8. Click on the Go to Parent button to go to the top level of the Planet sub-material. In the name slot, type in **Planet** and click the Go To Parent button once again to return to the top of the Blend material hierarchy. The name Planet now appears in the Material 1 slot along with the material type (currently Standard).

7

9. Click on Material 2 to open its Basic parameters section. Click on the Diffuse map button (as you did earlier) and select Noise as the material type. In the Noise Parameters section, set the Noise type to Fractal. Name the material **Clouds**.

10. Use the Material/Map Browser to go directly to the top of the Blend material hierarchy and set the Mix Amount to 60. This represents a 60 percent blend of Material 2 into Material 1. In this way, you can blend two or more materials (by using multiple Sub-Materials) to create very complex material attributes.

11. Name the entire material **myEarth** and click the Put to Library button. You will be prompted for a name (you can use the same name); then click OK. The material has been saved for future use. Save this material because you use it again later.

A blend material can blend only two materials. To Blend more than two materials, set the Blend Sub-Materials to the Blend Material type. In this way, complex hierarchical Blends can be created under a single hierarchy. To stay organized, it might be best to use the Material/Map Navigator to traverse the Material tree.

The UVW Modifier

Some objects such as imported meshes or Compound objects (such as Booleans) do not generate their own Mapping coordinates. When using objects that do not have mapping coordinates, MAX has no way to know how to apply an image map to the object's surface and cannot render that map. If you drag and drop a material that contains maps on an object without mapping coordinates, the maps will not display in the viewport, even if Show Map in Viewport is turned on. No warning will occur and you will wonder what went wrong. Take that as a sign. If you do not see any applied maps, even though Show Map in Viewport is turned on, you need to add a UVW Modifier to the object with that material.

If a UVW Modifier is not added, at Rendering time an error message appears notifying you that the listed objects do not have mapping coordinates and that MAX cannot render those objects correctly.

To correct the error, you must supply MAX with a basis for mapping coordinates. To do this, add a UVW Modifier. This modifier adds a Gizmo that can be positioned, rotated, or scaled to accommodate the object's mapping requirements.

Mapping Coordinates

We've been talking about mapping coordinates, but what are they? Mapping coordinates are the basis in which materials are positioned, rotated, or scaled on an object's surface. An object's mapping coordinates are based on the object's geometric shape. Objects that are cylindrical, for example, are typically given a cylindrical mapping algorithm. By matching the mapping most closely to the shape of the object, better mapping is achieved.

Without mapping coordinates, you have no control over how materials are placed on objects, and because all objects are not the same, using the same mapping coordinates for every object simply would not return realistic results when rendered.

Figure 7.6 shows some primitives with the same checker material applied. No mapping was added or changed. This is the default mapping supplied with these types of objects. As you can see, the objects all have mapping that positions the material correctly on the object with minimum overlap or truncation.

FIGURE 7.6.

These five primitives use the default mapping generated by MAX when the object was created.

Unlike the default mapping provided by the objects seen in the previous figure, Figure 7.7 shows what the same objects would look like if a spherical mapping algorithm was used on every object. Judging by the image, these results would not be acceptable in real world graphics or animation.

When you drag and drop a material onto a primitive that can generate its own mapping coordinates, these coordinates will turn on automatically. This will not occur on custom created geometry. Although this might seem confusing, understand that because primitives are created and optimized by MAX, the mapping coordinates are built in. For custom geometry, you simply need to add a UVW Modifier.

7

Using the same mapping coordinates for different objects would not provide adequate results, as is seen by these objects that have all been given the same mapping coordinates.

Mapping coordinates can also be controlled through the Unwrap UVW Mapping Modifier, which offers the best control for selective mapping inside MAX. Applying the Unwrap Modifier to selection sets of faces allows you to get exact positioning of bitmaps on complex geometry.

Advanced Materials

Now that you have the mapping coordinates understood, it's time to use them to your advantage. There are advanced material techniques that utilize the mapping coordinates to create more realistic surface illusions by applying greater control over surface attributes. Such attributes such as surface bumps, transparency, and refraction are controlled by changing the maps for those attributes. These attributes require that you understand how a material is mapped to an object so that you can predict how the surface will render and prepare their surfaces accordingly.

Bump Maps

One of the most commonly used mapping techniques is the Bump map. Through the use of the Bump map, the object can be made to look as though its surface is smooth as glass, rough as rock, or somewhere in between. The Bump map works by altering the object's surface normals according to the luminance value of a supplied bitmap image or procedural map.

Although Bump maps are great for simulating surface texture, they do have their flaws. Figure 7.8 shows two objects with Bump maps applied. The sphere uses a procedural noise and the box uses a bitmap. Although both are effective for adding surface texture to the object, notice the edges around the sphere. The Bump map works on surface normals and not actual geometry, so the edges are unaffected by the Bump map. Using Bump maps are great when the object is an insignificant part of the scene or if the surface texture is not too severe, but nothing replaces good old-fashion geometry.

If you want to use a map to affect the geometry, use the map as a Displacement map. Displacement mapping is not found in the Material Editor, but rather as a space warp or Object Modifier. Be forewarned however that the complexity of the geometry required usually is prohibitive and precludes extensive use of this technique. Displacement maps are best used when simple geometric displacement is needed.

FIGURE 7.8.

A sphere and a box with different Bump maps applied. Notice how the edges of the sphere are unaffected by the Bump map and continue to be smooth. This is because Bump maps work on surface normals and not object geometry.

For each material property that utilizes maps, you have three controls. These controls are found under the Maps parameters listing and are described here.

- *On/Off check box*   Preceding the name of each property is a check box. When checked, this property is on. When the check box is clear, the property is not set. This enables one to experiment and turn properties on and off while refining a material.

7

- *Amount*   This spinner sets the amount of the effect. With the exception of Bump property, the Amount spinner can be set from 0 to 100. The Bump amount spinner has a limit of 999 but is typically set to something much less. The default value is 30, but for most practical applications, an amount of 200–500 is sufficient.

- *Map Button*   This button has a default label of None, indicating that no map has been applied to this attribute. When the Map button is clicked, the user is asked to select from the various maps types. When the map type is selected (by double-clicking on the selection or highlighting the selected type and clicking OK), the Material Editor is advanced to the new material attribute. The On/Off check box is also automatically checked when a new map type is selected.

To Do: Applying a Bump map

1. Reset MAX and create a Box in the Front view with the following dimensions: Length 175 units, Width 300 units, Height 12 units. Because MAX can be set to different measuring units, use what is comfortable for you.

2. Open the Material Editor and click on the Maps Rollout (see Figure 7.9). Notice the different attributes that can have maps applied to them.

3. Click on the Bump Map button labeled *None*, along the side the Bump property Amount spinner.

4. The Material/Map Browser opens up and the Browse From filter should be set to New. Single-click on the Noise type. A small sample is shown in the upper-left part of the Browser.

5. To select this Noise type, double-click on the Noise name or click OK. The Noise map type is applied to the Bump property of the current material and the Material/Map Browser will close.

6. Click on the Go to Parent button to access the Maps parameter section. Set the Bump Amount to 60. Apply the material to the box object by dragging the material sample on the box or clicking the Apply To Selection button (provided the box is selected). The box changes color to reflect the material just applied, but the bump is not yet visible in the viewport.

7. Perform a quick rendering by clicking on the QuickRender button, located on the upper toolbar. Your box is bumpy.

    Although that is the most basic application of applying a Bump map to an object, take it one step further. In the following steps, you apply a Bump map that coincides with a Diffuse map to the same box object.

8. Open the Maps parameters in the Material Editor for the material created in the previous steps. Drag any of the buttons labeled *None* on the Bump Map button. This clears the current Bump map so that you can start fresh.

9. Click the Bump Map button and choose Bitmap as the Map type from the Material/Map Browser.

   You need to add a bitmap image to the Bump map property. This can be achieved by clicking on the Bitmap button located under the Bitmap Parameters section of the Bump map, or you can use the Asset Manager. If you haven't used the Asset Manager, you're in for a treat.

10. From the Utilities Panel, find the Asset Manager button. If it is not located on the Utilities Panel, select the More button and choose Asset Manager. Open the Asset Manager by clicking on the Asset Manager button.

11. The Asset Manager works like a file browser, with directories on the left side of the window and contents on the right. Open the MAX directory and then open the Maps directory.

12. In the Asset Manager filter drop-down list, choose All Images as the filter type. The Asset Manager builds small icons of the images found in this directory. Wait until this is finished. A full install of MAX has a lot of maps added to your hard drive, so this can take some time.

13. When the images are loaded into the Asset Manager Cache, you can easily view all image maps visually instead of by name. Scroll down to find BrickRuf.gif. Drag the icon on the Bump bitmap button. The Material's Bump map is now set to the BrickRuf.gif image. Set the Bump Amount to 300. Leave the Asset Manager open.

14. Click the Go to Parent button in the Material Editor. From the Asset Manager, drag the BrickTan.gif file onto the Diffuse Map button. The map is now used as the Diffuse Map for this material. Close the Asset Manager.

15. Use the Render Last button to rerender the same image with the new attributes applied. Now you've really hit a brick wall.

The Asset Manager is an invaluable resource for quickly loading maps for materials and placing them into a material's property. In this exercise, you used two versions of the same map so that the Bump and Diffuse map coincide to create a realistic illusion. To check how much realism the two added, rerender the image with the Bump map attribute turned off. The wall is not nearly as realistic.

7

FIGURE 7.9.

Clicking on the Maps rollout in the Material Editor reveals all the attributes that can have Maps applied to them.

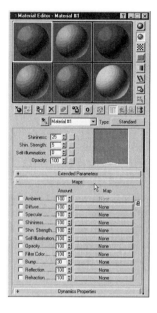

Opacity

Opacity is the property that makes a material opaque or transparent. The more opaque the material, the less transparent it is. Materials that are 100 percent opaque have no transparency, such as steel or wood. As the opacity value of a material decreases, the object becomes more transparent, meaning more light passes through the material. Materials such as glass are highly transparent, though materials can have any level of transparency, such as some translucent plastics.

Opacity Mapping takes a map and uses its luminance values to create areas of transparency in the rendering. It uses the luminance values only and disregards the hue and saturation values. Black areas of the map are treated as transparent, white as opaque. Remember "Black hole, white wall" if you are confused. Some paint programs, notably Adobe Photoshop use the opposite method when working with transparency.

Accompanying the Opacity setting is the Falloff setting found in the Opacity section of the Extended Parameters rollout. In truth, even the most transparent object is not invisible. There will be a degradation of visibility when looking through even the most transparent materials. The Falloff setting is used to simulate the variance in the transparency of a material. For example, when looking through a transparent object with a curved surface, there will be less transparency where the surface curves because there is more of the material to look through, as in looking through a clear drinking glass. The Falloff setting is based on the angle of the surface normal relative to the camera. When Falloff is set to In, the transparency increases as the angle of the surface normals relative to the view get closer to zero. When Falloff is set to Out, the transparency increases as the angle of the object's surface normals gets closer to 90 degrees relative to the view. For a typically curved glass surface, such as a drinking glass, setting the Falloff to In gives the glass less transparency when looking through the curved portion of the glass.

Creating a realistic transparent materials is one of the most difficult illusions to create properly. Because the light in MAX is simulated, materials such as glass (which allow lots of light to pass through) must be created with great care to get the proper material settings. Part of the challenge is that we all know what glass looks like and how it reacts with light. What most people don't know is that a lot of physics is going on as the light passes through the glass. Some key components to remember when creating a transparent material are listed here.

- *Opacity*   To make a material some degree transparent, the Opacity setting must be less than 100. For typical glass, it is less than 10. To create a translucent material, Opacity should be set between 20 and 35. For more realistic Opacity settings, use a map in the Opacity parameters. Better results are obtained by using a map than by simply changing the Opacity value.

- *Shininess Strength/Shininess*   Set these values high. More often than not, transparent materials have a very shiny surface. Set the Shininess Strength very near or at 100 and the Shininess between 20–30 percent lower than the Shininess Strength.

- *Falloff*   For transparent curved edges, set the Falloff to Out. Set the Falloff to In for an opaque edge. Setting Falloff to In causes the inside of the object to be transparent, as in glass, where setting the Falloff to Out causes the edges of the object to be transparent, as in smoke.

- *2-Sided*   Transparent materials should be set to 2-Sided so that both sides of the material can be seen. Because the material is transparent to some degree, the inside faces that are not normally visible, will be rendered.

- *Refraction*   Curved transparent edges also refract or bend light. That is why a magnifying glass has a curved edge. Set the index of refraction rate to a value between 1.0 and 1.8, depending on the material. Refractive values are published in many books stating the index of refraction for listed elements. Air has a refractive value of 1.0 and objects in the real world rarely have a refractive value of 2.0 or greater. There are refraction value tables found on the online reference system that ships with MAX. Go to the Help menu, Online reference and perform a search on refraction.

7

Using Extended Parameters

In conjunction with the Opacity settings, the Extended Parameters provide more control for the overall transparent effect. These controls control how light is affected as it passes through the material, such as refraction, color filters, and opacity falloff.

- *Falloff*   As previously described, this parameter changes how transparency is applied to an object, with the surface based on the angle of the surface normals.

- *Opacity Type*   As light passes through an object, the color of the light might change color to reflect the material it is passing through. Each of the Opacity types (Filter, Subtractive, or Additive) have their own effect and change the way light exits a transparent surface.

- *Filter*   Sets the color of the light passing through an object to the color specified in the Filter color swatch. The Filter method uses transmission color and does not have to reflect the Diffuse color of the transparent object. In real-world lighting, light that passes through transparent objects is affected by the transparent object's transmission color.

- *Subtractive*   Subtracts the transparent object's Diffuse color from the Diffuse color of the object that is receiving its light. Using the Subtractive method has a tendency to darken the appearance of the transparent object and even makes it appear less transparent.

- *Additive*   The light transmitted through the transparent material is added to the color of the objects that receive its light. This has an effect that tends to give the object more luminance and works well when applying the material to objects such as car headlights or beams of light from a street light.

- *Reflection Dimming*   This parameter controls how reflection maps are rendered when within a cast shadow. The default value turns off Reflection Dimming. When turned on, the Dim Level affects the portion of the reflection map that falls within a shadow, and the Refl. Level affects the portion of the map that is in direct light. The Dim Level is a percentage value where 1.0 equals 100 percent reflective; in essence Reflection Dimming is turned off. Because the Refl. Level increases the luminance of the material in the area outside shadows, this level might need to be adjusted to compensate for the added luminance.

- *Wire Size*   This parameter is only effective when the Wire Basic Parameter is checked. The Size parameter is used to change the thickness of the wireframe used when rendering the material. The thickness is measured in either Pixels or MAX Units, as described next. For an interesting effect, try using Wire combined with Diffuse mapping.

- *In Pixel/Units* Choose between Pixels or MAX Units when rendering in Wire mode (set by checking Wire in the Basic Parameters section). When choosing Units, the rendered wireframe changes as the distance of the object changes. When set to pixels, the wireframe retains the same thickness regardless of the object's distance from the camera. Using Units enables the wires in the distance to be rendered smaller than those in the foreground, using pixels forces all the wires to be rendered with the same thickness, defeating the illusion of perspective.

The Extended Parameters are used to add subtle effects to the material's opacity features. When working with opacity, reflection, and refractive parameters, it is important to remember that a material that looks great in one scene might not work as well in another. Opacity, reflection, and refraction are three attributes of a material that work directly on the light in a scene. They are also highly sensitive and not as forgiving as a Bump map, for example. MAX provides a glass material that is great for some cases but is not intended to be an end-all solution for glass. Experiment with the parameters of the glass material to suit the lighting and material needs required of the scene. You might find that you use a different variation of the glass texture each time you use it. Remember to save each variation in your Material Library (don't forget to change the name) so that you can build a library of various glass materials. You'll be glad you did.

The Shininess and Shininess Strength Properties

All surfaces in the real world reflect light. Objects with a high gloss shine reflect more light than surfaces with a matte finish, which reflect very little light. This reflected light is not to be confused with the Reflections property. The Shininess of an object is used to calculate the amount of specular light that is reflected. The Shininess Strength property is used to affect how intense the specular light is reflected.

When thinking of specular light, picture a very shiny surface such as a polished red apple or a highly polished piece of chrome. Where the light reflects, you see a specular highlight, which appears as a white (typically) hotspot of more intense light than the rest of the surface. If you look around the room, you can immediately spot specular highlights on every polished surface. Look at your computer keyboard and you might even notice one there, although it might be very slight and spread out. This is because the surface of the keyboard leans more toward a matte finish than a smooth glossy surface.

The Shininess and Shininess Strength parameters work together, which is the reason for the visual graph in the Material Editor. As can be seen in Figure 7.10, the Shininess graph is rounded, resulting in a matte surface texture, seen in sample slot 1. When the Shininess Strength and the Shininess property is increased, the result is a glossy surface, as seen in Figure 7.11.

7

FIGURE 7.10.

Low Shininess Strength and Shininess values create a matte or dull surface. The Shininess graph indicates the matte surface by the rounded curve.

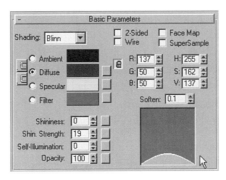

FIGURE 7.11.

By increasing the Shininess Strength and the Shininess parameter, the surface becomes increasingly glossier. The glossy surface is reflected in the Shininess graph as a sharp spike, as opposed to a smooth bell curve.

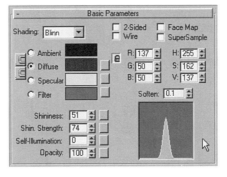

Reflection/Refraction

Though listed here together, reflections and refractions are not the same phenomenon. Both are affected by the amount of light present, but react differently. Objects that reflect work like a mirror to some degree. Images of the surrounding environment appear on the object's surface. Refractions occur in objects that have some degree of transparency and distort the view of objects seen through them. A shiny Christmas ornament ball reflects all the lights and decorations around it. A fish tank refracts and distorts the fish in the tank, especially when they swim past a corner in a square tank. If you stand at the correct angle, the fish looks like two fish because the two separate plates of glass are refracting the image of the fish separately.

The real world is full of reflections and refractions. Look around you, no matter where you are, and take notice of how many things reflect the environment. It might surprise you how many surfaces actually have some degree of reflectivity. Though not as prevalent as reflections, almost every transparent glass object has some degree of refraction. A perfect example of this is a magnifying glass, which uses refraction in a positive way to make images larger.

In the wonderful world of 3D, it's a whole different game. Reflection is based on the light reflected by objects onto the surface of another object and then reflected onto our eyes. For a computer to do even a single reflection is a mathematical nightmare. Refractive surfaces are no different. Both require plenty of power and can really slow down rendering. To expedite the process, MAX uses various methods of applying reflections and refractions on objects.

- *Mapping*   Using the mapping method, reflections are simulated by mapping the environment onto the reflective surface of the object. This is a much quicker method of adding reflections to a material but not the most accurate.

- *Raytracing*   A real number cruncher, raytracing calculates the reflections on an object's surface by following each light ray from its source back to the camera to calculate how objects and the environment are reflected. This is a more accurate method of producing reflections but at the price of increased rendering times. Though it varies with each scene and the exact settings, raytracing reflections can add an additional 40 percent rendering time to even the most basic of scenes for every object with a Raytrace Material applied.

When creating quality work, sometimes there is no way around spending the rendering time, so reflections and refraction must be added. At the very least, you have options as to how good you can make your reflections. To add reflections to your object, you need to edit the reflection parameter.

Here are some keys to creating a good reflection:

- *Image color*   When using a reflection map, use a map with colors that closely resemble the scene. For complex scenes, it might be quicker to render the scene without the reflected objects and then use the output image map as a reflection map on an object in the scene. Apply the map to the object's reflection map parameter and rerender. It's quicker than raytracing.

- *Blur reflection maps*   Add blur to your reflection by changing the Blur setting and the Blur offset. These two parameters give the reflection a more realistic look because almost nothing reflects a perfect image, other than mirrors.

- *Change map angles*   Instead of applying a reflection map straight on, try changing the angle of the mapping. Though a subtle change, it can sometimes make a nice improvement on the overall look of the material.

- *Make some noise*   MAX has a built-in Noise parameter for the Bitmap material type. Use this noise to "dirty up" the surface reflection so that it does not become a perfect mirror type reflection.

7

- *Don't set Reflection Mapping to 100%*   In most cases 30% to 70% gives much more realistic results. Many beginning 3D artists love to add reflections to everything. This effect is as overdone as the infamous lens flare. Use good judgment when applying reflections to an object and be aware of how objects in the real world reflect.

Thin Wall Refraction

The standard Reflect/Refract map works well as a generic refraction material, but some types of surfaces produce a better effect when using the Thin Wall Refraction material type. Unlike the Reflect/Refract Map that simulates a built-in curved refraction algorithm, the Thin Wall Refraction can be set to a specific amount of refraction and therefore achieves a more realistic refractive surface. The Thin Wall Refraction type is also quicker than the Reflect/Refract map type.

The Thin Wall Refraction type has only a few parameters, some of which have been used before in other materials, such as the Blur parameter (also found in the Reflect/Refract map type). The Thin Wall Refraction map is best when used on objects that are not perfectly round transparent objects.

- *Blur*   Like the Blur parameter in the Reflection map, this option also blurs any objects seen through the refractive surface. Adding blur to the refractive property adds a bit of roughness to the glass surface, sometimes a desirable effect. Typically, almost all maps should have some amount of blur applied to smooth out the edges.

- *Render Parameters*   Thin Wall Refraction can be calculated every frame, the first frame only, or every specified number of frames. Because refractions are very processor intensive, reducing the number of refraction iterations can substantially cut down on rendering time, without the loss of quality as one might expect. Choosing the First Frame Only option is the quickest because the refraction is only calculated one time. The problem is that during the course of animation, if the camera or the object move, the subsequent refraction output will be incorrect. Check the Use Environment Map option if you want to calculate the background map into the refraction calculations. When not checked and when the refractive material passes in front of the background Material (if one is applied), the rendered image will be geometrically incorrect.

- *Thickness Offset*   This parameter sets the distance (10.0 is maximum) the refraction can appear to be higher, based on the thickness of the material. Because this is simulation, you must experiment with each case to see the value of which thickness offset is best. The final result is that the refracted image is shifted an amount based on the Thickness Offset parameter. This makes it appear as though the material has apparent thickness.

- *Bump Map Effect*   This parameter is used to scale the effect of a map present in the Bump map when calculating refraction. When refracting irregular surfaces, a phenomenon occurs known as secondary refraction. This parameter is used to control the secondary refraction by using this parameter value to scale the Bump map. If a Bump map is present and the refraction is too great, reduce this number to a value less than 1.

Matte/Shadow

One of the tricks you will quickly learn is how to improve rendering speed. The simplest way is to reduce the polygon or face count. For some complex scenes, this is simply not possible. There are ways around that, though. Examine the scenario of creating a scene where there are lots of ornate columns in the scene. After running some test renders, you find that each frame takes 15 minutes to render. (It's a big temple.) Instead of running out and spending $30,000 on a small rendering farm, there are alternatives.

Enter the Matte/Shadow material type. This mild-mannered material can save incredible amounts of time for unique rendering situations. The process in which it works is a relatively simple concept.

To Do: Using a Matte/Shadow material

1. Render out a single frame of the scene without the characters. This will be the background map. In the scenario previously stated, this is all the columns and nothing else.

2. Save the resulting image as an image file.

3. Replace the ornate columns with simple cylinders of the lowest possible face count.

4. Create and apply a Matte/Shadow material to all the columns. This material will use the background as the map.

5. Add all other elements to the scene, including characters and any other objects. Also, load the rendered frame from step 2 as a background map.

6. Render the scene as usual. The simplified columns will not be rendered but their shadows will be cast, and they will block the geometry of objects that move behind them. Because of the background map rendered previously and the fact that the replacement columns are invisible, the columns in the rendered background will appear to be in the rendered scene.

Using the Matte/Shadow material requires a little preplanning. There is also the overhead of rendering the background image and the Matte/Shadow material to consider. If your scene has three objects, it might be quicker to just render the scene as is. If your scene has many items that are static and do not move, these are candidates for using the Matte/Shadow material. Although this does save time when substituting complex objects, replacing simple objects with a Matte/Shadow material might actually increase rendering time.

To Do: Using Matte Shadow material

Matte Shadow material can also be used to place elements of the background bitmap in front of geometry. Here's the technique:

1. Set up the background so it renders the way you want it to.

2. If you are using a Camera, Create a Grid and activate it.

3. Activate the Camera view and then Align the Grid to the View. Position the Grid so it is between the camera and the actual geometry in the scene.

4. Use Create Spline to draw in the Camera view to trace key background elements to be moved to the foreground. Be sure to set the initial and drag types of your line to Smooth or Corner, avoid Bezier.

5. Add Extrude modifiers set to 0 to the drawn shapes. This gives spline objects faces instead of just edges.

6. Add Matte/Shadow materials to the shapes and render.

Multi/Sub-Object Materials

Creating complex materials is somewhat easier with the Multi/Sub-Object Material. Unlike Standard materials that are applied to an object as a whole, the Multi/Sub-Object Material is applied to the entire object; then the Sub-Materials are applied to specific faces on the object. For example, if you want to create an elaborate chessboard with a different wood grain on the both the light and dark squares, using the Multi/Sub-Object Material, it's a breeze.

To Do: Creating and applying a Multi/Sub-Object material

1. Open submat.max from the accompanying CD-ROM. This file contains a single box object constructed with multiple segments. This is intentional so that a Multi-Sub-Object Material can be applied.

2. Open the Material Editor and click on the Type button to change the type from Standard to Multi/Sub-Object.

3. When the Material/Map Browser appears, change the Browse From filter type to New and choose Multi/Sub-Object.

4. When requested to either Discard or Keep old material, check the option to keep the material as a sub-material and click on OK. The pre-existing material is now part of the new material.

5. When the Multi/Sub-Material is chosen, the Material Editor opens the new material at the top level, revealing 10 sub-materials (see Figure 7.12). Notice the material in the first slot is the material that occupied that sample slot prior to changing the material type.

6. Because you are only going to use three materials in this exercise, click the Set Number button and enter 3 in the number slot.

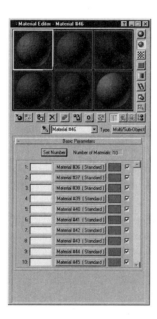

Clicking on any of the material buttons accesses the material properties, as at the top level of the Material Editor. In this exercise, you replace the materials in the material slots with materials that ship with 3DS MAX 2.5.

7. To change a sub-material to a material stored in a library, open the sub-material and click on the Type button. Set the Browse From filter to Mtl Library and choose one of the existing materials. Repeat this procedure for the other two sub-materials.

8. When all three materials have been set, apply the material to the box object, close the Material Editor, and click on the Quick Render button. Notice how each of the sides have a different material applied.

Building Multi/Sub-Object materials is similar to building standard materials; the only difference is in the parenting. All these sub-materials now reside under a single-parent material. Now that you created the material, you need to apply it specifically to the object. This is done by adding a Mesh Select modifier to the object so that you can access individual faces on the object's surface.

7

9. Select the box object and add an EditMesh Modifier. Open the Sub-Object selection and choose Face as the Sub-Object level of selection.

10. In the Edit Surface rollout (see Figure 7.13), at the very bottom is a button labeled Select by ID and a field above it labeled ID. Click the Select by ID button and choose 1 as the ID Number. Notice that the faces on the top of the box object turn red, indicating the Sub-Object selection.

11. With the top faces selected, use the Alt key to remove all four corner faces from the selection. This gives the selection set a shape similar to a cross or plus sign (see Figure 7.14).

12. Now that just the middle faces are selected from the top plane, change the Material ID to 3 using the spinner or by typing a 3 in the Material ID slot.

13. Click the Render Last button to see how the material has been reassigned to the new faces.

Multi/Sub-Object Materials are applied at the Face Sub-Object Selection Level and as such, either a MeshSelect or EditMesh Modifier must be applied if a Face Sub-Object Selection Level cannot be achieved otherwise. You can also collapse the parametric object to an Editable Mesh and gain direct access to the faces although any Modifiers applied to the object become permanent and are no longer accessible.

FIGURE 7.13.

The EditMesh Modifier is used to select specific Sub-Object levels of an object. At the Face level, individual object faces can be selected and their Material IDs can be set.

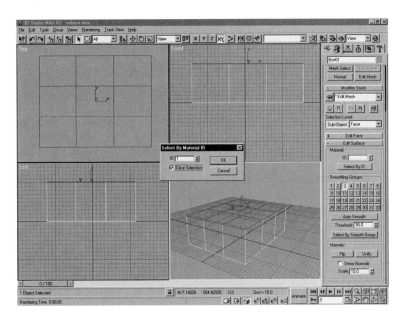

FIGURE 7.14.

Using the EditMesh Modifier, the top faces of the box have been selected by Material ID. Using the Alt key, the corner faces have been deselected so that only the middle faces are still selected (shown darker).

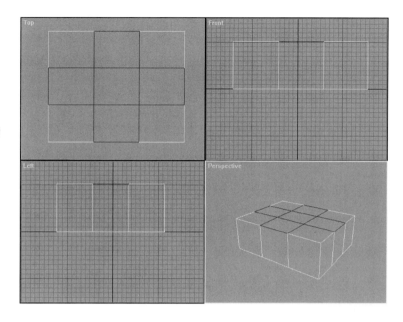

Note The EditMesh Modifier can be memory intensive and so alternative methods, such as the MeshSelect Modifier, are preferred when possible.

Raytrace Materials

The processor hog of them all, raytracing produces fantastic reflections and refractions, but at a severe increase in rendering time. MAX has a unique solution to that problem: Raytrace the objects that need raytracing and use faster rendering algorithms for those that do not need all that processing power. This translates to major savings when rendering reflective surfaces.

Visualize this scenario: a scene in a greasy-spoon diner. There is a lot of chrome, silverware, cooking utensils, and lights. Raytracing the entire scene can take an enormous amount of computing power and time to create even a small animation. Now imagine if you raytrace only the chrome and use standard reflection maps to render everything else. The worn vinyl stools and booths don't need to be raytraced. The counter top can be so worn that it won't be shiny enough to require raytracing. By selectively choosing which objects or even portions of objects require raytracing, you can optimize the rendering process.

7

With that said, how do you go about using the Raytrace Material type? You can find the Raytracer in two places: as a Raytrace material and as a Raytrace map. They are identical in their performance of raytracing; the difference is that one is applied to an entire material and the other to a specific property within a material.

Using the Raytrace material or Raytrace map involves many parameters. To avoid confusion, we will discuss the basic parameters used to produce a common reflection.

To Do: Creating a basic Raytraced material

1. Reset MAX and open raytraz.max from the accompanying CD-ROM. This scene file contains a torus on a box with two cylinders in the center.

2. To speed things up, set the rendering output to 320×240. Render the scene using the QuickRender button while the Perspective view is the active view. Notice the lack of reflections on the cylinder objects in the center.

3. Open the Material Editor and select the material in the first sample slot (named MyRays). Change its type to Raytrace by clicking on the Type button and selecting Raytrace from the Material/Map Browser.

4. Render the scene to see the difference between the previous material and the one converted to the Raytrace type. You shouldn't see a perceivable difference.

   The reason that there is no difference between the materials is that the Raytrace parameters are based on the luminance value of the color swatches. As you can see in Figure 7.15, the color swatch for reflection is black. When using the Raytrace material, the closer the color swatch is to black, the less the effect. For more reflectivity, shift the color swatch closer to white.

5. Click on the Reflect color swatch to display the color selector. Set the Whiteness value to midway to create a midlevel gray, about the same color as the Diffuse color swatch. Rerender the scene. The torus and the box object are reflected on the cylinders.

6. To increase the reflection, set the Reflect color swatch closer to white. The result is a more distinct reflection.

You can use the Raytrace material for either reflection or refractions with more accurate results than you achieve using the Reflect/Refract map described earlier. Regardless of which way you use the Raytrace material, the degree of the property is based on the value in the color swatch with the effect decreasing as the color gets closer to black and the effect increasing as the color swatch moves closer toward white.

FIGURE 7.15.

Use the color swatch to control the amount of effect for all the controls in the Raytrace material.

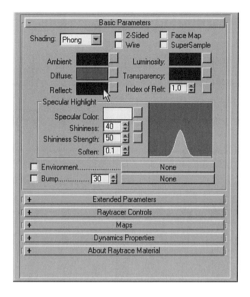

Animating Materials

One of the powerful built-in features of MAX is that nearly every attribute or property can be animated. This includes materials and their properties. Colors and transparency amount can be changed; even maps can be changed over the course of the animation. By animating materials, objects can be made to age, disappear, or completely change surface characteristics.

For the most part, animating a material is no different than animating any other aspect of MAX. Simply set the initial parameters, turn on the Animate button, set the time slider, and make the changes. The changes span the time between the initial frame and the current frame. To create an animated material that spans the entire length of the animation segment, set the initial parameters at frame zero and the changes at the final frame.

When materials are animated, the attributes can be adjusted using the TrackView window. Working in the TrackView window is explained later in this book. For now, you need to know that when the animated parameters are keyed (meaning key frames are created for the changes), TrackView enables you to move those keys to different times or change the values of the key parameters.

7

To Do: Creating an animated lava material

1. Reset MAX and create a geosphere in the Front view.

2. Open the Material Editor and select the first sample slot. Click on the Diffuse Map button, next to the Diffuse color swatch (see Figure 7.16), and select Noise as the material type from the Material/Map Browser.

3. In the Noise parameters section, click on the Color #1 color swatch (Black) and change it to a bright red. Then click on the Color #2 color swatch (White) and change it to a bright yellow. Set the Noise Type to Fractal.

FIGURE 7.16.

Clicking the Diffuse Map button takes you directly to the Diffuse Map properties. From here, you can set Diffuse map proper-ties, change type, or animate Diffuse map properties.

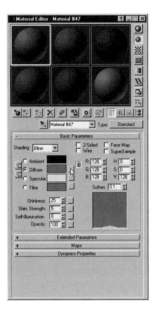

To animate the features, you must turn on the Animate button. When the Animate button is on (shown in the down state and glowing red), all changes are recorded as key frames, resulting in an animated feature.

4. Turn on the Animate button and set the time slider to the final frame by clicking the Go to End button (shown in Figure 7.17).

5. In the Noise Parameters section of the Diffuse Map, set the Phase value to 5. Turn off the Animate button.

6. Click on the Go to Parent button and access the Maps section at the Parent level. You will see the Diffuse Map has been set to a Map# with the material type in parentheses (see Figure 7.18).

7. Drag and drop the Diffuse material over to the Bump Map button. When prompted choose Instance. This creates an instance of this material on the Bump property as well. Any changes to this material is reflected in both the Diffuse and the Bump properties.

FIGURE 7.17.

When the Animate button is turned on, all actions are recorded and parameter changes will be animated. The time slider must also be advanced, otherwise the change will be instant, resulting in a change that isn't noticeable, because it would occur in a single frame.

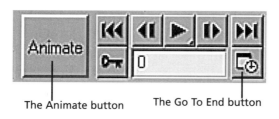

The Animate button   The Go To End button

FIGURE 7.18.

The Diffuse Map button shows the Map number and the name of the material or bitmap used for that map.

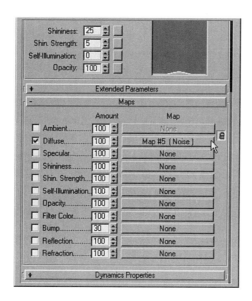

7

You have animated your first material and now you can see how it looks. You can render the entire scene to an .avi file (which can take a while) or you can read the next section for an easier solution to see what an animated material looks like. For the sake of time, don't render the scene, read on.

Making an Animated Material Preview

You decided you want to take the quick approach to see how an animated material performs, as opposed to rendering out the entire scene. Good choice. For any but the most basic scenes, that means waiting a while just to see if your texture looks right. Fortunately, MAX provides a quicker solution. Just render the material.

To render out just the material, you simply need to select the material in the Material Editor and use the Make Preview button, located on the Material Editor (see Figure 7.19). You have a few options to create a material preview, as listed here:

- *Active Time Segment*   When checked, this renders the material for the entire length set for the scene.

- *Custom Range*   Choose a range of frames to render. Use this if the animation length is longer than the animated material or when just a portion of the animated material is in question.

- *Every Nth Frame*   For lengthy animations, using the Every Nth Frame option instructs 3DS MAX 2.5 to render 1 of every frame specified in the value slot. For example, setting the value to 2 renders every other frame. Setting it to 3 renders every third frame, and so on.

- *Playback FPS*   Use this to set the frame rate of the animated material preview. When working in different mediums, such as CD-ROM playback versus film, the frame rates would be different. If the animated material frame rate was not set accurately, the intended effect would not be achieved when the material was rendered.

- *Percent of Output*   Change this parameter to create a larger or smaller output size. This can be set to make the output larger than the material sample slot by putting in values greater than 100, or smaller than the sample slot by putting in values smaller than 100.

After the Make Preview button has been pressed, the options selected, and the animation created, MAX starts the Media Player and loads the material preview. MAX saves all previews using the default name of _medit in the Previews directory under the MAX directory. This means that subsequently created material previews will write over existing previews, unless saved.

FIGURE 7.19.

The Make Preview button is used to create an animated preview of the selected material. When created, the preview appears through the standard Windows MediaPlayer in the form of an .avi file.

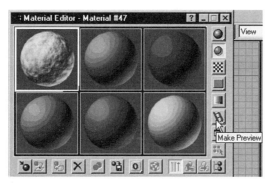

The Make Preview button is a flyout menu that has Play Preview and Save Preview buttons on it. If you decide you want to make previews of multiple materials, each will have to be saved so that it is not overwritten. For saving a material preview, use the Save Preview button and save as you save any other file. Use the Play Preview button to load and play previously saved or rendered material previews.

To Do: Animating clouds on a Planet material

▼ To Do

1. Reset MAX and open the Material Editor. In a previous exercise (Changing a Map Type), you created a Planet material with clouds. Load that material or load the myEarth material from the tymax.mat material library found on the accompanying CD-ROM.

2. Using the Material/Map Browser, select the Clouds Sub-Material. Click on the Diffuse Map button to open the Noise material parameters.

3. In the MAX interface, set the time slider to 100. Click the Animate button to invoke Animate mode. You will know you are in Animate mode because the Animate button will be red and a red border will be drawn around the active view.

4. In the Noise parameters, set the Phase parameter to 5. Turn off the Animate button.

5. Click on the Make Preview button on the Material Editor to create a Preview of the animated material. Be sure the Preview Range is set to Active Time Segment and
▲ click OK.

MAX temporarily closes the Material Editor and a progress bar appears at the bottom of the screen. This indicates the progress of the preview for the selected material. When completed, the standard Windows MediaPlayer activates and the current material animated preview appears as an .avi file. Click Play on the MediaPlayer to watch the animated clouds roll by.

7

The Camera Mapping Modifier

MAX does an excellent job of creating mapping coordinates for objects. Although these work great, at times you might want to use a camera angle as the mapping angle. Whenever you need the mapping to coincide with that of the camera, use the Camera Mapping Modifier. This Modifier applies planar mapping coordinates to the selected object, based on the camera chosen from the Modifier's parameters.

There are two types of Camera Mapping Modifiers. One is World Space; the other is Object Space. The World Space Modifier will move with the camera so that as the camera changes position during the animation, the mapping is repositioned parallel to the plane of the camera. The Object Space Modifier is the opposite, creating a mapping coordinate based on the position of the camera at frame 0. After that, the movement of the camera has no effect.

The World Space Camera Mapping Modifier has unique instances when you use it. Suppose you have an object that you want to blend into the background. By applying the same map as the background and using the Camera Mapping Modifier, you can match the angle of the material mapping to that of the camera. If the object is moved, or the scene is shot from a different angle, the material is remapped to the object based on the chosen camera's mapping angle. This type of effect is also useful for projecting images on both the background and objects, such as logos. Using Screen environment mapping, the entire map can be seen on the background and any objects using this Camera Mapping Modifier. The Camera Mapping Modifier is applied in the Modify Panel, just as other Modifiers are applied.

The Object Space Camera Mapping Modifier enables you distort the background bitmap for Terminator II style effects. Suppose you want to animate a concrete floor suddenly bulging up. You load in background video, Camera Match it, and then create geometry to replace the floor. Add an Object Camera Mapping Modifier so the background video is perfectly mapped to the new floor. Now if you bulge or distort the floor, it appears to be happening in the background video.

Dynamics Properties

The Dynamic Properties rollout is used to apply physical characteristics to the material. When applied in this manner, materials can be used for both visual effect and physics simulation, based on the type of material. The Dynamics Property is discussed in a later chapter and is mentioned here because it is found in the Material Editor. Changing parameters in the Dynamics Properties rollout has no effect on the way that materials are rendered. The parameters of the Dynamics Properties rollout are used exclusively by the Dynamics Utility, found on the Utility Panel.

Summary

Creating materials for 3D models is an art in itself. Remember that being creative in using the tools to get the right effect accounts for more than anything else in the field of 3D graphics. Some materials are easy to create, others more difficult. Do not let the limitations of your tools be the limit of your imagination.

One important note about materials: Don't make your materials too perfect. One of the biggest mistakes that beginning 3D artists make is to make materials too perfect. In real life there are scuffs, scratches, dents, and dirt. Unless you create scenes that depict sterile product promotion, your object's materials should not be completely shiny and unflawed. This is the first giveaway that the scene is computer generated.

It's common for 3D artists to joke about the Make Art plug-in. The truth is, some people believe you need a tool for everything, every modeling or material situation. The reality of the matter is that will never happen, nor should we hope for it. Just as an oil painter uses a palette of colors to create a beautiful painting, so must we use the palette of tools provided to us. Regardless of whether we are modeling or creating materials, let your mind set the limit, not the tools.

Q&A

Q When using the Material/Map Browser, I noticed that occasionally a map has a red parallelogram next to it. What does that mean?

A When a map has a red parallelogram next to it, the map is currently used in the scene and the map has the Show Map in Viewport option turned on.

Q How can I animate the diffuse map to completely change from one map to another? Even though I activate the Animate button when changing maps, the same last map overrides the first.

A To animate a diffuse map (or an map), there are two solutions. First, you can use an .avi file of the animated maps when assigning a map. Though that works, it requires you to render the animated sequence of maps in another program, such as Adobe Premiere. Another method is to make the material type of the attribute a Blend material type. Using this method, simply animate the amount of blend from 0 to 100 to coincide with the timing required to simulate the effect. This method is easier and lets 3DS MAX 2.5 do the morphing work for you. Each has advantages and it is really a matter of situation to decide which method is best for you.

7

Q **Why does the Raytrace Material I've applied an object not reflect the surrounding objects?**

A Check the color used in the Reflect color swatch. The Raytrace Material uses luminance values of the grayscale color swatch to create reflections. As the color gets closer to black, there is less effect applied to the object. Conversely, as the color moves closer to white, the effect increases.

Q **I've created a number of special materials and saved them into a Material Library, but I can't located them on my hard drive. Where are libraries stored and how can I view them?**

A Unless the material was stored in the default library, you must create your own name for any saved libraries. The default directory for all libraries is in the MAX directory under the Matlibs sub-directory. All Material Libraries are given the extension .mat, so search for that if a saved library is not found in the default directory. To load existing or saved libraries, Press the Get Material button, select Mtl Libraries in the Browse From filter, and click on Open in the File section of the Material/Map Browser. Simply select the library from the default material directory or browse for one placed elsewhere.

DAY 8

Lighting and Atmosphere

Someone famous once said, "Let there be light." Movie directors are always commanding, "Lights! Camera! Action!" It certainly gives the impression that perhaps light is an important element in both life and art. This couldn't be more true than it is in 3D computer animation.

Every scene intended for still imagery or animation depends highly on lighting to give it life. By today's lesson, you've become familiar with the MAX interface and discovered how to use MAX to create models and materials. Today's lesson starts the second week of learning MAX and covers the final element to complete your composition—lighting.

Illumination and Atmosphere

In the real world, we can't see anything without light. The same is true in the virtual world. Lighting provides many things to your scene, but two basic effects of lighting are illumination and atmosphere.

Consider illumination as the minimal application of lighting necessary to allow you to see the objects in your scene. MAX realizes the concept of minimal light for illumination, so it actually supplies default lighting in your scene. This way, the objects in your scene will always be visible—even if you don't add any lights your-self. After you add your own lighting, MAX turns off its default lighting to give you complete control on how light affects every object. You'll explore each type of light and its unique attributes later in this chapter in the section "Types of Lights."

The second basic effect of lighting is atmosphere. Webster defines atmosphere as "environment; predominant aspect or mood." Thus, carefully planned lighting has a dramatic effect on how your scene is interpreted by your audience. Consider the two scenes in Figure 8.1. The image on the left has basic white lights distributed evenly throughout the scene. The resulting image is flat and very sterile. It simply has no life; it appears artificial. The image on the right has more natural yellow and white lighting with careful placement of shadows. This image has depth and a soft, realistic feel.

FIGURE 8.1.

Lighting plays a very important role in how your scene is perceived by your audience.

> **Tip**
>
> When you light your scene, imagine you are a set designer or interior designer. Your scene is your set, or room. By creative placement and use of color, you allow your scene to take on characteristics of its own. For example, don't limit yourself to placing lights at the ceiling level as you might have in any room in your home or office. Instead, create dramatic areas of light and shadow by adding spotlights at the floor level shining up, creating interesting shadows of room objects on the walls and ceilings. The techniques of each type of light available are discussed in the following chapter. However, it's your creative use and combination of these lights that will set your scene apart.

Types of Lights

8

MAX offers the following seven types of lights to create different effects:

- Omni
- Target Spot
- Target Direct
- Free Spot
- Free Direct
- Sunlight
- Ambient

The first five are actual light objects found in the Lights section of the Create Panel. Sunlight is a System that creates a directional light that is automatically animated at the proper rotation and movement of the real-world sun given a specified date and time. Ambient light refers to general lighting that illuminates every object in your scene. Ambient light is set in the Environment dialog box. Take a close look at creating each of these types of lights; start with a basic MAX scene with a few objects and no lights and then add different light types to see the effects.

 Note

As mentioned, Sunlight is what MAX terms a System. A *System* combines geometry and some predefined links and possibly motion to simulate complex object creation or animation. Sunlight is a good example that creates the directional light for the sun, and also the accurate rotation of the sunlight object based on your input date and time.

Creating Omni Lights

Omni lights are similar to natural lighting because they cast light in all directions and have the option of casting shadows. You might want to start lighting your scene by adding one or two Omni lights to properly illuminate the scene and then adding different lights for added effects.

To Do: Setting Omni lights

1. Open the file lighting.max from the accompanying CD-ROM and save it to your hard drive. Periodically save your work as you progress through the next few sections. You'll use this same file for the "Adjusting Lights and Shadows" section later in this chapter.

2. Make sure your Camera viewport is set to display Smooth and Highlights by right-clicking on the viewport name and making the appropriate selection. This enables you to see the effects of moving your lights around in real-time.

3. To create an Omni light, click the Create tab to view the Create Panel; then click the Lights icon to view the light types. Figure 8.2 shows the location of these buttons as well as the buttons for the various types of lights.

FIGURE 8.2.

You access all the light objects by clicking the Create tab and the Lights icon.

4. Click on the Omni icon and click anywhere in any viewport to add the light.

After you add the Omni light, which is the first light you created in this scene, the default lighting MAX supplies will be turned off. Because you are always free to move the light around, it really doesn't matter where you click to add the light.

 Note   When you select Smooth and Highlight in a MAX viewport, you only see the illumination effects of any light. You won't see any shadows.

5. Click the Select and Move tool from the toolbar and select your Omni light. Move it around the scene to see the dramatic differences in scene lighting you can achieve with just one light.

6. This is also a good time to name your light. As you add more than one light, it will be easier to go back and edit any given light if it has a descriptive name. Click in the text entry field in the Name and Color section of the Lights Panel (refer to Figure 8.2). Name this light Omni Backlight (you'll see why in the next step).

7. Select the Top viewport and position the light opposite the camera object, behind the box. See Figure 8.3 for the positioning of this and the next two Omni lights.

FIGURE 8.3.

The positioning of three Omni lights around your objects can provide good, even lighting as a basis for illuminating your entire scene.

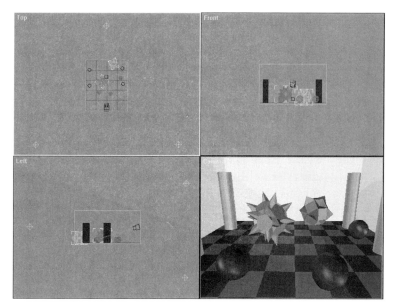

8. Use the same procedure above to add two more Omni lights. Position each using the Top viewport. Place one in the lower-left corner and the other in the lower-right corner as shown in Figure 8.3.

9. Select your second light and switch to the Left viewport. Using the Select and Move tool, move the light up until it is above the box. Select the third light and move it down below the box as shown in Figure 8.3.

▲ 10. Save the changes to mylighting.max.

The positioning of these three Omni lights provides a good basic lighting for your scene. In most cases, you will not want to stop with basic lighting. Although it illuminates the objects, the look is flat and lacks any depth. You'll look at the specific parameters for Omni lights later. For now, add a different type of light.

Creating Target Spot and Free Spotlights

Spotlights are the equivalent of real-world flashlights or theater spotlights. They create a focused beam of light you can point at different objects or areas. You have full control over the width and intensity of the beam of light and whether they cast shadows. Add one of each and see the difference between the two.

To Do: Adding Target Spot and Free Spotlights

1. In the Lights Panel, click Target Spot.

2. You create the spotlight and its target by clicking the left mouse button and dragging. The first click sets the spot, and the drag sets the direction of the target. When you release the mouse button, the target is created. In the Left viewport, click in the upper-left corner and drag toward the middle of the floor and release.

Notice the cone that is created between the spot and its target as you drag to set the target (shown in Figure 8.4). This represents the spotlight's beam of light. It is made up of two parts called the Hotspot and the Falloff. You adjust these settings in the Spotlight Parameters section of the Lights Panel; they will be covered in the next section. By default, the cone will disappear when you release the mouse. For now, just notice the spot and its target.

FIGURE 8.4.

Spotlights create a cone, or beam of light, much like a flashlight or theater spotlight.

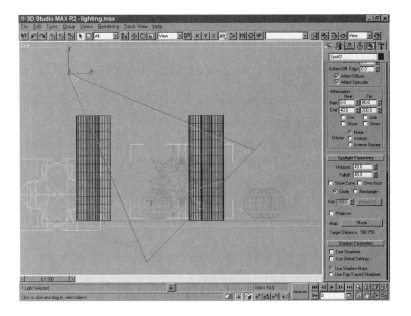

You can select either the spot or its target and move it any way you like. Both can be animated to move across your scene or even to follow an object through your scene. Each object can also be animated independently of the other. For example, you can animate the spot object moving to the left and the target object moving up. Now create a Free Spot.

To Do: Creating a Free Spot

1. In the Lights Panel, click Free Spot.

2. A Free Spot has no target object. Its cone (beam of light) will be created from the point where you click in a direction away from the spot.

3. Click somewhere in this room scene in any viewport and notice how the spot and its cone appear.

4. Use the Select and Rotate tool to align and direct your Free Spot as needed.

▲ 5. Save the changes to lighting.max.

The light you create will not be affected in any way by creating a target versus a Free Spot. The main advantage to a Free Spot is you have only one object to adjust when animating its movement. This is especially convenient when you animate a light along a path; it will be easier to direct the light along a path with only one object to worry about.

Adjusting a Spotlight's Hotspot and Falloff

Spotlights have a unique setting for their beam of light, referred to as the cone in MAX. Think of the Hotspot as the area that will be uniformly lit. Falloff determines the area extending outward from the Hotspot. This area is filled with diminishing light that gradually fades to transparent. Use Falloff to give your beam of light a soft edge. Figure 8.5 shows two different settings for a spotlight. On the left, little use of Falloff results in a hard edge to the spotlight. The image on the right uses Falloff to soften the edges of the beam, or cone, of light.

FIGURE 8.5.

Hotspot and Falloff settings dramatically affect the appearance of a spotlight.

Explore how you display a spotlight's cone in MAX's viewports, and how you adjust both Hotspot and Falloff.

To Do: Displaying a spotlight's cone

1. Select one of your spotlights and click the Modify tab to access its parameters.

2. Pan the Modify Panel until you see the Spotlight Parameters rollup section.

3. Check the box next to Show Cone. This turns on the display of the cone in all viewports.

4. By default, the Falloff is set slightly larger than the Hotspot. This setting gives you a hard edge spotlight. Select the Camera viewport and click the Quick Render button in the toolbar to render the default settings. Your image should resemble the left image of Figure 8.5 (without the shadows).

5. Change the Hotspot, making it smaller. Change the setting from 43 to 25. Notice how the cone has changed in the viewport. The Hotspot is the inner cone and shrinks as we reduce its size (see Figure 8.6).

FIGURE 8.6.

You change how your spotlight appears with settings in the Spotlight Parameters rollup in the Modify Panel.

6. Click Quick Render again to rerender the image and see the difference. Your image should resemble the right image of Figure 8.5 (without the shadows).

  7. Save the changes to lighting.max.

Creating Target Direct and Target Free Lights

Directional lights, in the forms of Target Direct and Free Direct, are similar to spotlights in that they have a Hotspot and Falloff cone. The difference is that directional lights project light in parallel lines in one direction. The best way to differentiate between spots and directional lights is the shape of their beam of light. Spotlights create a flared cone-shaped beam, and directional lights create a consistent size cylinder-shaped beam. Directional lights are great for sunlight. In fact, a directional light is used in the built-in Sunlight System in MAX. The creation method for Target Direct and Target Free lights is exactly the same as Target Spot and Free Spot.

Creating the Sun

Now that you know what a directional light is, let's see the best use for one—creating the sun. MAX has a great built-in System enabling you to input a date and time for your scene. After you do that, you simply click to add the sun and MAX does the rest. You can animate the movement of the sun throughout the day, or create different animation accurately portraying the sun's position at different times of day.

Add the sun to your MAX scene and see how easy Systems are to use.

To Do: Using Systems

1. To best see the results of the Sunlight System, hide all the lights you added. Using the same lighting.max scene, select all the lights in your scene by clicking the Selection Filter drop-down menu in the toolbar. When the menu drops down, select Lights, as shown in Figure 8.7.

FIGURE 8.7.

The use of the Selection Filters can assist in selecting only certain types of objects.

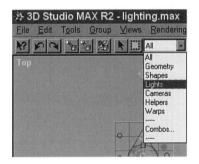

2. Now click the Edit menu and the Select All command. Because you designated Lights in the Selection Filter, only lights will be selected.

3. Click the Display tab and the Hide Selected button in the Hide rollup as shown in Figure 8.8.

FIGURE 8.8.

Use the Display Panel to hide objects you don't currently need in your scene but might need later.

4. Click on the Create tab and the Systems icon.

5. Under the Object Type rollup, click Sunlight, as shown in Figure 8.9.

FIGURE **8.9.**

Systems, such as Sunlight, are found in the Systems icon on the Create Panel.

6. When you click Sunlight, you see the Parameters rollup. You can designate the exact time of day, year, and time zone for your sun. Click the Get Location button and select a geographic location.

7. Figure 8.10 shows the Geographic Location dialog box. You can click on the map, or scroll the locations and pick a city near your desired location.

FIGURE **8.10.**

The Sunlight System enables you to pick an exact geographic location for you scene.

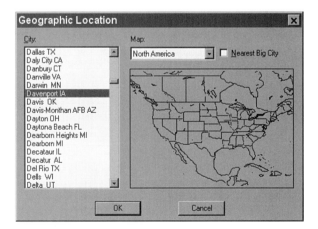

8. After you set the location, click once in the center of the room in the Top viewport. Placing the sunlight takes two clicks; this first click places the light in the scene.

9. After clicking once, drag the cursor to set the Orbital Scale. This simply sets the distance between the sun's directional light and its target. Drag until the light is beyond the boundaries of your room; then click a second time to set the light (see Figure 8.11).

FIGURE 8.11.

The Sunlight System places a directional light that orbits around its target.

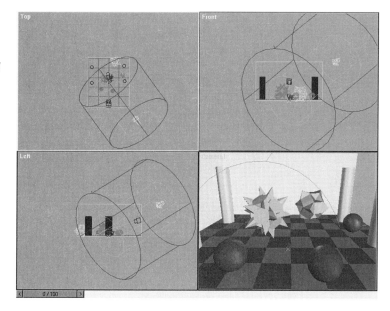

10. With the sunlight selected, click the Motion Panel to access its Control Parameters. Adjust the time of day or month settings to see the sun orbit the target (see Figure 8.12).

11. Save the changes to lighting.max.

FIGURE 8.12.

Access the Sunlight's Control Parameters from the Motion Panel to make changes, or to animate the sunlight.

Adjusting Lights and Shadows

Placing any type of light in MAX with default settings is easy and will give you adequate scene illumination. But that's about it. Fortunately, it is equally easy to adjust just about every aspect of each light. In addition to ease of adjustment, it's also possible to animate most every aspect of each light. In this section, you review many of the common settings of all the light types you will use regularly.

Note

Lights, perhaps more than any other feature in MAX, take experimentation with each unique project. Don't become frustrated if you find yourself spending an hour adjusting lighting aspects to get the right mix. Everyone who spends time working with lights will see the benefits in his final image or animation. This is not an area you can afford to simply accept the default settings.

Attenuation

Attenuation describes the distance over which a light illuminates or otherwise affects objects in your scene. The use of this setting helps you simulate the real-world property of light. Your lights diminish the farther away you get from their source. By default, MAX lights affect every object in your scene regardless of distance. Using attenuation creates more realistic lighting and saves in rendering time. It also keeps your scene from being over-lit. Imagine you create a neighborhood scene and add a porch light on a house. You don't want that light illuminating the neighbors' house three doors down the street. Rather, it should have a distance of 15 feet or so. Using attenuation, you set those limits.

Return to your example MAX files to see how to set attenuation.

To Do: Setting Attenuation

1. Click the Display tab, and the UnHide All button in the Hide rollup to unhide the lights in this scene.

2. In the Top viewport, select one of the Omni lights and click the Modify tab.

3. To make your changes very obvious, change the color of the light to red. In the General Parameters rollout, click the gray square next to the Color On check box. In the Color Selector dialog box, click on the palette to select a bright red. Figure 8.13 shows the Color Selection square and the Attenuation area of the General Parameters rollup.

FIGURE 8.13.

The Attenuation settings in the Modify Panel.

There are two setting for Attenuation: Near and Far. You might want to think of these as ways of fading the light in and out from the source. Each has a Start and End setting that moves a visible ring around the light in the viewports. To set Far attenuation for this example, perform the following steps:

4. Check the boxes for Use and Show for Far Attenuation as seen in Figure 8.13. Use the spinners to set the Start and End settings. You can see the results of adjusting the spinners in the viewports—watch while you drag the spinners to see what happens. Set Start to 754 and End to 793. This makes the light affect the scene to a point about halfway through the room.

5. Select the Camera viewport and click Quick Render in the toolbar to see the results of your Attenuation settings.

▲   6. Save the changes to lighting.max.

Figure 8.14 shows a comparison of this light with and without attenuation.

FIGURE 8.14.

Attenuation determines the effective range of any given light in your scene.

Color and Intensity of Lights

Lights, just like materials in MAX, have color. You can create a light that is blue, red, white, or whatever you like. You can even animate a light's color (covered later in this chapter in the "Animating Lights" section). MAX describes colors, as all computers do, in combinations of RGB (red, green, blue). However, you can manipulate colors in a variety of ways.

Figure 8.15 shows the Color Selector dialog box you get when you click on the Color Picker square in the General Parameters rollup for any light you create. From this dialog box, there are many ways to adjust the color. The large box on the left allows you to select a hue as a starting point. Hue is basically what most people refer to when they talk about the color of an object. From there, you can adjust the Blackness slider along the box's left side or the Whiteness slider along the right. These settings do what you expect them to; Blackness makes the color darker and Whiteness lightens the color.

FIGURE 8.15.

The standard MAX Color Selector dialog box, as displayed when you edit the color of a light.

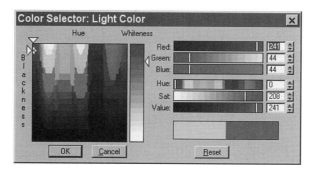

Adjusting the Whiteness setting for a color actually adjusts the Saturation level. Adjusting the Whiteness slider up is increasing saturation, creating a pure form of the color that is not being mixed with other colors. Adjusting the Blackness affects the Value or relative darkness of lightness of the hue (color). Although it is helpful to realize what is happening as you adjust these sliders, the most important aspect is to learn how to quickly get the results you need. It's not necessary to master an understanding of MAX's HSV or RGB color model.

Why will you want to change the color of light? Because by default, MAX assigns each light a RGB color value of 180, 180, 180. This gives a dull off-white light that is good for illumination but not very natural in appearance. Experiment with more yellow-white light for natural lighting. You can create much softer lit, realistic environments with the proper use of color.

Including and Excluding Objects

If you take a look back at the General Parameters rollup in Figure 8.13, you see an Exclude button. Use this button to limit the objects in your scene that are affected by any given light you create. Figure 8.16 shows the Exclude/Include dialog box you get when you click the Exclude button. In this figure, Sphere01 and Sphere03 have been excluded from all effects of this light. You simply click on each object name, or multiple-click names while holding down the Ctrl key. You add the objects to the Exclude list by copying them to the list box on the right using the arrow keys between the two lists. Note the radio buttons for Exclude or Include at the top of the dialog box. You can easily switch the list from an Exclude to an Include list by switching this selection. Similarly, you can change the designation of what is excluded or included by switching the radio buttons for Illumination, Shadow Casting, or both.

FIGURE 8.16.

The Exclude/Include dialog box enables you to select from a list of all the objects currently visible in your scene.

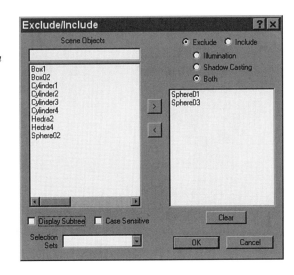

Each light has only one Exclude or Include list. Although this is fine under most circumstances, the situation can arise in which you have items on the list you want different exclusions for. For example, you might want to exclude shadow casting for Sphere01 and Sphere02 but only want to exclude illumination for Sphere01. In this case, you can't select the Both setting in the Exclude dialog box, so what do you do? Fortunately, each object has its own object properties. In this, and similar situations, you have to use the objects' individual settings.

To Do: Setting exclusions

1. Open the lighting.max file again.

2. Right-click on the Sphere02 object located in the lower-left corner when viewing the camera viewport. This brings up the Object Properties dialog box shown in Figure 8.17.

3. In the section labeled Rendering Control, remove the check in the check box for Cast Shadows. This setting is only for the Sphere02 object and solves your little dilemma.

▲ 4. Save the changes to lighting.max.

FIGURE 8.17.

The Object Properties dialog box adds another level of control for excluding individual objects from casting shadows.

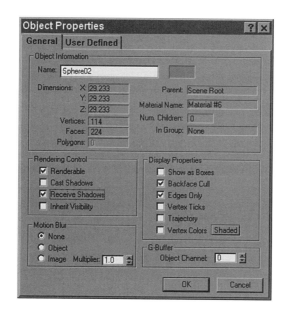

8

Using Shadows

Where there are lights, there are shadows. Just as the proper use of light can add a great deal of realism to your scene, the proper use of shadows can create the convincing depth and real-world believability your scene might need.

Obviously, all projects are different in their needs, but when shadows are not used, the scene definitely suffers from a lack of depth. The downside to shadows often is increased rendering time. Depending on the type of shadows you define, this added rendering time can be dramatic. MAX gives you two types of shadows: Shadow Maps and Raytraced Shadows.

In MAX, any light can cast shadows. The process of turning shadows on is two-part. First, you must turn shadows on for each light, and then you need to tell MAX to render shadows when you set the render parameters. Read on to learn how to cast some shadows in your lighting scene.

Shadow Maps

The quickest way to render shadows is by applying a Shadow Map. Shadow Maps are actually bitmaps MAX creates during the rendering process and applies to the image. The shadow created has a soft edge, and although it might work for most instances, it is not the most accurate way to create shadows. The trade-off it offers for its less accurate method is a quicker rendering time than the Raytraced Shadows alternative. This method works for most instances, unless you need to work with shadows from objects that are rendered in wireframe, or are in any way transparent. Use the same lighting.max file you've been using and adjust some of the lights to cast shadows.

To Do: Casting shadows

1. Open lighting.max.

2. Select the spotlight and click the Modify tab.

3. Pan the Modify Panel, if necessary, until you see the rollups called Shadow Parameters as seen in Figure 8.18.

FIGURE 8.18.

The settings for shadows your lights cast are in the Shadow Parameters rollup of the light's Modify Panel.

We've mentioned panning the various panels alongside the viewports many times to see a particular rollup section. We wouldn't actually be doing the program justice if we didn't use the rollups when it is convenient. Each section, referred to as a *rollup*, has a title bar with a plus or minus symbol on its far-left side. A plus means it is rolled up and you can expand it by clicking on it, and a minus means it is expanded and you can roll it up by clicking on it. Using the rollups might be faster than using the grabber hand to pan the panels. How you navigate the interface is up to you. A right-click in an open area also brings up a list of all the rollups available. For very long rollups, this is a handy way to jump to the place you need to go.

4. Click the check box next to Cast Shadows to turn shadows on for this light. Notice the default shadow type is to use Shadow Maps.

5. Select the Camera viewport and click the Render Scene button in the toolbar to set up the rendering with shadows.

6. Figure 8.19 shows the portion of the Render Scene dialog box where you tell MAX whether or not to render shadows. By default, this check box is checked and shadows are rendered.

FIGURE 8.19.

You tell MAX whether or not to render shadows in the Render Scene dialog box.

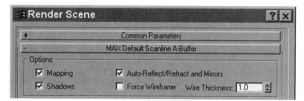

8

7. Click the Render button to see the default shadows cast from this light. Your image should resemble Figure 8.20.

▲ 8. Save the changes to lighting.max.

FIGURE 8.20.

The default settings for shadows using Shadow Maps provides quick rendering and soft edge shadows.

Tip

As mentioned, the Cast Shadows check box is checked by MAX as a default, so shadows render without you having to make any change to this setting. However, as you work, you might want to check or remove the check mark from this box depending on whether you want to wait for shadows to render or not. Many times, during the design stages of your project, you'll be rendering many times over just for positioning and movement and won't need to see things such as materials and shadows. To help speed things up, MAX provides two settings for rendering that you can set up: one for final production and one for proofing draft renderings. You might want to set up the draft mode without materials and shadows. Day 13, "Rendering," covers these setting in the "Render Scene Dialog Box" section.

As with everything in MAX, the default settings get you started and the rest is up to experimentation. For example, it is possible to get shadows with slightly less soft edges than what you see with the default settings for Shadow Mapped shadows. You do so by adjusting the Map Size and Sample Range in the Shadow Parameters. However, adjusting the Map Size can create slower renderings by creating a more demanding bitmap Shadow Map and increasing the sampling to create more defined edges, which runs the risk you will see some jaggedness to the edges.

The last item to take note of is the check box for Use Global Settings. If you decide to experiment with the different settings for a particular light, you need to decide whether you want to make the settings global (affecting every light in the scene) or specific to only the one light. If you want the settings global, check the Use Global Settings option.

Raytraced Shadows

Now that we've added shadows, let's take the next step. Really cool shadows. Raytraced Shadows represent the ultimate in accurately created shadows. The process actually traces light through the scene, from the light source to the objects in the scene. So you can be fairly certain that if you add a lamp in a room and set its light to raytracing that the rendered image is a good representation of the conditions you created.

However, there are a few drawbacks to this method. The first and foremost is the rendering time. Depending on your scene, the complexity, and the number of lights using Raytraced Shadows, you can easily see frames that take 30 seconds with Shadow Maps take 4 or 5 minutes with Raytraced Shadows—and some might comment that those numbers are conservative. The bottom line is, use them only if you gain enough advantage in your final product.

The second potential drawback is the hard edge of the shadows. This does create a great defined shadow, but it might appear artificial because it is too well defined. In the real world, with natural lighting, there are few shadows with truly defined edges such as those raytracing creates. The best scenes probably contain a combination of each type of light.

With all this being said, change your light to a Raytraced Shadow light and compare the output.

To Do: Comparing different shadow effects

▼ To Do

1. Open lighting.max.

2. Select the spotlight and click the Modify tab.

3. Pan the Modify Panel, if necessary, until you see the Shadow Parameters rollup.

4. Click the radio button next to Use Ray-Traced Shadows. This toggles the selection, so you see the radio button for Use Shadow Maps become deselected.

5. Essentially, this is all you have to do, so click the Quick Render button on the toolbar to see the default shadows you get from Raytraced Shadows. Your shadows should resemble those in Figure 8.21.

6. Save the changes to lighting.max.

FIGURE 8.21.

The default settings for shadows using Raytraced Shadows creates images with well-defined edges but with potentially long rendering times.

Projecting Maps with Lights

How can you create shadows from a group of leafy trees as they appear on a street you have created, but the trees won't ever show in your scene—only their shadows? You don't want to go to the trouble of modeling and lighting each individual tree, so you create a Projector light. That is, you project a bitmap of your shadow object with one of the lights in your scene. It's really a simple concept that creates the effect you want, and no one will ever know the trees never existed. It saves you the modeling and rendering time the actual tree models demand. You can even make the Shadow Maps for the trees an animated bitmap, so your scene appears with moving leaves, branches, and so on.

To add a Projector spotlight to a typical MAX scene to see how it works, follow these steps:

To Do: Working with Projector spotlights

1. Open projector.max from the accompanying CD-ROM.

2. This basic street scene contains the sidewalk and a simple building, along with three lonely teapots just to add some life to our scene. Click the Create tab, and the Lights icon.

3. Click Target Spot, and in the Left viewport, click in the upper-right corner and drag to where the sidewalk meets the building as shown in Figure 8.22.

FIGURE 8.22.

Click in the Left viewport and create the Projector Spotlight pointing toward the base of the building.

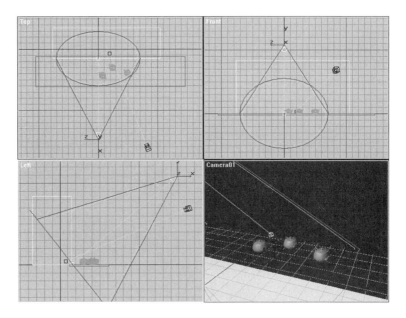

4. Because you'll be working with a rectangular image map for the shadow, select the Rectangle radio button for the shape of the spotlight's cone (changing it from the default Circle).

5. Check the check box for Projector, and then click the None button next to Map to select the image map you'll use for the projected shadows.

6. In the Browse From section of this dialog box, check the radio button next to Mtl Editor (for Material Editor). You see the premade image made for this example. In your actual projects, you can choose your bitmap from any predefined material, or from a bitmap file (see Figure 8.23).

FIGURE 8.23.

*The Material/Map
Browser dialog box
opens to let you select
your Projector Shadow
Map.*

7. Select the Shadow Projector material and click OK. When the dialog prompts you to choose an Instance or a Copy of the material, select Instance. Choosing Instance instead of Copy ensures that any changes made to the material later will be updated in the light's Shadow Projector.

8. Click the Bitmap Fit button in the Spotlight Parameters and select the bitmap file shadows.jpg on the accompanying CD-ROM. This scales the aspect ratio of the light's cone to match that of the bitmap used in your Shadow Projector material.

9. Type in a setting of 70 for the Hotspot to make sure the projection covers your wall.

10. Also turn on Cast Shadows, using Shadow Maps, in the Shadow Parameters rollup for some added life to your teapots on the sidewalk.

11. Click the Quick Render button to see the projected shadows. Your image should be similar to Figure 8.24.

FIGURE 8.24.

*Projecting shadows
through your lights is
a quick way to simu-
late shadow-casting
objects in your scene
without having to
model them.*

Animating Lights

You will undoubtedly have the need to animate the movement of lights over time. You already saw how one type of light, the Sunlight System, automates a sun's movement; now you can see how to animate any other light. As with anything in MAX, don't limit yourself to moving, for example, just the target of a spotlight. If the effect works in your scene, animate the changing of size of the Hotspot or Falloff, and change the color or intensity of the light.

Regardless of your ideas for your lights, you can find a way to get the animated affect you dream of. You'll cover the specifics of the animation process on Days 10 and 11, but for now, just realize that light objects are no different from any other objects when it comes to the control you have over them. Through various ways of linking objects to lights or lights to objects, you can have your light follow or lead other objects through the scene. You can even set the motion for a light by having it follow a path you designate.

Working in a Light Viewport

When you manipulate the position of your lights, you have the option of doing so through one of your MAX viewports. In this way, you see what the light sees, as if the light were a camera and you were looking through its lens—much like the Camera viewport.

To set a viewport to display the view of one of your lights, do the following.

To Do: Displaying light views in a viewport

▼ To Do ▲

1. Right-click the label of any viewport.

2. The flyout menu lists the available views you can select, including any lights in your scene.

3. Simply highlight and click on the Spot01 name and the viewport shows you what the light sees (see Figure 8.25).

FIGURE 8.25.

Designating a viewport to display the view of a light is a great way to fine-tune the placement of your light object.

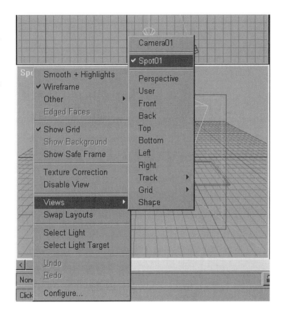

When you work in the Light viewport, your viewport navigation tools in the lower-right portion of the screen resemble the tools available for a Camera viewport. You can interactively change the Hotspot, Falloff, and Roll of the light, as well Dolly (move toward and away from the target), Track (move side to side), and Orbit the light. Orbit allows you to move the light in three dimensions about its target and is a great way to experiment with multiple possible positions quickly, with minimal effort.

    Dolly Light

    Light Hotspot

    Roll Light

Zoom Extents All

 Min/Max Toggle

 Orbit Light

 Truck Light

 Light Falloff

To Do: Using navigation tools for a light viewport

1. Click the Orbit Light icon in the viewport navigation tools section on the lower-right area of the screen.

2. In your Spotlight viewport, click and hold in the middle of the scene.

3. While holding the mouse button down, move the cursor around the window. You actually manipulate the viewport around its target in multiple directions at the same time. This is a great tool for getting just the positioning you want.

What Is Atmosphere?

Earlier, we defined atmosphere as "environment; predominant aspect or mood." Besides this emotional, aesthetic property of atmosphere, there is a real-world physical definition. In simple terms, atmosphere is the air around us. In MAX, atmosphere includes the "air" portion of your scene, and for the sake of this discussion, the background image you might decide to include to create the backdrop to your virtual set.

Working with the Scene Environment

Aspects of the scene environment are set in a dialog box accessed by clicking the Rendering drop-down menu and clicking Environment as shown in Figure 8.26. This figure shows the four types of atmosphere that ship with MAX. Set up Fog and Volume Lights in this section. The scene environment helps you create a believable environment without involving extra modeling. By designating a background image, you can display a city or some other setting in the background of your scene just by creating one image of the view you want. The scene environment also enables you to add volume (a visible property) to the beam that emanates from a light. To add a background image to a scene, follow these steps:

FIGURE 8.26.

You add background images and atmospheric conditions from the Environment dialog box.

To Do: Adding a background image to a scene

1. Load the environment.max scene from the accompanying CD-ROM. This street scene is lit only by the default lights that MAX provides. You add your own lights later.

2. Click the Rendering drop-down menu and click Environment to bring up the Environment dialog box.

3. Click the Use Map check box next to Environment Map and click the long button underneath to select the map file you'll use from the Browser dialog box.

4. In the Browse From section, click the Mtl Library to choose from the Material Library. MAX ships with a sky image map, so scroll down the list until you see Reflection: (Sky.jpg). Click on the selection and click OK.

5. Because you'll use the Environment dialog box later, just minimize its window for now.

6. Click the Quick Render button to see the sky image added to the scene background. Your image should resemble Figure 8.27.

FIGURE 8.27.

The sky.jpg image has been added as a background image.

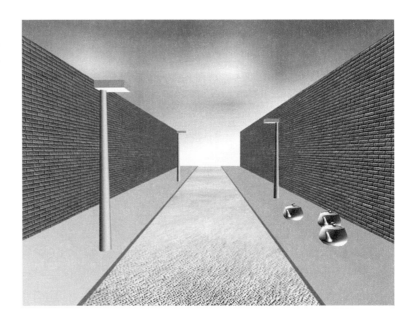

▲   7. Save the changes to environment.max.

Creating Fog

Fog allows you to create the illusion that your scene fades into the distance or background. Now use the same environment.max file and continue adding environment elements with Fog.

To Do: Adding fog

1. Maximize the Environment dialog box and click the Add button in the Atmosphere rollup section.

2. Click on Fog and OK.

3. Pan this window, if necessary, to see the Fog Parameters. This is where you can choose the color of the fog. You can choose a solid color by clicking the color square and using the Color Selector, but use an image to create your fog. Click Use Map next to Environment Color Map and then click the long button underneath.

4. Scroll the list in the Material/Map Browser and select the same file you used as your background (sky.jpg). Click OK after you select the file.

5. Minimize the Environment dialog box and click Quick Render to see the fog you created. Your image should resemble Figure 8.28.

FIGURE 8.28.

The sky.jpg image used as a background has also been used as a color map for the Fog atmosphere.

8

▲   6. Save the changes to environment.max.

Creating Volume Light

Now create even more atmosphere to your environment.max scene by replacing the default lighting with your own and also adding some volume lights for your street lights.

To Do: Replacing the default lighting

1. Select the Create Tab and click the Lights icon. Select Target Spot and drag to add the light starting directly under one of the streetlights and extending to the street in the Left viewport, as shown in Figure 8.29. If you put it in or above the light, the model creates a shadow or obscures the light.

2. Use the Select and Move tool to move the light in the Top viewport until it is aligned with the streetlight model. Figure 8.30 shows the light correctly positioned in all viewports.

3. Next adjust the cone of the spot so its falloff covers a greater area. Click the Modify tab and adjust the Hotspot to 90 and the Falloff to 130. Figure 8.30 shows the change to the light's cone.

4. In the Shadow Parameters, click Cast Shadows.

5. Now that you set up one light, create instances for the other two streetlights. Creating instances saves you time if you ever have to make changes to the lights— any changes made to the first light affects all its instances. Select both the light and its target with the Select and Move tool.

FIGURE 8.29.

Add the Target Spot for one of the streetlights.

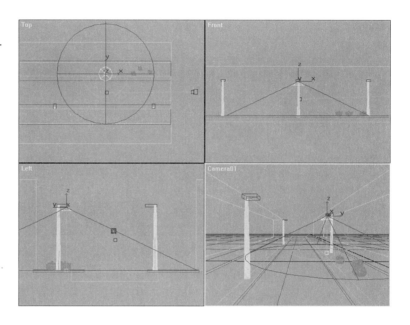

6. Hold down the left Shift key and click the Lock Selection Set icon located just below the timeline (it looks like a padlock). In the Top viewport, move the light until it lines up with one of the other streetlights in the scene.

7. When prompted with the Clone Options dialog box, select Instance and click OK. Repeat steps 5 and 6 once more for the remaining streetlight.

8. Click the Quick Render button and see the results of adding your lights before setting their volume properties. Your image should resemble Figure 8.30.

9. Enter the Environment dialog box again and click the Add button under Atmosphere. When the Add Atmospheric Effect dialog box appears, select Volume Light and click OK.

10. In the Volume Light Parameters rollup, click the Pick Light button to choose the lights you want as volume lights.

11. Because it can be hard to click on light objects, click the H key to bring up the Select By Name dialog box. You'll assign all the lights in this example, so click the All button and the Pick button to close the dialog box. Figure 8.31 shows the Environment dialog box with all three lights selected.

FIGURE 8.30.

*The streetlight spot-
lights before adding
volume lighting.*

8

FIGURE 8.31.

*The three streetlights
have been selected to
be volume lights in the
Environment dialog
box.*

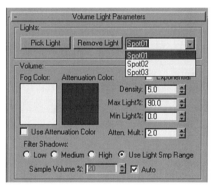

12. Adjust the color of the fog by clicking the Fog color square and inputing a value of 220 for R, G, and B.

13. In the Volume section, change Density to 3.0 and Max Light % to 75. Figure 8.32 shows the settings for steps 12 and 13.

14. Click Quick Render to see the results. Your image should resemble Figure 8.34.

▲   15. Save the changes to environment.max.

FIGURE 8.32.

The settings made to the volume light affect its color and density.

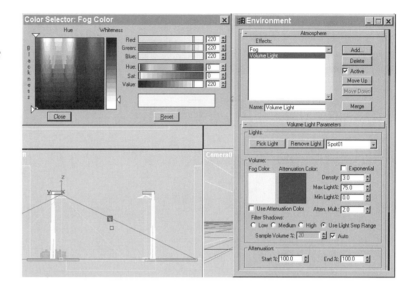

FIGURE 8.33.

Our final street scene complete with a background image, fog, and volume lights.

Summary

Lighting and atmosphere have as much to do with the design of your scene as the actual models you design. That statement holds true for rendering times as well. The best way to accomplish the look you want, and achieve the reasonable rendering times you hope for, is through experimentation. No one can tell you the correct combination of lights and scene complexity that will meet all your expectations. In fact, be prepared to accept some type of trade-off. Good lighting quite often involves enough shadows and raytraced lights to drag out your rendering at least minimally.

You saw how easy it is to switch the shadow creation method between Shadow Maps and Raytraced Shadows for each light. Use this to your advantage during design stages. Set up your scene, add some lights, and switch back and forth, rendering each type and noting the render times. Decide for yourself if the trade-off between enhanced images and longer rendering times is warranted.

When planning your lighting, keep these key points in mind.

- Lights serve two basic purposes: illumination and the creation of atmosphere.
- Use the right light for the right reason. Omni lights, for example, are great for general lighting, but you can't focus their light in one direction as you can with spot and directional lights.
- Use features such as Attenuation and Exclude/Include to limit the affective range of each light. Doing so speeds up rendering and prevents your scene from becoming overlit.
- Shadows add depth and realism, but the trade-off is rendering time. Spend enough time adjusting and experimenting with your settings to get the best trade-off between imagery and performance.
- Everything you create in MAX can be animated, and lights are no exception.
- Add atmosphere to your scene when the situation calls for fog, or fire, or smoky lights in a dimly lit room.

Q&A

Q **How many lights do I need in my scene?**

A Each scene will be different, depending on the effect you are designing. Try starting with two Omni lights: one behind and slightly below the subject, and one in front and slightly above the subject. This should give good, basic lighting. Where you go from there is up to you.

Q   **Can I tell MAX not to render my atmospheric conditions such as fog and volume lights while I'm rendering proof images during the design stage?**

A   Yes. Just like turning on or off shadows, tell MAX whether or not to render environmental effects by selecting and deselecting the Render Atmospheric Effects check box in the Render Scene dialog box.

Q   **What happens in areas where spotlights overlap?**

A   In areas where spot or any other lights overlap, you get mixed colors. This is actually a great way to create mood and color in your scene. Try it, try it, try it—the combinations you create will surprise you.

DAY 9

Cameras

Concepts of Using Your Virtual Camera

Before this discussion gets too complicated, let's understand the basic idea
behind the camera, virtual or otherwise. The function of any camera is to record
a snapshot of the events within its view. In MAX, your camera (or cameras)
exist to make an animated or still image representation of what you create in
your 3D scene. In today's lesson, we'll take a look at the camera object you
create in MAX and learn the following:

- How to create a Target and Free camera, similar to a Target and Free
  spotlight.
- How to adjust a camera as if it were a real-world camera.
- How to animate camera objects along a path or to follow an object
  through your scene.
- How to adjust your camera when using atmospheric effects such as Fog.
- How to adjust your camera for tight close-ups.
- How to use Video Post to create focus effects.

Applying Real-World Methods

The MAX camera is much like a real-world 35mm camera or video camcorder in that it gives you the capability to change lenses and adjust your field of view. Working with your camera object is similar also in the way you move it to see different things. It's really as if you were standing in your scene looking through the lens of your 35mm. The advantage a MAX camera object holds over its real-world counterpart is the capability to go anywhere and see anything. This means you can send a camera into an anatomical model or inside a tiny mechanical part you design. You can record things with your virtual camera you can't even see in the real-world.

With the knowledge that the MAX camera is similar to using your real-world camera, you can start applying some tried and true methods of capturing your scene and motion. Knowing how you will record your scene with your camera(s) should have an affect on how your scene is designed and modeled.

| Tip | Think of your scene as the set of a movie and your camera object as the movie camera. Hollywood sets don't have completely built houses; they only have the portion of the house built that is visible in any given camera shot. The point is that if the camera doesn't see it, don't waste time including it in your model. Therefore, it's a good idea to plan your camera shots early enough to possibly save yourself some modeling time. |

Lenses and Field of View

Figure 9.1 shows the series of stock lenses MAX provides (derived from real-world cameras). Aside from using stock lenses, you also have the ability to type in any lens setting you want. This means you can literally have any lens length you desire. Before we get into the details of creating cameras and changing lenses, let's start with a few definitions.

- **Lens Length:** This defines the distance (to use a real camera analogy) from the lens to the film in the camera where the image is recorded. Through the use of different lenses and variable length zoom lenses, the real camera changes its lens length. In MAX, this is set in the Parameters rollup of the camera Modify panel as shown in Figure 9.1. (Figure 9.1 identifies the properties of the MAX camera object.) Lens length is represented in the MAX viewports as a straight line extending outward from the camera (see Figure 9.2).

FIGURE 9.1.

The MAX camera parameters rollup provides stock lenses for your cameras or you can type in any settings you want.

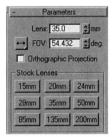

- **Field of Vision**: Referred to in MAX as FOV, this represents the visible range of the camera expressed in degrees as seen in Figure 9.1. Think of this as peripheral vision in the human eye. The FOV includes everything you can see. It's represented in the MAX viewports as a cone, extending outward from the camera (see Figure 9.2).

Lens length and FOV settings are inversely related—that is, when one setting increases, the other decreases and vice versa.

FIGURE 9.2.

Camera objects display the lens and FOV parameters as a cone in the viewports.

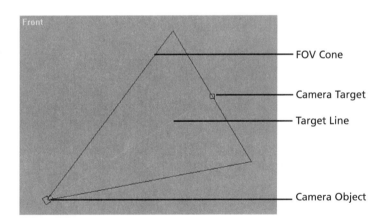

Note

If you're familiar with real-world cameras, you may be familiar with a term called *depth of field*. This describes the effect of some background items becoming out of focus as the camera focuses on its subject matter in the foreground. This is one feature MAX cameras do not recreate. You can, however, simulate depth of field by adding your own focus effects in a MAX feature called Video Post. We'll cover Video Post and many of its effects on Day 14.

Creating a Target and Free Camera

You create a Target camera much like you do a Target spotlight. You'll be creating two objects: the camera and the target. Each can be manipulated separately from the other, but when you make modifications to the camera's lens or FOV you need to select and modify the camera object, not its target.

To Do: Modifying the camera object

1. Open cameras.max from the accompanying CD-ROM.

2. Click the Create Tab and the Cameras icon. Pick the Target button in Object Type rollup.

3. In the right viewport, click and drag from the upper-right hand corner (creating the camera object), releasing the cursor over the dinosaur model (creating the target).

Note

MAX defines two types of cameras: Target and Free. They are created and perform in the same way a Target Spot and Free Spot work as covered in Day 8. A Target camera has a "target" and a Free camera does not. If you plan on assigning a camera movement along a path, you may opt for the Free camera as it only has one object to adjust. For most situations, however, you may find the Target camera is easier to adjust.

You create a Free camera much like you do a Free Spotlight. With a Free camera, you only create one object.

4. In the Cameras panel, under the Object Type rollup, click the Free button.

5. Because Free cameras are created from the point you click in a direction pointing away from you, let's create the Free camera in the Front viewport. Click in the Front viewport directly over the first camera you created. Watch all the viewports to see where the camera is created, it should be directly over the dinosaur at the center of our grid.

6. Let's point the Free camera at the dinosaur. Click the Select and Move tool and constrain to the Y axis by clicking the Y button in the toolbar.

7. In the Top Viewport, move the camera down until it is the same distance below the dinosaur as the Target camera is above the dinosaur (see Figure 9.3).

8. Click the Select and Rotate tool and click the Free camera object in the Right viewport. Rotate the camera on its Z axis by dragging the mouse up. Manipulate the camera until you match the view shown in Figure 9.3.

FIGURE 9.3.

A Target and Free camera, each with similar settings.

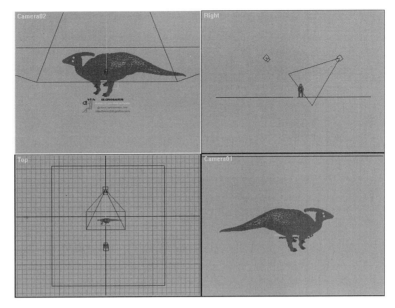

9. Change the Perspective viewport to the first camera view by right-clicking the viewport label and selecting Camera01.

10. Change the Front viewport to the second camera view using the same method.

▲ 11. Save changes to mycameras.max.

As you can see, each camera can easily capture the same view of your scene. It often takes less steps to move a Target camera's target object to point to any object than it does to rotate and move a Free camera.

Adjusting a Camera

Adjusting the position of your camera is where you realize the full control you have over how you record your images or animation. Basic movements (placing cameras and their targets at different locations at different times) are easy to accomplish with the Select and Move tool in the toolbar. Cameras are treated just as any other object in the scene. In this section, we'll take a look at some of the ways to fine-tune the camera position.

Working in a Camera Viewport

On Day 8, we discussed working with a viewport that was assigned the view of one of the lights in your scene. You can do the same thing when you designate one of the viewports to display what your camera sees. In the previous section, we designated two viewports to display each of the two camera views. Aside from simply viewing the scene, the Camera viewport can be used as a camera positioning tool.

When a Camera viewport is the active viewport, the navigation tools in the lower-right hand corner of your screen change to accommodate camera movements. (If you want to experiment with each tool as it is described, open the cameras.max file and activate one of the Camera viewports).

To Do: Working with a Dolly Camera

 Dolly camera: Dolly is a term taken from traditional filming technique where the camera (on rollers) moves closer to or away from its target.

1. Click the Dolly Camera button, then click and hold in the Camera viewport.

2. Drag the mouse up to move closer to the target and down to move away.

Dolly movements in the Camera viewport are the equivalent of moving the camera object closer to the target object. The target object is unaffected. Using Dolly camera is easier than using the Select and Move tool and trying to stay on a steady course to or from the target.

To Do: Adjusting the FOV and Dollying

Perspective: This adjusts the FOV and the amount of perspective flare you notice in your camera view. It does this while also using dolly to maintain the same compositional view. This means the perspective tool dollies the camera object closer to or away from its target to avoid changing what is visible in the view as a result of the perspective change. Use perspective to adjust how three-dimensional your scene appears. By adjusting the FOV and dollying at the same time, you can create a very flat perspective or a very flared perspective of the same view.

1. Click the perspective button, then click and hold in the Camera viewport.

2. Drag the mouse up to increase FOV and increase the noticeable perspective. Notice the scene composition (viewable objects) does not change.

3. Drag the mouse down to decrease FOV and decrease the noticeable perspective, ultimately rendering a flat scene.

To Do: Working with a Roll Camera

 Roll camera: This simply rotates the camera object about its axis.

1. Click the Roll Camera button, then click and hold in the Camera viewport.

2. Drag the mouse from side to side to roll (or rotate) your camera.

To Do: Adjusting FOV

 FOV: Just like adjusting FOV in the camera's Modify panel, this tool accomplishes the same thing from the Camera viewport.

1. To use this tool, click the FOV button, then click and hold in the Camera viewport.

2. Drag the mouse up to increase FOV and down to decrease FOV.

 The FOV tool differs from the Perspective tool in that it does not dolly the camera. So changing FOV is like changing lenses as well; your composition view changes.

To Do: Working with the Truck Camera

Truck camera: This is similar to panning in any non-Camera viewport. It moves the camera object up, down, or side-to-side.

1. Click the Truck Camera button, then click and hold in the Camera viewport.

2. Drag the mouse according to how you want the camera to move (up, down, left, or right).

To Do: Adjusting the Orbit/Pan Camera

 Orbit/Pan camera: Potentially the greatest camera positioning tool you find in MAX. There are actually two tools here: Orbit and Pan. You access either one via a flyout menu you bring up by clicking and holding the button. Orbit rotates the camera about its target and Pan rotates the target about its camera. This tool moves the camera on multiple axis at one time, making it a quick way to manipulate your camera in one movement.

1. Click the Orbit Camera button, then click and hold in the Camera viewport.

2. While holding the mouse button, drag the cursor around the screen and notice how you are moving around the camera target.

3. Now click and hold the Orbit Camera button until you see the flyout menu. Select the Pan Camera button.

4. Once again, click and hold in the Camera viewport and move the mouse around. Notice how the camera target is actually moving around the camera object.

Setting the Environmental Range

In Day 8, we discussed atmospheric conditions such as Fog. Those atmosphere settings are what MAX terms as the environment. When you have environmental effects in your scene, you can control the way they are rendered by setting the camera's Environmental ranges as shown in Figure 9.4. The two settings are for Near range and Far range. If you check the Show checkbox, you see a representation of these ranges in the camera's viewport as shown in Figure 9.5.

FIGURE 9.4.

Environmental effects settings for Near and Far ranges are located in the Modify panel for each camera.

FIGURE 9.5.

You can display the Environmental ranges you set in the Camera viewport.

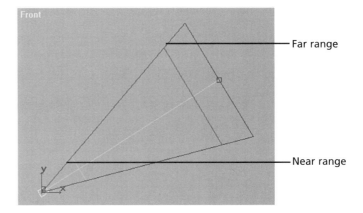

When you designate the settings for atmospheric effects, such as Fog, you are inputting ranges (see Figure 9.6). Let's see how this works.

To Do: Designating settings for atmospheric effects

1. Open ranges.max from the accompanying CD-ROM.

2. Click the Rendering dropdown menu and select Environment.

3. In the Atmosphere rollup, click ADD, select Fog, and click OK.

   In the Fog Parameters rollup, find the section labeled Standard. It has two inputs: Near and Far. These work together with the Near and Far ranges of the camera. The settings for Near and Far in the Environment dialog tell MAX a percentage of the fog color that should be rendered at the Near of Far distance set in the Environment ranges section under the Camera Parameters rollup.

4. Leave the setting in the Environment dialog at their defaults and click OK. The scene now has the Fog effect added.

5. Click the camera01 object and then click the Modify Tab to see the camera parameters.

   In the Environment ranges section, notice that Show is checked. If you look at the viewports, you'll see the ranges indicated. The Far range extends to the end of the ship, and the Near range is actually not visible because it is at the camera position.

FIGURE 9.6.

The Near and Far settings for atmospheric effects work together with the Near and Far settings for your camera.

9

FIGURE 9.7.

You can display the Environment ranges in MAX's viewports.

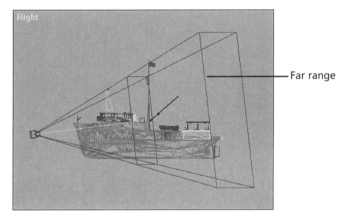

6. Activate the Camera viewport and click the Quick Render button in the toolbar. Your image should resemble Figure 9.8.

With our current range settings (Far range at the back of the ship), the fog is rendered at 100% from the back of the ship away from us (remember the default Fog setting of Far:100% in the Environment dialog). The Fog is rendered as a gradation of 100% to 0% from the back of the ship towards the camera (remember the default Fog setting of Near:0% in the Environment dialog).

FIGURE 9.8.

With the Environment range for Far set to the back of the ship, this is the image you should see rendered.

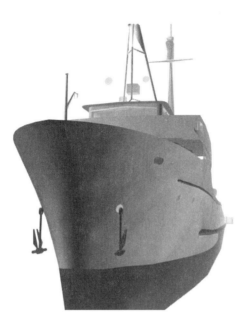

7. In the Environment ranges dialog for the camera, change the Far range to 20000 (this scene was modeled in centimeters). Notice the Far range displayed in the viewports. It moves closer to the camera.

8. Click the Quick Render button to see the difference when you move the Far range toward the camera. Your image should resemble Figure 9.9.

▲

FIGURE 9.9.

The image on the left has the Environment range for Far set to the middle of the ship. The image on the right has the Far range set towards the front of the ship.

Setting the Clipping Planes

As the camera approaches an object, you may start to see parts of your objects disappear. This is known as clipping. Clipping planes have many purposes, but basically they exist to exclude some portion of your scene from rendering. Much like Environmental ranges, Clipping planes have a Near Clip and a Far Clip. Quite simply, anything closer to the camera than the Near Clip and anything further away from the camera than the Far Clip will not be rendered.

MAX sets a default for the Clipping planes that is active unless you set your own ranges. You do so by checking the Set Manually checkbox in a camera's Modify panel as seen in Figure 9.10.

FIGURE 9.10.

If you display the camera's cone, you can see the Clipping Planes as well.

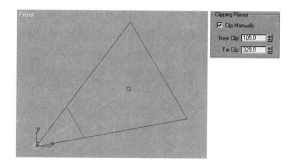

One possible use of Clipping planes is to create a cutaway view of what you've modeled. Let's say you've created a prototype of a piece of machinery. The exterior design is approved, but now you need to demonstrate how the machine is designed internally. If you are going to use a static (non-moving) camera in your animation, you could use Clipping planes to dissect the machine.

| **Caution** | Clipping planes are relevant to the position of your camera. If you move your camera, the amount of clipping that occurs is affected. If you're doing a cutaway shot of your model and need to move the camera throughout the animation, you'll want to use another method, such as Boolean operations, to create actual cutaways of your object. |

To Do: Creating cut-away views

1. Open clipping.max from the accompanying CD-ROM.

2. For simplicity, this example only has two tube objects, one inside the other. Activate the Camera viewport and click the Quick Render button to see the normal (non-clipped) view. It should resemble Figure 9.11.

FIGURE 9.11.

The tubes rendered view before manual clipping is applied.

3. Select the camera object and click the Modify Tab to access the camera parameters.

4. Check the Show Cone checkbox.

5. In the Clipping planes section, check the Clip Manually checkbox.

6. While watching the viewports, use the Far Clip spinner to adjust the Far Clip to a position just beyond the tubes and the Near Clip to a position in the middle of the large tube. Do not penetrate the small tube with the Near Clipping Plane (see Figure 9.12).

FIGURE 9.12.

Align the Near Clip in the middle of the large tube to create a cutaway.

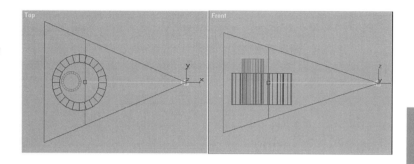

9

7. Activate the camera view and click the Quick Render button to see the resulting cutaway of your models. It should resemble Figure 9.13.

▲

FIGURE 9.13.

The tubes rendered view with manual clipping applied to create a cutaway view.

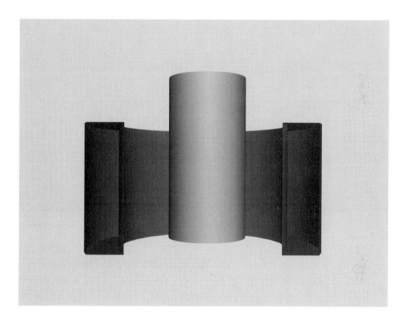

Caution

When creating a cutaway with Clipping planes, you have to render all materials as 2-sided (unless their materials already are designated as 2-sided). Doing so prevents some or all of the models' faces from rendering transparent. You can tell MAX to render all faces as 2-sided by checking the Force 2-Sided checkbox in the Options section of the Render Scene dialog.

Animating a Camera

Many beginning animators tend to forget they can animate camera movement. It doesn't take long to realize, however, that camera movements can add a tremendous amount of interest to your scene. Nothing shows off the true 3D aspects of your creations more than a camera flying through the scene.

Most camera parameters are animatable, including lens length, FOV, Environmental ranges, and Clipping planes. Imagine generating animated Fog rolling into or out of your scene. Load the digital movie rollfog.avi from the accompanying CD-ROM to see a short animation of fog rolling out of a scene. In Day 10, we'll explore just how animation works. For now, just realize what you can animate relative to the camera object and its parameters.

Following Paths

Moving your camera around your scene is easy enough, but there are times when you will want to dictate an exact path for the camera to follow. You can do this by applying a trajectory path for the camera. The path can be a simple spline object you create, basically a line you create and tell the camera to follow. We'll cover the specifics of creating paths and trajectories in Day 10. For now, let's see an example of a file where the trajectory path has already been applied.

To Do: Understanding trajectory paths

▼ To Do

1. Load cameras2.max from the accompanying CD-ROM.

2. Notice the curved line surrounding the dinosaur model in the Right viewport. This spline is drawn as a path for the camera to follow as it rotates around the model from top to bottom. Click the camera path object.

3. Click the Display Tab and the Hide Selected button to hide the spline path. We don't need it for this example because the path trajectory has already been applied to the camera.

4. Click the camera object and the Motion Tab.

5. In the Motion panel, click the Trajectories button. When you do this, you see the trajectory path the camera is set to follow. It is the exact shape of the spline object it was created from. Figure 9.14 shows the trajectory path.

▲

FIGURE 9.14.

The camera object has a trajectory path assigned from a spline object created in MAX.

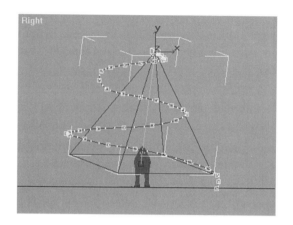

9

If you want to see a rendered animation with this camera path applied to this scene, load pathcam.avi from the accompanying CD-ROM.

Summary

Today we took an initial look at setting up a camera and how to finely tune its placement. We've also seen that, as with most things in MAX, cameras and all their settings can be animated. Even the environment depends on settings for the camera that you can animate. When setting up your cameras, keep the following in mind.

- The MAX cameras work similarly to real-world cameras. Basic knowledge of lenses and field of view can help you plan your scene.

- Target cameras and Free cameras both accomplish the same basic job, although you might opt for a Free camera if you plan on having your camera follow a trajectory path through your scene.

- Use the Camera viewport as much as possible for fine-tuning movements. It's time-saving and is probably the best way to make adjustments to your camera.

- If you zoom in close to your objects and start experiencing disappearing faces, turn on Set Manually for Clipping planes in the Camera Parameters rollup.

- You can use Clipping planes to dissect your objects and create a dramatic cutaway image. As long as your camera doesn't have to move through the scene, you can keep a consistent cutaway view.

Q&A

Q **Do I have to learn photography to understand how to use MAX's cameras and all their lenses?**

A No. Although MAX provides many stock lenses that are familiar to the traditional photographer, they are provided just as a starting point. Any knowledge of traditional photography will be an advantage, but it's not necessary.

Q **Can I set up more than one camera for my animation, or do I need to do everything with one camera?**

A Use as many cameras as you need. When you storyboard your animation, you plan different shots within each scene. You may wish to create a different camera for each shot. You'll be able to use Video Post to coordinate the transition between multiple camera views.

Q **Does moving the camera target further away or closer to the camera affect its FOV or lens length?**

A No. Moving the camera target has no affect on the camera settings at all. The target exists simply to show where the camera is pointing.

WEEK 2

DAY 10

Animation Part I

General Animation Concepts

It's time to take a look at the main feature of MAX and the reason most every-one buys the program—animation. Previously, you used MAX to model your objects, arrange your scene, and create lighting and camera views. Each day, you read that practically all features of MAX can be animated. Today, you take a look at basic animation features, how to use them, and how you can animate many of MAX's features. You cover the following topics and return on Day 11 to continue with even more animation concepts:

- Understanding how MAX animates objects using the Animate button
- How to work with the objects in your scene to make them perform as you have planned
- How to best use Track View to edit keyframes
- How to make objects follow a path through your scene
- Controllers and when to use them

Understanding What Happens When You Move Objects

When you move objects around your scene over time, the most important button in MAX is the Animate button. Without it, you would simply be moving and changing the static position of your objects.

In traditional animation, there was a master animator and the assistant animators. The master animator drew the character in its initial position and then in the next important, or *key*, position. This drawing was called the *keyframe*. The assistant animators drew all the in-between frames, between the original position and the keyframes drawn by the master animator.

In 3D Studio, you are the master animator and MAX is the "in-betweener." You press the Animate button, advance to the point in time where you want to set a key frame, and reposition, rotate, or scale your objects—this is the process of keyframe animation.

- The Animate button (shown in Figure 10.1) tells MAX to create a Key at a particular point in time—a process called *Keyframing*.

- A key is a way of representing the transformational (position, rotation, and scale) state of any object at a specific point in time.

- Every change to an object property that happens over time is represented by a key. This is done by creating a key on a timeline for every change you make to your object.

When objects change (creating different keys) at different frames on a timeline, you have an object that changes (in one or more ways) over a given time. This is the basis of the animation process. So the most basic example of animation is to start with an object at frame 0, move to a nonzero frame (for example, frame 30), turn on the Animate button, and move the object to a different position or otherwise alter the object. MAX fills in all the in-between positions from frame 0 to frame 20 to make it appear as if the object is moving from one location to the next.

MAX actually gives you more than one method of keyframing your animation: one automatic and another manual method. The Animate button is the automatic method where MAX instantly inserts the keys necessary to represent the changes you make in your scene. Even if you select and change multiple objects at the same time, MAX inserts individual keys for each object affected.

FIGURE 10.1.

When the Animate button is on, it turns red, telling you and MAX that any movements you make are to create a moving object. In this figure, the ball moves across the screen in 30 frames. You only need to set the initial and end positions, and MAX fills in the rest (called In betweening).

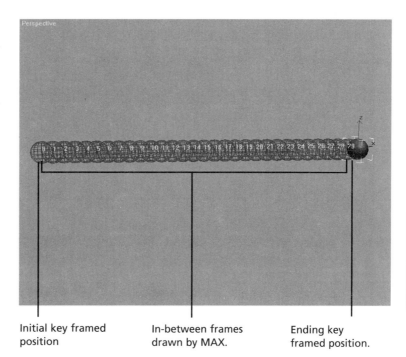

10

| Initial key framed position | In-between frames drawn by MAX. | Ending key framed position. |

However, there are times when you want to insert keys on your own. MAX enables you to do just that in the Track View window. The Track View (see Figure 10.2) displays your animation timeline. In Track View (covered in more detail in the next section), you manually insert a key at any frame on the timeline to record the state of any object at that particular frame. In most animation projects, you let MAX create the initial movements with the Animate button, then you fine-tune movements by manually editing and creating keys in Track View.

Note

It is extremely important to check—and double-check—the state of the Animate button. When you want your changes animated, the Animate button and active viewport must appear highlighted in red. If they aren't, and you proceed to move objects and change settings you want animated, you risk the order of the composition you have worked so hard to create. Without the Animate button on, you'll be changing the relative state of your objects. Get in the habit of noticing when the Animate button is on or off. It will save you many headaches down the road. If you want, you can turn the entire time slider red, by setting "Enable TimeSlider while animating" in the 3dsmax.ini file. See the readme for instructions.

FIGURE 10.2.

The Track View window displays the timeline for your animation.

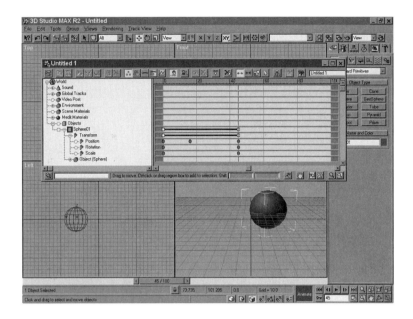

As you use the many tools MAX provides to create animation, you'll discover important terms you might not be familiar with. The following sections describe some of the terms and concepts you should develop an understanding of before going any further.

Pivot Points

When you apply a transform such as rotate or scale to an object, the command occurs about the object's pivot point. By default, an object's pivot point is positioned at the center of its local coordinate system. The important thing to remember here is that objects will be transformed about their local coordinate system, and not about the scene's world coordinate system. Each object will act independently from the rest of the objects in the scene. Figure 10.3 shows a sphere with its pivot point at the default location at the center of its local coordinate system.

MAX enables you to adjust pivot points to make objects behave as you need. As you create more complex models, where objects must move relative to other objects in the same model, pivot points become increasingly important, for example, animating the bones in your hand. Imagine the bones in one of your fingers. The pivot point of each bone must be located at the point where one bone meets with the next bone. Take a quick look at how this relationship works.

FIGURE 10.3.

An object's pivot point, identified by two arrows extending along the XY axis, determines how it will be affected by any transforms.

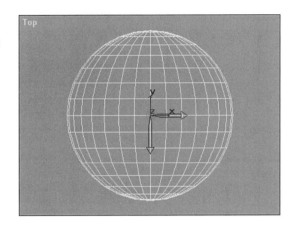

10

Note

Each object has its own coordinate system—that's how it's oriented in 3D space. An object's coordinate system is not always aligned with the scene's world coordinate system. Based on the way an object was created, it might have a completely different system. What this means is the X axis in world space might differ from the X axis of any particular object. So rotating an object about its X axis might create different results from object to object. It's a good idea, in many situations, to have objects that need to move in relationship to one another share the same coordinate system. It makes for more predictable results.

To Do: Working with Pivot Points

To Do

1. Load pivots.max from the accompanying CD-ROM. This simple scene contains three boxes that represent the three bones of a finger.

2. Click any one of the bones to see where the default pivot point is located. Looking at the Top and Front viewports, notice the pivot point is at the center and bottom of the object.

3. Click the Select and Rotate tool and click on the middle bone in the Front viewport. Rotate the bone 15 degrees on its Z axis. As you can see in Figure 10.4, rotating the middle bone with its default pivot point causes quite a painful broken finger.

4. Click the Undo button once to undo the rotation.

5. Adjust the pivot point to make this rotation work. Click on the Hierarchy Tab and click the Pivot button to display the Adjust Pivot rollup.

FIGURE 10.4.

The default location of an object's pivot point might have to be adjusted.

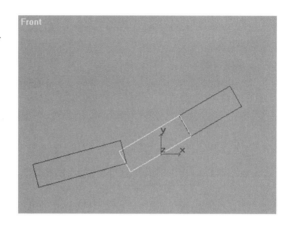

6. With the center bone still selected, click the Affect Pivot Only button. Notice the large Pivot Point icon that displays over the object's Local Coordinate Center icon. With this button highlighted, any Transform tool you use will only be affecting the object's pivot point and not the object itself.

7. Click the Select and Move tool. In the Front viewport, select the Pivot Point icon and move it to a position directly between its bone and the bone to its left as shown in Figure 10.5.

FIGURE 10.5.

Moving the center bone's pivot point allows proper rotation of the center bone object.

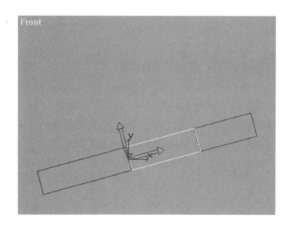

8. Click the Affect Pivot Only button to deactivate it, and click the Select and Rotate tool again.

9. Rotate the center bone 15 degrees on its Z axis and notice the difference the new pivot point makes. By applying these same steps to the next bone to the right, you can create a properly bending finger similar to the one shown in Figure 10.6.

FIGURE 10.6.

Adjusting pivot points for each object allows the correct bending of the finger.

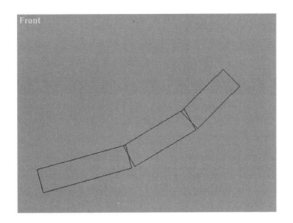

10

Note

> The bone objects in this example were linked together in a *hierarchy*. The analogy used is one of parents and children. The first object in the linked hierarchy is the parent, and all objects linked to it are the children. When the parent object is moved, the children follow, inheriting all the transforms applied to the parent. Transforms applied to a child object do not affect the parent but do affect children further down in the linked hierarchy. This linking of objects is critical for any animation that requires multiple objects to move in relation to one another. Linking and Hierarchies will be covered in more detail on Day 11.

Pivot points become extremely important for objects included in a hierarchical chain, such as the finger example. Any animation including objects with multiple parts, such as character animation, requires you to spend time adjusting the pivot points of each object to assure predictable motion.

Ghosting

Ghosting is derived from a traditional cel animation process called *onion skinning*. Cel animators draw on thin paper that can be laid over the previously drawn frame. This way, the animator can draw the next position of the animated character or object as it appears in succession using the underlaying previous frame's drawing as a guide.

Ghosting is a new feature in MAX 2.5. It refers to the ability to view a faded-colored representation of the position of your selected objects before and/or after the current frame. This ghosted view is helpful in fine-tuning movements for smooth motion. Figure 10.7 shows a bouncing ball as it appears with ghosting turned on for five frames before the current frame.

FIGURE **10.7.**

Ghosting enables you to view positions of your selected objects any number of frames before or after the current frame.

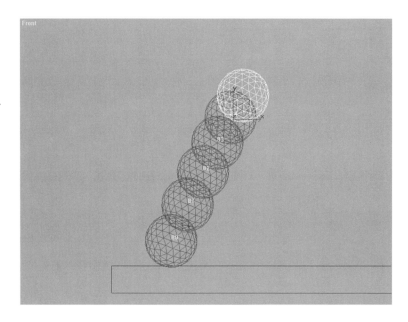

Ghosting is off by default. To turn it on, click the View drop-down menu and click the Show Ghosting selection. You toggle Ghosting on and off by selecting this option again from this menu. To edit the Ghosting properties, click the File drop-down menu and select Preferences. The Ghosting parameters are found under the Viewports tab. Both dialog boxes for Ghosting are shown in Figure 10.8.

FIGURE **10.8.**

You turn Ghosting on in the View drop-down menu, shown on the left. You edit Ghosting settings in the Preferences dialog box, shown on the right.

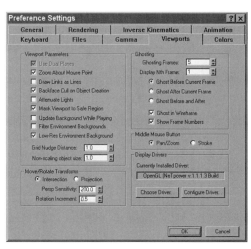

Adding Motion Blur

Have you ever noticed the way moving objects are captured on film by standard 35mm cameras? There is a blurred effect around the object that is moving, along with a slight blurring on the object itself. Why does this happen? Simply put, multiple positions for the moving object are being imaged onto the film between the time the shutter opens and closes, creating a blurred image. This is why cameras come with adjustable shutter speeds. A faster shutter speed means the film is exposed for a shorter period of time, ultimately capturing a single position on film, even for fast moving objects.

MAX gives you the ability to simulate motion blur in three ways: object motion blur, image motion blur, and scene motion blur. Although the objectives of each method are similar, they each have a distinct use as explained in the following definitions:

- *Object Motion Blur*   Use this method when you want to create a blurred effect only for individual objects in your scene. This method does not affect anything besides those objects you specifically assign to render Object Motion Blur.

- *Image Motion Blur*   Similar to Object Motion Blur, you assign this to individual objects, but you also have the option to blur the environment. Use this method when you want to blur selected objects and/or the environment background. Image Motion Blur can be affected by camera movements if the Apply To Environment option is applied.

- *Scene Motion Blur*   Used more for special effects trails, Scene Motion Blur works on the entire scene and is actually a Video Post image filter event. That means MAX renders your entire scene, and then Video Post applies a motion blur to the entire rendered image. Scene Motion Blur will be affected by camera movements.

It's a quick and easy method to add any of the motion blur methods. What takes the most time is fine-tuning the settings for whatever method you use to get exactly the look or effect you want. Now set up motion blur in a bouncing ball animation.

To Do: Working Motion Blur

1. Load blur.max from the accompanying CD-ROM. This scene contains an uneventful ball that bounces once on your ground object. There is no object blur set for this animation. To see the rendered animation, load noblur.avi from the accompanying CD-ROM. Use this file to compare to the motion blur files you're about to create.

2. First add Object Motion Blur. Select the ball using the left mouse button and then click it using the right mouse button. When the pop-up menu appears, click Properties to brings up this ball's Object Properties dialog box.

3. In the Motion Blur section in the lower-left side of the dialog box (see Figure 10.9), click ObjecZt and then click OK. That's all it takes to assign the default Object Motion Blur settings to the ball.

FIGURE **10.9**

You turn on Object or Image Motion Blur for each individual object in the Object Properties dialog box.

4. The last step comes when you prepare to render the animation. Click the Render Scene button. In the Render Scene dialog box (see Figure 10.10), scroll the window until you see the rollup labeled MAX Default Scanline A-Buffer. In that rollup is a section for Object Motion Blur and Image Motion Blur. Click the Apply button for Object Motion Blur because that is the only method you have assigned for this scene.

5. Click the Render button to render the scene. Watch each frame in the Virtual Frame Buffer as it is rendered. Notice that each frame is rendered with the blurring effect happening at the same time as the object is being rendered. This animation results in blurring of the ball only. Load objblur.avi from the accompanying CD-ROM to see the final animation.

6. Select the ball using the left mouse button and then right-click the ball and enter its Object Properties once again. This time select Image for the Motion Blur type.

7. Click the Render Scene button and remove the check mark from the Apply button for Object Motion Blur, and check the Apply button for Image Motion Blur. Click the Render button and watch as this animation is rendered. Notice that for each frame, the scene is rendered first and the blur effect is rendered in a second pass of

the same scene. This method of rendering the blur by using the already rendered scene image enables the possible blurring of the environment. Load imagblur.avi from the accompanying CD-ROM to see this animation.

FIGURE 10.10.

If you assigned Object or Image Motion Blur in your scene, you must apply the effect in the Render Scene dialog box in order for it to render.

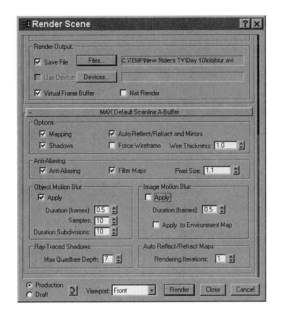

10

> **Note**
>
> Notice there is not much difference between the default settings you used for Object and Image Motion Blur. As you adjust the Duration settings in the Render Scene dialog box for either method, the differences become more dramatic. With longer durations, the Image Motion Blur actually begins to create a rendering of the object that makes it appear that the object is being deformed in some way. Using the default settings for either method provides excellent motion blurring to enhance the appearance of smooth motion of moving objects. Either method is a good alternative to using Render Fields, which enables for smoother motion when rendering to videotape. Because you can't render to Fields when rendering to a digital video format, the Motion Blur methods are a good solution. The topic of Render Fields are covered on Day 12, "Rendering."

8. Now try one more setting. Click the Render Scene button again and look at the setting for Image Motion Blur.

9. Click the Apply to Environment Map button to affect your scene background ▲   bitmap image, and click OK.

To make the effect more noticeable, change the Duration setting to 3.0. The resulting animation not only blurs the ball object but the background as well. Load imagenvblur.avi from the accompanying CD-ROM to see this animation.

The third type of motion blur is Scene Motion Blur. This is applied as an Image Filter Event in Video Post, which is covered on Day 14, "Video Post and Compositing." For now, you can load sceneblur.avi from the accompanying CD-ROM to see the special effect type of blur you can create with Scene Motion Blur.

Working in Track View

Think of your animation as occurring over a period of time starting at frame 0 and including as many frames as necessary for the time designated at the frame rate your output demands. For instance, for NTSC (TV) standard videotape, you have a frame rate of 30 frames per second (fps). Given that output demand, a five-second flying logo for your company's TV commercial would consist of 150 frames. You view these frames, and the events that make up your animation, on a timeline. In MAX, that timeline is the Track View. Everything you can animate in MAX is given a Track to log specific instructions on that particular object property and how it is to be animated. Figure 10.11 shows a sample Track View of the 40-frame animation used in the Motion Blur example file, blur.max. Notice that everything, including the creation parameters for the ground box and the bouncing ball, has its own track to display particular changes and settings.

FIGURE 10.11.

Every aspect of every object, including lights, cameras, and just about everything else you can create in MAX, is represented in the Track View with its own track.

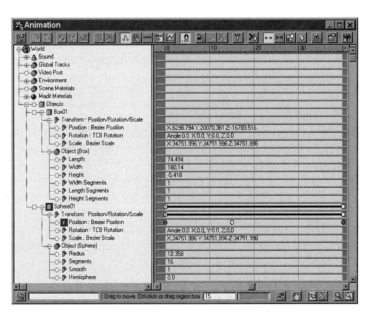

You can display the Track View in one of two ways. Most useful is to click the Track View icon in the toolbar to display a floating dialog box similar to every other dialog box in MAX. It can be rescaled to enable you to see as much or as little of its information as you need. Because it's a window, you can minimize it when you need to work in the viewports and maximize it whenever you need to access the tracks again. Leaving it open remembers the state of the hierarchy list you had designated. So if you have the branch of a particular object expanded, you won't have to keep expanding that branch as you would if you kept opening and closing the Track View window.

The second method actually replaces one of your viewports with the Track View. This is particularly handy if you want to track the specific keys of objects as you manipulate them in another viewport. Here's how this works.

To Do: Working in Track View

1. Select New from the File drop-down menu to start a new scene.

2. Click the View drop-down menu and select Viewport Configuration.

3. Click the Layout tab and select the diagram that displays one long horizontal viewport on top and two standard square viewports on the bottom. By default, the Top view is on top, the bottom left is the Left view, and the bottom right is the Perspective view. When you click the diagram, the larger display of the viewports on the bottom of the screen display your selection.

4. Now change the Top view to display the Track View. Right-click on the Top viewport to bring up a pop-up menu of alternate selections for the viewport. Select Track and New as shown in Figure 10.12.

FIGURE 10.12.

Choose the viewport layout that works best for displaying the scene view you need to manipulate and the Track View.

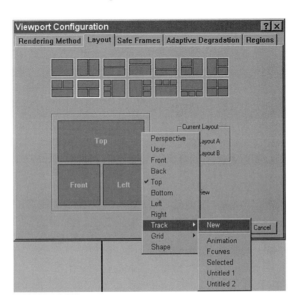

5. Click OK and MAX switches the current viewports to match your selection. Figure 10.13 shows the Track View as one of the viewports.

▲

FIGURE 10.13.

If you find yourself working back and forth regularly between Track View and the viewports, you can change the display of one of the viewports to show the Track View.

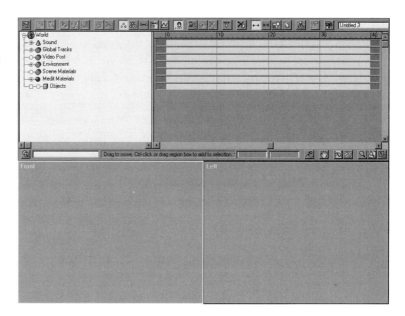

Understanding the Track View's Hierarchy List

To the left side of the Track View dialog box is the Hierarchy List, which lists everything in your World from sounds and object parameters to special effect space warps. The Hierarchy List works much like the Explorer in Windows 95 or NT. Each entity has a box or circle next to it. If an icon has a plus (+) sign in it, that means you can click that icon to expand that branch of the hierarchy and display more parameters or other linked objects beneath that object in the hierarchy. A minus (-) symbol means that branch has already been expanded to show all it contains.

With this amount of information available, the Track View becomes a very busy dialog box very quickly, which might confuse you. Thankfully, you can customize how information appears by using filters. Now take a look at how you might weed out the information you might not need, as well as some shortcuts to use in the Hierarchy List.

To Do: Using Track View's Hierarchy List

1. Load blur.max from the accompanying CD-ROM.
2. Click the Track View icon in the toolbar to open the Track View dialog box.

3. In the Hierarchy List, left click the + sign in the square icon next to Objects to display the objects in the scene.

4. Instead of clicking each of the two objects' + sign icons to expand their branches, use a shortcut. Right-click the word Objects, which is the Parent of the Objects branch, and select Expand Tracks. In one mouse click, you opened every track within the Objects branch of the Hierarchy List. Using the menu available through the right mouse click can save you a few mouse clicks. Figure 10.14 shows the available shortcuts using the right mouse button.

FIGURE 10.14.

The right mouse click menu within the Track View's Hierarchy List offers many shortcuts to accessing only the information you need.

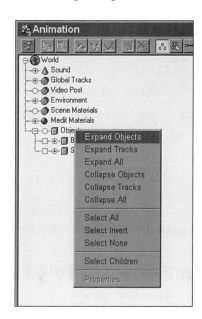

5. Minimize the Track View window and select the Sphere01 object. Now maximize the Track View window and you see another shortcut to minimizing what appears in the Track View.

6. Right-click the first icon on the left side of the Track View dialog box. This button is the filter button, but right-clicking it is a quick way of accessing some common filters. Figure 10.15 shows the filter button's right click pop-up menu.

7. Click Selected Objects Only and notice that only the Tracks pertaining to the Sphere01 object now appear in the Track View. This filter remains selected until you once again enter this menu and turn it off. This makes the filter interactive.

8. Click the box object in one of the viewports and then look at the Track View window. The Tracks for the Sphere01 object are replaced with those of the Box01 object.

Figure 10.15.

The right mouse click menu of the Filter Button has some common filters for quick access.

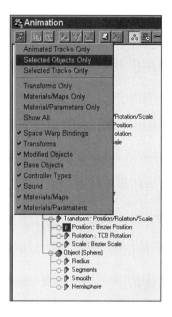

By left mouse clicking the Filter button, you have access to every possible element that appears in the Track View. You have the option of turning each Track on or off. As you use the Track View in your own animations, you'll find the ability to turn certain things on and off to be a major help in uncluttering the Track View dialog box.

Understanding the Track View's Edit Window

The right side of the Track View dialog box is the Edit window. Here you see the actual timeline for your animation. Similar to the Hierarchy List, you can customize how information appears. Many times you'll be interested in seeing in what frame range a certain movement occurs. Other times you'll want to see more specific details of what keys are located within a particular range. By expanding or collapsing the various tracks and using familiar viewport navigation tools, you gain access to more and more detailed information.

Adjusting, Zooming, and Panning the Edit Window

Take a quick look at ways to adjust how information appears in the Edit window.

To Do: Adjusting the Edit Window

1. Open blur.max from the accompanying CD-ROM.
2. Select the Sphere01 object and click the Track View icon.

3. Right-click the Filter button and click Selected Objects Only.

4. Right-click Objects in the Hierarchy List and click Expand All (see Figure 10.16). This opens all the tracks for only the selected object in your scene.

FIGURE 10.16.

Using Selected Objects Only and Expand All expands all tracks listed under the selected object.

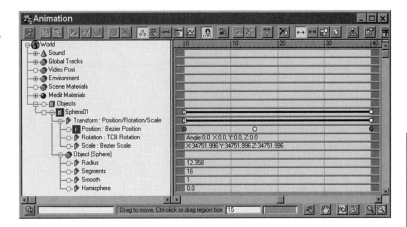

10

5. You're currently looking at the Keys view for the Edit window. Now change the display to show only range bars. On the Track View's toolbar, select the icon that looks like a black line with two white boxes on either end, called the Edit Ranges button. This changes the display from showing keys to showing the range those keys occupy. Use ranges when you don't need to edit individual keys. Figure 10.17 shows each of the two types of displays.

FIGURE 10.17.

The Edit Window can display information by showing individual keys (top), or range bars (bottom).

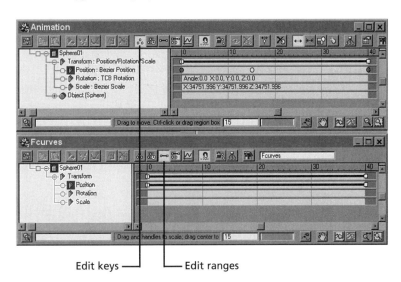

Edit keys ─┘   └─ Edit ranges

6. The lower-right area of the Track View dialog box has the view navigation tools, many of which are the same as viewport navigation tools. They include Pan, Zoom Extents, Zoom, and Zoom Region. Select Zoom Region and click and drag the mouse to draw a square around the first and second key for the Sphere01 object. Release the mouse button and the Edit Window zooms to include only the area you defined. Figure 10.18 shows how to define a Zoom Region.

FIGURE 10.18.

You can zoom regions and otherwise navigate the Edit window just as you can any viewport.

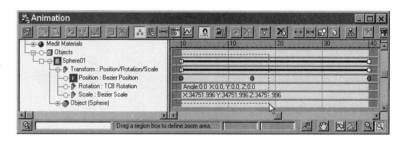

Creating, Moving, and Deleting Keys

What MAX offers you, by way of the Animate button, is a quick and basic set of keys. After you create motion, or change some animated settings in your scene, you'll see these basic keys in Track View. Although the motion can be acceptable, in many situations it needs help. As you define the motion in your animations, you will quite often need to add, move, or delete keys of your own or adjust the in-betweens. Now learn how to work with keys in an actual animation.

To Do: Working with the Animation Keys

1. Load tank.max from the accompanying CD-ROM. This simple scene has a tank turning away from the camera, driving off in the distance, and then turning around and driving back toward the camera.

2. Examine the basic keys created by MAX as you adjust the tank's position using the Animate button. Right-click the Track View Filter button and click Selected Objects Only.

3. Click the Select By Name button from MAX's toolbar to bring up the Select By Name dialog box. Click the object named FT17-BER, which is actually a Grouping of all the objects that make up the tank.

4. In the Track View, Click the + sign in the Box icon next to the Object header. Then right-click on the FT17-BER name and select Expand Tracks to display the tracks for the tank. You see the keys for the tank as shown in Figure 10.19.

FIGURE 10.19.

*The basic keys MAX
added for your tank
movement are shown
in Track View.*

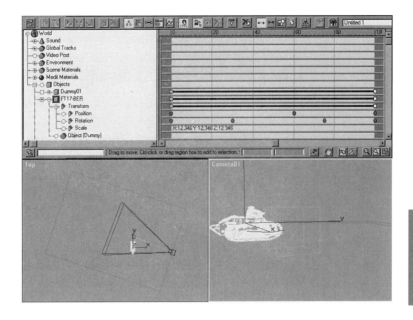

The viewports in this scene are set to display objects as bounding boxes in
order to speed up screen performance. Bounding boxes are created at the
size of the boundary extents of your objects, so their size is accurate. If you
work with objects that are complex and take a long time to view onscreen
as they are animated, try to work in Bounding Box mode. You select this
option by right-clicking on any viewport name and selecting the Other
option and one of the five possible Other options MAX supports. Figure
10.20 shows this viewport fly-out menu.

FIGURE 10.20.

*Displaying a viewport
in quick-rendering
Bounding Boxes can
speed up your work.*

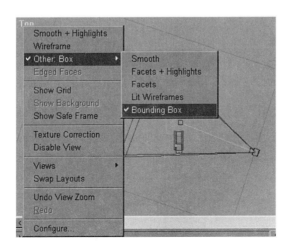

10

5. Activate the Camera01 viewport and play the animation by clicking the blue arrow pointing to the right in the section at the bottom of your screen that resembles VCR controls. Figure 10.21 shows these controls.

FIGURE 10.21.

VCR type controls enable you to rewind, play, or step through your animation frame by frame.

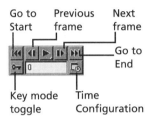

6. Tanks tend to completely finish their turn/rotation before they drive off in any direction, so adjust your movement. Looking at the keys in the Edit window, you see a starting key for both Position and Rotation at frame 0. These are the starting points for your tank. The next rotation key at frame 30 is the first turn the tank makes. You want the position of the tank to remain the same until that turn is complete at frame 30. To do so, you need to copy the tank's frame 0 Position key to frame 30. Hold down the left Shift key as you click the frame 0 Position key and drag it until the readout at the bottom of the Track View window reads 30, or simply align it with the frame 30 Rotation key.

7. If you play the animation, you notice things aren't quite right yet. Although the keys for frame 0 and 30 are the same, there is movement between them. That's because MAX, by default, uses smooth tangents between keys. This needs to be changed anytime you want hard turn, corners, or more abrupt movement. To change the tangent type between keys, enter the Key Info dialog box by right-clicking the frame 0 key for Position. Figure 10.22 shows this dialog box with the available tangents MAX supports.

FIGURE 10.22.

The Key Info dialog box provides a way to fine-tune each key and shows how your animation will behave between keys.

8. The In tangent affects the animation before a key, but you're interested in the Out tangent to affect the animation after frame 0 and before frame 30. Click and hold the Box icon under the Out tangent setting, and drag to select the icon that looks like three white boxes with straight lines between them. This is the tangent as seen in Figure 10.22. After you select this tangent, click the arrow to the right of the tangent box to copy this same tangent to the In tangent box of the next key. If you advance to the second key by clicking the right arrow at the top of this dialog box, you see the same tangent in the In tangent box.

9. Play the animation and notice the tank holds position for 30 frames while turning. Rotation keys have a similar setting called Continuity that is set for smooth motion at each key. This needs to be changed in your animation because you want hard turns for your tank. Right-click the first Rotation key and change the Continuity setting to 0; then click the advance frame arrow at the top of the dialog box and make the same change for each of the four Rotation keys. Figure 10.23 shows this dialog box.

FIGURE 10.23.

Rotational keys have their own settings, as shown in the Key Info dialog box.

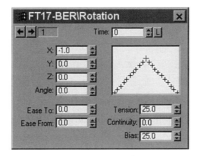

10. As you approach frame 60, the rotation needs to stay constant. Click on the Rotation key at frame 30 while holding the left Shift key down. Drag the key to frame 60 to make a copy and release the mouse button.

11. Play the animation to see how you're doing. The last change you need is to make the tank's position remain constant during your final rotation that happens from frame 60 to frame 75. Using the Shift-click method, copy the Position key at frame 60 to frame 75. Play the animation to see the results.

12. Make one final adjustment to the tangents for the Position keys. Right-click the second Position key and change its tangent to the tangent that looks like a straight line pointing down, and click the arrow next to it to copy to the next key.

13. Click the advance frame arrow to go to key 3. Change its Out tangent to the linear motion that looks like three white boxes connected by straight lines. Click the arrow to copy to the In tangent of key 4. Continue on to key 4 and assign the straight line tangent to its Out tangent and copy it to key 5. That should give you the stop and turn motion you want.

14. Save the changes to tank.max to your hard drive.

▲ 15. You can load the tank.avi from the accompanying CD-ROM to see the final rendered animation with the hard turns you added.

Along with the ability to move keys, you might also have the need to add or delete keys. Adding keys using the Add Key button creates a key at the current frame that contains a snapshot of the object's current state at that particular frame in time. You might decide you need to add a frame after setting an object in motion. Take a quick look at how you might add a key to your tank scene.

To Do: Adding a key to an animation

1. Load the tank.max file you have been working in from your hard drive. If your animation didn't quite match the description, you can load tankpart2.max from the accompanying CD-ROM.

2. Add a bump for the tank to run over as it approaches the camera. Scroll the timeline, or jump to frame 82. Click the Add Key button in the Track View toolbar. It looks like a round key icon with a yellow starburst. Now click the Position Track at the current frame to add a key representing the present state of the tank. Adding this key enables you to make changes to the tanks position after frame 82 while assuring you the position of the tank from frames 75 and 82 will remain unaffected.

3. Because you also want the rotation to remain the same between frames 75 and 82, you need to make an adjustment to the rotation track as well. You don't need to add a key for rotation because the tank isn't rotating after frame 75. Use the Shift-click method to copy the Rotational key at frame 75 to frame 82. If you play the animation at this point, you notice that adding this key hasn't changed anything.

4. Advance the animation to frame 87.

5. Activate the Left viewport and press the F key on your keyboard. This shortcut changes the viewport to the Front view.

6. Using the Zoom Region tool, draw a region box around the tank object. Rotate the tank to make it appear it is driving over a bump on the ground.

7. Click the Animate button to turn it on; then click the Select and Rotate tool and select the tank object. Rotate the tank about its Z axis 12 degrees.

8. Use the Select and Move tool to move the tank on its Y axis until it appears slightly airborne, as shown in Figure 10.24.

FIGURE 10.24.

Work in the Front viewport to adjust the tank's rotation.

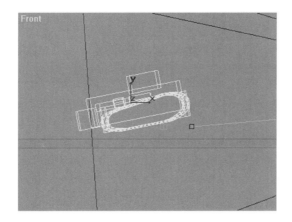

9. Advance to frame 91. Now you have to return the tank to its previous rotation and readjust its position so it's back on the ground. In Track View, Shift-click the Rotation key at frame 82 and copy it to frame 91. The tank resumes its prebump rotation.

10. Use the Select and Move tool to move the tank along its Y axis until it touches the ground object.

11. You need to make one last adjustment to the tank's Position In and Out tangents. Right-click the Position key at frame 75. Because your tank will have very jerky motion, change all the In and Out tangents to the straight line tangent.

12. Save the changes to tank.max to your hard drive.

13. You can see the changes by loading tankbump.avi from the accompanying CD-ROM.

Adding a Visibility Track

You might encounter many situations where you want an object to suddenly appear in the scene—and perhaps disappear just as suddenly. To do this, you can add a Visibility Track for the object in Track View. Here's an extreme use of this feature in your tank scene.

To Do: Adjusting for Quick Entrances and Exits

1. Load the tank.max file you have been working in from your hard drive.

2. Click the Display tab and the Unhide All button. You see the Red Alert text object appear in the Camera view as seen in Figure 10.25.

▲ To Do ▼

FIGURE 10.25.

Any object, such as the Red Alert text in this scene, can be assigned a Visibility Track so you can toggle its visibility on and off.

3. In Track View, click Red Alert Text in the Hierarchy List to highlight it.

4. In the Track View toolbar, click the Add Visibility Track icon. It looks like an eye. You see a Visibility Track added just above the Transform Track for the highlighted object. By default, when you add a Visibility Track, the visibility is set to ON—represented in the track by a solid blue line as shown in Figure 10.26.

FIGURE 10.26.

A solid blue line in the Visibility Track indicates a visible object.

5. Click the Add Key button and add a key in the Visibility Track at frame 10. This turns OFF visibility at frame 10.

6. Continue adding keys every 10 frames through frame 100. You should have a track that looks like Figure 10.27.

FIGURE 10.27.

As you continue to add keys to the Visibility Track, you will be turning the object on and off repeatedly.

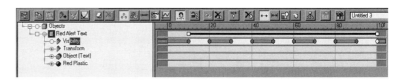

7. Save the changes to tank.max.

8. You can see the flashing Red Alert text by loading tanktext.avi from the accompanying CD-ROM.

Working with Controllers

If you were in charge of thinking up a name for the type of plug-in that controls all the animation processes you assign in MAX, what would you call it? How about a Controller? Good idea, because that's what they're called, and that's what they do. Whether you realize it or not, you've already been using them. When you animate anything in MAX, it is assigned a controller to manage the changes. You can access Controllers in the Track View; they are identified by a green rectangle. So far you've dealt with Visibility, Position, and Rotation that are all Controllers.

Using Bézier and TCB Controllers

For the most part, Controllers are of the Bézier type. That means they create a smooth, adjustable spline between keys that you can adjust to get the motion you want. You did this earlier in today's lesson when you adjusted the In and Out tangents for the Position keys of the tank you animated.

Now reenter the same animation you used to examine editing keys to get a better feel for the Bézier type Controller.

To Do: Working with Bézier Controllers

1. Load tank.max from your hard drive.
2. Select the tank object.
3. In Track View, click the Position Track for the tank to hightlight it.
4. Click the Function Curves button in the Track View toolbar to display the spline-based curve representations of the animation. Because you assigned all linear tangents for your animation, there are no curves currently displayed. You should see a display similar to Figure 10.28.

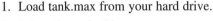

Edit keys   Function curves

FIGURE 10.28.

Displaying Function Curves in Track View gives you a visual representation of the straight or curved splines that control how the animation occurs.

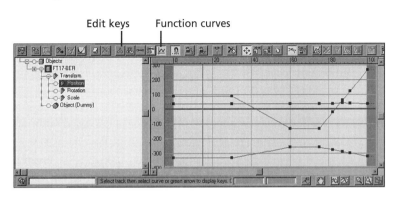

5. The black squares represent keys. The colored lines are the X (red), Y (green), and Z (blue) coordinates of the objects position. Click the Edit Keys button in the Track View toolbar to display the keys once again.

6. Right-click the first Position key and change the In and Out tangents of the first two keys to Béziér Splines, which is the bottom choice on the tangent fly-out menu you see when you hold the Tangent icon down.

7. Click the Function Curves button and click the Red line representing the X axis. When the vertices representing the keys appear, click one of the first two vertices. Notice the tangents extending out from either side of the key. Click and hold one of the tangents and move it up or down to adjust the curve as in Figure 10.29. This adjusts the movement between keys in an attempt to create smoother motion. If you play the animation, you see the tank now has some movement prior to frame 30 that it didn't have before.

FIGURE 10.29.

Tangents on Bézier Splines allow fine adjustments for smooth motion.

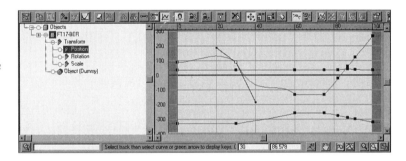

In animations where smooth motion is desired, you can use the tangents to finely tune the subtle adjustments needed before or after a change in your object's direction.

Another frequently encountered Controller is the TCB type. This type uses three settings for Tension, Continuity, and Bias to adjust the smooth spline between keys. You also used this type of Controller when you edited the Rotation keys of your tank animation.

Using Path Controllers

So far, your experience with Controllers has occurred in the background, without your direct knowledge of what was actually happening. However, some movements benefit from direct interaction with Controllers. For example, keyframing animation by moving objects around your scene one move at a time is great and works for many situations. But when you use more detailed movements including tens or hundreds of adjustments, you can take advantage of a Path Controller. A popular use for a Path Controller is an architectural walkthrough. If you intend on animating a camera as it makes its way from room to room in a house, attaching the camera to a spline path using a Path Controller is the only way to go.

Animating Objects Along a Path

Any spline you create in MAX or import from another program can be used as a path. You can even use drawing programs such as CorelDraw and Adobe Illustrator to develop complex shapes to import into MAX as .ai or .dxf files. It's often easier to create very complex shapes in full-blown vector drawing programs than it is to use MAX's tools. Make a quick walkthrough of a building to see how this works.

To Do: Animating objects along a path

▼ To Do

1. Open walkthru.max from the accompanying CD-ROM. This store model might represent the design for your client. But before building the actual structure, they want to walk around and through the building making cost-effective changes to the virtual building.

2. Create a path for a camera that walks the entire circumference of the building and then enters the building moving around a bit inside. Activate the Top viewport and you create your spline path.

3. Click the Create tab and the Shapes icon. Choose the Line Object Type and scroll the panel so you can see the Creation Method rollup. Make sure Initial Type is corner and Drag Type is Bézier.

4. Click once at the bottom of the Top viewport to set the starting point. Move the mouse to the left as if you are following the hour hand of a clock over the Top viewport. Click the mouse and hold it down when you reach the number 8. With the mouse button held down, drag to the left and up slightly. When you drag, you define the curvature of the point you just made. Try to create a smooth curve, but don't worry about getting it perfect because you can fix it later. Continue placing points around the building and into its interior to resemble something similar to Figure 10.30.

5. After you place all the points and create the spline into the building, click the Modify Tab and add an Edit Spline modifier. Work on each vertex until you have a nice smooth path to follow.

6. Click the second vertex on the spline and adjust its position with the Select and Move tool, as well as adjusting its handle bars until you feel you have a smooth corner. Proceed with all the vertices on the spline until you have something similar to Figure 10.31. You might even decide to delete some of your vertices if they are not necessary.

10

FIGURE 10.30.

A spline path drawn around, and into, the building will serve as the basis of the Path Controller.

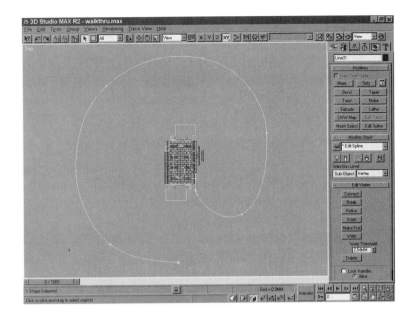

FIGURE 10.31.

Use the Edit Spline modifier to refine the shape of your spline until you have a smooth path to follow.

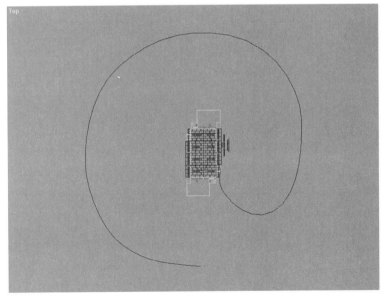

7. Create a Target Camera in the Top viewport. Place the camera object around the start of the spline and the target object at the center of the building. This way you can get a preview and decide if there are any adjustments that need to be made.

8. Now assign the Path Controller to the Camera and see how you're doing. With the Camera01 object selected, click the Motion tab and highlight Position: Béziér Position in the Assign Controller rollup.

9. Click the Assign Controller button just above the scrollable window that looks like a green arrow and a black arrow pointing to the right.

10. The Assign Position Controller dialog box opens as shown in Figure 10.32. Choose Path and click OK.

FIGURE 10.32.

The Assign Position Controller dialog box lists all the available Controllers for your object.

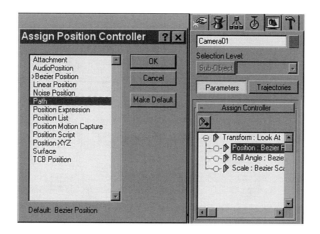

11. Pan down the Panel until you see Path Parameters as shown in Figure 10.33, and click the Pick Path button. In any viewport, click the spline path you created. The camera object should snap to the beginning of the path.

FIGURE 10.33.

Click the Pick Path button to select the path from any viewport.

12. Play the animation to see how you're doing. Pretty good—until you reach the steps to the store. At that point, you can use a view that looks up the stairs instead of so closely at the side of the building. If you look at Figure 10.32, you see a section labeled Look At Target, for which you accepted the default of the actual Camera01.Target. This works, but you need to realize that this can have been any object, or dummy object, you selected. To help your animation, you need to animate the position of the target starting at this problem point at frame 50.

13. Select the camera target object and open the Track View. Jump to frame 49, and add a key for the camera target's position at frame 49 because you don't want the target to move prior to frame 50.

14. Jump to frame 55 and turn on the Animate button. Use the Select and Move tool to move the camera target until it is just outside the doorway the camera will enter. See Figure 10.34.

FIGURE 10.34.

Move the camera target to eliminate a problem view.

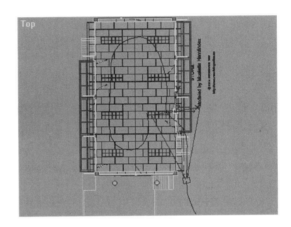

15. Jump to frame 61 and return the camera target back to the center of the room. This fixes the door problem but doesn't allow the user to see the ceiling at all. Now make one last adjustment to the camera target.

16. Jump to frame 78 and, with the camera target still selected, open the Track View. Shift-click to copy the camera target's frame 61 position to frame 78.

17. Jump to the last frame. Use the Select and Move tool in the Front viewport to move the camera target along its Y axis toward the ceiling as shown in Figure 10.35. Turn the Animate button off, save the file, and play the animation to see your walkthrough.

▲

FIGURE 10.35.

Further adjust the camera target to show a view of the ceiling.

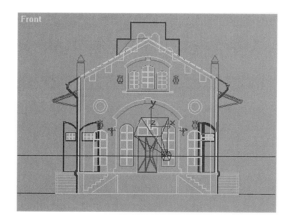

Configuring (and Reconfiguring) Time

If you were to render the walkthrough animation you just created, you'd see that it flies by at the speed of light. You created this animation, did all this work, and didn't think about how long it should last. Obviously, 100 frame (just over three seconds), isn't enough. It probably should occur over 1,000 frames if you really want your client to see what you designed. Don't worry; there is a simple solution. Located next to the frame number display in the lower-right corner of the screen is the Time Configuration button. This is where you should initially set up information such as number of frames and frame rate.

Up to this point, you covered quite a few animation techniques without putting much thought into preparation of your scene in regards to output. Now fix your walkthrough animation, and at the same time, learn how you should have set up the animation to begin with.

To Do: Adjusting time in your animations

1. Open the walkthru.max file from your hard drive. If your animation doesn't look quite right at this point, you can load walkthrupart2.max from the accompanying CD-ROM.

2. Click the Time Configuration button.

3. In the Time Configuration dialog box, in the section labeled Animate, click Re-scale Time.

4. In the Re-scale Time dialog box, enter 1,000 for the Total frames and click OK. Both dialog boxes are shown in Figure 10.36.

5. Save the file and then open walkthru.avi to see the final rendering of the walkthru animation.

FIGURE **10.36.**

*The Re-scale Time fea-
ture enables you to
increase or decrease
the total number of
frames without affect-
ing anything but the
speed of your anima-
tion.*

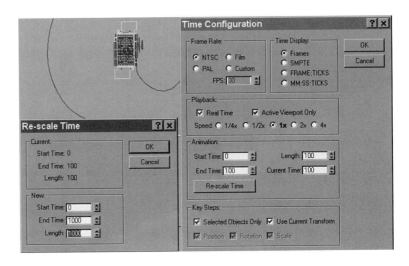

Summary

Today, you covered many basic and some advanced animation concepts and techniques.
This information serves as a good basis for Day 11, "Animation Part II," where you
examine some animation techniques for more complex sequences dealing with Inverse
Kinematics and detailed hierarchical links. Here are some of the key points from today's
lesson to remember:

- Always check and double-check that the Animate button is on or off, depending on
  what you need. I can't stress enough that this saves headaches.

- Use Ghosting to study how your objects move to help you make fine-tuned adjustments.

- Motion Blur can add just enough blur to moving objects to make motion appear
  smooth and realistic. You can also use it to create special effects for fast-moving
  objects by over exaggerating the settings.

- Track View is your timeline for your animation. Use it often and get to know the
  many ways to customize its display to see only the information you need to see.
  Good animation can become great with the right amount of time spent working in
  Track View adjusting keys.

- Keyframing each move is one way to animate your objects, but explore Controllers
  such as the Path Controller to automate some of the tedious work keyframing
  requires.

Q&A

Q What do I do if I have made quite a few changes to my scene and realize I forgot to turn the Animate button on?

A The only thing you can do is use the Undo button to undo all the moves and rely on your memory to redo the moves with the Animate button on. Then write a note to yourself and stick it to your monitor that reads "Check the Animate Button!"

Q What is the best method of motion blur to use?

A There is no best method, but depending on your intended effect, there might be better choices. To smooth motion, low duration settings for Image Motion Blur create a good effect. For special effects, Scene Motion Blur might be the better choice. Experimentation for your particular need is the best way to determine the best method.

Q I don't understand what Controllers are and how to use them. Can I still effectively use MAX?

A Yes. Remember that most of the Controllers are behind the scenes and don't require you to actually think about adding them. Simply adding a change in an object's position or rotation adds a Controller, although you didn't think about it. By familiarizing yourself with more interactive Controllers, such as the Path Controller, you can expand you abilities tremendously. Exploration into the world of advanced Controllers is well worth the time.

10

DAY **11**

Animation Part II

Choreographing the Elements

If you ever watched college football games, you probably sat through your share of marching bands. What makes the bands movements so intriguing is the order and complimentary fashion in which they happen. Waves of motion and flowing lines of band members march in step with one another. They twist and turn their instruments in time to the music and draw your attention to the field. Somehow, hundreds of individuals spread out over a huge field and seem to be working together as parts of the same animated object. Marching bands are a collection of finely choreographed individual movements, and they are a great example of what you need to accomplish with your animations.

Second only to having a great story to tell, the way you set up your scene and have all the elements work together is the key to great animation. Every move should have a purpose and receive the attention to detail it demands to move in a proper manner. Today, you explore the relationship between individual objects and how they work together to form more complex animated objects and motion. Here are some of the key topics covered today:

- How to create a proper hierarchy for the most predictable motion
- How to create an inverse kinematics animation for characters and mechanical objects
- How to use Morphing to change object appearance
- How to tap the power of MAXScript to add more control over objects and streamline tedious processes

Natural and Mechanical Motion

If you want to over-generalize motion, you can say there are two types: natural and mechanical. You might define these types further as smooth or rigid. Human motion is natural, or smooth. Machinery, for this general purpose, exhibits mechanical, rigid motion. Most objects, living or machine, have the capability to incorporate both types of motion. The same is true in MAX. You can assign either type of motion to any object in your scene. You need to consider each object's physical characteristics carefully to determine which type of motion is appropriate. For example, although you might animate the motion of an athletic teenager as smooth, the motion of a ninety-year-old man walking with a cane might take a mechanical appearance.

As with most steps in creating your animations, the time you spend refining each object's motion will pay off in results closer to what you intended. Many not-so-obvious aspects of your individual objects have a great deal to do with the type of motion that is perceived. Take the ninety-year-old man with a cane example. Posture plays a large role in the perception of motion and the type of character you are creating. Range of motion and speed of movements are also areas on which to focus some critical attention. Swaying of the hips and shoulder movements for character animation tell a lot to the audience, as well as how the character interacts with the environment. Consider a couple of example movies of block skeleton figures walking across a room. With no facial or bodily features rendered, you still get a strong sense of their physical characteristics from their posture, speed, range, and type of motion.

To Do: Block animation examples

1. Load ballet.avi from the accompanying CD-ROM. This animation shows the fluid motion of a ballet dancer. Notice how movements seem to blend into one continuous motion.

2. Now load cane.avi from the accompanying CD-ROM. Set your movie player so it automatically repeats and you immediately see the rigid motion that portrays an elderly or injured person walking with a cane. Notice that even though walking with a cane indicates an injured leg, the rigid motion is evident throughout the entire body.

Note   These movies were created by using a plug-in for MAX called Character Studio. The motion data is from BioVision, a company that creates motion data files by motion capture of actual real-world movement. If you use Character Studio, you can access some motion data to plug into your characters from the Kinetix Web site (www.ktx.com). However, the basic principle of motion does not require the plug-in—nor does the animation of such movements.

Relationships between Objects

To animate convincing motion of humans, machinery, or any object, you have to spend some time studying how that object moves and interacts with other objects. Consider the movements necessary, and the multiple objects involved, to animate someone swinging an axe.

To Do: Relationships between objects in animation

1. Load chop.avi from the accompanying CD-ROM. This animation shows the motion capture data applied to a skeletal figure in MAX.
2. To emphasize the motion, take a look at the series of images in Figure 11.1.

FIGURE 11.1.

Even if one part of the body does most of the work, it usually affects other connecting parts as well.

The purpose of viewing this animation, and studying the still images, is to see the effect of someone swinging an axe. At first, it is seen as something you do with your hands and arms, but when you really look at the motion you see a complete body movement. When you begin to realize this type of relationship between connecting objects, you're ready to create properly moving objects in your animation. The next two sections look at how you apply these types of motion in MAX through Linking and using inverse kinematics.

Linking and Hierarchies

For objects consisting of a collection of smaller objects, such as a human figure or a machine, you need a way to define relationships between each individual object. You do this with a process called *Linking*, which uses a Parent-Child model. Imagine your individual objects in this method as links on a chain. The first object (or link in the chain) is the Parent, and all objects linked to it are its children. If you link each object in the chain to the object directly next to it on this chain, you create a series of parent-child relationships (see Figure 11.2).

FIGURE 11.2.

In the example of a simplified human model, the pelvis is the ultimate parent for the lower body, and the torso is the parent for the upper body.

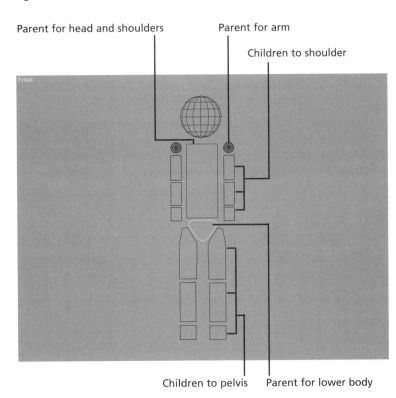

Before any linking can be done, you must understand how your object moves and how each individual part affects any other parts on the same object. Thus, the previous sections on understanding motion are very important. Don't let this intimidate your animation process, however, because you can always unlink, relink, and add other links as needed if you're not getting the motion you planned. You will eventually end up with an object, or objects, that serve as the ultimate parent object(s) for the composite object being animated. This ultimate parent object(s) controls all, or most of, the entire structure, meaning each movement of this ultimate parent object moves all of its children. However, you can choose two main ways to link objects to this ultimate parent object(s). You can select all the children and link them all directly to the parent object. This creates a two-link hierarchy. Or you can select individual objects at the end of the chain and link each object to the object directly above it in the progressive chain to the ultimate parent (see Figure 11.3). The decision depends on the type of motion you need to send through this chain of objects. If you want every object to move each time the ultimate parent moves, link each object directly to the parent object. If, however, you need only certain objects to move when the ultimate parent moves, create a multilinked chain from each object back to the parent. Such a model would be a human body.

FIGURE 11.3.

Link each of the weights on the bar directly to the bar, but create a multilinked chain of objects for complex objects such as humans.

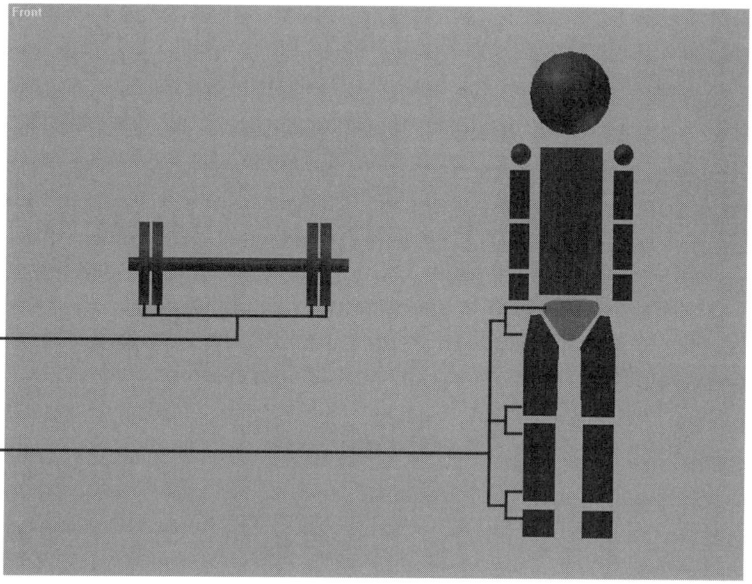

All four weights linked directly to bar

Links

Although the ultimate parent object controlling the body might be the torso, you don't want every finger and toe twitching each time you move the body's torso. What you do want is the upper legs moving when the torso moves (under certain restrictions discussed later), the lower leg moving when the upper leg moves, and the foot moving when the lower leg moves. If you find yourself singing, "the foot bone's connected to the ankle bone, the ankle bone's connected to the leg bone," you might think it was written by someone trying to figure out a linked hierarchy for a character animation. Now proceed with some of the details of linking.

Working with Parent and Child Objects

When linking, you use two buttons on the toolbar: Select and Link, and Unlink Selection. Figure 11.4 shows the two buttons and their locations. These buttons act just like the Transform buttons. They select an object and enable you to then select its parent.

FIGURE 11.4.

Use Select and Link and Unlink Selection to set up the hierarchical relationships of your objects.

To Do: Linking parent and child objects

▼ To Do

1. Load dog.max from the accompanying CD-ROM. This file contains a very crude model of a dog created from standard primitive shapes in MAX.

   Review this animal and think about how it will move. You can separate it into four basic sections to identify one parent object for the entire body, and three separate areas where objects will act as independent branches linked to that parent. Figure 11.5 shows how you section off this simple model. The torso object is the ultimate parent, controlling every other object making up the dog. The tail is a branch of one object, the legs make up another section, and the head the third. Actually, each leg is a branch independent of the other legs, each connected to the body parent. But the three major sections remain the same: head, tail, and legs, all as children to the torso (the parent for the entire body). This is similar to the way you might section off a human body with head, arms, and legs, each attached to the torso or pelvis as the parent of each section.

FIGURE 11.5.

If you first section off the major parts of the objects, you can begin to see how each individual object must be linked.

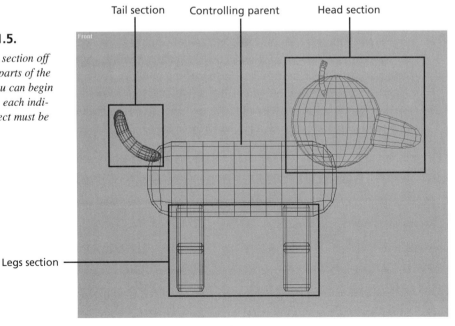

Within sections with multiple objects, such as the legs, you start with the object that is farthest from the parent object and work your way back to the parent.

2. Click the Select and Link button on the toolbar.

3. Start by linking each lower leg to its upper leg. Click on any of the lower leg objects. Notice the Link icon that replaces the cursor when you hold the cursor over the selected object.

4. Hold down the left mouse button and move the cursor off the selected object. Notice the Link icon disappears.

5. Drag the icon over the upper leg object. The Link icon now reappears, telling you that it is possible to link to this object. Before releasing the mouse button on the upper leg, drag the icon back over the lower leg object. Notice the x'd out icon that appears. This tells you that you cannot link to this object, in this case, because it is the same object you have selected. Drag back to the upper leg object and release the mouse button when the Link icon returns. The lower leg object is now a child of the upper leg—it's parent.

6. Repeat the above steps until each lower leg object is linked to its upper leg.

7. Now link all the upper legs to the torso in one step by selecting all the upper leg objects and linking them to the torso object. Because all four upper legs share the same parent, you can link at the same time.

8. Because the head and tail sections contain only one object per section, linking is one simple step. Use the Select and Link button to select both the tail and head, and link them to the torso.

9. Save the file to your hard drive as mydoglinks.max.

At any time, you can use the Select By Name dialog box to view the hierarchy you establish through linking. To do so, click the Select By Name button in the toolbar. When the dialog box opens, check the Display Subtree check box. This might help you to see the chain of command from the parent to the last child.

To Do: Viewing created hierarchies

1. Select the four upper leg objects; then click the Select By Name button.

2. In the lower-left corner of the Select By Name dialog box, check the Display Subtree check box. You can now see the relationship of all objects in the scene. Each indentation identifies another child object link, as seen in Figure 11.6.

FIGURE 11.6.

You can see a visual display of the hierarchical tree you create by linking by using the Select By Name dialog box.

To have control over individual objects at the end of the hierarchical chain, independent from every single torso (parent object) movement, you must link in this multilinked chain method. This is also a good time to mention that child objects, such as the lower leg in this example, can move independently from their parents.

To Do: Child objects that move independently

1. Select the lower leg object with the Select and Move tool.

2. Move the lower leg around in any direction, and right-click to cancel any permanent movement. Notice that the upper leg (its parent) is unaffected.

3. Select the upper leg and move it around in any direction. Its child, the lower leg, follows each and every movement it makes.

Just like the real world, children in MAX don't always listen to their parents. As the animator, and ultimate controller of the parent-child relationship, you dictate which instructions from its parent each child listens to or ignores. You can limit the transform (move, rotate, and scale) instructions a child listens to by locking certain axes, so the object will not change its orientation about those axes. You can also limit which transforms are inherited by each child from its parent. Consider how the parent-child relationship works with the dog object you are working on. Because dogs' legs don't usually rotate about their center, you start by locking some axis movements to prevent unwanted movements.

To Do: Finer control over child-parent relationships

1. Open mydoglinks.max.

2. Select all eight leg objects. Locking axes can be done for multiple objects at the same time.

3. Click the Hierarchy tab and the Link Info button. This exposes the Locks rollup menu.

4. In the Rotate section, check the X and Z check boxes. This prevents the leg objects from rotating about these axes. Your dogs legs now rotate only forward and backward, as they should. Figure 11.7 shows the locks you applied.

FIGURE 11.7.

Locking axes for your objects can prevent unwanted movements.

11

5. In the User viewport, use the Select and Rotate tool to select any of the upper leg objects and click on them to rotate. Notice that they rotate only about the Y axis.

6. Use the same procedure for the torso object, locking its X axis rotation.

7. Save the changes to mydoglinks.max.

The dog object is now completely linked, with the torso object serving as the ultimate parent that can move the entire dog. But the dog is not quite ready for animation. Something is still not working as it should. The next section fixes your dog and makes it animation-ready.

Inheriting Properties from Parent Objects

What's the problem with your dog? It has to do with heredity. No, this dog didn't inherit bad animation traits from its virtual ancestors, but it might not be inheriting all the right information from its parents. To be exact, it's inheriting too much information from its parents. MAX enables you to control what transforms each child inherits from its parents. This is done much in the same way as locking axes was done in the previous section.

To Do: Controlling what the child inherits

1. Load mydoglinks.max. Take a look at what is wrong with the inherited links.

2. Use the Select and Rotate and rotate the front right upper-leg object in the user viewport. Notice that the rotation not only affects the upper, but also the lower leg as seen in Figure 11.8. This is not what you want. The lower leg should remain attached to the upper leg, as if it were pinned to it at its pivot point, but it should not rotate.

FIGURE 11.8.

By default, all transforms are inherited by child objects. Here the rotation of the upper leg also rotates the lower leg.

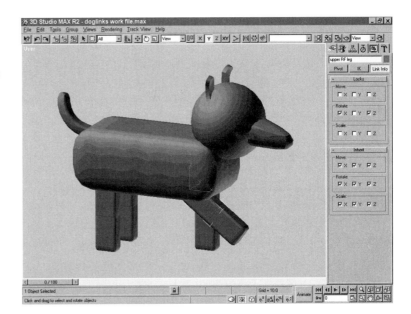

3. Undo the rotation.

4. To make adjustments regarding inherited traits to the child object, select the lower-leg object of the same leg and click the Hierarchy tab. You should see the Inherit rollup in the Hierarchy Panel.

5. In the Rotate section, remove the check in the Y check box.

6. Select the upper-leg object and rotate it once again. This time, the lower-leg object behaves as it should, appearing as if it is pinned to the upper leg, but not rotating. This looks more like a natural dog leg movement as shown in Figure 11.9.

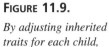

FIGURE 11.9.

By adjusting inherited traits for each child, you can create correctly moving links.

▲

7. To complete the dog, repeat the steps for the other three legs and save the file as mydoglinks.max.

11

The dog's legs now move as they should—to an extent. You need to do more to assure proper movement. The dog's legs now rotate only forward and back, and they bend as they should. But if you want to, you can rotate the leg in a complete circle—obviously not what you want. In the next section, you see how you can use inverse kinematics to limit ranges of motion.

Inverse Kinematics—The Tale That Wagged the Dog

There are two methods of animating objects in MAX: forward and inverse kinematics (IK). Forward kinematics is used by default and might seem most logical to most people. It works on a hierarchical linkage from the parent down through its children. This means you animate by moving the parent object. Each move is passed down the hierarchy to the children of that parent, and so on. This method is used in this book. Inverse kinematics is just the opposite. You animate by adjusting a child object, and its transformations move up the hierarchical chain to its parent object, and potentially up to its parent, and so on up the chain. Inverse kinematics is usually easier to animate than forward kinematics. However, it takes more thought and time to set up properly.

Tip

When do you use forward kinematics and when do you use inverse kinematics? The deciding factor might be the detail and amount of movement your object will have. For example, if you have a human model that will take two steps and stop, that is probably quicker to set up with normal forward kinematics. If that human model will be running through the scene and walking up steps, or some other complicated motion, it's well worth the time to set up the correct IK parameters. Every situation will be different, but these are good starting points on which to base your decision.

IK gives you the ability to limit the range of motion for each object (link) in the hierarchy. This helps you solve your object rotation problems in your dog example. The next section explores how to define the ranges for each linked object.

Defining Joint Parameters

The point at which two objects are linked is called a *joint*—just like your elbow is the joint between your upper and lower arm. Your elbow links the two parts of your arm together, and it also defines the limits or ranges of motion for your lower arm. Moving up in this human body analogy, the shoulder is the joint between the torso and the arm, which controls the limits or ranges of motion for the arm as a whole. In the dog example, each object has a joint that must be adjusted to get predictable motion during IK animation. Adjusting every joint takes forethought and time; that's why the initial work for IK is so much more intensive than normal forward kinematics. The payoff is well worth it, so take the time to learn IK.

MAX supports two types of joints: sliding and rotational. A sliding joint slides, or moves, along one axis away from the point at which it is linked to its parent. You probably won't encounter any sliding joints in your body, but you definitely might in a machine or man-made object. A good example of a sliding joint is a telescoping handle on a folding luggage cart.

Rotational joints are what you have in your body—elbows, knees, shoulders, and so on. These allow the child objects to rotate about the point at which it is linked to its parent. Figure 11.10 shows each type of joint.

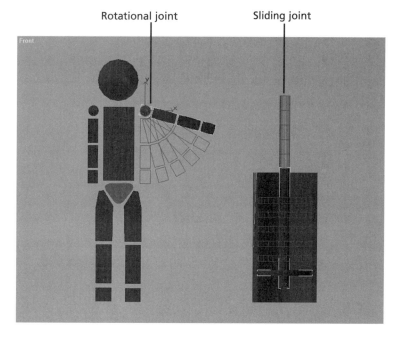

Rotational joint   Sliding joint

FIGURE 11.10.

The shoulder on the human model is a rotational joint, and the plunger in the cylinder on the right is a sliding joint. The ghosting feature highlights how each type of joint moves.

11

Take another look at your dog to see how you adjust the joints and correctly animate with IK.

To Do: Adjusting joints for proper IK animation

▼ To Do

1. Load mydoglinks.max.

2. Click on the Hierarchy tab and the IK button.

3. Close the first two rollups until you see the rollup for Rotational Joints.

4. You'll create four dummy objects, one under each of the four lower-leg objects. They will serve as a handle for each leg. The use of the dummy object allows proper rotation of the lower leg. Click the Create tab and the Helpers icon; then select the Dummy button. Draw a small box under each of the legs. This is easiest to do in the Top viewport. You then have to move the boxes in position under the legs. You should now have a setup similar to Figure 11.11.

5. Use the Select and Link tool to link each dummy to the lower leg it is beneath. The dummy objects are now the end effectors (the end of their respective IK chains) for each leg.

6. Select any one lower-leg object and click the Hierarchy tab. Make sure all of the check boxes in the Inherit rollup are checked.

Figure 11.11.

Placing the dummy object under each of the four legs creates handles to control each of the four IK chains.

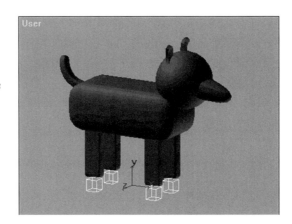

7. Now set the range limits for each object. Select the right-front lower leg and click the Hierarchy tab and IK button. Scroll the Panel until you see the Rotational Joints rollup.

8. Check the Active and Limited check boxes for all three axes. Adjust only the Y axis because it's the only axis you want potential movement on. Leave the From: spinner at 0 but adjust the To: spinner to 100. Watch the leg bend as you drag the spinner. When you reach 100, release the mouse and the object will snap back to its initial position. Repeat the steps for each lower leg object.

Tip

For objects similar to this dog, where you have more than one identical limb that requires the same setting, you might save time by creating one leg and then creating instances for the other identical limbs. That way, you have to adjust only the first object and the instances will automatically update. Think this through carefully, however, because every time you move that initial object, its instances will also move—no exceptions.

Tip

You can check the From: and To: position for any axis by clicking on the word From: or To: and holding the mouse button down. When you do, the object snaps to its current limit setting. When you release the mouse, it returns to its initial position.

9. Select the upper leg object on any leg and make the same type of adjustment to its limits. You can limit all axes but you need to adjust only the Y Axis. Set the Y limits at From: -60, and To: 30.

10. Next, after the legs, set the torso as a terminator. This way, adjusting the legs won't make the rest of the body (head, tail, torso) move. Select the torso object and access the IK Panel.

11. In the Object Parameters rollup, check the Terminator check box as shown in Figure 11.12.

FIGURE 11.12.

Setting termination for key objects constrains adjustments to a certain area of an IK chain.

12. Also set Rotational Joints to Limited for all three axes of the torso object. Adjust only the Y Axis at From: -33 and To: 0.

13. Select the tail object and set Limited for all three axes. Adjust the Y Axis at From: -2.5 and To: 49 and the Z Axis at From: -46 and To: 48.

14. The head will need Limited checked for all three axes, and it also needs adjustments on all three axes. Set the X Axis limits From: 39 To: 107, the Y Axis From: -31 To: 31, and the Z Axis From: -160 To: -40.

15. Now the best part—Auto Boning. Bones are the nonrendering control skeleton that are created inside your objects. When you have a structure that has limits set and is part of a hierarchy, Auto Boning simply creates the bones and respects all the settings you make. After you create the Bones, you work directly with the bones to animate your object. Click the Create tab, the Systems icon, and the Bones button. You access the Bones Panel as shown in Figure 11.13.

16. Click the Pick Root button and select the torso object in the viewports. MAX automatically creates the hierarchical linked bones system as shown in Figure 11.14. Click the Select and Move tool to exit the bones creation mode.

11

FIGURE 11.13.

After you do the hierarchy and limit setting work, use Auto Boning to create the bones for IK.

FIGURE 11.14.

The Bones MAX exists within your objects and respects the linking and limits you set up.

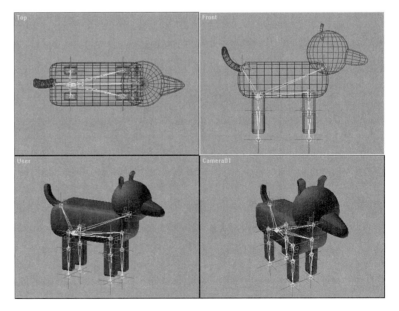

17. Your dog is now set up to work with IK. It's helpful at this point to set the Selection Filter to Helpers. That way you can only help objects and won't accidentally choose some other geometry. Figure 11.15 shows the Selection Filter entry field.

FIGURE 11.15.

When you want to select only a helper object, such as bones, set the selection filter to helpers.

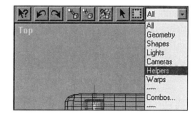

Caution

When you use Auto Boning, you don't have to check the IK button in the toolbar. If you do, the bones won't move.

18. Quickly add some running movement so you see how IK works. Select Bone01, which is the bone controlling the torso, the parent object for the entire dog. Maximize the Front viewport and zoom out a bit to pan the view until the dog is at the left edge of the viewport.

19. Go to frame 20 and turn on the Animate button. Move the Bone01 object along the X axis to the right and notice the movement of the dog's legs. Move the dog ahead about one body length.

20. Select the end effector (located within the dummy object) for one of the front legs, and move it on the XY axes up and forward. Do the same for the other front leg; then move each back leg so they are pushing back. Try to match Figure 11.16.

11

FIGURE 11.16.

The initial lunge forward for your dog, using IK.

21. Continue adjusting the legs and the torso to make the dog run across the screen. Play around with rotating the tail and head as well. Don't forget to save your first ever IK animation. You can load Ikdog.avi from the accompanying CD-ROM to see how you ran your dog around.

▲

Morphing Objects

Morphing is the ability to transform one object into another. For example, you can change a sphere into a sprawling puddle of water, or a cat into a dog. The possibilities are endless, but there are limitations. The two objects must be mesh objects and they must have the exact same number of vertices. These limitations can make it nearly impossible to morph certain objects. However, if you know you will be morphing two objects before you start creating them, you can usually make it work. The sure-fire way of creating morphable objects is to make one object and clone it. You then modify its clone into the shape of the second morph object. Depending on the complexity of the second object you're trying to create, this can be very difficult.

When you morph from one object to another over time, MAX does the tweening. That is, MAX calculates the inbetween frames so you see the animated transformation process. The morph occurs between an initial object called a Seed Object and any number of destination objects called Target Objects. The next section shows you how to perform the following tasks:

• Create morph targets by cloning and modifying the original object

• Animate between one or more targets

Creating Single Morph Targets

You'll probably never find two objects that just happen to have the same number of vertices, so you'll always be in the position of having to create your morph objects yourself. A simple example is a drop of water morphing to a puddle of water on the floor.

To Do: Creating single morph targets

1. Load morphsplash.max from the accompanying CD-ROM. This file has your 'morph seed sphere' object hovering above the floor object at frame 0 and hitting the floor at frame 10. You'll create the morph target and complete the animation. These are just standard primitive MAX objects.

2. At frame 0, Shift-click on the sphere in the front viewport and drag it down to the floor. When you release the mouse button, create a copy of the sphere and name it splash target. See Figure 11.17.

FIGURE 11.17.

Make a copy of the morph seed object and position it on the floor.

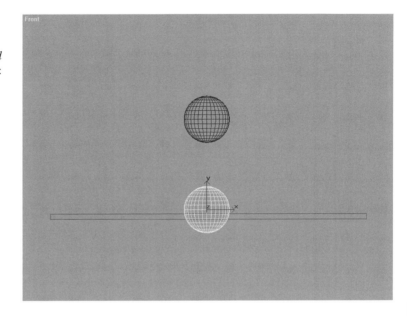

3. With the splash target object selected, click on the Modify tab and the More button in the Modifiers rollup.

4. Scroll the Modifiers dialog window to the bottom and click on Xform as shown in Figure 11.18. Click OK to add the modifier to the stack.

11

FIGURE 11.18.

Choose an Xform modifier before scaling the splash object.

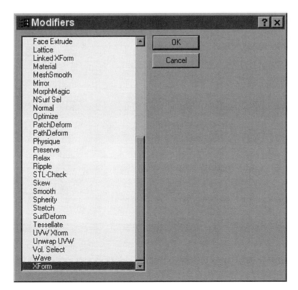

Note

Use the Xform (short for transform) modifier when you need to perform a nonuniform squash to an object at any point in its Modifier Stack. This allows you to perform the transform to a gizmo (a nonrendering bounding box around the object). If you don't use this method, the squash transform will not be created until the end of the stack, after all other modifiers (including the morph) have been executed. In this example, that would cause your morph to occur with the splash target object before it is squashed. That means the original sphere would be morphing to another sphere, and you wouldn't even see a difference.

5. Click on the Select and Scale icon and hold it down until you see the flyout menu. Drag the mouse over the last icon on the flyout menu. This is the Squash icon.

6. Click the Constrain to Y button on the toolbar and squash the gizmo for the splash target sphere into a pancake shaped object on the floor. The gizmo is a yellow-colored bounding box around the sphere. See Figure 11.19.

FIGURE 11.19.

With the Xform modifier in place, you can now scale the splash target object.

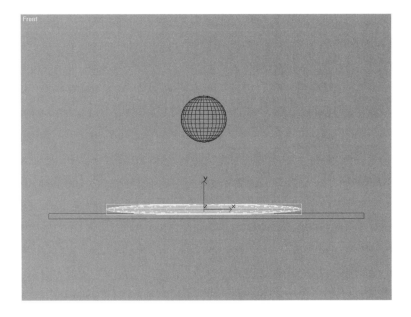

7. After you scale the gizmo for the sphere, click on the highlighted Sub Object button on the Modify Panel to exit the sub-object level for this object.

8. If you slide the timeline, you see your copy of the morph seed sphere object also copied the animation to the second sphere. Select the (now squashed) second sphere and enter the Track View dialog box. Expand the splash target object's Transform track and delete the two position keys to eliminate the movements. Close the Track View dialog box.

9. Select the morph seed sphere and go to frame 10.

10. Click the Create tab and choose Compound Objects from the selection field. Then click the Morph button in the Object Type rollup as shown in Figure 11.20.

FIGURE 11.20.

Morph is accessed through the Create - Compound Objects Panel.

11. Click the Pick Target button and check the Instance radial button. You'll create an instance, so you if you make any changes to the morph target, they will automatically be applied to the animation.

12. Click the splash target object in the viewport. You'll see its name added to the Current Targets window on the Morph Panel (see Figure 11.21).

FIGURE 11.21.

You can see the Morph Targets as you click on them, in the Current Targets window of the Morph Panel.

11

13. You're done with the splash target object, so you can hide it. But now you have to adjust the position of the morphed object to rest on the floor. Select the object and move it down onto the floor surface.

14. If you play the animation, you'll notice the morph occurs too soon. Select the morph object and open Track View. Expand the morph seed object Transform and Morph tracks to see the keyframes. Then click the Zoom Extents icon on the bottom of the Track View dialog box to see all 30 frames.

15. You actually need the morph to start at frame 10 and end at frame 20. Drag the morph key at frame 10 to frame 20. Then Shift-drag the morph key at frame 0 to frame 10 as shown in Figure 11.22.

FIGURE 11.22.

Use Track View to adjust the morph keys.

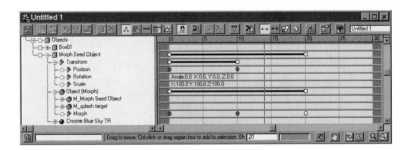

▲ 16. Save the file to your hard drive as mymorphsplash.max.

If you play the water drop animation, it looks realistic enough. The water drop even anticipates the morph by stretching out during its drop toward the floor. This is an effect of the default curved tangents MAX inserts at all keyframes as you saw on Day 10. It actually works great in this example and doesn't need any adjustment. On Day 12, you look at special effects that can add waves to objects that would be a nice touch to this animation. You can load morphwaves.avi from the accompanying CD-ROM to see how waves might be added to your morphing sphere.

Tip

> Not all morphs occur over multiple frames like the morphing sphere you just created. Consider creative uses of morphing that might have the objects transform over one frame, essentially occurring instantly. You might consider such a morph for popping balloons or breaking glass.

With a single morph target, you can toggle back and forth by defining multiple morph keys. This way, you can create a beating heart or another object that needs to change from one state to another repeatedly. Here's a quick example.

To Do: Defining multiple morph keys

1. Load morphtoggle.max from the accompanying CD-ROM. This animation, derived from your previous morphsplash example, has the droplet (sphere) bouncing across the floor. You'll add a morph as it hits the floor so the drop squashes into a puddle and then morph back to the drop as it jumps off the floor.

2. Go to frame 30. This frame is halfway between the frame where the drop first hits the floor and the frame where it will jump back off the floor. At this frame, you'll set your morph to the puddle object. Click the Create tab and select Compound Objects in the field selector for Geometry.

3. Click the Morph button and the Pick Target button in the Pick Targets rollup.

4. Pick the splash target in one of the viewports and notice the object instantly transforms into the morph target.

5. Turn on the Animate button and use the Select and Move tool to lower the morph object onto the floor object. After you do this, you can hide the splash target object.

6. Select the morph object and open the Track View window. Use both Track View and the morph Modifier Panel to further adjust the animation. Expand the morph seed object in the Track View to match Figure 11.23.

11

FIGURE 11.23.

Use Track View and the morph modifier settings to adjust the animation.

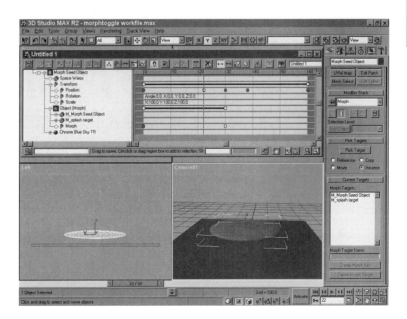

7. In the Morph Modifier Panel, you'll work in the Current Targets rollup. This lists both the Seed and Target object for this morph. Currently, you have two morph keys, as you can see in the Track View: the original at frame 0, and the first morph target at frame 30. You don't want the morph to start until the water drop hits the floor at frame 22, so you'll add another morph key at that frame. Go to frame 22.

8. In the Current Targets window, click the Morph Seed Object. When you do this, the two buttons under the window become active. Click the Create Morph Key and notice that it adds a key in the Track View and that the morph object in your viewport transforms back into the seed object (see Figure 11.24).

FIGURE 11.24.

You can use the Morph Modifier Panel to add morph keys.

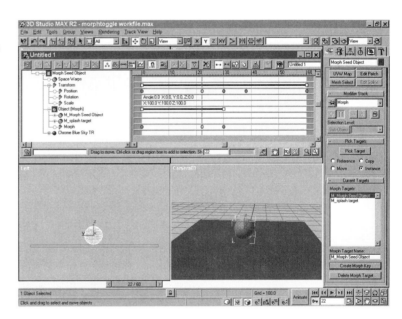

9. Go to frame 38. This is where the drop needs to jump off the floor, but you want it to once again transform back into the seed object. With the Morph Seed Object still highlighted in the Morph Targets window, click the Create Morph Key button and notice the change that occurs and the keyframe that is added.

10. Save the changes and play your animation. You can load morphtoggle.avi from the accompanying CD-ROM to see the finished rendering.

Creating Multiple Morph Targets

The previous example used two objects: one seed and one target. We eluded to the situation of having more than one morph target. The process is similar to using a single target—you just add additional targets to your list. You then have the ability to create morph keys for each object on the list. Furthermore, you have the ability to adjust the weight of each morph. That translates into the ability to have the morph object represent a portion of each target simultaneously. Weighted morphing is what is used for lip-syncing. Cloned objects of a person's mouth (or head and mouth) are created for different letter pronunciations. Each object becomes a morph target and speech is formed by the gradual (weighted) transformation and combination of different targets.

First, use multiple targets to have an object go through a series of transformations.

To Do: Using multiple targets in a series transformations

1. Load mymorphsplash.max. Now add some more morph targets to make the puddle of water move around on the floor.

2. Unhide the splash target object. You need to make a copy of this object in order to make more morph targets.

3. Select the splash target object and Shift—drag it to the left edge of the floor, creating a new object. Create a copy of the object and name it new puddle target.

4. With this object selected, click the Modify tab and the More button. In the Modifiers dialog box, click the FFD 4x4x4 modifier and click OK to add it to the stack. This is a Free Form modifier that creates a lattice of control points around the object allowing you to deform the object in any way imaginable. When you click the Sub-Object button for the FFD 4x4x4 modifier in the Stack, you gain access to the Control Points. Figure 11.25 shows the lattice with control points active for your object.

5. Use the Select and Move tool to select different control points and move them to deform the object. Move control points around until your object resembles Figure 11.26.

11

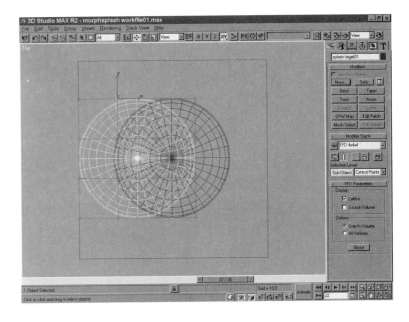

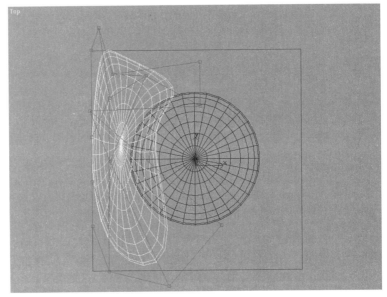

6. When you finish, click the highlighted Sub-Object button on the Modify Panel to exit the sub-object selection level.

7. Using the same methods in the preceding steps, create two more objects with the water moving to the top and right edges of the floor.

8. Click the Time Configuration button at the bottom right of the screen. In the resulting dialog box, enter 100 in the End Time field in the Animation section to add 70 frames to this animation. Click OK to add the frames and exit the dialog box.

9. Select morph seed object and click the Modify tab to see the morph information. Make sure Morph is selected in the Modifier Stack.

10. Move to frame 40 and click the Pick Target button. Click on the puddle to the left, which is splash target01.

11. Move to frame 70 and click on the puddle on the top side of the floor, splash target02.

12. Move to frame 90 and click on the last puddle on the right, splash target03. Your Morph Targets window under Current Targets should look like Figure 11.27.

FIGURE 11.27.

Add multiple morph targets for complex transformations.

11

13. Hide the morph target objects; then turn on the Animate button and go back to frames 40, 70, and 90 to adjust the position of the morph object as necessary.

14. If your morph object dips below the floor just after it hits at frame 10, you can adjust the tangent for the Position Key at frame 10 to have a straight line tangent (see Figure 11.28).

FIGURE 11.28.

Adjust the keys as necessary to fine-tune the motion of the water puddle.

15. Save your file and then play back the animation. You can load movingsplash.avi from the accompanying CD-ROM.

Now add some complexity to your animation such as lip-synching. For this example, you deal with only the mouth. For most lip-syncing animations, it's more convenient to create morph targets comprised of the entire head, complete with eyes, mouth, and so on.

To Do: Advanced animation complexity with morph targets

1. Load lips.max from the accompanying CD-ROM (just the lips because this is just an example).

2. The goal with lip-syncing is to create a set of lips forming most of the major sounds such as EE, AH, OH, TEE, HA, and so on. If you do this, you'll have the basis for most words. The first step is to clone the seed object. Shift-drag the lips neutral object to create a copy. Name it lips OH.

3. Click the Modify tab, and the More button in the Modifiers rollup. Add the FFD 4x4x4 modifier.

4. Using Figure 11.29 as a guide, deform the Sub-Object control points to form the OH-shaped lips.

FIGURE 11.29.

Create multiple clones of the morph seed object and transform them into different shapes for different sounds.

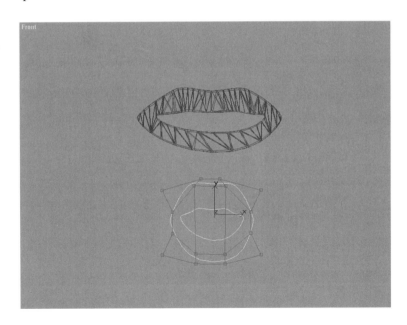

5. Unfortunately, you have to spend quite a bit of time creating the lips with all the shapes you need. But you can take the cheap way out for this example and animate whistling. Click the Display tab and Unhide All to unhide the third pair of lips.

6. You need to check where the pivot points for these objects are located. When you morph between these objects, the pivot points will be used to line them up. If the pivot points are located at different parts of the mouth for each object, you might get some bizarre movements. Click on the lips neutral object and make note where the pivot point is. Now click on the lips OH and see it's in a different location.

7. Click the Hierarchy tab and the Affect Pivot Only button in the Move/Rotate/Scale section.

8. Use the Select and Move tool to place the pivot close to the same location as it was for the seed object. When you're done, click the Affect Pivot Only button again to deactivate it.

9. To check how the two lips line up, click the lips OH object and the Align button in the toolbar. The cursor turns into the Align icon. When it does, click on the lips' neutral object. This brings up the Align dialog box as shown in Figure 11.30.

10. Click the X, Y, and Z position check boxes and the Pivot Point check boxes for both Current and Target objects. Don't click the Apply button, but simply move the dialog box aside so you can see if the objects line up. If they do, cancel the alignment and proceed. Simply use the alignment option to check your pivot placement. The objects don't have to be aligned because the morphing process aligns them. When you check your pivot alignment, you should have something that resembles Figure 11.30.

FIGURE 11.30.

Aligning objects can help you see how pivot points align and how morphing between the two objects works.

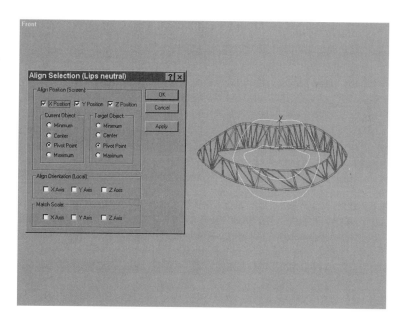

11. One last step before you assign the morph target. For each of the two target objects, select the MeshSmooth modifier in their stack to make sure it is active (see Figure 11.31).

FIGURE 11.31.

Toggle the Active/Inactive Modifier button back to active.

Active/Inactive toggle

12. Go to frame 15 and select the seed object. Click the Create Tab-Compound Objects-Morph button to access the Pick Targets rollup.

13. Click the Pick Target button and select the lips OH object.

▲ 14. Go to frame 30 and select the lips OOO object.

These steps create a basic multiple target morph. When you play the animation, you see the transformation from one to the next in the order you picked each target. If these are the only three lip shapes you need to use, you can continue on the timeline adding keys for any of the three shapes needed until the end of your animation. If you want complete control of the lips, you can access the key information for the morph keys in the Track View and adjust their weight. This is basically a percentage of each of the three targets that is visible at the same time. Figure 11.32 shows the Track View morph key information and the Percentage window. To change the percentage, simply highlight the name of the target and adjust the percentage spinner. Experiment to see the combinations you can create. You'll discover the seemingly unlimited lip-shape variations it enables you to create. This process is essential for proper lip-syncing.

Animating with MAXScript—A Basic Introduction

If you polled the animator profession, you'd probably find a mixed bag of programmer and nonprogrammer types. Among those nonprogrammers, you'd probably receive hostile responses from suggestions that they learn to use a scripting language to control aspects of their animation. After all, this is art, and why would an artist want to use code to draw pictures? The suggestion to use scripting, called MAXScript in 3D Studio MAX, is one that should be considered very seriously. In certain situations, using scripts can save valuable time.

FIGURE 11.32.

You can adjust the weight, or percentage, of each target used at any given key.

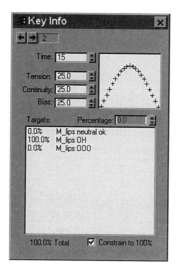

Think of the MAXScript feature as an option you should at least explore to discover what it offers. Although you can use MAX without ever writing, or using, one line of MAXScript code, you might find your animations can benefit quite a bit from your original, or prewritten scripts. Because you're dealing with only an introduction to this topic, you won't look at writing any code. MAX does come with a detailed help file on MAXScript that serves as a great reference to the MAXScript language.

Why Use Scripting?

Scripting can handle quite a bit of automation in your animations. Everything from terrain generation to automatically generating environments with land, sky, and water can be written into a script. You can use scripting to custom write your own plug-ins for features you want to have at your fingertips in MAX.

Writing and Sharing Scripts

The best news for nonprogrammers is that you can share scripts with other animators. The scripts are not written for anyone's particular system, so you can load them on anyone's MAX system and run them perfectly. Thankfully, there are a number of individuals and companies interested in writing and distributing/selling scripts that offer a wealth of functions. One particular Internet site at www.max3d.com keeps an updated list of downloadable MAXScripts. Here are two examples with a tremendous amount of capabilities. First, run Environment System, written by Frank DeLise (www.FrankDeLise.com). It is currently in Beta so some features don't work, but you get a sense of its overall functionality.

To Do: Working with MAXScripts

1. Start a new scene in MAX.

2. Click the Utilities tab and the More button. Select MAXScript and click OK (see Figure 11.33).

FIGURE 11.33.

Load MAXScript from the Utilities Panel.

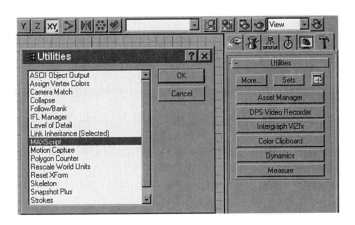

3. In the MAXScript rollup, click Run Script and select env92.ms from the accompanying CD-ROM.

4. In the Utilities entry field, you see the name Environment System.2. Click the down arrow button to expand the list and then click on the script's name to open its rollups (see Figure 11.34).

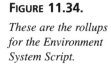

FIGURE 11.34.

These are the rollups for the Environment System Script.

11

5. There are many settings for this script that include the sunlight system—fog, land, sky, and water generation—just about everything for a complete environment. But you don't have to do anything to get a basic environment created. For now, just click the Create Environment button and see what it creates. Figure 11.35 shows the rendering of the default environment.

You can then enter the rollups for Sky or Water—or any element—and further adjust the settings to get the effects you want. Play around with these settings, but remember that at this point this beta version has some features missing.

This second script is called Galaxy System, written by Tetsuya Takee (takee@tky0.attnet.or.jp). It is also in beta so some features might not work. This script automatically creates a galactic backdrop for your animation, generating stars and nebulas.

FIGURE **11.35.**

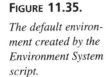

FIGURE 11.35.

The default environment created by the Environment System script.

To Do: More script examples

▼ To Do

1. Reset MAX to start a new scene.

2. From the MAXScript Panel, run the script called Galaxy11.ms from the accompanying CD-ROM.

3. When you run the script, its rollups appear as shown in Figure 11.36.

4. Similar to the Environment System script, simply clicking the Create Galaxy button generates the default galaxy. You can then modify by changing the settings. Figure 11.37 shows the rendering of the default settings.

▲

FIGURE 11.36.

The rollups for the Galaxy script give you access to all its settings.

FIGURE 11.37.

The default galaxy created by the Galaxy System script.

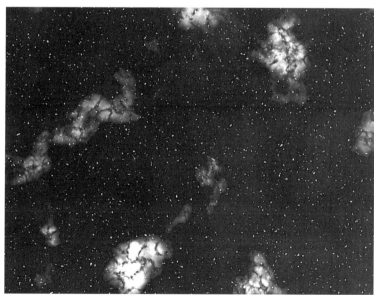

11

You can explore these scripts by opening them and reviewing the code. Many MAXScripts include good documentation to tell you what sections of the code are doing. You open a script in the same fashion you run a script. Just click on the Open Script button and select your script. A window opens that enables you to see the code, as shown in Figure 11.38.

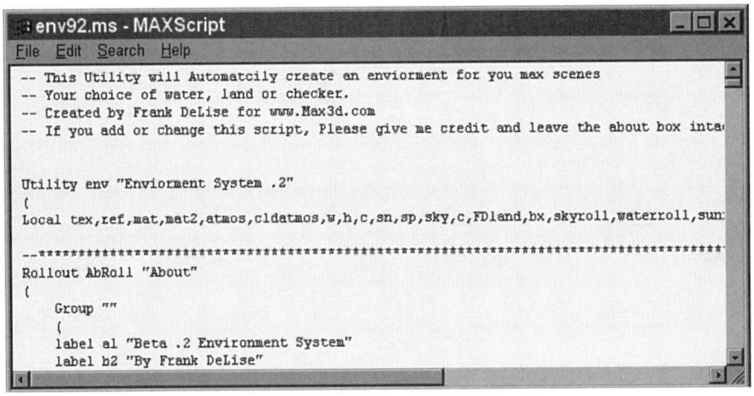

FIGURE 11.38.

By reviewing existing scripts, you can begin to understand how to write one.

Summary

Today you took a look at some of the advanced animation capabilities of MAX. Here are the important subjects to remember:

- The way your objects must move and react to other elements of your scene will dictate how you create those objects and what methods you will use to animate them. Put enough forethought into your animations to make the right decisions about modeling and animation.

- Linking objects and creating complex hierarchies is the way to animate complex movements. Once again, take the time to think through the possible movements of each object to assure you have the linkage set up properly.

- You can create predictable motion by locking the axes of objects in directions they should not be allowed to move. Similarly, you can control what aspect each object in your hierarchy inherits from its parents. These two settings are essential for proper movement.

- Inverse kinematics takes quite a bit of time to set up, but the payoff is easier animation of complex movements. Learn by experimentation how to set the limits of the joints on your objects. After you establish the limits and a hierarchy, use Auto Boning to create the skeleton you use for IK.

- Morphing enables you to create some dynamic object transformations. With the right amount of planning, you can create the shapes you need that are capable of morphing. Remember to start with one object and modify its clone to keep the same amount of vertices for each object.

- Explore MAXScript, even if you aren't a programmer. It's worth your time to surf the Internet of popular MAX Web sites to find the latest scripts that animators are sharing.

Q&A

Q What's the best way to determine the order of my linked hierarchy with complex objects such as humans?

A The best way is to work out some sketches of the object and diagram the hierarchy, thinking through possible movements. But you can experiment in MAX as well. You can always unlink, relink, or add links as necessary to make adjustments.

Q IK seems too labor-intensive. Why should I go to all the trouble?

A IK can be extremely time-intensive to set up. The benefits might come into play only when you set up complex animations with human characters walking and running, or climbing steps. Judge the complexity first and then decide which animation method is best.

Q MAXScript is a programming language and I hate programming. Can't I do these same things without writing code?

A For all MAXScripts, the results can be created right from within MAX without ever writing one line of code. After all, the MAXScript is basically a collection of commands for MAX to follow. However, using the scripts might save you hundreds of steps and hours of animation or modeling. Plus, you can reuse the script in other animations. Even if you hate programming, you might have an idea for a script you can approach a programmer with and have him write it for you.

11

DAY 12

Special Effects

Particle Systems and Space Warps

You know how to create objects and arrange your scene. You also know how to animate the objects. After all the creation is complete, the lights are set, and the animated moves keyframed, what next? What if you need to add some pizzazz to your animation? How about special effects? MAX provides two types of special effects: particle systems and space warps. With these systems, you can create effects ranging from rain and snow to explosions. You can also apply the laws of physics to your objects with dynamics, allowing you to create blowing rain by adding wind to your particle system rain. Today, you explore these special effects and learn the following techniques:

- How to create rain and snow with particles
- How to set up space warps in a scene
- How to explode objects with space warps
- How to add real-world physics, such as wind, to your scene

Working with Particle Systems

Particle systems are appropriately named because they create multiple sub-objects (particles) based on the parameters you set. These sub-objects might take the form of drops of water, flakes of snow, or parts of a cloud. Although you can't edit these particle objects directly, you can control them through their creation parameters. You even control how they render by having the option of assigning materials to the particles or allowing them to render as geometric shapes such as triangles. Because particles are created over time, they create great animated effects. Figure 12.1 shows an example of the great snow effect possible with the standard MAX particle system. You can see the animation this frame came from by loading snow.avi from the accompanying CD-ROM.

FIGURE 12.1.

Adding snow is an automated process with the use of particle systems.

Emitters and Common Parameters

Particle systems are accessed under the Create tab. You must click the Geometry button and select Particle Systems from the geometry type selection field as shown in Figure 12.2.

FIGURE 12.2.

Particle Systems are found in the Geometry/Particle Systems Panel under the Create tab.

There are six basic Particle Systems that ship with MAX.

- *Spray* Good for creating rain, water droplets, or any type of spraying particles such as sparks. See Figure 12.3.

FIGURE 12.3.

The box represents the Spray Emitter (defined in the next section), and the dots are the particles.

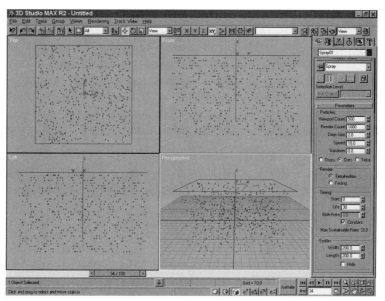

- *Snow* Good for creating snow (That was probably obvious). Figure 12.1 shows an example of snow.
- *PArray* This enables you to choose an object in the scene as an emitter. From this emitter object, you can generate the particles in your scene. You can choose to have the particles resemble fragments of the emitter object (for explosion effects), or the particles can be instances of the emitter shape (an emitter object of a dog bone emitting particles shaped like dog bones). Figure 12.4 shows an example of PArray. You might also load parray.avi from the accompanying CD-ROM to see this animation using PArray to blow bubbles through a bubble wand.

FIGURE 12.4.

The ability of PArray to use objects as emitters and templates for particles shapes opens a tremendous amount of creativity for your particle effects.

- *Super Spray*   This takes Spray to a whole new level. It gives you greater control over the formation of the particle spray and the particle type, just to name a few enhancements.

- *Blizzard*   Much like snow, this one's predictable; it creates blizzard-like conditions using particles. It gives you greater control over particle timing and size than snow allows.

- *PCloud*   When you need to fill a 3D space with a cloud, use PCloud. It uses a 3D object in your scene as a boundary for your Particle Cloud. Figure 12.5 shows an example of PArray using carbonation bubbles floating out of a glass. The glass, in this example, was used to define the direction of the bubbles. You can load pcloud.avi from the accompanying CD-ROM to see this animation.

FIGURE 12.5.

PCloud particles fill 3D spaces and can use objects to define their boundries and direction.

Particle systems vary greatly in what they accomplish, but they all share some common elements:

- *Emitters*   This is a nonrendering object from which the particles are generated (emitted). In that sense, it's similar to any other Helper object in MAX, such as tape measures or dummy objects. For particles systems, think of it as the nozzle on a hose. You set the timing for your particles telling MAX when to turn on the hose (the Emitter). This is the object you animate to create particle streams such as shooting stars or smoke behind an airplane.

- *Size/Speed/Variation*   The three main settings for particle generation are based on these three parameters. They tell MAX how big the particles are, how fast to generate them, and if the generation of these particles should be constant or vary over time.

- *Start/Lifes* This tells MAX at what frame to start the particle generation and how long the particles live (remain in the scene).
- *Viewport Count/Render Count* These two settings enable you to control how many particles are created and displayed in your viewports and how many are actually rendered. This gives you great flexibility when trying to keep your viewport display speedy when you need to render thousands of particles.

Obviously, each particle system has its own set of parameters specific to the type of particle it is creating. For example, Spray and Snow are two basic particle systems with almost identical parameters. Two more advanced systems are Blizzard and Super Spray. Each of the latter adds numerous parameters for particle type, rotation, and motion. Knowing the basics helps you understand the any particle system and enables you to easily adapt to unique settings with more advanced systems.

To Do: Creating rain with the Spray particle system

Creating Rain or Snow is relatively easy because each has a specialized particle system. This example uses Rain and sets up the particle system.

1. Open rain.max from the accompanying CD-ROM. This simple street scene is a familiar one; you add rain and adjust the settings to get the effect you need.

2. Click the Create tab and with the Geometry button selected, pick Particle Systems from the selection field.

3. Click Spray and draw a box in the Top viewport along the street object as shown in Figure 12.6.

12

FIGURE 12.6.

Draw the box emitter for the Spray Particle System just as you would draw a standard box object, in the Top viewport.

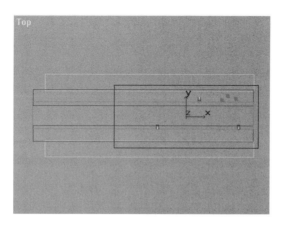

4. Because the box emitter is created at ground level, switch to the Front viewport and move it up along the Y axis until the top is above the building lining the street. Activate the camera view and press the Play button.

At this point, you covered the most basic procedures necessary to create rain in your scene. You can render the animation to see what the rain looks like by default. You can also scroll the timeline and see representations of the rain particles in the MAX viewports. Although the rain is there, you don't have enough drops defined to give the effect that it's raining. You need to increase the amount of drops to simulate actual rain.

5. Select the emitter object and click the Modify tab to access its parameters as shown in Figure 12.7.

FIGURE 12.7.

The Modify Panel gives you access to the particle emitters parameters.

6. Change the Render Count to 1,000 and render the animation. Because this setting is only for the renderer, the viewports will not be affected, leaving your screen redraws as fast as possible.

At 10 times the previous amount, you can notice the raindrops. However, based on the size of your scene and the size of the emitter, you might have to increase this setting even higher. Judge for yourself, based on your individual expectations, but take a look at raining.avi from the accompanying CD-ROM. This file was rendered with a Render Count setting of 10,000. To see how the rain particles look by themselves, load rain.avi; this was rendered with no other objects visible.

The raining.avi file also incorporated changes for the Speed and Variation settings.

7. In the Particles section, click the Dots radial button that changes only the viewport display of the particles. Dots are a little easier to see than Drops.

8. Change the Speed to 5.0 from 10.0. This slows down the rainfall.

9. Because you slowed down the rate at which the raindrops fall, it now takes them longer to reach the ground. This creates a problem you need to fix in the Timing section. The current Life setting is for 30 (frames). That means each drop only exists for 30 frames and then it disappears. Your drops used to reach the ground in 30 frames, but at the slower speed it will now take 50 frames, so adjust the Life setting to 50.

▲

Caution

When you render the scene as you have it set up, or even when you drag the timeline, notice the emitter begins creating the particles at frame zero from the emitter object. Based on the Speed and Life settings, it now takes 50 frames for the drops to reach the ground. That means it appears that the rainfall is just starting in your scene because the first drops start at frame zero and won't reach the ground for 50 frames. If you want to have it raining from the first frame in your animation, you can either start rendering at frame 50, or you can set the Start setting in the Timing section to -50 (for frame -50).

12

The more you experiment with different settings with particle systems, the more realistic results you receive. You can also assign a material to the emitter that, in turn, assigns that material to all the sub-object particles. This leads you to the ability to map materials to the particles. Although it's not necessary for rain, it is for other particles such as snowflakes. The next section covers mapping particles.

To Do: Mapping materials to particles

By default, all particles are generated as some geometric shape. The raindrops you created, for example, rendered as Tetrahedrons. That was great for rain, but the default shapes don't always work. As an alternative, you can select the Facing option in the particle system's Render section. This renders the particles as squares, with their faces always oriented toward the camera. You can map any material you want to these particle faces and create dramatic effects. This is how you create snowflakes, smoke, and so on. Because you can use normal mapping techniques, you can create opacity maps to make transparent areas in your materials, as needed.

1. Load snow.max from the accompanying CD-ROM. Use the familiar street scene and add the snowfall with a snowflake pattern (shown in Figure 12.8) mapped to the particles.

FIGURE 12.8.

The image used for the Diffuse and Opacity maps for the snowflake particles.

2. Select the emitter object - Snow01 and click the Modify tab.

3. In the Particles section of the Parameters rollup, change the Viewport Count to 200 and the Render Count to 2,000. This gives you a good representation in your working viewports and enough particles in the rendered scene to make a believable snowfall.

4. In the Render section, click the Facing radial button. This changes the particles to square objects that enable you to map materials to them. Figure 12.9 shows the needed settings.

5. Click on the Material Editor button to open its dialog box.

   Because you cannot directly edit any one particle, you assign the material to the particles by assigning it to the emitter. You create a material that uses the snowflake bitmap as both a Diffuse and Opacity map. The same image of the white snowflake on a black background works for each type of map. The Opacity map setting tells MAX that all the black pixels in the map should be rendered transparent, leaving you with only the white shape of the snowflake when you render your scene.

6. Click the Get Material button and select New in the Browse From section of the Material/Map Browser window. In the window on the right, double-click the Standard type to start a new material in the active slot in the Material Editor dialog box (see Figure 12.10).

FIGURE 12.9.

Set the parameters for the Snow01 emitter to set up the rendering of the snowflake material on each particle.

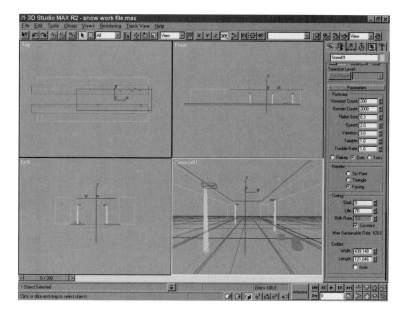

FIGURE 12.10.

Start a new standard material for the snowflake particles.

12

7. Close the Material/Map Browser dialog box, and name this material snowflake mask.

8. Leave all the settings as they are and click to expand the Maps rollup.

9. Click the check boxes for Diffuse and Opacity. Then click the map selection bar to the right of the Diffuse map that currently is labeled None. See Figure 12.11.

FIGURE 12.11.

Use both a Diffuse and Opacity map to create the snowflake material.

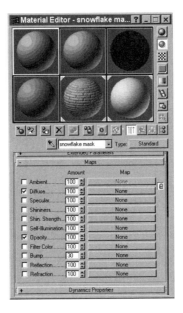

10. When the Material/Map Browser opens, make sure the New radial button is selected in the Browse From section. Then double-click the Bitmap type in the window on the right and click OK.

11. In the Bitmap Parameters rollout, click the Bitmap file selection bar and choose snowflake.tif from the accompanying CD-ROM. Change List of File types to *.* if necessary. When you select the bitmap file, your setting appears as they are in Figure 12.12, including the rendering of the snowflake on the sphere in the preview section of the Material Editor dialog box.

FIGURE 12.12.

Select the snowflake.tif file as the bitmap for the snowflake material.

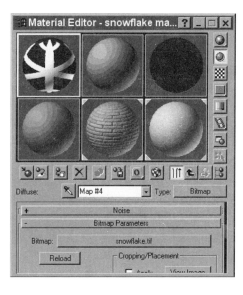

12. Click the Go To Parent button to return to the main level in this material. Because you want to use the same map for the Opacity map, click and drag the Diffuse map selection bar (which now reads snowflake.tif) down to the Opacity map selection bar. When it prompts you to choose what type of Copy to make, choose Instance. That way, changing one map setting changes both.

13. By clicking the Background button (Checkerboard icon), you see that this material now renders transparent around the white snowflake as shown in Figure 12.13. Save the material and then apply it to the selected emitter object.

FIGURE 12.13.

The transparent background is essential in making the snowflake material work.

14. If you want the snowflakes to appear bright white, set the self-illumination on the material to 100%.

▲

That should do it. Rendering the scene reveals a fairly realistic snowfall with snowflakes, not just triangles, for particles. Further adjustments made to the number of particles, the speed at which they fall, and the amount of tumbling for each particles can further enhance the effect. You can load snowflakes.avi from the accompanying CD-ROM to see what the final animation looks like with a few of these further modifications.

Working with Space Warps

Space warps represent the second standard special effect built into MAX. Space warps are objects that you create in your scene to affect other objects. The space warp is not rendered; it exists as an object in world space (your scene being the world) and might create such effects as waves, ripples, or explosions. When an object has been bound to a space warp (explained in the next section), dragging the object over/through the space warp creates animated effects such as waves or ripples for water. Virtually any object can be bound to a space warp and reflect the special effects that the Space Warp feature offers. In this section, you explore the basic concepts of the space warp and see how to:

- Create space warps and bind other objects to them
- Animate Space Warp parameters
- Add a Wind Space Warp to a snow scene to create blowing snow
- Explode objects with the Bomb Space Warp

Different space warps affect different types of geometry or particle systems. All space warps are found in the Create tab under the Space Warps button. You select the type of space warp by using the field selector that provides you with a drop-down list of all the types available.

Common Procedures for Creating a Space Warp

You can add space warps at any time in the animation process. You might choose to create your animation and add the space warp last. The process involves creating the Space Warp object and adjusting its parameters as needed. You then bind the select objects in the scene that should be affected by the space warp.

You have two ways of adjusting a space warp: through its own parameters and with the move, rotate, and scale transforms. Because space warps are objects, like most others in your scene, they can be adjusted in much the same manner.

To Do: Creating a space warp

▼ To Do

Creating a space warp is a straight forward process. Set up a few in a new scene to see how it's done.

1. Click on the Create tab and the Space Warps button.
2. Click the Wave button.
3. Click and drag from the center of the Top viewport and define a box roughly 90 units in Wave Length as you monitor the Parameters rollup for the monitor. Then release the mouse button.

4. There is a second setting for this particular space warp that sets the wave amplitude. Move your mouse around until you create an amplitude of around 8; then click the mouse to set the parameters.

That's all there is to creating a space warp. You can use the standard transforms to move, rotate, and scale this object as needed to arrive at the proper positioning in your scene. Figure 12.14 shows a few examples of space warp objects and how they appear in your scene.

FIGURE 12.14.

Create as many space warp objects as you need in your scene.

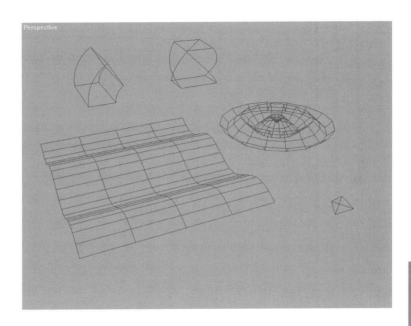

By simply creating the space warp, you have not altered or affected anything in your scene. So the next step to set up a space warp is to tell MAX which objects in a scene are to be affected. This is done through a process called Binding. Let's see how it works.

To Do: Working with the binding process

1. To create an object to be affected by the Wave Space Warp, make it a sphere. Size and location don't matter. For this example, put it next to the Wave Space Warp.

2. Click the Bind To Space Warp button located on the MAX toolbar next to the Select and Link and Unlink Selection buttons as shown in Figure 12.15.

FIGURE 12.15.

You associate the space warp with the objects it affects with the Bind To Space Warp button.

3. Click on the sphere and, with the mouse button still selected, drag the cursor to the space warp. When the cursor is over the space warp, it changes to display the Bind To Space Warp icon. Release the mouse to bind the two.

The binding is complete, and the sphere will now be affected by the Wave Space Warp. You should already see the sphere transform in shape depending on the location of the space warp and its current parameters. If you move either the sphere or the space warp, you see the changes in the sphere object.

Exploding an Object with the Bomb Space Warp

If you watch enough television and movies, you begin to think animation was invented to explode objects for special effects. With that in mind, someone has created the Bomb Space Warp. With it, you can explode most any object you create. Here's how it works.

To Do: Working with the Bomb Space Warp

1. Load bomb.max from the accompanying CD-ROM. Here's the street scene again. This time you add three Bomb Space Warps to blow up the three teapots.

> **Note**
>
> You can bind more than one object to each space warp, and you can also bind more than one space warp to each object. In the bomb example, however, you had to create a bomb for each object, because there is only one detonation for each bomb, and you wanted three separate explosions.

2. Click the Create tab and the Space Warps icon to access the space warps.

3. Select Bomb and click in the Top viewport to create the first Bomb. Place it over one of the three teapots.

4. Use the Shift-left click method to create two copies of this Bomb Space Warp and place them over each of the other two teapots. When prompted, make these new Bombs copies of the original. Your scene should resemble Figure 12.16.

FIGURE **12.16.**

Place the Bomb Space Warps directly over each teapot in the Top viewport.

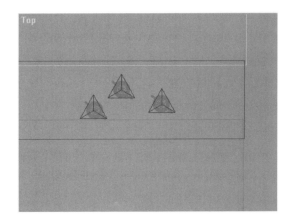

5. In the Top viewport, select the Bind To Space Warp button and bind each of the teapots to the space warp that is directly over it.

6. Select the first Space Warp icon and click the Modify tab to access its parameters. The settings you use are shown in Figure 12.17.

FIGURE **12.17.**

The Bomb settings should be identical for this example, with the only change occurring in the Detonation setting.

12

7. Set Strength to .1 under the Explosion section.

8. Set Min to 5 and Max to 12 in the Fragment section.

9. Set Gravity and Chaos each to 1 in the General section.

10. Set the Detonation frame for the first Bomb to 10. Then proceed to change the Detonation for the second teapot to frame 25 and the third teapot to frame 40. These are the only necessary changes; leave all the other settings as they are.

▲   11. Drag the timeline slider to see the results in your viewports and then render the animation. You can load bomb.avi to see the final animation with these settings.

Working with Dynamics

One of the potential downfalls to 3D animation happens to be a feature that actually makes it so appealing in so many other ways. That downfall is that animation programs don't normally account for physical properties of objects. For example, you can have a car cross the center line of a two-lane road and collide with another car coming in the opposite direction. When the cars intersect, they actually pass directly through one another with no interaction at all. Of course, you can manually keyframe the resulting impact and motion of each vehicle, but it's nice when the software takes care of it for you.

MAX provides a method for detecting collisions between objects and acting upon those collisions in the most accurate fashion. This means when you push a desk object across the floor in your animation and it strikes a lamp, the lamp will fall. The method by which MAX calculates these collisions does not deform the objects at all; it simply makes them react accordingly with a resulting movement.

Note

Dynamic simulations can be time-consuming to set up. The number of objects in your scene that will be affected are partly what determines how long it will take. With this being the case, the use of Dynamics follows much the same line of thought as the use of Inverse Kinematics. If you have complex movements and interactions in your scene, especially if there might be future revisions to the scene, using Dynamics can be a great benefit. However, if you create a one-time simulation involving two objects colliding once or twice, it might be quicker to keyframe the motion yourself.

Dynamics can be added to your scene at any time, even after all the modeling and keyframing has been completed. You can even use Dynamics in conjunction with space warps such as Wind. You can combine different space warps and Dynamics to create the effects you want. Imagine using Wind to blow a branch of a tree so it strikes a window on a house. As the branch hits the window, the dynamics you have set up detect the collision and the branch reacts by pulling away from the window. You have full control over the properties of the objects that will be affected by Dynamics. In the next sections, you see how to

- Set up objects for Dynamics
- Set up your scene for the use of Dynamics
- Create Wind and Gravity in a Dynamics simulation

Setting Up Collisions with Global Settings

You can set up each individual object with its own physical attributes for collision detection, or you can designate the entire scene for collision detection. When you need to work with individual objects, settings can become numerous and quickly add up as you add more objects to the list of potential collision objects.

When you designate dynamic properties by object, you decide which other objects in the scene the current object will collide and react with. Next you see a basic demonstration using both methods for collision detection.

To Do: Working with collision detection

1. Start a new scene in MAX.
2. Click the Create tab. Under Standard Primitives, select the Sphere button under Object Type and create two similar spheres and a box in the Top viewport, forming a straight line as in Figure 12.18.

FIGURE 12.18.

Create three objects forming a straight line in the Top viewport.

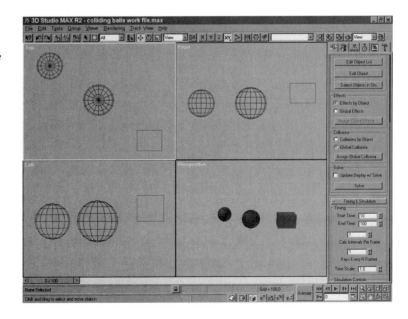

12

3. Click the Zoom Extents button so you can see everything in all viewports.

4. Click the Utilities tab (hammer icon) and select the Dynamics button in the Utilities rollup as shown in Figure 12.19.

FIGURE 12.19.

You apply physical dynamics to object from the Dynamics Utility Panel.

5. The first step is to create a Simulation Name by clicking the New button. You can use the default name or enter a descriptive name.

> **Caution**
>
> As projects become complex and you add more objects with their own individual dynamic simulations, make sure you use a descriptive name for the simulation. Descriptive names help when creating your objects and when you need to edit the scene particular to one or two objects. Dynamics00 doesn't tell you much, but 'branches hitting' will easily identify the simulation that controls the branches of a tree.

6. Next you must identify the objects in your scene that will be included in this simulation. Click the Edit Object List in the Objects in Simulation section. Select all objects and click the arrow pointing to the right to transfer all the selected objects to the Include window (see Figure 12.20).

So far, you only identified which objects to include, but you still need to define how they should react to each other. Start by defining Global Collisions to affect all the objects you included. Then follow up by editing each individual object to see the difference between the two methods.

FIGURE 12.20.

Move all the objects in this scene to the Include window.

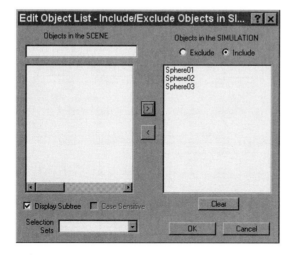

To Do: Defining global collisions to affect all included objects

1. In the Collisions section, click the Global Collisions radial button. This assigns the collision settings to all objects in the scene you included in this simulation.

2. Click the Assign Global Collisions button to open its dialog box. This dialog box works the same as the Object list dialog box, only this time you're including them in the actual collision list. Select all the objects and click the arrow pointing to the right (between the windows) to transfer them to the Include window.

3. Go to frame 10 and click the Animate button; it should be highlighted red.

4. Move the first sphere until it just touches the center sphere, as shown in Figure 12.21. Be careful not to intersect the spheres or the dynamics won't work.

▲ 5. Click the Animate button again to turn it off.

12

FIGURE 12.21.

Move the first sphere on the left along its X axis until hit touches the center sphere.

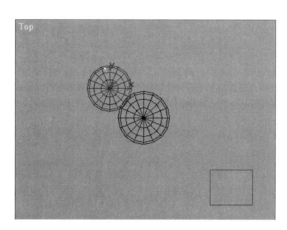

In order for the collision to be as accurate as possible, you need to edit the Collision Test method for each object. There are four methods available: box, cylinder, sphere, and mesh. Each represents the bounding box surrounding each object used in the detection of a collision. You should try to pick the shape that most closely resembles your object. If that's impossible, use mesh, but realize the mesh method takes longer to compute.

To Do: Editing the collision test method for each object

1. Click the Edit Object button in the Objects in Simulation section to open its dialog box as shown in Figure 12.22.

FIGURE 12.22.

Edit the Collision Test method for each object.

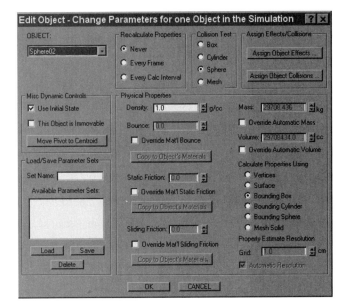

2. In the Collision Test section, select the method that closely resembles the object shown in the Object field in the upper-left corner of this dialog box. Because you used primitive shapes, this is easy to do. Continue with the other two objects in the scene and then click OK.

3. Check the Update Display w/ Solve box. In the Solve section of the Dynamics Panel, click the Solve button. MAX calculates the position of the three objects at each frame of the animation.

4. Hit the Play button to see the result. Take a quick look at what happens when one of the objects is not included in the simulation.

5. Click the Assign Global Collisions button and select the Box01 object in the Include window. Click the arrow (between the windows) pointing to the left to transfer the Box01 object to the Excluded window.

6. Click the Solve button and see what happens. The first collision is fine, but the second sphere passes through the box object.

   The methods used for the Collision Test can make a dramatic difference in the outcome. For example, if you review this animation frame by frame, you notice the second sphere does cross over the edge of the box, actually entering its object space. See what happens when you switch the Collision Test method for the Box01 object.

7. Click the Edit Object button and select the Box01 object from the Object field selector.

8. Change its Collision Test method to Mesh and then click OK.

9. Click the Solve button to recalculate the animation. This time, the collision is more accurate.

▲

Notice, in this last example, the behavior of the box object. Depending on the height of the box, the sphere strikes it at different angles that might add tumbling movements. If you move the box up along its Y axis in the Front viewport until it is half way up the height of the spheres, you get a dramatic tumble (see Figure 12.23).

FIGURE 12.23.

Moving the objects in your scene can make dramatic differences in the collision results.

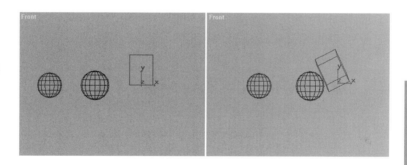

12

  Be aware of the potential for the Mesh method of Collision Test to require quite a bit more calculation time. Sometimes it's not worth it, but other times you will have to use it to get the correct results. Try the other methods first to see if the results are acceptable; you might save yourself valuable calculation time.

Setting Up Collisions by Object

The Global Collision solution is great for simple scenes or when most or all the objects in the scene will collide with each other. Many times, however, you might only be dealing with one or two objects in a scene of hundreds of objects. This is a better situation for using the Collisions by Object method. Where Global settings made every object in the simulation interact with every other object, the By Object method allows some objects in the simulation to be ignored by other objects. The By Object method creates a list for each individual object of the objects that it will interact with. You have to specifically set this list for every object involved. You do so by choosing the Collisions by Object radial button in the Dynamics Panel's Collisions section.

FIGURE 12.24.

When you use the Collision By Object method, you have to select the objects each object can collide with.

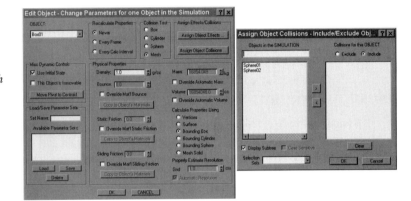

Figure 12.24 shows the Edit Object dialog box. In the upper-right corner, you see the Assign Effects/Collisions section. By clicking on the Assign Object Collisions button, you open another window you've seen before. It lists all the objects (besides the one currently selected in the Object selection field on the previous dialog box) in the simulation that can collide with the current object. Just select the ones you need and copy them to the Include window by using the arrow button between the windows. This is the only difference between the methods. Clicking the Solve button reveals the calculated motion of the selected objects.

Planning for Interactions and Collisions

Carefully planning your collisions makes easy work of setting the dynamics parameters. Figure out how you expect the results to look and see if you can match your expectations. You might even discover an unpredictable result works better than your original expectation. Regardless of what you end up with in your final animation, begin with a plan that gives you a starting point.

If your objects are real-world objects such as cars, desks, baseballs, and so on, you have a reference for setting up your scene. Object Mass is a good place to focus some of your attention. MAX lets you designate object mass for any objects involved in collisions. This enables you to make a tree quite a bit heavier than a tennis ball, so when the tennis ball flies across the yard and hits the tree, it doesn't knock it over. Continuing on that line of thought, you can make a car quite a bit heavier than the tree so when you drive the car into the tree, it can knock it over. Here's how to add mass to your objects.

To Do: Designating object mass

1. Load mass.max from the accompanying CD-ROM. This is your collision demo. Adjust the mass of the box to see how it can affect the animation.

2. Click the Utilities tab and the Dynamics button.

3. In the Object in Simulation section, click Edit Object.

4. Set the Density in the Physical Properties section to 250 and then click OK.

5. Solve the dynamics solution and then play the animation to see how the box moves slightly, but its larger mass sent the sphere backward.

To Do: Mixing space warps and dynamics

Dynamics add quite a few creative possibilities to your animations. After you set up the objects with the proper settings, you can save a lot of time on complex movements. Here's how Wind and Gravity affect a stack of checkers.

1. Load dynamics.max from the accompanying CD-ROM. Someone obviously spent some time stacking these checkers on top of each other. But now the wind has blown in the room from an open window and knocks them over, causing them to tumble onto the ground.

2. Click the Utilities tab and the Dynamics button.

3. Click the New button to start a new simulation.

4. Click the Edit Object List button and add all the objects in the scene to the simulation.

5. In the Collisions section, click Global Collisions. Then click the Assign Global Collisions button and add all the objects in the simulation to the Global Collisions list.

6. Click the Create tab and the Space Warps button, and change the Space Warps category to Particles & Dynamics in the selection field.

7. Click Wind and create a Wind icon in the Front viewport directly over the checkers.

8. Set the Strength for Wind to 25 in its Parameters rollup.

9. Use the Select and Move tool to move the Wind icon back away from the stack of checkers as shown in Figure 12.25. The direction of the Wind is indicated with a large arrow icon. Make sure the arrow points toward the checkers.

To Do

To Do

12

FIGURE **12.25.**

Move the Wind icon so it points to the stack of checkers.

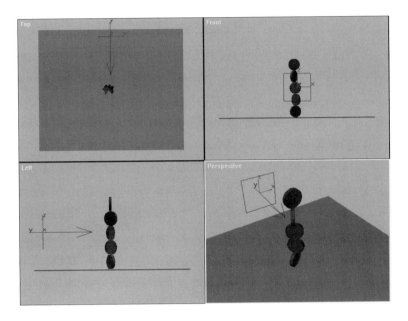

10. When the Wind blows the checkers over, you need them to fall to the floor. The Gravity Space Warp allows this to happen. It's created just like Wind. Click the Gravity Space Warp and draw a box for its icon in the Top viewport. Notice its arrow points down, indicating the direction gravity will pull objects. Your scene should now look like Figure 12.26.

11. Enter a Strength setting of 25 for Gravity in its Parameters rollup.

    You have just a few more settings before this will work. There are three things you are concerned with. First, the checkerboard object should be involved in the collision but it shouldn't move. Second, you have to add the Space Warp effects to the Dynamics simulation. Third, the Collision Test method for the checkers needs to be set to Cylinder. These are easily done.

12. Click the Utilities tab again to access the Dynamics settings.

13. Click the Edit Object button and select the Box01 object from the selection field under Object.

14. Directly under the selection field is the Misc. Dynamics Controls section. Check the check box labeled This Object is Immovable (see Figure 12.27). This way the checkboard will not move when the checkers fall on its surface, but it will still be a factor in the collision, making the checkers bounce.

15. Also check the Move Pivot To Centroid check box. This moves the pivot point of the checkboard (box01) object to its center. This speeds up calculations.

FIGURE 12.26

The Gravity icon resembles the Wind icon, with its arrow indicating the direction of gravitational pull.

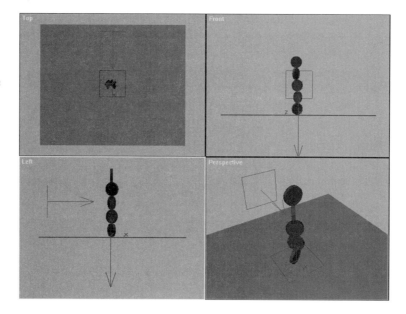

FIGURE 12.27.

Making an object immovable is essential for including floors or similar nonmoving objects in dynamic simulations.

12

16. The space warps in your scene will not affect dynamic simulations unless they are added to a simulation. In the Effects section of the Dynamics Panel, click the radial button for Global Effects, click the Assign Global Effect button, and then add the Wind and Gravity effects to the Include window.

17. Click the Edit Object button and set the Collision Test method for all the checkers to Cylinder to match their shape.

18. Click Update display w/solve. Now click the Solve button and MAX calculates the scene. If all goes well, the checkers will be blown off each other and tumble onto the checkboard.

This turns out pretty good except the checkers move too fast. There is a way to slow up or speed up the dynamic simulations. In the Timing & Simulation section (see Figure 12.28), there is a setting for Time Scale. By default it is set to 1.0, which creates constant dynamic motion. To slow the effect down, make it as low as .1. Try it and see what happens. You can load the final animation with the Time Scale setting at .4 by loading dynamics.avi from the accompanying CD-ROM.

FIGURE 12.28.

Use the Time Scale setting in the Timing & Simulation section to slow down or speed up the simulation.

Summary

Today you covered the special effects standard in MAX 2.5. You have the tools to create just about any effect you need. Here are some of today's key points:

- All particle systems are based on using an emitter object to produce the particles. This object is like the nozzle on a hose; everything comes from the emitter when you turn it on.
- Particles such as Spray (for rain) and Snow are easy to create. Take the time to play around with their settings to get the best results possible.
- Particles can render as geometric shapes, but using materials to map images to the particles can give you great looking particles for snow, smoke, and so on.
- Space warps are nonrendering objects you create with the purpose of affecting other objects in the scene. You can bind multiple objects to the same space warp, but you might have to create more than one of the same space warps to get the results you need. Remember the multiple bombs you had to create for multiple explosions because there is only one detonation frame per Bomb Space Warp.
- Dynamic and Particle Space Warps such as Wind and Gravity add realism to your scene, as well as help you create accurate animations respecting the laws of physics.
- Think through your scene to plan accordingly for dynamics and particles. Most are easy to set up if you have an idea of what results you want.

Q&A

Q Can I use particle systems with dynamics such as wind?

A Yes. For example, when you create rain, add wind to blow the raindrops.

Q Is there a quick way to animate complex movements of particle systems?

A There is. Under the Space Warps tab, you select Particles & Dynamics and the Path Follow Object Type. This enables you to assign your particle system to follow any spline object in your scene. You can use this to create a burning fuse where the sparks from the lit end of the fuse slowly burn along the length of the fuse spline.

Q Is there a way to create other real-world dynamic forces besides collisions?

A Yes. Two space warps enable you to create pushing and rotational torque forces that come in handy for mechanical simulations. They are called Push and Motor.

12

DAY 13

Rendering

Exploring Output Options in MAX

Until today, you learned how to use the various tools in MAX to create practically any scene or animation imaginable. That's fantastic. It's fun. And it's probably why you're interested in 3D graphics. Over the past 12 days, you saw how to construct a pretty good animation in MAX. But how good are your creations if they aren't in the right format for the right project? After you spend valuable time planning, modeling, and animating your wonderful, creative ideas, you still have to evaluate all the output options available to find the one best-suited to you particular needs.

The best way to make the best output decision is to find out enough about all, or most, of the options available. Sometimes, delivering your animations or still images works best from a digital format, and other times analog videotape is the best medium. When it comes to either delivery method, you'll encounter a number of decisions that have to be made along the way. The decisions you make affect the quality of the presentation and might affect the way in which you set up your scene as well.

Today, you explore the many options available to give you a good understanding of each option. You cover the following options:

- Popular digital formats available in MAX and which ones are best for your project
- Differences in production to consider when using digital or analog playback
- Understanding the MAX Render Scene dialog box and all its options
- The basics of how to render animations and stills
- Ways to maximize the quality and production time of your productions

Popular Digital Formats Supported

FIGURE 13.1.

You choose how to output and save your renderings from the Render Scene dialog box.

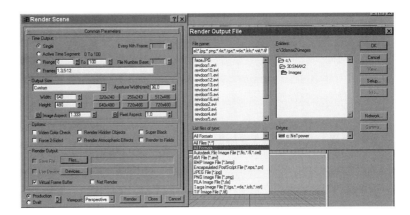

From the Render Scene dialog box, you choose how to save your files (see Figure 13.1). MAX supports just about any format your projects might require. Some have been left out of the base program, but third-party plug-ins have filled the voids and created output capabilities for those MAX formats left out. Here are currently supported animation output formats:

- Autodesk Flic Image File (.flc, .fli, .cel)　This stems from Autodesk Animator, the DOS-based cel animation program. The formats are very useful for creating digital animations in 256 colors, especially for use in interactive media and Internet design.
- Microsoft Video For Windows (.avi)　This is the most popular digital media format on the Windows platform. Various compression codecs are supported that allow you to create varying degrees of quality and color depth for animations.

Because every project is not based on animation, most of the popular still image formats are also supported. Many of these still image formats are also used in creating animations by rendering sequentially numbered single image files that are later converted to a digital video format. They include the following:

- *BMP Image File*   This Windows bitmap format can be saved with 256 colors or 16.7 million colors. Its versatility in color depth makes it a useful format for many applications including Internet and interactive media. The files tend to be larger than some of the compressed images.

- *EPS Encapsulated PostScript File (.eps, .ps)*   If still image output with page layout compatibility is your goal, this format is the one to consider.

- *PNG Image File (.png)*   Portable Network Graphics. This format was designed for use on the Internet/World Wide Web. It gives you palette options from 8 bit (256 color) to 48 bit, to grayscale. It also allows for Alpha channel and Interlaced graphics. Interlacing graphics is used on the Internet to display larger graphics rapidly by drawing them in multiple passes. Each pass adds more clarity until the full image loads. This is the only format MAX directly writes to that supports interlacings.

- *RLA Image File (.rla)*   This is an SGI-compatible format. It's a flexible format that allows the user to include MAX channel information within the file. Such information includes Material Effects channel data as well as object ID and zbuffer information.

- *TIF Image File (.tif)*   Tif images give you the ability to render in 24-bit color, or grayscale. It provides maximum compatibility with page layout programs.

- *JPEG (.jpg)*   JPEG is a high-quality compression format used in both animation and still imagery. When used in animation, sequential JPEG files are compiled to play back as a complete animation. Specialized hardware is required that enables the user to specify how much compression should occur, thereby giving you the control over quality versus file size. The rule is the smaller the file (more compression), the greater the loss of quality in the image.

- *Targa Image File (.tga, .vda, .icb, .vst)*   One of the most popular files used in both animation and still imagery. When used in animation, sequential targa files are compiled to play back as a complete animation. Specialized hardware or software is required. When used as a still image format, you have a quality 24-bit image that has the capability to store alpha channel information for compositing. (You cover compositing on Day 14.)

13

Now that you know what digital formats are supported, look at some popular formats not supported. Where applicable, a solution is provided to help you find a way to work with that particular format if you absolutely have to have it.

- *GIF (.gif)*   This 8-bit (256-color) format is probably the most popular Internet-based format. The advantage of GIF is its relatively small file size and the capability to interlace graphics for speedy Internet downloading.

  GIF SOLUTION: Consider using JPEG or PNG files if your Internet software supports them. Otherwise, render to BMP or some other format, and use a paint package such as Adobe Photoshop to open each of your files and resave them as GIFs with the settings you need.

- *Quicktime (.mov)*   With the release of version 3 of this Macintosh-based format, Quicktime movie creation has now officially crossed over to the PC. Quicktime is very common in multimedia titles and Internet Web sites.

  QUICKTIME SOLUTION: Plug-in to the rescue. Future releases of MAX are sure to address the Quicktime issue now that it will be supported on Windows machines, but until then, there is a third-party plug-in available that gives MAX Quicktime rendering capability. You can find this and many other useful plug-ins by browsing the Kinetix Web site at www.ktx.com.

- *MPEG (.mpg, .mpv)*   This digital video format has gained tremendous support in multimedia titles and the Internet due to its incredible compression capabilities and good quality output. Among the revisions of the MPEG format, MPEG 1 is still the most common. Most newer video cards, including laptops, now have built-in hardware accelerated MPEG playback. The quality of MPEG is good but not superb, especially with text or when it is enlarged any more than twice its native 352×240 resolution. MPEG 2 has a native resolution of 720×480 and has tremendous quality (although much bigger files). Files sizes are almost always much smaller than similar files written to .avi or .mov formats. MPEG1 looks best with natural video and might not be the choice for RGB graphics such as animations. (But don't rule it out without trying it on your particular animation.) MPEG2, however, is far superior to any other digital video format. If your end product requires digital playback and your hardware supports MPEG2, you need to consider it for the best option.

- *MPEG SOLUTION*   A third-party developer (DARVISION, www.darvision.com) has developed a low-cost driver for Windows 95 and NT that allows any program capable of rendering to .avi to use their DVMPEG .avi codec to render to MPEG video. It does so by creating a dummy .avi file while it is actually writing an MPEG1 or MPEG2 file. The rendering time is very fast (it doesn't add any time to MAX's normal rendering time) and the quality is outstanding.

Deciding on the Right Output

Now that you're thoroughly confused with all the choices, how do you decide on the right one? That question can be decided only by your project's criteria. Base the decision on the following:

- How will the final animation or still images be presented to your target audience? Via TV, videotape, laser disc, CD-ROM, or digital video from a computer hard drive or over the Internet?

- Do you need to use a high-color palette, displaying more than 256 colors?

- Is the file size of the digital video file an issue? This is a big consideration for Internet and CD-ROM delivery.

The first decision is digital versus analog playback. This is usually obvious. Will your project be played back from a computer or traditional means such as a videotape player? One thing to consider is the possibility that it will be displayed both as a digital movie and on videotape or TV. This can play a key role in how you set up your animations. Because of the final rendered resolution of TV versus most digital formats, small details will be more obvious for TV playback. In other words, small details, or so-so modeling will be noticeable at the TV resolution of 720×486 but might not be noticeable at the digital resolution of 320×240. Even larger digital movies at 640×480, or smaller videos stretched to fill a larger screen, might not show all the details like TV does. Use this to your advantage when designing your animation.

Be aware of the limitations of the format you use. One example of how planning for all possible outputs can help is a project where you initially design the animation for output to a digital video format such as MPEG 1. Its 352×240 resolution is fine for most screen playback, but the details can get lost (especially if it's played back at full-screen resolution). Later in the project, your client decides it likes your project so much it's going to use parts of the animation on a new TV commercial. Suddenly, shortcuts you took in modeling become very apparent at the higher TV resolution, forcing you to remodel some of your objects. If this were a true story, redoing much of the modeling work wouldn't be fun or the best way to spend your time.

13

Think through all possible scenarios for output; it can save you major headaches later. Here's a good rule of thumb. If there's any chance that your animations will be used for broadcast-quality presentations, render them at full resolution (whatever that might be for your equipment). The reason is you can always resave a higher-resolution format down to a smaller digital format with minimal degradation—the reverse is not true. Always create and render for the best quality necessary for your project.

The next decision deals with color depth. If you work with broadcast animations, you need 24-bit color. Highly detailed and colorful image maps used in your scene will be worth the effort and show up in the final production. If you're final output is Internet-based, or CD-ROM-based, you'll probably only be dealing with a 256-color palette. Due to this limitation, you can scale back on some material details and color usage, as the results might not even show up in the final product.

A third decision stems from file size. This is not an issue with broadcast animations rendered direct to tape or to a realtime playback system, but definitely an issue for digital formats. The exception to the rule might be MPEG and MPEG 2. Although their file sizes can become large, most playback will be aided by a hardware playback card or built-in acceleration in a video card that handles the file size nicely. For other digital video formats, especially those being played over the Internet, file size is a huge consideration. Adjusting the playback size you render to and the compression quality for the digital video codec are ways to keep file sizes manageable.

Color Depth

Color depth refers to the total number of colors available to your images. The output format you choose determines the color depth of the image or movie file. The following are most important to your animations:

- *8-bit color*   Refers to a palette of 256 colors. There is no set 256-color palette from which these files are created; rather, the palette is determined from the colors used in the scene. Any colors in the scene that are not represented in the 256-color palette are simulated by a process called dithering (described in the next section, "Dithering"). The 8-bit files are common for digital formats and for use in CD-ROM development and Internet delivery. Many of the compression codecs for Video for Windows (AVI) support 256-color animations. Another format that is designed for 8-bit color is FLI.

- *24-bit color*   Refers to a palette of 16.7 million colors. This is also referred to as true color. Also used for broadcast (TV) animations and video, 24-bit color gives the most accurate, true-to-life colors. This is also used for high-color computer displays. However, due to large file sizes, digital formats often opt for 8-bit color.

- *32-bit color*   Refers to a palette of 16.7 million colors with the extra 8 bits representing alpha channel information. This information determines transparency of an image and is used for compositing in Video Post or other video editing packages. This topic is discussed on Day 14, "Video Post and Compositing."

Although 256 colors are limiting, they are necessary for speedy delivery over the Internet and from most CD-ROM applications. One of the limitations shows up in gradations. Many times, there are simply not enough colors available to create a smooth gradation between colors. This problem is solved through a process called dithering, described in the next section.

Dithering

Dithering is the way in which the computer handles the translation of millions of colors your MAX scene contains, to the 256-color palette used in most digital video formats. It also helps smooth the edges of objects by looking at the colors of pixels next to each other on object edges, and creating intermediate colored pixels around the edge to make a less harsh color change. The process of dithering output can be turned on or off in the Preferences dialog box (see Figure 13.2). For most situations, you'll want to leave it on. The process simulates the potential millions of colors by mixing different colors within the 256-colors available.

FIGURE 13.2.

You can turn dithering on or off in the Preferences dialog box.

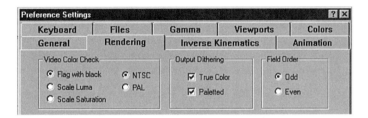

Without dithering, it's almost impossible to create smooth gradations, which will become noticeable in many of the shaded areas in your scene. Figure 13.3 shows two images; the one on the left has dithering turned off and the one on the right has dithering turned on. The image on the left suffers from *banding*. These bands of color are the result of the lack of enough colors to create the smooth gradation needed. Unless you have a need for this type of look, keep dithering turned on.

FIGURE 13.3.

The image on the left suffers from banding; the image on the right corrects the problem with dithering.

 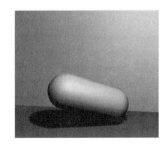

Preparing for Analog Videotape Playback

Analog playback of your animations with traditional videotape is still one of the most commonly used ways of distribution. This has been the norm since the early days of computer animation. Because so many people have access to videotape players, it probably won't go away very soon, even with the push to DVD and CD-ROM technology.

What has changed in recent years is the way you record your animations to videotape. Previously, you used a technique called single-frame recording. This consisted of your animation computer equipped with a frame-accurate controller card and a professional videotape deck. As each frame of the animation was rendered, it was sent to the videotape deck and recorded. The tape deck would then rewind itself, play to the position at the end of the last frame recorded, and wait for another frame to be sent from the computer. This method yielded great results because the images were never compressed. But it was a costly setup that was also very time-consuming. Another downfall was edits and corrections. If you discovered the animation needed changes, you either had to rerender the entire animation to tape a second time or pay for someone to edit the corrections in to the first rendering.

Although you can still render directly to videotape and laserdisc (MAX supports the Accom WSD Digital Recorder), the most popular method today involves rendering directly to a dedicated high-speed SCSI hard drive with the assistance of specialized compression and playback hardware. The beauty of this method is that it plays back from the hard drive without any delays of rendering a single frame to a tape deck. After the entire animation is rendered, you simply play the animation with the output from the specialized playback hardware connected to a videotape deck and it records in realtime. On this dedicated hard drive are sequentially numbered files from the animation. Using the hardware, these files are played back at standard video frame rates depending on your specific need. (In the U.S., the rate is 30 frames per second, the NTSC standard.)

Note

> Because the individual files are stored on the hard drive, any corrections to the rendered animation can be rendered directly over the old files for the frames that have changed. It's not necessary to rerender the entire animation. The changes, when rendered, play back immediately with no editing necessary.

The use of these specialized hardware setups also makes it possible to archive your rendered files on a backup in case they are ever needed again. You can also take sequentially numbered animation files from other computers and have the hardware import them as an animation. In other words, you don't have to render directly to these hard drives to record the animation. You can record to any hard drive in your system and use the hardware system's own software to import the files later.

There are many systems available and the following list does not attempt to list them all. These are but two of the most popular, manufactured by the following companies:

- Digital Processing Systems (DPS)   The Personal Animation Recorder, the Perception Video Recorder, and the Hollywood Recorder are all exceptional products that directly support MAX.

- TrueVision   The Targa boards are well used in the animation and nonlinear video industries—and have been from the start. Much of the new video editing systems moving from Mac and SGI now support the Targa 2000.

The cards range in their degree of compression and hard disk requirements, with some offering realtime playback of totally uncompressed video. This gives the best image quality but has hefty hard disk requirements. The dedicated hard disk drives need to be large (4 gigs or more) and fast (AV rated). Each board setup uses a plug-in interface to enable you to work with their animation files from within MAX (see Figure 13.4). The plug-ins enable you to select the board as a device to render to. You can even select the systems as a frame buffer. Doing so allows you to preview your work by rendering through their cards and out to a video monitor for proofing.

FIGURE 13.4.

The plug-in from DPS enables you to work directly with the animation files on the dedicated video hard drive from within MAX.

13

Understanding the Render Scene Dialog Box

Throughout this book, you render to see the results of your modeling and animation. But we haven't covered many of the options available. Let's start with the basic definition of what you want to render. MAX enables you to render any active viewport. That includes orthographic views as well as cameras and lights. Within that viewport, MAX gives you four options of how it will be rendered:

- *View*   This renders the entire viewport as you see it on your display.

- *Selected*   This only renders those objects in the scene that are selected.

- *Region*   This enables you to define a region in the viewport by setting the corners of a Marquee box. After you define the region, you simply click OK and MAX only renders that region. Use this in complex scenes to render and rerender tests.

- *Blowup*   With Blowup, you define a region just as you do with the Region option. When you click OK, MAX renders just that region but enlarges (blows up) it to the output size you designate in the Render Scene dialog box. This allows you to isolate around details in a scene and render them as large as you need them. Use this for still image details from larger scenes.

Here's a quick example of how these selections work. Figure 13.5 shows the area where you define your view to render.

FIGURE 13.5.

Tell MAX exactly how you want to render any viewport by selecting one of four options from the toolbar.

To Do: Using the Render Scene dialog box

1. Load render.max from the accompanying CD-ROM. This simple scene has a camera in a room full of primitive objects. There is one Omni light in the center of the room and a spotlight casting light in through windows in one of the walls.

2. Suppose you were working on this scene and were concerned with the way light from the spotlight strikes the torus knot object. Every time you make an adjustment to the lighting, you don't want to rerender the entire scene just to see one area. That's when you use the Region setting for the renderer. Activate the Camera01 viewport and click on the Region Type selection field. Select Region from the drop-down menu, as shown in Figure 13.6.

FIGURE 13.6.

Select the type of view you want to render from the Render Type drop-down menu in the toolbar.

3. Click the Render Scene button in the toolbar and notice the Marquee selection box and OK button that appear in the active viewport.

4. Define the region you want to render by positioning each of the four corner handlebars for the Marquee box. In the example given, you can define only the region on the torus knot that you are working on (see Figure 13.7).

FIGURE 13.7.

Use the Marquee box to define the region you need to render.

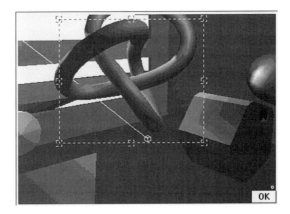

5. When you finish defining the region, click OK to start the rendering. The frame buffer displays the rendering of only the defined region, as shown in Figure 13.8.

FIGURE 13.8.

The results of rendering only a region of a viewport.

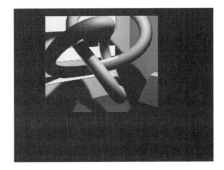

13

Defining Time and Size

As you explore the Render Scene dialog box, the first section is the Time Output section where you define the frames you want rendered. You can specify ranges or frames, individual frames, or instruct MAX to render every Nth frame. N is the variable you replace with a number. If you enter 2, MAX renders every other frame; enter 3 and MAX renders every third frame, and so on.

MAX enables you to define segments of your overall project to work on. Basically, you're isolating a particular range of frames. If you work with a segment, you can tell MAX to render the currently defined segment in the Time Output section. Here's how to set up a segment.

To Do: Setting up a segment with time and size

1. Click the Time Configuration button in the lower-right corner of the screen to open its dialog box(shown in Figure 13.9).

FIGURE **13.9.**

Define segments of your project to work on in the Time Configuration dialog box.

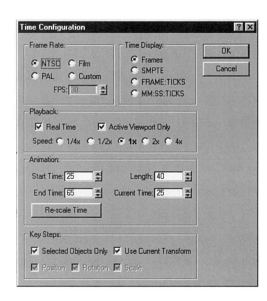

2. This animation is 100 frames long, but you just want to concentrate on frames 25 through 65. In the Animation section, change the start time and end time to 25 and 65, respectively.

3. Click OK and the timeline now represents only those frames. You can then select Active Time Segment in the Time Output section of the Render Scene dialog to render only the active frames.

Render Options

Most options you set in your scene that affect the way things render must be turned on in the Render Scene dialog box. For instance, Shadows, Atmospheric Conditions, and Motion Blur (covered later in this chapter) are all set up in your actual MAX scene, but they won't render unless you check their check boxes in the Render Scene dialog box. Here's an example in the render.max file you have open.

To Do: Exploring more rendering options

1. If you don't still have render.max open, load it from the accompanying CD-ROM.

2. Activate the Camera01 viewport and click the Quick Render button. Your rendered scene should look like the top image in Figure 13.10.

FIGURE 13.10.

If you forget to check the appropriate check boxes in the Render Scene dialog box, the outcome can change dramatically.

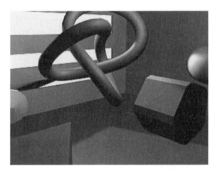

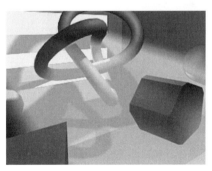

13

3. Click the Render Scene button to open its dialog box. Notice that Render Atmospheric Effects and Shadows are both not checked. Check each check box and rerender. The resulting image should resemble the right image in Figure 13.10.

Figure 13.10 is a perfect example of how certain settings won't render until you turn them on in the Render dialog box. Although this simple example makes this seem too obvious to overlook, it is possible when animations become more complex. If you think something isn't rendering correctly as you create your animations, make sure you have each of these check boxes checked.

Using the Frame Buffer

Because the virtual Frame Buffer is such a useful tool to preview your work and monitor changes you make, learning to use it can be a big help. One of the more useful features it has is the capability to clone itself. By doing so, you can open a second frame buffer window. The advantage is in proofing your scene.

To Do: Working with the Frame Buffer

1. Click the Quick Render button to render this scene.

2. Click the Clone button to create an identical Frame Buffer window displaying the scene you just rendered.

3. Click the Render Scene button and deselect the check boxes for Render Atmospheric Effects and Shadows. Then click the Render button. This way, the new rendering will be different from the first.

You now have two Frame Buffer windows: the current and previous renderings. If things still need adjustment, you can continue cloning the Frame Buffer as many times as you need to aid you with your changes. Figure 13.11 shows the Frame Buffer window and its clone.

FIGURE 13.11.

Cloning the Frame Buffer window allows you to see the previous and current rendering of your scene.

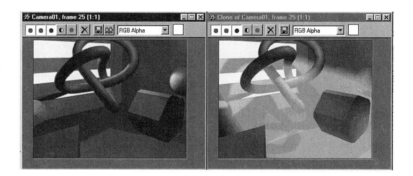

Predefining Production and Draft Settings

There are a lot of settings in the Render Scene dialog box, and you want to avoid constantly changing back and forth between settings optimized for proofing and those set for final output. Kinetix was aware of this and provided a way to toggle between Production and Draft settings.

To Do: Differentiating between proofing and final settings

1. Click the Render Scene button to open its dialog box.

2. Notice the two radial buttons on the bottom of the dialog box labeled Production and Draft, shown in Figure 13.12. By default, the Production radial button is checked. Scroll the dialog box and notice such things as Antialiasing, Render Atmospheric Effects, and Shadows are checked. The render size is set to 640×480, which is the final resolution for a high-resolution digital video file.

FIGURE 13.12.

Using the toggle between Production and Draft render settings can save you a lot of work in the Render dialog box.

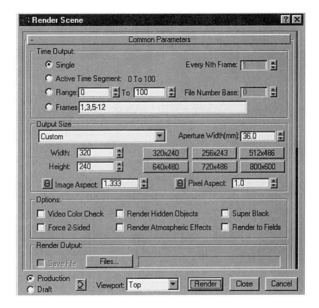

3. Click the Draft radial button and notice the changes. The settings mentioned above are now deselected and the size is set to 320×240. These settings render much quicker, allowing you to work through your proofing stage much faster.

   You can also toggle between the two settings from the toolbar, without entering the Render Scene dialog box.

4. Click and hold the Quick Render button in the toolbar until its flyout menu appears.

5. The two icons that appear represent the two choices. Production settings are represented by the color icon, and the gray icon represents the Draft settings (see Figure 13.13).

13

FIGURE **13.13.**

*Access the Production
and Draft render set-
tings directly from the
toolbar and the Quick
Render button.*

Rendering to Fields and Using Motion Blur

MAX presents two ways for you to smooth motion in your animations: Rendering to
Fields and Motion Blur. Rendering to Fields is used only for analog (videotape) playback
(see the previous section, "Preparing for Analog Videotape Playback"). Motion Blur,
although having special effects uses, is a good method for providing smoothness of moving objects for use in digital movies.

Rendering to Fields

Analog video is interlaced, meaning each frame displays a two-pass process. In one pass,
only have the horizontal lines making up the picture appear. The second pass fills in the
other half of the lines, completing the image. This is why TV screens (and some older
computer monitors) flicker. When you render animations meant for analog playback, you
can take advantage of interlacing and render your animation to fields. By doing so, you
render two images for every frame. Both images are intermediate representations of the
moving object's previous frame position and its current frame position. It adds more
information about the moving object because you're now drawing two pictures for every
frame. When you don't render to fields, the same image appears in each field (two fields
per frame). You turn on field rendering by checking the Render to Fields check box in
the Options section of the Render Scene dialog box.

Because rendering to fields renders two images for every frame, you will be increasing
your render time. If you have enough motion in your scene, however, the increased
smoothness of motion is almost always worth the wait.

Another thing to be aware of when rendering to fields is the order in which MAX renders the fields. The two fields per frame are referred to as Even and Odd. There is no
correct order in which to render these, but different hardware vendors require different
settings. Before rendering to your equipment, check your hardware specs or try rendering
a few frames with both even and odd and observe the difference. You can set the order in
the Preferences dialog box by checking the appropriate radial button (see Figure 13.14).

FIGURE 13.14.

When rendering to fields, the order in which the fields are rendered needs to match your hardware specifications.

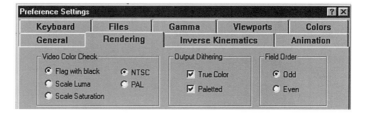

To Do: Using Motion Blur

You can use Motion Blur to add enough blur to an object's motion to provide it with a smooth edge resulting in smooth motion. There are actually three types of Motion Blur: Object, Image, and Scene. Object is best for one or two objects moving in the scene with no need to blur the environment or entire image. Image Motion Blur and Scene Motion Blur both affect the environment map (if there is one) and act upon camera movement, affecting the entire scene instead of single objects. Here you set up an object Motion Blur to smooth the motion of your digital movie file.

1. If you don't already have render.max open, load it from the accompanying CD-ROM.

2. Click the Display tab and the Unhide All button. You see an animated sphere object moving through the scene from frames 0 to 40.

3. Object Motion Blur must be assigned to each object and then turned on in the Render Scene dialog box. Select the Sphere01 object; then using the right mouse button, click on the sphere01 object again to access its flyout menu as seen in Figure 13.15.

FIGURE 13.15.

Right-clicking on a selected object accesses its flyout menu.

13

4. Click Properties on the flyout to access the Properties dialog box shown in Figure 13.16.

FIGURE 13.16.

You set Motion Blur for individual objects in the Object Properties dialog box.

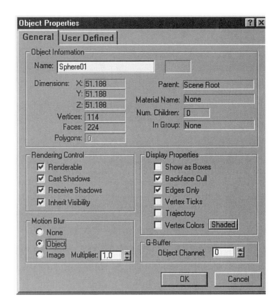

5. Click the Object radial button in the Motion Blur section and click OK.

6. Now you must Apply Motion Blur to the scene in the Render Scene dialog box. Click the Render Scene button.

7. In the Motion Blur section, make sure the Apply check box is checked (see Figure 13.17). You don't have to worry about deselecting the Image Motion Blur check box because no objects in the scene have Image Motion Blur defined so it will have no effect.

FIGURE 13.17.

You apply Motion Blur in the Render Scene dialog box.

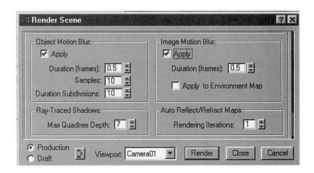

8. Set the Time Output to frames 0 through 40, the Size Output to 320×240, and click the Files button in the Render Output section. When the Render Output File dialog box opens, save the file with the name blur.avi and click OK (see Figure 13.18).

FIGURE 13.18.

Designate where to save the file with the Files button.

▲   9. Click the Render button.

You can load blur.avi from the accompanying CD-ROM to see the final animation. The blur settings used in this example are subtle; to see an exaggerated example of object motion blur, load blur2.avi from the accompanying CD-ROM.

Rendering Still Images

MAX is designed for animation, but imagine the possibilities for creating still images. With very few exceptions, most plug-ins and effects in MAX can be used for both motion and still images. If still images for print or multimedia are your targeted output, consider the options in the Render Scene dialog box.

Photographers and those familiar with traditional photographic terminology will rejoice in the many presets MAX provides for rendering output. Figure 13.19 shows the Output Size section of the Render Scene dialog box with the predefined options exposed. If you output to high-resolution slides, transparencies, or video, MAX supplies the basic resolutions for many popular formats.

FIGURE 13.19.

Predefined output sizes provide a starting point for most projects.

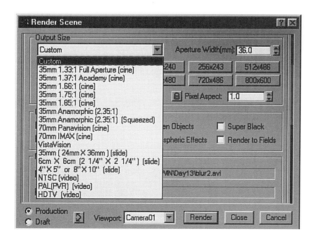

13

Because each preset has a different aspect ratio that affects what appears in the final rendering, MAX provides you a way of previewing what your output aspect settings are, in the viewports using the Safe Frames feature.

To Do: Working with Safe Frames

1. To turn on Safe Frames, select it by right-clicking on any viewport's label.

2. When its flyout menu appears, click Safe Frames (see Figure 13.20).

FIGURE 13.20.

Turn Safe Frames on by right-clicking a viewport's label and accessing its flyout menu.

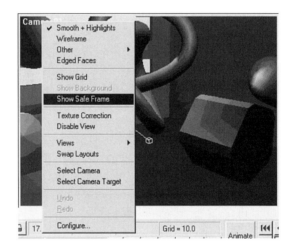

Three safe frames appear. The outermost is the yellow safe frame representing your current screen aspect ratio. The middle green safe frame represents the area considered safe to place your scene action (meaning it won't get cropped off by a television set). The innermost blue safe frame is the safe area to place titling in your scene. By changing the output size of your animations, the aspect ratio of the safe frames adjust accordingly as the aspect ratio of the output changes. Figure 13.21 shows the safe frames displayed on a camera viewport.

FIGURE 13.21.

Safe Frames are a guide for placing titling and containing action in your scenes to prevent cropping by the limits of a TV monitor.

Network Rendering—Use It If You Can

Unlock that back room where you have last year's old Pentium 90s stored and dust them off. What is too slow for production can now help out in rendering. MAX R2 took great steps forward in the network rendering feature. We won't cover how you set up a network but will tell you that all you need for network rendering is the most basic of setups. Kinetix has provided an excellent step-by-step help file for setting up your network and getting it to work with MAX. After you take the time (allow a few hours) to get the network set up, you won't believe you ever lived without network rendering. What takes all day on even the most robust Pentium II system can take hours on a network rendering setup with only three slower Pentiums. You won't want to dig out any 486 computers, but just about any computer that can run MAX can add some speed to your project renderings.

13

Summary

Today you covered the rendering techniques in MAX R2. There are a lot of settings to turn on or off or to set in some way, so take the time to look over the Render Scene dialog box. Remember some of today's key points:

- MAX supports many digital formats; experiment enough to know which is right for your needs.

- Effects such as shadows and atmospheric effects must be assigned in your scene but won't render unless turned on in the Render dialog box.

- Rendering to fields and object motion blur can help smooth out motion in your animations.

- Shortcuts such as the Production and Draft settings in the Render dialog box save you from continually changing the same settings when you render proofs and final images.

- Network rendering, although not detailed in this book, is worth setting up. Consult the documentation that came with MAX; you'll be glad you took the time to set it up.

- Use the frame buffer's clone feature to create multiple copies of a rendered image for comparisons during proofing stages.

Q&A

Q MPEG, AVI, Quicktime—there are so many digital video formats—so how do I choose?

A Consider any programs you might be using to put together your interactive or multimedia presentation. Many have preferred formats they want to use. Other times, trial and error might show better results with one over the other.

Q How do I determine the resolution of my output for animations?

A Most every output will be determined by the format you use. For example, AVI's are typically 320×240 or 640×480. MPEG 1 files have to be 352×240 and MPEG 2 have to be 720×480. If you use a realtime recording solution, the hardware manufacturer will dictate what its hardware solution requires.

Q How do I determine the resolution of my output for prints?

A Consider how the image will be printed. The settings for printing to your 300dpi
laser printer will differ from those needed when printing to a 1,200dpi Linotronic.
Here's the formula to follow. Double the line screen used by your printer (laser
prints are typically 60lpi and high-resolution printers can be 120 to 150 on average) to determine the pixels per inch for your image (that is, a 60lpi printer
requires a 120ppi setting). Take that ppi number and multiply it by the width and
height of your final print to get the appropriate rendering width and height. So if
you are printing to your 60lpi laser printer, you ppi requirement for decent output
is 120. If your final print size will be 10-inches wide by 8-inches high, the width
and height setting you enter in the Render Scene dialog box would be 1200×960.

Q What if I want the best possible output for my poster print?

A You should consider rendering using the preset 4×5 transparency setting and out-
putting to film. You can then have the print photographically enlarged from its high
4,000 or 8,000 line resolution. The output will be stunning.

13

DAY 14

Video Post and Compositing

Rome wasn't built in a day, and quite often, the images you render for your animations won't be complete with a single pass of the MAX renderer. MAX enables you to render an incredible variety of things when you click the Render Scene button, but sometimes it's necessary to use other programs to create the image or effect you need. Or you might need to use special effects filters within MAX by using Video Post. That's where compositing comes into the picture. *Compositing* is the procedure you use to create a single (composite) image from one or more images, or as MAX calls them, layers. Compositing is used in both still images and animations. Today, you explore the uses of compositing and how to create composites using MAX's Video Post feature. Here's what you learn:

- What types of files Video Post works with
- How to set up a Video Post sequence
- What are some uses of Video Post

What Can You Do with Video Post?

Video Post enables you to do more than just composite two or more images; it also enables you to create special effects through the use of standard- and third-party effects filters. Consider using Video Post for compositing whenever you encounter these two basic situations:

- You think you can create the effects or images you want faster by using another program and then combining them with your MAX scene.
- You know there is a Video Post filter event that creates the image or effect you want.

Imagine wanting to add a lens flare that mimics the effect you get when sunlight creates a glaring effect on a real-world camera. You see this streaking light effect in real photographs, but how can you create this in MAX? You can create an object that can be deformed to create streaks of light and receive a transparent, glowing material. But that's a lot of work and might not yield the results you want anyway.

Luckily, MAX supplies a standard filter event for use in Video Post that creates just such an effect. Look at Figure 14.1 to see an example of a lens filter applied to an image using Video Post. This MAX scene contains nothing more than a few primitive objects and an Omni light. When in Video Post, the Lens Effects filter is loaded and instructed to act on the Omni light to create its effects. Special Effects filter events such as lens flares can be animated as well, so you can have a glimmer appear and then fade away over time. By animating such an effect, you can create a sparkle, flash, or just about any effect you need.

FIGURE 14.1.

Using Video Post is an easy way to add effects such as Lens Flares, which is a standard filter event with MAX.

Here's another use of compositing that is used quite often in movie and video production. Imagine you have a scene that requires animated text to appear in which the camera flies around a lake. Do you go to the trouble of creating the lake and surrounding terrain, or do you use actual video footage of a lake as a backdrop image for your animated events? Of course, if the video fits your needs, it is much easier than creating the objects and animating the lake fly-around yourself. Video Post enables you to take the two separate images (digitized video of the lake and the new animated text you create) and composite them to form one image. Figure 14.2 shows the previously described scenario.

Even if you want the lake and surroundings to be created with animation (to match a certain look your animation requires), you still might want to use compositing to put two separate renderings together (foreground animated text and background lake and surroundings). Why? One good reason is speed of creation and speed in revisions. The complex animation of the lake fly-around might take hours to render, but the animated text alone might take far less. If you render each separately, any future revisions to the animated text will require you to only rerender the text alone (without the background). You can use the original animation for the lake when you recomposite the new text after revisions are made and rendered. It can save valuable time.

The potential uses are endless. One of the most valuable uses to those without video editing software or equipment is the ability to render different camera views, different frame ranges, and to combine rendered animation from other MAX scenes and transition between the different scenes. Using Video Post, you can do basic video editing with transitional effects similar to those in dedicated video editing packages. You can render, and

14

edit together, title slides or title animations for your scenes all in Video Post. It makes a great proofing method before editing final versions of your work and might provide enough tools for your final project in many cases. You can also cut from camera to camera in Video Post to mimic cuts previously only possible with video editing.

Video Post works as though it is a separate, full-blown video editing package you can access within MAX. If you use it to its full potential, you open up a whole set of creative possibilities for your productions.

Explaining the Role of the Alpha Channel

How does MAX composite multiple images to create one image? The answer lies in an extra 8 bits of information stored with the images involved in the composite process. This information is known as the *alpha channel*. Normal RGB images contain 24 bits of information, broken down as an 8-bit Red Channel, an 8-bit Green Channel, and an 8-bit Blue Channel. Compositing requires 32-bit images. The extra 8 bits define the transparency of the image. From within MAX, when images are saved as 32 bit with alpha channel information, all areas that contain no imagery (where nothing is being rendered) are treated as transparent. You can even create images with areas that are varying percentages of black (shades of gray) that are treated as semitransparent.

In the previous example of the text being composited over the lake, the object for the word text was rendered against a blank background. The resulting image designated the blank areas as the alpha channel of the image. When you composite it over the lake image, all areas designated as the alpha channel are regarded as transparent, allowing the underlying lake image to show through. You can see the alpha channel from within MAX after the image renders. You do this in the frame buffer window. Take a look at how you view alpha channels.

To Do: Viewing alpha channels

1. Start a new scene in MAX.

2. Click the Create tab and create any number of primitives in any arrangement you like. Don't worry about what you create or where you create them.

3. After you have your scene moderately filled with some different objects, click the Render Scene dialog box to render the image to the frame buffer window. Figure 14.3 shows a sample scene.

FIGURE **14.3.**

Arrange any objects in any fashion, to set up the alpha channel rendering.

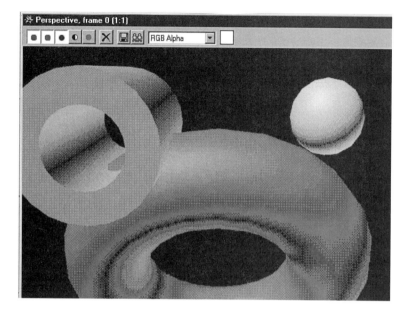

4. Working in the frame buffer window, you have a series of buttons that determine how the image appears. By default, the RGB channels are visible. You can see the three buttons for RGB are selected. The next button to the right is the Display Alpha Channel button. By clicking this button, the RGB buttons become deselected and only the alpha channel is visible. Click the Display Alpha Channel button. The image displayed in the frame buffer window is now a black-and-white image. The white represents the objects in your scene and the black represents the blank areas. Figure 14.4 shows the alpha channel for the RGB image shown in Figure 14.3.

If any of the objects have a material that adds transparency to the object, that transparency shows up in the alpha channel as well. In this case, you have no transparency in the objects, so they are solid white.

Any image you want to use in compositing must be saved in a 32-bit format with alpha channel information. The most commonly used formats that support alpha channels are Targa, TIFF, and JPEG. Any paint program should work with, and save images as, these formats for your use in composite images and animations.

14

FIGURE 14.4.

This is the alpha channel for the scene in Figure 14.3. When compositing, the black areas (alpha channel) are treated as transparent.

Working in Video Post

When you use Video Post, you do all your rendering from within the Video Post window. You do not use the Render Scene dialog box because it will not apply the filter effects.

To Do: Setting up a composite animation or still image

To set up a composite animation or still image, you need to take the following basic steps:

1. Create the one or more images you want to composite. These can be scanned images, images created in external paint or vector-based drawing programs, digitized video, MAX scene sequences, or prerendered animations. Because you can use outside sources for images, you don't even need to use a current MAX scene. You can use Video Post as if it were a standalone compositing program that just happens to reside within MAX.

2. Open MAX and enter Video Post.

3. Add the events that will comprise the composite image(s). The Video Post dialog box contains two windows: the Queue and the Edit windows (explained later in this section).

4. Add any filter events to the Video Post Queue. Transitions between scenes, special effects, or any other effects filters are added to individual or groups of images.

5. Add an output event. The output event tells MAX how and where to save each rendered composite image or entire animation.

6. Execute the Video Post Queue. This renders the events you defined in Video Post in the order you defined them, creating the proper composite image.

Exploring the Video Post Queue and Edit Windows

Video Post is comprised of two main windows: the Queue and Edit Windows (see Figure 14.5). The Queue window, on the left, is where you enter the events for your animation. There are five types of events:

FIGURE 14.5.

The Video Post dialog box and its two main windows.

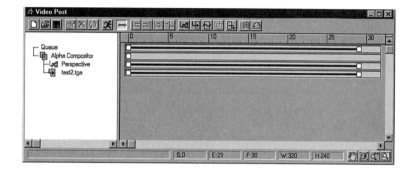

- *Scene Events*   These are the actual animation scenes loaded in MAX. The particular MAX scene file must be open in order for you to work with the scene as a Video Post Event. If you want to combine animations from more than one MAX scene in the same Video Post session, you need to use a combination of a Scene Event and an Image Input Event (described next).

- *Image Input Events*   Any image file format supported by MAX can be used in Video Post. This is how you import still images or digital video/animation files from other programs. You also use this type of event when you need to include more than one MAX scene in your Video Post session. Because you can have only one MAX scene open at one time, open any secondary scene file and render it to an AVI digital video format and add it to Video Post as an Image Input Event.

- *Image Layer Events*   These act on one or more events in the queue to create a compositing or transitional effects. Such events include Adobe Premier Transition Filter (you can use any Premiere transition), Alpha Compositor (using the alpha channel for layering images), Cross Fade Transition (fading from one to the next image), Pseudo Alpha (for images saved without an alpha channel; you designate a color to serve as the alpha channel), Simple Additive Compositor (also used when the image has no alpha channel; it uses the images HSV values to determine alpha), and Simple Wipe (a left to right or right to left transition from one image to the next).

14

- *Image Filter Events*   These are your special effects events. MAX ships with 10 standard Image Filters that are outlined next. There are many third-party filters being developed to create just about any effect or transition you can ever need.

- *Image Output Events*   Just as important as the images you input is how you output the animation or images. You can add any output type supported by MAX. This event simply instructs Video Post how to save the sequence you define in its Queue.

The Queue creates a hierarchy of the different Events you add. This hierarchy tells MAX the order in which to render and composite the different layers of images. If the order is wrong, the results can vary drastically. Events are executed from the top of the queue to the bottom. Those events listed first are rendered, or executed, first. Because of this, any image you want rendered in the background of your final image must appear first in the Queue. You can think of the Queue as your canvas.

As you begin to paint, you start with the background imagery and add layers of paint until you finish with the highlights and foreground images. The Queue is the same way. It's easy to get confused, so test render a few times to see if the compositing is turning out the way you anticipated. Figure 14.6 shows an example of events added to the Queue with the execution order identified.

FIGURE 14.6.

The order you add events to the Queue plays a significant role in how your final image appears.

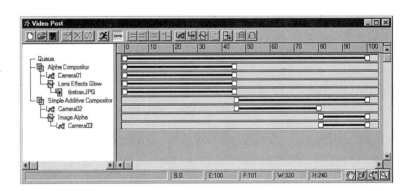

The Edit window is a timeline for each event you add to the Queue. This timeline shows the range of frame over which the events occur. If you add a scene event for camera 1 that occurs from frame 0 to frame 45, and another for camera 2 that ranges from frame 40 to frame 90, the edit window resembles Figure 14.7. All events, including Image Filters and Output Events have a range bar associated with it on the Edit window's timeline. The Edit window is similar in appearance and function to the Track view.

FIGURE 14.7.

The Edit window range bars tell you the frames each event occupies.

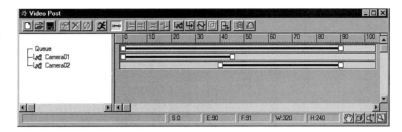

Filter Events

Filter Events, for the most part, offer some type of special effect. MAX ships with the following standard Filters Events:

- *Adobe Premiere Video Filter*   If you own Adobe Premiere, you can use any of its filters in Video Post. This is actually not even limited to filters developed by Adobe for Premiere. A number of third-party vendors develop 100-percent compatible Adobe Premiere filters that can be imported as well. This opens up a tremendous amount of filters for use directly within MAX.

- *Contrast*   Enables you to adjust the brightness and contrast of the image. This offers basic functionality, but remember that all things can be animated. That's the advantage over simply using this type of tool as you would in Photoshop.

- *Fade*   Enables you to fade an image in or out.

- *Image Alpha*   This replaces an image's alpha channel with a mask file you define. Once again, creative freedom reigns with the ability to use any alpha channel you want by creating your own.

Note

A *mask* is a file that defines areas of opacity and transparency that can be used in conjunction with many alpha-type filters in Video Post. Masks define these areas in black-and-white silhouette images where the black areas are transparent and the white areas are opaque. Any areas of gray are varying degrees of transparency.

- *Lens Effects*   Any number of lens effects including flares, glows, highlights, and focus can be created.

- *Negative*   Creates a negative of the image or scene, much like a 35mm camera negative.

14

- *Adobe Photoshop* Any third-party Photoshop 32-bit filter can be used in Video Post. You have full control over the effects, just as you have in Photoshop while working on still images. This is a great way to automate work you might normally do in Photoshop when you need it done over a series of images in an animation. Note that most filters that ship with Photoshop will not work here. Adobe has a scheme where these filters check to make sure you are using Photoshop and no other program. Some filters, such as those found in the plug-ins/effects folder in the default Photoshop program folder (and other supplied filters from other venders) will work.

- *Pseudo Alpha* This enables you to create an alpha channel for non-32 bit images by designating the pixel color or the upper-left corner pixel as alpha for the image. For example, if that pixel is blue, all blue pixels in the image are recognized as transparent.

- *Simple Wipe* A simple transition from left to right or right to left between two images.

- *Starfield* This very cool filter generates a starfield that moves based on the camera movement in the scene. The results are realistic movements as if you were flying the camera through the starfield. Load starfield.avi from the accompanying CD-ROM to see an example of this filter. The only downfall to this filter is it doesn't generate moving starfields along the axis of travel. For example, if your spaceship is traveling straight ahead along one axis, the stars will not move so no motion will be detected (that means no streaking starfields as you shift into hyperdrive).

Setting Up a Video Post Sequence

> **Caution** Video Post is quite simple but has the potential to become quite complex when you add layer on layer and multiple effects to each layer. Once again, having a clear idea of the results you need before you start to enter any events into the Video Post Queue will help you quickly arrive at your final image with fewer headaches.

 ### To Do: Putting a sequence together

After an introduction to all the components used in Video Post, you can see how to put a sequence together. Start with a basic scene and then add some image filter events and image layer events to create a fully edited scene. You'll quickly discover Video Post turns you into a fully functional video editor. It's quite addictive, too.

1. Load videopost.max from the accompanying CD-ROM. This simple scene of a tree falling into the water will work for this demonstration. It contains three cameras' views of the fall. You'll add three Scene Events, one for each camera, and then add transitions between the three events.

2. Click the Rendering drop-down menu and select Video Post to open the Video Post dialog box.

3. Click the Add Scene Event button from the Video Post toolbar to open the Add Scene Event dialog box shown in Figure 14.8.

FIGURE 14.8.

The Add Scene Event dialog box adds scene events to the Video Post Queue for any of the active views in your MAX scene.

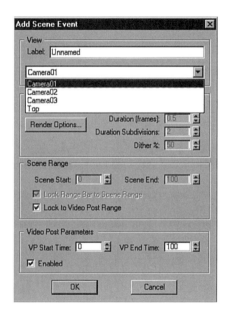

4. The view assigned enables you to select any of the active viewports in your MAX scene. It defaults to Camera01, which is what you want, so click OK to add it to the Queue.

5. Repeat steps 3 and 4 two more times to add scene events for Camera02 and Camera03.

6. Click the Zoom Extents button on the lower-right corner of the Video Post dialog box to see the entire extent of the Edit window. Your Video Post window should now look like Figure 14.9.

14

FIGURE 14.9.

Three scene events have been added to the Video Post Queue.

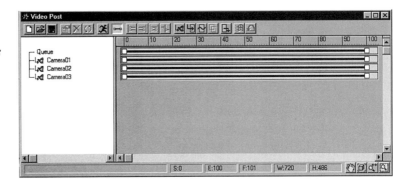

At this point, you successfully added three scene events to be rendered as part of your final Video Post production. There is one problem, however, with the way this is currently set up. Each scene event occurs over the same range of frames on the Video Post timeline. Now see how to adjust the three to make this work.

The Video Post timeline is separate from the MAX scene timeline. Don't confuse the two. Think of the Video Post timeline as a separate timeline for your overall project. The MAX scene timeline defines the timeline for one particular scene that you might add to your Video Post timeline. For example, your MAX scene timeline might contain 100 frames, but your Video Post timeline might contain three similar animations from different MAX scenes or different views in the same scene that create a 300 frame Video Post animation.

7. Click and hold the mouse button over the second scene events range bar in the Edit window.

8. Drag the range bar to the right while watching the display at the bottom of the Video Post dialog box. Two displays, marked S and E, tell you the Start and End frames for the range bar. Drag the range bar until the S frame reads 100 and then release the mouse.

9. Use the Zoom Time icon so you can see 300 frames in the Video Post window; then right-click to turn it off. Repeat steps 1 and 2 on the third scene event and drag it until its start frame is 200. Your Video Post dialog box should now resemble Figure 14.10.

FIGURE 14.10.

The scene events as adjusted so they do not overlap.

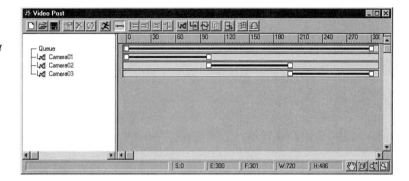

10. Click above the word Queue to make sure no individual event is selected. If you fail to do this, the Image Output event you add will appear indented and only be for the selected tracks. Click the Add Image Output Event from the toolbar and the dialog box shown in Figure 14.11 appears.

Note

> Notice the Devices button and the Devices dialog box shown in Figure 14.11. You can output Video Post animations directly to real-time video recorders and laser disks if you have one available.

FIGURE 14.11.

The Add Image Output Event dialog box enables you to designate how your animation should be saved.

11. Click the Files button to bring up the familiar Save As dialog box. Type in the name videopost.avi and click OK. Your Video Post dialog box should now resemble Figure 14.12.

14

FIGURE **14.12.**

With the Image Output Event added, the Video Post Queue meets the minimum requirements to output an animation.

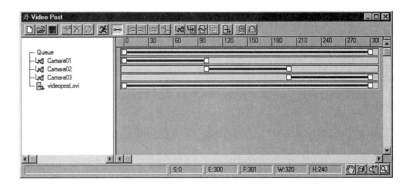

You need to set one more setting to correctly render the three views. You want each camera view to render scene frames 0 to 100, but by default, each scene event's scene frame range is locked to the Video Post range.

12. Double-click on the range bar for the Camera02 scene event in the Edit window. The Edit Scene Event dialog box appears.

13. In the Scene Range section, deselect the check box for Lock to Video Post Range.

14. Change the Scene Start to frame 0 and press the Tab key to advance the cursor from the Scene Start frame box. When you do so, watch the Scene End frame box; it changes to frame 100 because it's locked to the Scene Range (which is set to 100 frames).

15. Repeat steps 1 through 3 for the Camera03 scene event, changing its Scene Range to frames 0 through 100.

    You told MAX that although the Camera02 scene event is occurring from Video Post frames 100 to 200, it should render Scene frames 0 to 100. If you leave it locked to the Video Post range, it will try to render scene frames 200 to 300, which do not exist. Now render this animation.

16. Click the Execute button in the toolbar. It looks like a person running. The Execute Video Post dialog box appears as shown in Figure 14.13.

17. Check the Range radial button and make sure the From and To boxes read 0 and 300 to render the entire Video Post sequence.

18. Set the size to 320×240, enable the virtual frame buffer so you can watch the progress, and click the Render button. You can load the finished animation by opening videopost.avi from the accompanying CD-ROM.

▲

FIGURE 14.13.

*You render your Video
Post animations by
using the execute Video
Post dialog box.*

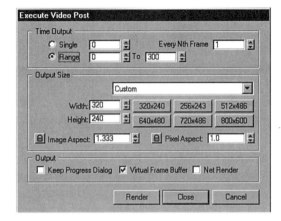

To Do: Adding image input events

When you need to add titles or still images, you do so with the Image Input Events feature. As mentioned earlier, any image file format MAX supports can be used with Video Post.

1. Be sure nothing is selected in the videopost Queue; then click the Image Input Event button on the Video Post toolbar. The Image Input Event dialog box appears as shown in Figure 14.14.

FIGURE 14.14.

*Add images with the
Add Image Input Event
dialog box.*

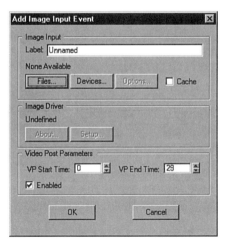

14

2. Click the Files button and add title.jpg from the accompanying CD-ROM.

3. Because you need the title to be rendered at the beginning of the animation, click and hold the mouse on the title.jpg name in the Queue and drag it until it is over the word Queue; then release. It should now be the first event in the Queue.

4. You also need the animations to start rendering after the title slide stays on the screen for the default 29 frames. To do so, select all the scene events in the Queue by Shift+clicking each name, or Ctrl+clicking the first and last events.

5. Now click the Abut Selected button in the toolbar. It looks like two range bars divided down the middle by a vertical line. This snaps the three scene event range bars to the end of the first events range bar. (Abut Selected always snaps to the end of the earliest occurring range bar.) Your Video Post dialog box should now resemble Figure 14.15.

FIGURE 14.15.

The title slide has been added and the rest of the scenes have been adjusted accordingly.

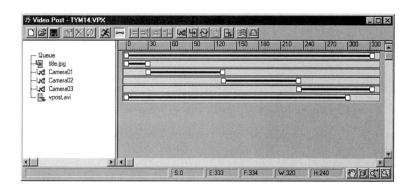

Now you have your scenes rendering properly and you added a title slide. All the basics are in place. In the next section, you start to have a little fun and jazz up the presentation a bit by adding some effects filters.

To Do: Adding Image Filter Events

Quite often, you'll want to add some effect to the images in your Queue for title slides and so on. In your example, you use a filter to fade up on your title.

1. Click the title.jpg event in the Queue. When you add filter events, you must have the image you want it to effect selected.

2. Click the Add Image Filter Event in the toolbar and the Add Image Filter Event dialog box appears shown in Figure 14.16.

3. Select the Fade filter. This filter can fade in or fade out an image.

4. Click the Options button and choose the fade In radial button. Also, set the range from frame 0 to frame 15 for a short fade in. Then click OK to add it to the Queue.

FIGURE **14.16.**

The Add Image Filter
Event dialog box adds
a filter for the selected
event in the Queue.

If you look at the current Queue, shown in Figure 14.17, notice the indentation. This
indicates a filter event where the Fade filter will affect the title.jpg event. The order in
which the rendering will occur is the title.jpg image will be loaded and then the Fade filter will act on it.

FIGURE **14.17.**

Indents identify the
hierarchy between fil-
ters or layer events
and the rest of the
Queue.

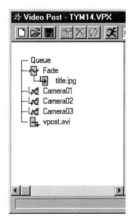

▲

To Do: Adding Image Layer Events

Things are shaping up. But you only have straight cut edits between your scenes. It
might be a smoother transition to add a crossfade between each scene event. You do this
by adding an Image Layer Event. This is also the same procedure you use to composite
two scene events using their alpha channels.

14

1. To create crossfades, you need to have the different events overlap on the timeline. Click the title.jpg event and drag the right end of its range bar until the ending frame is frame 45. That gives you a nice overlap with the Camera01 scene event.

2. Click the Camera02 scene event and drag it to the left until its start frame is approximately frame 116, giving an overlap between the Camera01 and Camera02 scene events.

3. Do the same for the Camera03 scene event, dragging it to the left until its start frame is approximately frame 203. Your Video Post dialog box should now look like Figure 14.18.

FIGURE 14.18.

Overlapping areas between events prepare the sequence for crossfade layer events.

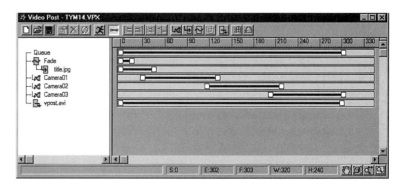

4. To add an Image Layer Event, you have to select two events you want the effect to occur between. Select the Fade filter event and the Camera01 scene event by using the Ctrl+clicking method. With both highlighted, click the Add Image Layer Event button to open its dialog box shown in Figure 14.19.

Note

Notice that you selected the Fade filter event and not the title.jpg. That's because the Fade filter event is the last item to effect your title graphic, rendering it with its alpha channel effect. You must always select the most recently executed event in the Queue when adding additional events.

5. Select the Crossfade Transition and click OK to add it to the Queue.

6. Adjust its range bar in the Edit window until it matches the overlap area between the Fade filter event and the Camera01 scene event. If you know the range of frames that make up the overlap, you can double-click the Crossfade Transition event and enter the range in its dialog box. Your Video Post queue should now resemble Figure 14.20.

FIGURE 14.19.

The Add Image Layer Event works on two selected events in the Queue.

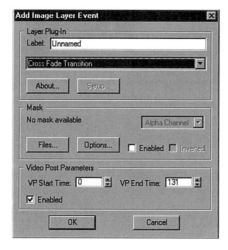

FIGURE 14.20.

The Queue, with added Image Layer Events, can become confusing quickly.

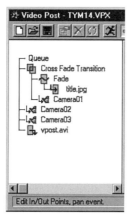

7. Now add another crossfade layer event between the Camera01 scene event and the Camera02 scene event. To do so, select the Crossfade Transition event and the Camera02 scene event; then click the Add Image Layer Event button.

8. Choose the Crossfade Transition filter and enter a frame range of 116 to 131. Click OK.

9. Add the final Crossfade Transition between the one you just added and the Camera03 scene event.

14

10. The last step is to make sure your Image Output Event length still matches the length of your Video Post sequence with all the additions and changes you made. With no events selected, the Start and End frames reported at the bottom of the Video Post dialog box are for the overall sequence. Double-click the Image Output event and make sure the frame range settings match the overall settings. You might also want to change the name of the rendered output file to vpost.avi so you don't overwrite the previously rendered file videopost.avi. When you finish, your Video Post dialog box should resemble Figure 14.21.

FIGURE 14.21.

The completed Video Post sequence with all filter and layer events added.

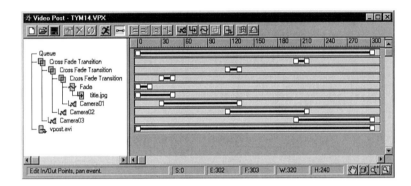

That's just about everything you can add to a Video Post sequence. Obviously, there are many variations on what you covered here, but you covered the basics. Execute the sequence and watch it render to get an even better understanding of how MAX works its way through the Queue. See if you got it right. You can view the final rendered animation by loading vpost.avi from the accompanying CD-ROM.

Summary

Today you covered compositing capabilities in MAX's Video Post feature. Based on your needs, Video Post can do everything from simple straight cut edits between images or scenes to complex image composites for stills or animations. Here are some of today's key points to remember:

- Video Post can save you a tremendous amount of time, as well as make a wide variety of special effects available to your animations.

- For compositing to work, you must use 32-bit images with the alpha information saved in the file. This defines the transparency for the image.

- Every image, special effect filter, or MAX scene you add to the Video Post window is called an event.

- Every event used in Video Post is added to the Queue.

- The order of events is extremely important in Video Post. MAX executes the events in the Queue from the top down, so background images must be entered first and foreground images last. Be careful what you select when you add an event. Certain events will not be available unless there are the correct selections in the Queue.

Q&A

Q I have three computers that I use to network render my animations. Can I still use the network and Video Post?

A Yes. Video Post has no effect on network rendering; it works the same as when you have just one computer rendering Video Post. The only thing you have to do is check the Net Render radial button in the Execute dialog box.

Q What if I make a mistake and need to undo things? Can I undo my mistake in Video Post?

A Unfortunately, you can't. The MAX Undo and Redo buttons do not work in the Video Post dialog box. So the trick is to use the Hold and Fetch feature often. You can save your Video Post sequences as Video Post files. Before you try anything too intensive, save a version of your current Video Post sequence. As you create more changes, keep saving versions before making too many changes. Doing these incremental changes will create a history of files you can revert to if you make a mistake or need to change things.

Q What programs can I use to create images to work with MAX for compositing purposes?

A You can create images in any paint or draw program that can work in one of the MAX-supported formats. However, if you plan to use the image as a composite image to place over another image in Video Post, the program you use must save 32-bit file formats with alpha channel information.

14

INDEX

W

X–Y–Z